Airlines and Air Mail

Airlines and *Air Mail*

The Post Office and the Birth of the Commercial Aviation Industry

F. Robert van der Linden

THE UNIVERSITY PRESS OF KENTUCKY

Publication of this volume was made possible in part
by a grant from the National Endowment for the Humanities.

Editorial and Sales Offices: The University Press of Kentucky
663 South Limestone Street, Lexington, Kentucky 40508–4008

06 05 04 03 02   5 4 3 2 1

Library of Congress Cataloging-in-Publication Data

Van der Linden, F. Robert.
    Airlines and air mail : the post office and the birth of the commercial
aviation industry / F. Robert van der Linden.
    p.   cm.
    Includes bibliographical references and index.
    ISBN 0-8131-2219-8 (cloth : alk. paper)
    1. Aeronautics, Commercial—United States. 2. Air mail service—
United States. I. Title.
    HE9763 .V36   2002
    383'.144—dc21
    2001007229

This book is printed on acid-free recycled paper meeting
the requirements of the American National Standard
for Permanence in Paper for Printed Library Materials.

Manufactured in the United States of America.

Contents

Illustrations

Preface

Conventional historiography generally concludes that the involvement of the federal government in U.S. airline industry regulation began with the Civil Aeronautics Act of 1938. Historians unfamiliar with aviation see this New Deal legislation as one more step taken by the Roosevelt administration to bring order from chaos in a nascent industry struggling to survive the ravages of unfettered competition as a direct result of inadequate government supervision. Although there is some validity to this argument, a better argument to the contrary can be made.

The airline industry was born in the mid-1920s and thrived under the watchful eye of the federal government, which fostered its creation and growth long before Roosevelt took office. In fact, American commercial aviation was largely the creation of the federal government. Under the Coolidge and, particularly, the Hoover administration, air transport companies were formed to take advantage of lucrative airmail contracts awarded by the Post Office Department. This use of an indirect subsidy to foster a fledgling industry and provide it with a market and a source of capital until it could stand on its own was a typical American response to the traditional antipathy of the public toward direct federal involvement in business. It is also a story that has received little scholarly attention.

The leaders behind this application of government funds were Progressive Republicans, who remained committed to their ideals despite the supposed passing of their time. Indeed, these Progressive Republicans applied Theodore Roosevelt's concepts of New Nationalism in creating, in essence, a group of "good trusts" in the aviation industry, which, through their firm financial backing together with substantial government incentive and guidance, could create and develop aviation as a new industry acting in the public interest, avoiding the predations and inefficiencies witnessed in the expansion of an earlier transportation industry, the railroads.

President Herbert Hoover himself was an active participant and an influential promoter of aviation at this time, as the recent work of Ellis Hawley has shown. Hawley's landmark works have provided a new and richer interpretation of the accomplishments and motivations of Hoover, both as commerce secretary and as president. Hawley's *Herbert Hoover as Secretary of Commerce: Studies in New Era Thought and Practice;* "Herbert Hoover, the Commerce Secretariat, and the Vision of the Associative State, 1921–1928," published in the *Journal of American History;* and, especially, "Three Facets of Hooverian Associationalism: Lumber, Aviation, and Movies, 1921–1930," published in Thomas McGraw's *Regulation in Perspective,* bring a clarifying insight to Hoover's presidency. Hawley's work, particularly "Three Facets," explores Hoover's active involvement with business and industry and examines Hoover's role in promoting aviation, but it is interested only in the creation of formal governmental safety regulation through the Department of Commerce and the promotion of aviation. The story of the most critical role, that played by the government through the activities of the Post Office in creating the airlines before and during Hoover's tenure in the White House, is left untouched.

Hawley's seminal work, *The New Deal and the Problem of Monopoly,* carries this interpretation of the difficult interwar years into the Roosevelt administration while placing Hoover's and Roosevelt's approaches to the question of public policy toward monopoly within the context of Progressive attitudes. It lucidly illuminates the juxtaposition of the conflicting ideologies of Republican Theodore Roosevelt's New Nationalism and Democratic Woodrow Wilson's New Freedom. Hawley's thesis provides the foundation for this book's new interpretation of the creation and development of America's air transportation system.

Among the many works analyzing Hoover, none examine his role in the development of commercial air transportation. Despite the detailed analyses of the political and economic sphere of Hoover's administration provided by Martin Fausold, David Burner, Joan Hoff Wilson, Eugene Lyons, and others, little is known or said about perhaps Hoover's greatest legacy, that of America's airline industry. Morton Keller follows Hawley's interpretation of Hoover's role in aviation but concerns himself only with the creation of formal aviation safety regulation in the Commerce Department while ignoring the role played by the Post Office in its de facto regulation of the airline industry.

In his *Regulating a New Economy: Public Policy and Economic Change in America, 1900–1933,* Keller aptly underscores the many conflicting and convergent policies of the nation's political economy and how public policy, in a rapidly evolving economy, reacted differently in each case with respect to the question of antitrust actions. His thesis is that both persistence in the dependence of regulators on established legal and political mechanisms to rein in monopoly and pluralism in public policy decisions resulted in the various responses to emerging industries. His argument that the aviation industry was still in its infancy and was generally left alone is accurate to a point but overlooks the tremendous progress made by Hoover by the beginning of the 1930s, the de jure regulation over the aircraft industry by the Aeronautics Branch of the Department of Commerce, and the de facto regulation of the airline industry by the Post Office.

By the end of the period covered by Keller's work, which coincides with the last months of Hoover's administration, aviation had largely come of age through the positive guidance of the federal government, though much work remained. In his *Leviathan*, Robert Higgs's presumption of the state as a negative influence in economic development is not accurate in the case of Hoover and aviation. Far from restraining and injuring aviation, Hoover's policies actively promoted the new industry through rational regulation and judiciously applied subsidies and incentives, which resulted in a national transportation infrastructure within a remarkably short span of only four years. Despite the crucial role played by the Post Office Department in the regulation of the air transportation industry, only one historian up to now has attempted to examine the tenure of Hoover's visionary, though irascible, postmaster general, Walter Brown. David Lee has produced two excellent articles that detail much of this unheralded administrator's critical work.

Walter Folger Brown was by far the most crucial figure in this story. In previous treatments of this period, Brown has been described as "a Toledo attorney" who reorganized and rationalized the system, creating a national network of airlines by awarding airmail contracts primarily to three large, well-financed aviation holding companies. Brown was indeed "a Toledo attorney," but he was much more than that. He was also, at one time, the boss of Toledo, the leader of the Ohio Republican Party, Theodore Roosevelt's campaign manager during the 1912 presidential campaign, chairman of the Joint Congressional Committee on Reorganization of the Executive Departments, and assistant secretary of commerce in the Coolidge administration, working immediately under Secretary Hoover. Brown's promotion of Hoover greatly influenced the Republican Party's decision to nominate Hoover for the presidency, and Brown's reward was the powerful post of postmaster general.

During his tenure, the visionary Brown fostered development of a national network of airlines. The airlines would operate, in his words, "from somewhere to somewhere," unlike trains during the nineteenth century's chaotic expansion of the railroads, and always under his definition of the public interest. While his definition often conflicted with Congress's and that of the small airline operator, Brown built the vast domestic air transport network that in essence exists today.

Lee's articles aptly summarize Brown's career but do not concentrate on the postmaster general's motivations or detail the effect of Brown's decision and philosophy on the airlines themselves. Only Henry Ladd Smith's excellent *Airways*, published more than fifty years ago, has attempted an analysis of this critical period of American air transportation, but even Smith's evaluation falls short.

Smith, a journalism professor, was limited in his methodology. Writing only shortly after the events occurred, he could not gain sufficient perspective on the issues. As expected in a journalistic approach to historical questions, his research is heavily dependent upon interviews and contemporary periodicals, particularly newspapers and published congressional hearings. He did not have access to the public papers of the government or the private papers of most of the participants, both of which are available today. Nevertheless, Smith accomplished a truly remarkable task. Up until now, his work remains the sole authoritative study, despite its age. Unlike most analyses before and since, *Airways* is ambivalent toward Walter F. Brown. Smith's conclusions are far less damning than he had originally intended, having assumed, as did all subsequent historians of the New Deal, that Hoover's airmail policy was corrupt.

Not possessing the benefit of Ellis Hawley's analysis of this period and not understanding the dominant role played by Progressivism in Brown's approach, Smith is at a loss to explain Brown's actions. Other volumes have attempted to detail the development of commercial aviation in the United States, but all without exception depend heavily on Smith's understanding and provide few, if any, new interpretive approaches. R.E.G. Davies's superlative *Airlines of the United States Since 1914* accomplishes the monumental task of examining virtually every airline that has ever flown in America and remains the definitive popular reference work on the subject. It relies heavily on Smith's account for the crucial formative years of the industry and, because of its vast scope, does not dwell on this important period. *Bonfires to Beacons: Federal Civil Aviation Policy Under the Air Commerce Act, 1926–1938,* Nick Komons's equally impressive official analysis of the formative period of formal federal regulation, concentrates on the important role played by the Commerce Department in establishing safety regulations and a nationwide infrastructure for air transportation. Komons examines the Post Office within this context but does not explore in depth its crucial role in fostering the airline industry. Carl Solberg's *Conquest of the Skies: A History of Commercial Aviation in America* is also heavily dependent upon Smith's work and does not provide additional original insight, despite its thoroughness, as Solberg, along with Davies, relies on a wealth of secondary source material only. All other aviation histories, without exception, rely on these works for an understanding of this crucial period.

This book places the critical role played by Brown within the context of Progressivism and answers the questions posed by Smith about Hoover's postmaster general. When seen in the light of Hawley's conclusions concerning Progressivism and the government's policy concerning monopoly, Brown's actions and those taken by Progressive Democrats in response readily fall into place.

Walter Brown, a New Nationalist in the mould of Theodore Roosevelt, saw the expenditure of public monies through airmail contracts as a means to create and guide a nascent airline industry. He made sure these monies were spent supporting a few financially sound companies that could expand this new industry under the watchful eye of the federal government. Although this led to an oligopolistic control of the industry, it ensured that the aviation holding companies operated within Brown's vision of the public's interest. He regulated the industry and its oligopolies in virtually the same manner as the Civil Aeronautics Board later would do for four decades. This book is the first to make this connection.

In 1934, Senate investigations led by Progressive Democrat Hugo Black exposed the machinations of the Brown years to public scrutiny. Black's view of the relationship between monopoly and the federal government was that of Wilson's New Freedom: all monopoly is inherently bad and should be dissolved. In emotionally charged and heavily politicized hearings the relationship between the Post Office and the airlines was examined in partisan detail. As a result, new postmaster general James Farley recommended and President Franklin Roosevelt ordered the suspension of the airmail contracts and the carrying of the mail by the U.S. Army. After several well-publicized airplane accidents, Roosevelt was forced to return the contracts to the airlines. Under new legislation, however, the aviation holding companies were broken up and the airlines forbidden to own any interest in the aircraft manufacturers.

The airmail crisis marked Roosevelt's first major, public defeat, yet it is generally overlooked by historians. It was critical, however, for the airmail crisis marked a turning point in FDR's attitude toward, as Ellis Hawley has said, "the problem of monopoly."

As is often the case in writing accounts of military conquest, the victors write the history. This adage is equally applicable in politics. Since 1934, a spate of Roosevelt biographies have either ignored the airmail crisis entirely or have accepted the interpretations of New Deal historians without question as complete. Most have treated the question of the airmail and the airlines briefly, if at all. As with Hoover's biographers, the story of the creation of the air transportation industry and its informal regulation by the federal government before 1938 is generally overlooked. Historians, such as Frank Friedel in *Franklin D. Roosevelt: A Rendezvous with Destiny,* state only that "Roosevelt created a furor by canceling all commercial contracts for carrying airmail on the grounds that they were not competitive. . . . Roosevelt then obtained legislation placing firm safeguards on contracts and returned the carrying of mail to commercial airlines." William Leuchtenburg comments only briefly, while James MacGregor Burns ignores the story altogether. Only Arthur Schlesinger Jr. mentions the airmail contract problem. He devotes ten pages to the question and provides a fair analysis—the only Roosevelt biographer to do so. He is not reluctant to remark that the crisis damaged FDR's reputation and sowed the seeds of future trouble with business, James Farley, and Charles Lindbergh. He is also fair to Walter Brown, although Schlesinger fails to understand Brown's methodology, concluding only that "Brown was neither so selfless and farseeing as he presented himself to the Committee nor so wicked as Black proclaimed him to the press."

Generally, when the subject of Roosevelt and the airmail is mentioned, the conclusions are based on subjective accounts and therefore overlook the larger questions of public policy and government business relations. Kenneth Davies's *FDR: The New Deal Years, 1933–1937* accepts the interpretation of the airmail situation only from the perspective of the Roosevelt administration and the independent airlines against the larger, airmail contractors. As such, his work draws unsubstantiated conclusions and accepts flawed secondary-source material as fact. His claim that "the Hoover Administration, obviously, had come into office with a clear and definite federal aeronautics policy, shaped by corporation lawyers and approved in corporate boardrooms, without the benefit or hazard of public debate" is simply wrong, as this work will show. Public debate did indeed occur in Congress, and when the contracts or extensions were let, they were done so legally, within the scope of the Watres Act and with the approval of the comptroller general. Statements that the aim of the Watres Act "was to replace competition with cooperation among large airlines—that is, to destroy the free market in commercial air transport," ignores the simple reality that regulation of an infant industry does exactly that, deliberately, for the betterment of the public, while purposely excluding those companies incapable of providing the necessary service in the public interest. Uncritically accepting opinion as facts, Davies also declares that "this in turn involved blatant violations of antitrust law and of the laws requiring open, competitive bidding for government contract and their award to the lowest bidder that met specifications." This, too, is simply wrong.

That the New Nationalism of Progressive Republicans was replaced by the New Freedom of the Progressive Democrats in the aviation industry is, in sum, the essence of my book. The result of this confrontation, nevertheless, was that the industry remained essentially the same. Although the aviation trusts were abolished, the airline business quickly returned to normal, as the same financially strong airlines that were created by previous administrations continued their industry dominance until almost half a century later, when under deregulation, the government acknowledged the maturity of the airline industry, at long last opening the market to competition.

Today's modern airline system is a direct result of the work of those farsighted Progressives who, understanding the nature of government-business relations in the United States, were responsible for the creation of a sophisticated air transport system. Far from taking a passive role, the federal government played a crucial, controlling role from the very beginning.

Though I alone am responsible for the content of this manuscript, no work is the sole product of its author. In the course of the research and writing of this book, I became indebted to a host of supportive people who generously gave their time and advice. Without their assistance, this book would not have been possible.

Dr. William H. Becker, Professor of History at The George Washington University, introduced me to the field of business history and inspired me to apply these lessons to the study of the aviation industry. I am indebted to Dr. Leo Ribuffo and Dr. Edward Berkowitz, also of the Department of History, for their profound knowledge, advice, and encouragement. I must also express my thanks to Dr. Chris Sterling, who to my surprise also shares my interest in commercial aviation.

To my friends and colleagues at the Smithsonian Institution's National Air and Space Museum (NASM) I express my profound appreciation for their support and encouragement. The positive intellectual atmosphere of the Aeronautics Division, led at various times by Donald Lopez, Dr. Von Hardesty, Dr. Tom Crouch, and Dr. Dominick Pisano, was instrumental in furthering my work. I am indebted beyond measure to R.E.G. Davies, the doyen of airline historians, for his unfailing encouragement and for instilling in me the fascination and enthusiasm of the history of the air transport industry. Dr. Howard Wolko provided sage advice and gave his moral support that helped keep me on track despite constant distractions on the job. I must also extend my thanks to the rest of the staff of the Aeronautics Division for tolerating my endless monologues on the early history of U.S. air transportation, especially Alex Spencer, Dorothy Cochrane, and Rick Leyes. Though visiting scholar Dr. David Lee's stay at NASM was brief, he willingly shared his profound knowledge of Walter Brown and provided me with invaluable research advice. My conversations with former Verville Fellow Jacob Vander Meulen were of particular value. I am especially grateful to Dr. W. David Lewis, Distinguished University Professor at Auburn University, for his keen insights into aviation history and for organizing the International Conference on the History of Civil and Commercial Aviation in Lucerne, Switzerland, where I first publicly presented my ideas on Walter Brown and the progressive movement's effect on the development of commercial aviation in the United States.

The staff of the NASM's Library and Archives was indispensable in providing the reference sources so necessary for this work. Archivists Marilyn Graskowiak, Paul Silbermann, and Larry Wilson were particularly helpful in cataloging and making available the Clement Keys papers. Reference Librarian Phil Edwards gave me much appreciated advice and access to the museum's arcane holdings.

Most of the research was conducted at the National Archives and Records Administration just before its difficult move into new quarters in College Park, Maryland. Despite this, the entire staff remained highly cooperative and pointed me in new directions that invariably produced results. I am especially in the debt of Aloha Smith and Jerry Clark of the Civil Records Division and Joe Schwartz at the Center for Legislative Archives. The holdings of the Manuscript Division of the Library of Congress also proved a veritable gold mine of previously unearthed material. The staff was always helpful. It is a blessing for all historians that these two excellent federal facilities are so well maintained and centrally located for all to use.

The staff of the Herbert C. Hoover Presidential Library and Archives in West Branch, Iowa, were most gracious with their time and advice. Dale Mayer, Wade R. Slinde, and their colleagues ensured that my brief stay was extremely productive. This jewel of an archive houses not only Hoover's records but also those of William MacCracken and significant, though small, holdings on Walter Brown.

At the Boeing Company's Historical Services Division, former archivist Marilyn Phipps was exceeding in her generosity in allowing me access to the company's records. Her vast knowledge of the history of this important company was of inestimable use. Archivist Tom Lubbesmeyer and former Boeing historian Paul Spitzer were similarly helpful. I am also always grateful to the ever-knowledgeable Jay Spenser, with whom I have enjoyed countless enlightening discussions. Boeing is one of the few companies that are actively aware of their rich history. It is a credit to the management of Boeing that they have preserved their heritage.

Greg Kennedy, the former director of American Airlines' C.R. Smith Museum, made available his airline's collections and enabled me to visit his and other facilities. Barb Hansen of United Air Lines generously permitted me to use the company's small but useful archival collection in Chicago. I would also like to thank Dr. Larry D. Sall, Associate Library Director for Special Collections at the University of Texas at Dallas, for access to the Aviation History Collection.

Dr. Deborah Douglas, Curator of Science and Technology at the MIT Museum and former NASM denizen, has shared with me a similar interest in the history of this crucial period in aviation. I am grateful for her friendship and for the numerous hours we spent discussing our respective projects. I also greatly appreciate her unflagging support and her tireless efforts on my behalf.

This book is dedicated to my family for their patience and understanding. I thank my parents Frank and Lyn for teaching me English and a love of history. I owe too much to them to express adequately in words. One look in any university library catalog will reveal who is indeed the best historian in the family. I have a long way to go to catch up with my father. I am grateful to my mother-in-law, Nella, for her support, and to my late father-in-law, Carl, who understood better than anyone the value of education, I wish to say, "Thank you for the pen."

I would also like to thank my sisters Margaret and Anne, their husbands, Ryan and Greg, respectively, my sister-in-law Carla and her husband Trey, and, particularly, Kristin, David, and Michael, who I hope some day will read this and know that their Uncle Bob was thinking of them.

Most of all I wish to dedicate this book to my wife, Sue, who has lovingly shepherded this stressed-out curator and historian through life.

Chapter 1

Foundations

O n the morning of May 15, 1918, a crowd gathered around a single-engined
Curtiss JN-4H "Jenny" trainer parked at the Polo Grounds near the
Potomac River in the nation's capital. Thousands of spectators pressed against
rope barricades hoping to catch a glimpse of the festivities as five hundred
dignitaries arrived amid much fanfare. Present were Postmaster General Albert
S. Burleson and Second Assistant Postmaster General Otto Praeger, Secretary
of the Navy Josephus Daniels and his assistant secretary, Franklin D. Roosevelt,
members of the recently formed National Advisory Committee on Aeronautics, and numerous members of Congress. At 11:15 A.M. President Woodrow
Wilson and the first lady arrived to witness the inaugural flight of the U.S. Air
Mail Service.

Within minutes a truck arrived carrying four large bags of mail. Into one,
President Wilson placed a letter addressed to the postmaster of New York from
General Burleson. After a short presentation ceremony, the pilot, Lt. George L.
Boyle, climbed into his frail craft, started his reluctant 150-horsepower
Hispano-Suiza engine, and bounced down the Polo Grounds, crawling into
the air at 11:46, headed for Philadelphia. The plan was for Boyle to land at
Bustleton, Pennsylvania, where his load of mail would be transferred into an-
other Jenny and flown to New York. Fifteen minutes before Boyle took off, Lt.
Torrey Webb left from the Belmont Race Track on Long Island and headed
south for the same destination, thus opening two-way Washington–Philadelphia–New York service. That was the plan. Webb reached Philadelphia one
hour later without incident. Boyle was not so fortunate.

Navigating by a single road map, Boyle became confused while attempting to follow the railroad tracks north. Without the aid of an accurate com-
pass, Boyle found himself sixty minutes later over Waldorf, Maryland,

Lt. George L. Boyle opened air mail service when he took off in his Curtiss JN-4 from West Potomac Park in Washington, D.C., on May 15, 1918. (Smithsonian, SI# 2000-6152)

twenty-five miles southeast of Washington. Landing to seek directions, Boyle flipped his aircraft, fortunately damaging only his pride. When news of his accident reached Philadelphia, the connecting flight left for New York, on schedule, but without the Washington mail, arriving on time at 3:37 P.M.

In Philadelphia, Webb transferred his mail load into a Jenny piloted by Lt. James Edgerton, who took off with no trouble and smoothly proceeded to Washington, where he landed at 2:50 P.M. to the applause of numerous well wishers, including his sister and fiancée. Thus the first day of regularly scheduled air mail service drew to a close.[1]

Today, we think nothing of flying thousands of miles to conduct business, visit relatives, or spend leisure time vacationing halfway around the globe. The ability to travel these vast distances, by air, is truly one of the greatest social and technological accomplishments of the twentieth century. In the span of only ninety years, this new and revolutionary means of transportation has changed how we perceive the world and has conquered heretofore unconquerable obstacles of time and distance. Perhaps the greatest achievement of the industrial age, heavier-than-air, powered flight, went from birth to maturity in an unprecedented short period of time. Unlike previous transportation systems, which evolved over centuries, aviation developed almost overnight.

Today, the ability to fly is taken for granted. The average American citizen is aware of the story of the Wright brothers and their remarkable creation in 1903. Most people know that the airplane was quickly forged into a weapon of war that is today capable of prodigious destructiveness. They see the sky full of gleaming jet airliners effortlessly traversing the continent over invisible routes to distant destinations. These aircraft and the airlines that operate them have always seemed to exist. That their creation and development in the United States was the product of a conscious effort by the federal government is little known. That the very existence of the airlines is the product of an often-abused bureaucracy is imperceptible. Yet that is the case.

Since 1792, the Post Office Department, now the Postal Service, has borne the responsibility of uniting the country through the communications system of the mail. The Post Office provided the vital link between communities, the lifeline between businesses and friends, and the one national instrument capable of spreading information throughout the nation quickly and efficiently. So important was this mission that the American citizen has always been willing, though usually grudgingly, to accept the intrusion of the federal government and the expenditure of tax dollars, even at a loss, for the benefits of mail service. To this end, the Post Office has traditionally sought ways to improve service, particularly through improvements in speed.

Post roads were the first manifestation of the growing federal presence across the nation. These public roads, which proliferated in the nineteenth century, were usually the first reliable links between new and old communities, and there was constant pressure from an expanding country for the Post Office to keep pace with America's internal development. Concurrent with the boom in transportation technologies, first with the roads, then the canals, and soon the innovation of the railroads, the Post Office kept pace by placing the public mails on stage lines, ships, and rail cars. Through the use of contract mail carriers, the Post Office was able to spread the mails across the nation while directly supporting new transportation technologies through payments for services.

By the beginning of the twentieth century, contractors were carrying the bulk of mail between city centers and were dependent upon the federal largess to keep their burgeoning enterprises profitable. Subsidies, a term generally anathema to Americans, have always been an integral part of the functioning of the Post Office. The first subsidies were granted in the 1840s to promote the development of American steamship lines that were threatened by foreign competition. This action promoted the creation of improved ship designs, advanced the state of the ship builders' art, and directly benefited U.S. business. Regional opposition, particularly from the South and the West, curtailed the use of subsidies until the advent of World War I. During this conflict, the federal government once again employed the strategy of subsidies to support the domestic merchant marine. With British and German merchant ships engaged in combat, the United States was deprived of the use of much of the world's commercial fleet. Through the renewed implementation of postal subsidies, the federal government once again came to the aid of a developing industry. Thus, by the end of World War I, the concept of federal support for new transportation technologies clearly had been established.

Concurrent with federal support of transportation came the politicization of the Post Office as, over time, its power and influence grew. For almost one hundred years the Post office was the only visible manifestation of the federal government seen by the average citizen. As such, the control of local post offices and the appointment of local postmasters became crucial political tools and rewards for successful campaigns and the means for political parties to extend their influence throughout the country. With lucrative federal patronage available to the winners, control of the Post Office and its spoils was fiercely pursued. The position of postmaster general became the nation's preeminent patronage post, usually awarded to the victorious president's most trusted advisor. Commonly, the postmaster general was the party leader, campaign manager, and critical liaison with Congress. He controlled the money, and it was to him that local, state, and federal politicians petitioned for rewards. Despite the diminished influence of politics following the creation of a federal civil service through the Pendleton Act of 1883, which abolished many of the former patronage jobs, and subsequent reforms during the Progressive Era to rectify repeated scandals, the influence of the Post Office and the postmaster general remained great.

With the precedent of direct federal assistance to transportation technologies and the important political role of the Post Office thus well established, America entered a new era in the ongoing relationship between business and government when, late in the spring of 1918, the Post Office inaugurated the nation's first regularly scheduled air mail service.

That day was the culmination of the efforts of many in both the Post Office and Congress to reap the promised benefits of aircraft speed. As early as 1910, Congress began to show interest in the potential of aircraft to carry the mail. That year Rep. Morris Shepard introduced the first air mail bill, which unfortunately died in committee.[2] Despite this setback, Postmaster General Frank H. Hitchcock, a promoter of the air mail concept, pressed on. At an international air meet on Long Island, Hitchcock allowed a special air mail service to fly as part of the festivities. Thus, on September 23, 1911, pilot Earle Ovington was sworn in as America's first air mail pilot and, squeezing a full mail sack between his legs, took off in his delicate Queen monoplane for Mineola, some five miles away. Six minutes later, Ovington banked his aircraft and pushed the bag out of the cockpit. The bag fell to the ground near the local postmaster.[3] Although purely ceremonial, this was the first time aircraft officially carried U.S. mail.

Hitchcock's subsequent efforts to convince Congress to provide fifty thousand dollars for an experimental service fell on deaf ears. With the advent of Wilson to the presidency in 1913, the new postmaster general, Burleson, continued his predecessor's efforts to foster the creation of an air mail plan. Little was done, despite bipartisan efforts. A change occurred on September 1, 1916, when Otto Praeger, a former reform-minded newspaperman and Progressive city clerk of San Antonio, Texas, became second assistant postmaster general and administered the delivery of the mail. Praeger adopted Burleson's desire to push for air mail.

Immediately upon taking office, Praeger began to campaign for air mail service in Alaska and Massachusetts. Although these efforts met with failure, his determination to push through service between New York and Chicago convinced enough members of Congress to authorize an experimental service between New York and Washington, D.C. With the support of the National Advisory Committee for Aeronautics (NACA), the purpose of which was to foster aviation development, and of Standard Aircraft, which hoped that this undertaking would prove an outlet for its aircraft products, Burleson approved the project, and with the begrudging cooperation of the U.S. Army Air Service, which initially was to provide the pilots and aircraft, the service began in May. Burleson, a former Populist, had no compunction against the government entering what traditionally was the purview of business. Despite the tradition of contracting with private transportation enterprises for the delivery of mail over long distances, Burleson realized that this infant industry needed substantial government assistance during its formative stages.

Despite setbacks that any pioneering enterprise would expect, the new U.S. Air Mail Service quickly became a generally reliable service, completing an average of 91 percent of its flights.[4] In August 1918, the army withdrew, leaving the Post Office in complete control of the operation, equipped with its own aircraft and pilots. Under Capt. Benjamin Lipsner, new Standard biplanes, each with a capacity of three hundred pounds, were acquired and the base of operations in Washington shifted to College Park Airport (the oldest in the world) in nearby Maryland. Under Lipsner's direction the service grew with a specific goal: that of a proving ground for eventual civil aviation. According to Lipsner, this noble experiment was "the mechanical laboratory for the advancement of commercial aviation. . . . The first step toward the universal commercial use of the aeroplane."[5]

Once rational procedures and reliable accounting practices were implemented, Lipsner pushed for the logical extension of his vision: transcontinental air service. Realizing that the time savings afforded by the speed of aircraft could be realized only over long distances, the Post Office pressed for New York–to–Chicago service, which opened on September 5, 1919. By this time, specially modified de Havilland DH-4 light bombers were converted as mail planes and introduced into the schedules, soon becoming the ubiquitous symbol of the Air Mail Service. Conflicts with Praeger forced Lipsner's resignation and the replacement as chief of flying by James Edgerton, one of the original pilots on the inaugural route. Despite this and continuing battles with the army and Congress over control of the operation, Praeger pushed forward, Edgerton building the route infrastructure, writing the operations manuals, and selecting and training the pilots and crew as the operation expanded westward.[6] On May 15, 1920, two years to the day after opening service, the air mail reached Omaha, and on September 8 the transcontinental route to San Francisco was completed.

At this point, all schedules were flown during the day as neither the aircraft nor routes were equipped with measures to allow for night and bad weather flying. In a dramatic display of the possibilities of continuous operation and to counter the attacks by critics that the operation was too costly and inefficient, on February 22, 1921, just ten days before the new Harding administration took office, four pilots, two from each coast, took off. Only one of the four schedules was completed, but the event made headlines. Battling bad weather, which killed one pilot and grounded the other two, Frank Yeager pressed on over his night stage from Salt Lake City via Cheyenne to North Platte, Nebraska. Pilot Jack Knight relayed the mail from there to Omaha, where he was to hand it over to the connecting flight from Chicago. Unfortunately, that flight was grounded, and, braving the night and deteriorating weather, guided only by bonfires lit across Iowa, Knight completed his epic flight. Once in Chicago, the mail was again transferred and flown without incident to New York in the remarkable time of thirty-three hours and twenty minutes.[7] This astonishing achievement highlighted the potential of air mail service. Yet much work remained.

Incoming postmaster general Will H. Hays was less than enthusiastic about this aerial experiment. Hays appointed as the new second assistant postmaster Edward W. Shaughnessy, who promptly sought to increase cooperation with the army. Shaughnessy's background was in railroads and because of this, sought to turn over the air mail operation to commercial carriers. He quickly learned that no one would accept the tremendous risk of capital involved in such an unproven technology. It was clear that only a subsidy could entice investors into the air, but the country was not yet willing to underwrite such a

Col. Paul Henderson
(Smithsonian, SI# 83-8163)

controversial idea. His experience in contracting proved a failure, as Alfred Lawson, an early aircraft builder from Milwaukee and a promoter of unsteady personality, reneged on his lofty promises to open three air mail routes by April 1921.[8] Concentrating now on efficiency over diversity, Shaughnessy eliminated air routes where railroads offered almost comparable service, such as that between Washington and New York, and concentrated on transcontinental service while biding time for new legislation. The second assistant's tireless efforts to improve service and safety as well as lower costs came to an abrupt end when he was tragically killed in the infamous Knickerbocker Theater collapse during a Washington blizzard in February 1922. Shortly thereafter, Postmaster General Hays resigned to accept a more lucrative position in Hollywood as the film industry's morals watchdog.[9]

The new Second Assistant was Colonel Paul Henderson, who would soon prove to be as effective as Otto Praeger in his dedication and results. Henderson, a forty-year-old veteran from Chicago who served as an ordnance officer during the Great War, was well connected politically, having married the daughter of Congressman Martin Madden. His business acumen, first as president of his father-in-law's stone company and later as treasurer of the Andrews Engineering Company, together with his political connections made him the ideal candidate to serve the new postmaster general, Hubert Work.[10]

A staunch Republican who wanted the air mail service eventually turned over to private enterprise, Henderson nevertheless actively worked to improve the government's air mail system. Taking control of the army's experimental lighted airway between Dayton and Columbus, Ohio, Henderson used this short, eighty-mile route as a model for his plan to light the entire transcontinental route. Henderson used a system of powerful rotating beacons developed by the General Electric Company located at every regular and emergency field along the way. By the summer of 1923, the crucial section from Chicago to Cheyenne had been completed, with 289 beacons, five lighted primary landing fields, and thirty-four lighted secondary fields. Seventeen DH-4 aircraft were equipped with special flares, luminescent instruments, and navigation and landing lights. A highly successful four-day experimental schedule was tested in August 1923, and on July 1, 1924, regular overnight service was begun, cutting transcontinental delivery time by air from ninety-one hours to only twenty-nine hours (with the eastbound tailwinds). This was almost three days faster than possible by rail. By the fall of 1925, the entire lighted airways system was finished, at a cost of $550,000, greatly assisting the subsequent expansion of commercial service.[11]

With the completion of the lighted airway system and the inauguration of regular, reliable air mail service, the Post Office's pioneering days were coming to a close. Just as the U.S. military had pioneered new technologies of mass production at the Springfield armory a century earlier, when private capital was unwilling to invest, so too did the Post Office invest public funds into another new technology, that of aviation, in a successful effort to demonstrate the possibilities of a new technology to revolutionize communications.

When Paul Henderson resigned from the Post Office in 1925 he left behind a flourishing government enterprise operating in the public interest and proving every day and night that aviation was no longer the realm of the foolhardy, but a viable, though still infant, industry. The times were rapidly evolving, for aviation was undergoing a rapid and turbulent period of change.

Although the Post Office was making dramatic progress, the state of aviation as a whole in the United States was chaotic. There was no regulation of any kind to control or promote rational growth of aviation as a business or as a transportation system. Between the end of World War I and 1926, the air was filled with gypsy fliers, the so-called barnstormers, flying from town to town in war surplus trainers, willing to take daring local members of the community on exciting circuits of the field for a fee. Flight was portrayed as the realm of the thrillseeker, the unbridled domain of the risk taker, not a means of safe, reliable transportation. Without regulation to promote safety and coherent development, there would be no private contractors or, more important, no financial backers willing to accept the huge risks for little or no reward. What was needed was rational legislation promoting both the regulation of the operation of the industry and the establishment of necessary incentives to attract investors.

As early as 1921, a small special interest group of aviation executives and enthusiasts began to lobby the halls of Congress in search of a remedy. In the words of President Warren Harding's secretary of commerce, Herbert Hoover, to Rep. Frederick Hicks (R-N.Y.), "It is interesting to note that this is the only industry that favors having itself regulated by the government."[12] Herbert Hoover, in fact, would take the lead in the search for appropriate new legislation. Working in cooperation with the Aeronautical Chamber of Commerce (ACC), which represented the aircraft manufacturers, and the National Aeronautic Association, which represented wealthy public-spirited aviation promoters, Hoover was able to take the lead and forge a new consensus concerning his vision of the role that aviation might play in the future.[13] It is important to note the desire was for the creation of operating rules to promote safety, not for economic control of the aviation business.

Hoover applied his notions concerning the associative state, as described by historian Ellis Hawley, to forge a viable business-government relationship based on voluntary cooperation to the benefit of both parties. He urged the formation of professional organizations in the aviation industry, which until that time had little representation.[14] During his tenure at the Commerce Department, Hoover actively promoted public acceptance of aviation through a series of publicity campaigns as well as by speaking widely on the potential advantages to business and transportation offered by the airplane. The airplane promised greater efficiencies, and its development opened new vistas for business and an expansion of the national economy, all goals of his secretariat.[15] Hoover realized that a prosperous aviation industry, led by adequate government incentives, would help defray the cost of maintaining a large national aviation capability. Adequate and immediate legislation was required before any substantive progress could result.

Hoover's initial efforts to create sufficient federal regulation failed to reach fruition. Attempts to establish national regulation as outlined in the Wadsworth bill of 1921 were successfully attacked by southern states rights' advocates, who blanched at the thought of federal control over the airways.[16] A successive, weaker bill failed to satisfy the aviation community. Further attempts to increase the power of the federal government over aviation combined with ineffective floor leadership condemned the measure to its premature demise.[17] Despite subsequent revisions and a renewed offensive in 1923 and 1924 led by Hoover, civil air regulation failed to fire the imagination of Congress and the public sufficiently to force passage. But times were about to change.

Pressure to reform the airways came again from the Post Office. On Feb-

M. Clyde Kelly, author of the Air Mail Act of
1925 (Smithsonian, SI# A4164D)

ruary 2, 1925, President Calvin Coolidge signed into law the Air Mail Act of
1925. Better known as the Kelly Act, after its primary proponent, Republican
representative M. Clyde Kelly of Pennsylvania, the bill for the first time authorized the transfer of the flying of the air mail to contract carriers. Earlier attempts in 1921 by Rep. Halvor Steenerson, a Minnesota Republican and
chairman of the House Post Office and Post Roads Committee, met a lukewarm response. Without a provision for a minimum load payment, or a guaranteed three-to-five year contract, business simply was not interested in flying
the mail as it was still a highly speculative proposition.[18]

In February 1924, following deliberations with Congress and incoming
postmaster general Harry New, Representative Kelly proposed new legislation,
which sailed through the Sixty-eighth Congress with little debate. Signed into
law one year later, the Kelly Act authorized a special ten-cent-per-ounce air
mail rate. More important, Section 4 of the act authorized the use of private
contractors to fly the mail at a rate not to exceed four-fifths of the amount of
revenue received by the Post Office for the carriage of the mail on each designated route.[19]

This "fraction of postage" method of payment allayed the fears of the potential contractors by guaranteeing them 80 percent of the postal revenues.
This was a subsidy in the classic sense, but concern was deflected because the
payment came from only postal receipts, not from general tax revenues.[20]

Although the law did not specify the length required for the contract, the Post Office used its discretionary powers provided in Section 5 of the law to make the contracts for four years, the maximum allowed by existing precedent. It was hoped that this would allow the holder of the contract sufficient time to invest heavily in route development, equipment, and training while still having substantial time to realize a decent return on his investment.[21]

The Kelly Act of 1925 created the first successful airlines in the United States and supplied the needed impetus to push Congress toward passage of necessary regulation of the industry. Without the government promoting air safety, a reliable, trustworthy airline system simply could not exist. Without government financial incentives, the airlines could not survive.

The experience of pioneering airlines, such as the St. Petersburg–Tampa Airboat Line of 1914 and Aeromarine in the early 1920s, made it clear that despite the best efforts of knowledgeable individuals and well-financed, well-organized companies, some form of government subsidy was necessary, given the present state of aeronautics and the general inefficiency of current aircraft technologies.

The question of subsidy was the overriding issue confronting commercial aviation. All of the witnesses before the Steenerson committee called for government financial assistance but were unanimous in their opposition to direct subsidy, something that was prevalent in Europe and was correctly seen as debilitating rather than constructive. All were in agreement over the necessity of government economic support; the differences were focused over the definition of "subsidy," a word anathema to most Americans at that time. According to testimony, the operators wanted only enough money to cover costs and no more. To them, a "subsidy" meant "profit," and they were deliberately vague in interpreting a subsidy as "a grant of funds or property from a government to a private person or company in the establishment or support of an enterprise deemed advantageous to the public as a simple gift or a payment of an amount in excess of the usual charge for a service."[22]

In a report prepared for Secretary Hoover and the Commerce Department by the American Engineering Council in 1926, the industry flatly rejected subsidies, as they defined them. "Although every European air line is receiving subsidies," the report noted, "aircraft operators in the United States are practically unanimous that direct government subsidies are not needed or advisable in this country. . . . Traffic conditions in the United States are more favorable for air transport than in Europe, and with proper navigational aids it should be able to establish itself on a sound business basis without subsidies."[23]

This last point was crucial, for aids to navigation were not seen as a subsidy. In a September 1925 statement prepared for the Morrow Board, which was called by President Coolidge to investigate the state of American aeronautics following the caustic and disjointed attacks led by Gen. William "Billy" Mitchell, Secretary Hoover spoke clearly about his vision. "The Department of Commerce has been confident for the last two years that the development of the flying art has reached a point where it is near the possibility of self-supporting application to commercial transportation in the United States," he said. "In this belief we have advocated the creation of a Bureau of Civil Aviation that the Government might undertake to give services to commercial aviation comparable with those which the Government has over a century given to commercial navigation."[24]

In Hoover's view, precedent existed for federal assistance in the form of aid to shipping. Since the beginning of the country, the federal government had provided for the lighting and marking of channels for navigation, had produced detailed charts of the waterways, and had provided information concerning weather and geographical changes of the routes. Furthermore, the government had provided safety services in the public interest, setting safety standards in the shipping industry and conducting inspections to enforce the regulations. Standards were set not just for equipment but for the personnel operating the equipment as well. Washington had also assumed responsibility for the development and improvement of the waterways and ports. In Hoover's farsighted opinion, such regulatory action was essential for the industry's survival.[25]

The committee was composed of many of the leading figures in the aviation industry and was reflective of Hoover's associative views of voluntary business-government cooperation to solve national problems. Appointed in June 1925, the committee was composed of nine prominent individuals, including J. Walter Drake, who served as chairman; J.W. Roe, past president of the Society of Industrial Engineers, who served as vice chairman; Edward P. Warner, from the Massachusetts Institute of Technology; and C. Townsend Ludington, a prominent aircraft operator.

The committee outlined four fundamental problems in U.S. civil aviation. First, there was a lack of definite legal status and government control over civil aviation. Second, an absence of an established government policy to encourage the civilian and industrial uses of aircraft hampered development. Third, there were at present no aircraft or supporting equipment adapted to efficient and profitable commercial operation. This resulted, fourth, in the lack of public and business confidence and support.[26]

In order to address these issues, the committee recommended the immediate enactment of a civil aeronautics law to create the Bureau of Aeronautics within the Department of Commerce. This bureau would issue licenses for aircraft and pilots, establish regulatory guidelines, and enforce inspections while creating and maintaining national air navigation facilities. The committee as-

serted that the public possesses a right of free air navigation and further recommended that commercial aviation be regarded as common carriers, thereby
limiting the liability of future airlines. In an attempt to assuage local fears of a
possible growing and intrusive federal presence, it left to the states and local
governments the heavy responsibility for developing airports. Of greatest importance, the committee strongly urged that the government refrain from
nonmilitary flying that could be better served by private enterprise.[27]

Reflecting Hoover's associative state once again, the committee stressed
the importance of cooperation and sought the creation of interdepartmental
committees to coordinate all nonmilitary government air activities in order to
promote civil aviation in the best manner. If these steps were taken, the committee believed, a solid foundation would result, eliminating much risk and
thereby provide incentive for investment.[28]

The council's report clearly underscored Hoover's position concerning the
relationship between government and business in aviation. With this report
and the Kelly Act pointing the direction for the country, the road to rational
regulation seemed open. There remained one large obstacle.

One of the most prominent and controversial figures in American aviation during the 1920s was Gen. William "Billy" Mitchell. Returning from World
War I a hero and thoroughly enamored with the possibilities of air power,
Assistant Chief of the Army Air Service Mitchell embarked on a crusade to
establish an independent air force along the lines of Britain's recently formed
Royal Air Force. His overriding concern was to unify all aviation, both civil
and military, into a Department of the Air, under his control. This last goal
was a tactical error, as it alienated most of those individuals in civil aviation
who were otherwise in agreement with the general.[29]

Behaving in an undisciplined manner, using propaganda and political connections, and manipulating the press and public opinion, Mitchell thrust himself into public view, decrying the sorry state of American military aeronautics
while staging dramatic demonstrations of the potential of air power. To this
end Mitchell mobilized his forces in Congress, much to the consternation of
President Coolidge and the nation's senior officers, and called for a congressional committee to investigate the state of U.S. aeronautics.

Chaired by Rep. Florian Lampert (R-Wisc.), this committee sought to examine claims made by Progressive Republican representative John L. Nelson
of Wisconsin that the administration was protecting a so-called aircraft trust
attempting to monopolize commercial aviation. Most of the wild claims were
based on politics, as during the 1924 election, insurgent Republicans backed
another Wisconsin native for the presidency, Robert M. La Follette. Despite
Coolidge's overwhelming victory in November, the committee convened in

the Sixty-ninth Congress. Despite the fact that two of the five Republicans along with the four minority Democrats might undermine the administration's efforts, the committee behaved in a surprisingly professional way.

Mitchell's testimony before this committee and the sympathetic House Military Affairs contrasted with the sensible approach taken by Lampert. His outbursts against the administration in January and February 1925 angered the War Department and the White House. As a result Mitchell was removed from his post as assistant chief of the Army Air Service, transferred to the Eighth Corps in San Antonio, Texas, and reduced to his permanent rank of colonel.[30]

Mitchell did not go quietly. After spending several months in relative isolation, he once again burst onto the scene in September, following the crash of a U.S. Navy dirigible, the USS *Shenandoah,* during an Ohio thunderstorm and the disappearance of the navy's PN-9 flying boat during a record setting flight attempt from California to Hawaii. Having lost his close friend Cdr. Zachary Landsdowne on the *Shenandoah,* Mitchell claimed that the accidents were the result of incompetency and criminal negligence and the "almost treasonable administration of the National Defense by the Navy and the War Departments."[31] Such insubordination could not be tolerated. Coolidge called for Mitchell's immediate court-martial while countering his critics by forming a commission of his own choosing.

Coolidge stacked the deck in his favor placing on his board eight conservative Republicans and one Democrat. Two board members were officers, including Gen. Douglas MacArthur, and only one, Sen. Hiram Bingham of Connecticut, was an aviator. Bingham, in fact, was a vocal proponent of civil aviation legislation along the lines that Secretary Hoover was proposing at that time and therefore was ideal. Heading the board was Coolidge's close friend and partner in J.P. Morgan and Company, Dwight W. Morrow.

The Morrow Board performed precisely as expected. Delving into the state of America's aviation industry, it worked feverishly to complete its investigation before December, when the Lampert committee was set to release its findings.[32] Working diligently for eight weeks, the Morrow Board interviewed ninety-nine witnesses, most of whom had already testified before the Lampert committee.

The conclusions reached by Morrow, released on December 2, were conservative and predictable. The board rejected Mitchell's assertion for a unified military and civilian aeronautics department and confirmed the program outlined by Hoover and the Drake Committee, which was also advocated by most of the civil aviation community.[33] The Lampert committee's findings were surprisingly moderate as well. Although it recommended a single department of defense on military affairs, it rejected the concept of an air ministry and Rep.

William P. MacCracken
(Smithsonian, SI# 91-13613)

Nelson's accusations of a sinister "aviation trust" while endorsing Hoover's plan for an aeronautics branch within the Department of Commerce.

With the blessing of two committees, Hoover now turned to William P. MacCracken, a Chicago-born attorney, to lead his efforts to reform aviation. MacCracken first became interested in aviation during World War I, when he learned to fly. A friendly, unassuming man, MacCracken possessed a sharp mind and was a proficient debater. When he chose to write a paper on aviation law he discovered that the body of literature was virtually non-existent. He took it upon himself to concentrate on this new branch of law and by 1921 became chairman of the Committee on the Law of Aeronautics of the American Bar Association, leading the fight for legislation. When his interest brought him to Washington in 1922 to meet with a state aviation law committee, MacCracken was introduced to Rep. Samuel Winslow, chairman of the House Committee on Interstate and Foreign Commerce. Desirous of implementing strong federal regulation, Winslow introduced the bill that MacCracken wrote with Frederic B. Lee, an attorney on the staff of the House Legislative Drafting Service. MacCracken and Lee would eventually form an important law practice in Washington.[34]

Problems concerning federal versus states' rights doomed the Winslow bill as well as the far weaker Wadsworth bill it replaced.[35] Nevertheless, Sen.

Hiram Bingham (R-Conn.) reintroduced legislation to regulate commercial aviation. This bill spurred the young MacCracken into action.[36] By appealing to Reps. Schuyler Merritt and James S. Parker, who also sat on the Morrow Board, MacCracken managed to win approval of his much stronger bill, which possessed the strengths of the earlier Winslow and Wadsworth bills and few of their weaknesses. Giving federal authority precedence but leaving to the states and municipalities the control over airport development, the Air Commerce Act was passed and signed into law on May 20, 1926.[37]

The Air Commerce Act of 1926 reflected exactly Hoover's ideas on federal regulation of civil aviation. He now had the tools to direct the rational development of aviation. Not unexpectedly, William P. MacCracken accepted Hoover's invitation to become the assistant secretary of commerce for air in charge of the new Aeronautics branch of the department.

Thus was established the regulatory framework for the development of civil aviation in the United States. The federal government now had control over aviation and the authority to develop rational routes, to construct aids to navigation, and to promote the safe growth of the industry. With this structure in place, the way was clear for the next step in providing the country with a new transportation technology.

Chapter 2

The Birth of an Industry

Although the Kelly Act became law on February 2, 1925, it would take many months before private contract air carriers could begin to fly the mail. The Post Office was realistic in handling the situation. Relinquishing the routes would be done in a gradual, methodical manner to ensure the reliability and safety of the service. Because the airlines were new and unproven, the Post Office required that all potential applicants conform to rigid requirements of operation and finance. Routes were to be awarded through competitive bidding, the award going to the lowest responsible bidder. The Post Office would determine the definition of "responsible."

In one of his final acts as second assistant postmaster general, Col. Paul Henderson issued the department's new regulations, the most important of which was that both the pilot and aircraft had to receive a certificate of airworthiness from the Post Office. This requirement, made because proper civil aviation regulation as yet did not exist, ensured that the airline would operate safely or risk cancellation of their contract. Each company was required to post a minimum of ten thousand dollars in bonds to show good faith and serve as collateral if the company failed to comply with the terms of the contract.

The contract air mail carrier would receive four-fifths of the revenue from the special ten-cent-per-ounce air mail rate, as determined after an accurate count by local postmasters. The companies were encouraged to seek other sources of income, such as passengers, air express, and cargo, provided that none interfere with the carriage of the mail. Such contracts could also be sublet with Post Office approval. Each operator was required to maintain all primary and emergency landing fields and radio and navigation aids. American citizenship was required of all contractors, only American-made aircraft could be flown, and at least 75 percent of the company's capital stock had to be owned by U.S. citizens.[1]

The Post Office remained cautious. It was not about to hand over all of its routes immediately to untested neophytes but would let contracts first on the routes feeding the main, transcontinental route. Only when the operators demonstrated their proficiency would the Post Office offer the potentially highly lucrative New York–to–San Francisco line, the nation's most important business route. In opening up a new industry that held great promise for the future, the government was aware of what could and should result. In a prescient editorial, the trade journal *Aviation* summarized the prevalent state of mind of the Post Office and the industry. "The United States covers a large area," it noted, "and it is inevitable that the most obvious routes will be controlled by great corporations. But there will always remain plenty of routes where smaller companies can operate with good chances of success."[2]

With these thoughts in mind, Postmaster General Harry New called for bids on July 25. Sealed bids would be received until 4:30 on the afternoon of September 15, 1925. Bidders were expected to state the number and type of aircraft they were planning to use, complete with a physical description. All aircraft were required to have a fireproof mail compartment, and potential operators had to provide a bond with two or more individual sureties approved by the postmaster general. An average speed of ninety miles per hour was expected. All routes were designed to connect with the transcontinental route.

Eight routes with no more than six round trip flights per week were advertised:

1. Boston to New York by way of Hartford, Connecticut.
2. Chicago to Birmingham, Alabama, by way of Indianapolis, Louisville, and Nashville.
3. Chicago to St. Paul and Minneapolis by way of La Crosse, Wisconsin.
4. Chicago to Dallas and Fort Worth by way of Moline, Illinois; St. Joseph and Kansas City, Missouri; Wichita; and Oklahoma City.
5. Chicago to St. Louis by way of Springfield, Illinois.
6. Elko, Nevada, to Pasco, Washington, by way of Boise, Idaho.
7. Salt Lake City to Los Angeles by way of Las Vegas.
8. Seattle to Los Angeles by way of Portland and Medford, Oregon; Sacramento; San Francisco; Fresno; and Bakersfield.

Leading the Post Office's air mail service was a new second assistant postmaster general, Warren Irving Glover. Effective August 1, 1925, Glover advanced from the rank of third assistant and was placed in charge of the transportation of mail. Brooklyn-born, the new forty-five-year-old air mail chief entered the woolen industry after leaving high school at the age of eigh-

W. Irving Glover, Second Assistant Postmaster General, 1923–1933 (U.S. Postal Service, 122-38)

teen, eventually becoming a sales representative for the Phoenix Woolen Company. By 1908 he had organized both the Afton and Sussex Holding Corporations, which controlled construction firms in the New York City area. As a member of the Third Ward Republican Club, Glover first entered politics supporting Theodore Roosevelt for the governorship. After moving to Englewood, New Jersey, he entered Bergen County politics, eventually rising to the New Jersey State Assembly, where he served a record five terms in office. As the state house speaker, he led the difficult fight for the passage of the Nineteenth Amendment.[3]

He came to prominence in 1920, when, during a trip to Central America, he returned home on board the same ship as President-elect Warren Harding. Soon Postmaster General Will Hays appointed Glover as third assistant, launching his active and productive career in federal service.[4] For the next seven years, Glover would seize the opportunity presented him and lead the operation of the air mail. His stewardship would prove critical guidance through difficult times and would in turn prove controversial.

As advertised, on September 15, 1925, before a roomful of anxious reporters, Postmaster General Harry New opened the bids for contract air mail routes.[5] A total of seventeen bids were received for the eight routes offered. Of the eight, five awards were given. The Boston–New York route went to Colonial

Air Transport, the Chicago–St. Louis route was awarded to the Robertson Aircraft Corporation, the Chicago–Dallas–Fort Worth route was won by National Air Transport (NAT), the Salt Lake City–Los Angeles route was given to Western Air Express (WAE), and the Elko-Pasco route was acquired by Walter T. Varney.[6] Two routes were already in operation: CAM-6, Detroit to Chicago, and CAM-7, Detroit to Cleveland.

In a move that startled the aviation industry and lent immediate credence to the possibilities of commercial aviation, automobile magnate Henry Ford entered the fray. In 1923 he began to invest in a struggling company built by promising aircraft designer William B. Stout. Stout had developed a rugged single-engined transport with a high-mounted, cantilevered wing that carried all of its structural support within its thick cross-section and built the aircraft of tubular steel, covered with corrugated aluminum, similar to construction techniques popularized by Junkers, the German firm. After the tests on the transport were successfully completed, Ford purchased the assets of the Stout Metalplane Company for approximately $500,000 in the summer of 1925 and invested another $2 million in the new division of the Ford Motor Company.[7]

Stout and William B. Mayo, Ford's chief aircraft engineer and designer, immediately went to work improving the design of the 2-AT, and in the spring of 1926 they revealed the Ford 4-AT Tri-Motor, an aircraft destined to change the face of aeronautics. It was powered by three reliable Wright Whirlwind engines and capable of carrying ten passengers safely in unequalled comfort, for its time. It would quickly become the model for the industry.

On April 3, 1925, Ford opened cargo air service between Detroit and Chicago to speed delivery of auto parts between the factory and his suppliers. More important, the route was intended to demonstrate the reliability and soundness of the new Ford Air Transport and to impress the Post Office officials who were to weigh the bids along this air mail route. On July 31, the date Ford bought control of Stout, the auto manufacturer opened air service between Detroit and Cleveland.[8]

February 15, 1926, marked the opening of Ford Air Transport's inaugural air mail service and the first contract air mail route. In ceremonies attended by Second Assistant Glover and the postmaster of Detroit, Henry and his son Edsel Ford loaded the first sacks of mail into their Ford 2-AT *Maiden Dearborn 1* at Ford Airport in Dearborn, Michigan, for the flight to Cleveland. At 10:40 A.M. the large, Liberty-engined monoplane rolled down the grass-covered field, lifting off for its one-hour-and-seventeen-minute flight, escorted by a squadron of army fighters to the state line. Five and a half hours later a similar 2-AT took off for Chicago, and one hour and thirty-eight minutes later it touched down at Maywood Field.[9] Detroit was now only eight hours from New York and twenty-six hours from San Francisco.[10]

Clement M. Keys
(Smithsonian, SI# 2000-6119)

When Irving Glover accepted his new post in August 1925, he replaced Paul Henderson, the "father of the night mail," as second assistant postmaster general. Paul Henderson resigned his position, which he had held with such dignity and efficiency, to become the general manager of the most impressively financed company to emerge following the passage of the Kelly bill, National Air Transport.

National Air Transport was the first company founded specifically as an airline and was the brainchild of a Canadian, pioneer aviation financier Clement M. Keys.[11] Keys was perhaps the preeminent aviation financier and investor of his time. In 1920, he rescued the Curtiss Aeroplane and Motor Company from certain extinction when he took a gamble on the new industry by acquiring all of the company's common stock and borrowing heavily to sustain the fragile enterprise. He returned the company to profitability, in part to preserve its engineering expertise.[12]

Keys had another motive as well. Since graduating from the University of Toronto in 1897, he had been enamored with the power and efficiency of the large railroads. In 1901 he moved to New York, where he became a reporter for the *Wall Street Journal* and its railroad editor. Three years later, he became the finance editor of *World's Work*. His affinity for the well-organized, vertically integrated, railroad-holding companies was immediately evident in his numerous articles praising the railroad magnates, particularly E.H. Harriman of the Union Pacific. These individuals, in Keys's view, were not dangerous speculators but true industry pioneers who built huge, well-run enterprises that benefited the economy and served the public interest.

In 1911, Keys founded C.M. Keys and Company, a firm of investment brokers and bankers, becoming a noted speaker and author on financial subjects. Through his work he became known to most of the prominent financiers of the time, giving him the access to the Wall Street investment houses he needed to pursue his aviation interests. In 1919, Keys traveled to Europe as a member of the American Aviation Commission, which first interested him in aviation.[13] He took up the cause of aviation, hoping to produce, almost singlehandedly, an efficient enterprise from the confusion and waste generated during the Great War. He was imbued with the promises of commercial aviation.

When Keys returned to the United States, he sought to emulate his railroad idols and apply their methods to the new business of aviation. As owner of Curtiss Aeroplane, he sought to expand vertically by creating National Air Transport to make money carrying mail and to serve as a market for Curtiss products. As such, he joined with Howard Coffin, another prominent member of the American Aviation Commission, to take advantage of the new political and economic situation presented by the recent air mail legislation.

Keys brought together a diverse group of some of America's most prominent investors immediately after the passage of the Kelly Act and on May 21, 1925, formed NAT at a meeting held at the Drake Hotel in Chicago. With Keys as executive committee chairman, Howard E. Coffin, organizer of the National Aeronautic Association, head of the Hudson Motor Car Company, and wartime chief of the controversial Aircraft Production Board, took the lead in forming the new company. Among the prominent investors and members of the board of directors were Philip K. Wrigley as well as Wayne C. Taylor and Charles F. Glore of Marshall Fields of Chicago; Charles Lawrence, president of Wright Aeronautical and developer of the first practical air-cooled aircraft engine; Chester Cuthell, a prominent New York attorney; William A. Rockefeller of New York; Richard F. Hoyt, chairman of the board of Wright Aeronautical; Harold H. Emmons of Detroit; C. Townsend Ludington, a successful transportation investor; and Harold Pitcairn from Philadelphia.[14]

The company was capitalized for an astonishing $10 million, $2 million of which was sold to the organizers of the company. The original authorized capital comprised one hundred thousand shares of common stock, each with a par value of $100.[15] In order to prevent speculation, no stock was issued to the public at that time. So much money was raised, in fact, that most was reinvested as it was not needed.[16] This kind of financial backing was exactly what the Post Office wanted.

National Air Transport was the recipient of CAM-3, the coveted Chicago-Dallas route, and began operating at 6:05 A.M. on May 12, 1926, from Maywood

Field, Chicago. The promoters hoped they would eventually receive the coveted Chicago–New York route, once they had demonstrated their ability to carry the mail. Using specially built Curtiss Carrier Pigeon single-engined biplanes, NAT met immediate success over the one-thousand-mile route.[17] It was estimated that NAT brought air mail to more than twenty million citizens within four hundred miles of the new route.[18]

Although Ford and NAT were by far the best financed and most impressive of the new entrants, other entrepreneurs won contracts for the feeder routes. The route from New York to Boston, CAM-1, was awarded to Colonial Air Transport. Colonial had been in business since 1923, operating a Connecticut charter service known as the Bee Line. The company was reorganized in 1925 following the Kelly Act and brought in several prominent entrepreneurs, including Cornelius Vanderbilt Whitney; former Connecticut governor John H. Trumbull; W. Irving Bullard of Boston; Sherman M. Fairchild, a pioneer in aerial photography; Juan T. Trippe, a wealthy aviation enthusiast and future head of Pan American Airways who would serve as general manager and vice-president; and William A. Rockefeller, the same individual who was already investing in NAT.[19] Maj. Gen. John F. O'Ryan, a hard-nosed, prideful man of great energy, was named president of the company, bringing with him additional financial support from New York banking and industrial houses. O'Ryan had commanded the Twenty-seventh Division during the war and was now a practicing attorney with important political connections as member of the New York State Commission.[20]

Colonial opened service on July 1, 1926, and soon, unlike other contractors, was also attempting to carry passengers using single-engine Fokker Universals and, later, twelve-seat Fokker Tri-Motors. Despite difficult weather conditions along the New York–to–Boston corridor, Colonial managed to maintain reliable service within three months of the commencement of service.[21]

Maj. William B. Robertson, a successful St. Louis aircraft dealer, and his brother Frank, garnered CAM-2, the route from St. Louis to Chicago. The Robertsons had created a very profitable business buying and selling war surplus aircraft, forming the Robertson Aircraft Corporation in 1921. As with the larger aircraft manufacturers, the brothers sought an additional outlet for the sales of their aircraft and a chance to make a steady government guaranteed income, opening their air mail operation on April 15, 1926.[22]

Walter Varney, another pilot veteran of the war, operated an aerial ferry service across San Francisco Bay. When he learned of the opportunity for air mail payments he immediately placed a winning bid of 80 percent of revenues (eight cents per ounce), correctly gambling that no one else would think to bid on the obscure CAM-5 from Elko, Nevada, to Pasco, Washington. The route was not as obscure as it would first appear. When Varney opened service on April 6, 1926, this little airline was carrying mail from a connection on the transcontinental air mail route to a stop along the Northern Pacific Railroad that led into Seattle.[23]

Vern Gorst, the owner of a thriving bus line in Oregon, sought to acquire the direct connection to the Northwest when he successfully bid on the Pacific coast route from Los Angeles to Seattle. Gorst was concerned that CAM-8 would compete directly with his bus operations and attempted to head off a potential economic confrontation. After many months of careful planning and raising $175,000, Gorst opened service over this difficult route with his Pacific Air Transport (PAT) on September 15, 1926.[24]

Although a successful promoter, Gorst lacked essential knowledge about financial management.[25] While seeking advice from the Wells Fargo Bank in San Francisco, Gorst became acquainted with a young bank officer who would figure prominently in the immediate future of air transportation: William A. Patterson. "Pat" Patterson's advice concerning aircraft purchases and investment as well as loans greatly aided the success of PAT.[26]

The CAM-9 route from Chicago to Minneapolis proved troublesome to the Post Office. The contract was originally awarded to Charles Dickenson, who began flying on June 7, 1926. After only two months of flying and several crashes, Dickenson ceased operations. On August 1, 1926, a syndicate of Detroit and Minnesota businessmen headed by Col. Lewis H. Brittin assumed the contract and restarted the service on October 1 under the name of Northwest Airways. Brittin, originally from Derby, Connecticut, was educated at Harvard and served in the Spanish-American War as a corporal in Battery A of the First Massachusetts Volunteers and in World War I as a lieutenant colonel in the Quartermaster Corps. From that point onward, he was known as Colonel Brittin. In his civilian life, Brittin was an engineer for the Newhall Engineering Company and spent five years in Mexico constructing factories for the Sierra Madre Land and Lumber Company. Returning to the United States, Brittin accepted a position as manager of the National Lamp Division of the General Electric Company and later as the vice president and general manager of the Northwestern Terminal, a prosperous industrial center in Minneapolis.

In 1926, at the age of forty-nine, he organized Northwest Airways following the demise of Dickenson's operation. As vice president of the St. Paul Association of Public and Business Affairs, Brittin had already fought hard for a bond issue in St. Paul for the construction of an airport and was determined to bring air mail service to the area. As vice president and general manager of Northwest Airways, he implemented strict economies in operations, with his company ranking among the most efficient of the air mail operators, despite the difficult climate of the upper Midwest.[27]

Two more wartime veteran pilots entered the civil aviation scene along

CAM-10, the line between Atlanta and Miami, Florida. Reed Chambers and America's ace-of-aces, Edward V. "Eddie" Rickenbacker, organized the Florida Airways Corporation. Though it opened service on April 1, 1926, and was soon carrying passengers, the company eventually ceased operations following the loss of two aircraft. Chambers would become involved in the critical business of aviation insurance, while Rickenbacker would reenter the airline field in a few years.

Perhaps the most profitable airline possessed the shortest route. Clifford Ball, of McKeesport, Pennsylvania, operated CAM-11 from Cleveland to Pittsburgh, across the Allegheny Mountains. Organized as the Skyline Transportation Company but generally known as Clifford Ball, the airline made a substantial profit after the air mail payment rates were amended in mid-1926, starting service on April 21, 1927. Not coincidentally, Ball was the brother-in-law of Rep. Clyde Kelly, "father of the air mail."[28]

Colorado Airways was created to carry the mail from Pueblo, Colorado, through Denver to connect with the transcontinental route at Cheyenne, Wyoming, along CAM-12.[29] Despite operating at the maximum 80 percent rate, Colorado Airways ran into revenue problems because of low mail loads. Worse, it ran afoul of postal regulations when it was revealed that it had colluded with another potential operator to rig its bid. The company's contract was later turned over to Western Air Express.

Western was the creation of a prominent West Coast aviation pioneer and entrepreneur, Harris M. "Pop" Hanshue. A native of Mendon, Michigan, Hanshue accepted a job as chief factory tester for the Olds Motor Company following his graduation from the University of Michigan in 1902. The company sent the young Hanshue to California the following year to demonstrate and distribute their products along the West Coast. While there, he became intensely interested in automobile racing until his marriage in 1914. With his inherent fascination with speed, Hanshue took up the challenge of aviation in 1925, forming Western Air Express with the substantial financial backing of *Los Angeles Times* owner and publisher Harry Chandler and Richfield Oil magnate James A. Talbot. Together they bid successfully for CAM-4 from Los Angeles to Salt Lake City, opening service on April 17, 1926.[30] In no small part due to Hanshue's organizational ability as a successful businessman, the service operated without a hitch, cutting transcontinental travel time from Los Angeles to New York to only thirty hours. Not surprisingly, unlike most of the other operators, Western immediately made a great deal of money over this heavily traveled route.[31]

The first ten routes were awarded under the original payment plan, which allowed a maximum of four-fifths (80 percent) of the revenue collected by the Post Office to be given to the contract carrier. Costs were calculated along a zone system. Unfortunately, this unwieldy system required the local postmasters to count and weigh each letter mailed at each stop, a tedious method at best, which fostered delays and inefficiency. A concerned Clyde Kelly sought and received an amendment to his Air Mail Act of 1925, changing the method of payment to a poundage system.

As originally proposed by Postmaster General New, the new provision in the bill would allow payment at a fixed rate determined through negotiation with him. Sufficient members of Congress were concerned that this left too much discretionary power in the hands of the postmaster general. As finally agreed, the new legislation provided for a maximum payment of three dollars per pound for the first one thousand miles and no more than thirty cents per pound thereafter for each additional one hundred miles.

It was intended that the actual payment would be approximately the same, with 80 percent of revenue from the sale of air mail stamps going to the contractor. In reality, the amendment now separated the payments due the contractors from actual revenue.[32] In other words, the payment was no longer tied to the income generated from the sale of stamps, leaving open the possibility of excessive payments. Still, under this system, no subsidy was intended, and as a result most, though not all, of the airlines continued to lose money because of payments insufficient to cover the operating costs of unrefined and inefficient aircraft (despite the excellent management of most of the airlines). This also opened the door to direct air mail appropriations for the contract carriers in the form of indirect subsidy if postal revenues fell short of the contracted payment rates. In so doing, however, the 1926 amendment also encouraged the creation of numerous uneconomic short routes.[33]

With a solid core of well-financed companies flying the mail, and the air mail act amended sufficiently to permit greater efficiency, the Post Office Department prepared to relinquish its transcontinental route. The line would be divided into two separate routes, similar in practice to the railroads, none of which operated coast-to-coast: CAM-17 from New York to Chicago and CAM-18 from Chicago to San Francisco.

Late in 1926, the Post Office finally called for bids along the two new routes. National Air Transport's officials were already prepared; this route was their reason for being, and they had spent the last two years working toward that goal. To head off possible competition from a potentially powerful opponent, NAT initiated merger agreements with Colonial Air Transport during the summer of 1926 and entered discussions with WAE. Though the negotiations bore no fruit, Colonel Henderson well understood the nature of this new industry. "By the very nature of air transport," he asserted, "some sort of monopoly, such as this would indicate, is almost necessary to success."[34] Although neither

Colonial nor Western agreed to merge with National, in two years time, mergers and oligopoly would sweep the industry.

Barring an unsuspected bid from an unknown source, NAT expected to win the contract. When the postmaster general opened bidding on January 15, 1927, the attendees were astonished at the low bids. Three companies sought the contract. An unknown entity, Columbia Air Lines, bid $1.73 per pound for the first thousand miles. Colonial offered to carry the mail at $1.88, and NAT made two bids, one for $1.98 and the other a complicated sliding scale system ranging from $1.25 for loads over six thousand pounds per thousand miles up to $2.57 for loads of less than seven hundred pounds.[35]

Postmaster General New was concerned with the wide differences in the bidding. The numbers were so disparate that he chose to reject the original offers and call for new bids, by March 24. This problem of open, competitive, and possibly destructive bidding was manifested here for the first time. It would not be the last.

Three weeks before the new bids were opened, the comptroller general, J.R. McCarl, handed down an opinion concerning the power of the postmaster general to determine competent bidders. At stake was the definition of "responsible" bidder. New wanted an interpretation that would allow him to reject questionable bids. He requested the full authority of the law to decide the best bidder for the job, even to the exclusion of competitive bidding altogether. Despite the postmaster general's wishes, McCarl flatly rejected the notion that the routes could be awarded through negotiation.[36]

At noon on March 24, 1927, General New opened the resubmitted bids for CAM-17. Four bids were received this time. Colonial Air transport now dropped its offer to $1.68 a pound, NAT bid $1.24, and a new organization, North American Airways, bid $1.23. One New York speculator, E.F. Stewart, offered to carry all air mail and first-class mail for only 35 cents a pound. His bid was summarily rejected as not conforming to the requirements of the advertisement.

The challenge from North American Airways was another matter. This company had just been formed by a group of fourteen air mail pilots who were flying the eastern route together with Superintendent Carl Egge, subscribing to $100,000 in shares of capital stock. Underwriting the project was eccentric New York junk dealer and aviation enthusiast Charles Levine, with an additional $500,000 in capital supplied by Cleveland business interests.[37]

After much discussion, General New awarded the lucrative contract to NAT, considering it the lowest "responsible" bidder, even though Levine's group underbid them by a penny per pound. Paul Henderson had protested that North American Airways' bid was improper because government employees

William E. Boeing (Smithsonian, SI# 87-11937)

had illegally participated. Although Chief Justice Charles Evans Hughes of the Supreme Court disagreed, stating that North American's participation was in fact legal because the government employees were not officers in the company and, therefore, not "interested parties," the Post Office thought NAT the better of the two based on their experience operating CAM-3.[38] By September, NAT was flying to New York.

William E. Boeing of Seattle forged the final link in the transcontinental network. Born in Detroit, Michigan, the son of a wealthy German-born lumber magnate, the tall, bespectacled Boeing followed his father into the family business after attending Yale and making an independent fortune in the mining business, subsequently establishing his own lumber company in Seattle to exploit the vast potential of the magnificent forests of the Pacific Northwest. An astute businessman, Boeing invested well; he held controlling interest in Pacific National Bank, a decision that allowed him much freedom in pursuing his varied interests. The quiet young Boeing was introduced to aviation in 1914 at the age of thirty-two, when he flew as a passenger off nearby Lake Washington in an early Curtiss flying boat. In 1916, he pooled his resources with U.S. Navy commander G. Conrad Westervedt to produce the B&W floatplane, patterned after the Martin TA aircraft that Boeing had purchased earlier. The B&W aircraft performed well enough for Boeing to incorporate this new business as the Pacific Aero Products Company. In the age of wooden construction, the establishment of an aircraft company in the lumber-rich Northwest was a logical step. Quickly, a contract was received from the navy for trainers and Curtiss HS-2L flying boats under license during World War I. The firm was renamed the Boeing Airplane Company in 1917 and soon moved from its first site on Lake Union to a larger facility on the Duwamish River, south of the city.[39]

Military and naval contracts dried up briefly for the Boeing Airplane Company after the Armistice, temporarily forcing the company, with its force of skilled woodworkers, into the manufacture of furniture and boats. In search of new uses for aircraft and alternative sources of money, Bill Boeing first stepped into the field of air transport with an improved version of his Type C floatplane, which he had built for the navy and named the Model CL-4S. With this aircraft, Boeing, with pilot Edward Hubbard, flew sixty letters from Vancouver, British Columbia, to Seattle on March 3, 1919. Inspired after this flight, Hubbard flew a similar route, only now from Victoria, British Columbia, in October 1920 using a B-1 flying boat purchased from Boeing. With this flight, Hubbard Air Transport, later known as the Seattle-Victoria Air Mail Line, became the first to exercise a U.S. Post Office Foreign Air Mail contract and was able to cut one day off the delivery time of U.S.-bound letters arriving in Victoria on Pacific steamships and making the same improvement on the outbound journeys. This small, independent enterprise would continue until 1937. Eddie Hubbard himself would soon become a major figure in Boeing's plans for future air transport.[40]

William Boeing had already shown some interest in the possibilities of air transport when he flew with Eddie Hubbard from Canada in 1919, and he had remained close to Hubbard during the ensuing years. Hubbard had served as a Boeing Airplane Company test pilot while running his air mail operation. In 1926, Hubbard approached his friend with another idea. To seize the opportunity offered by the Post Office for the lucrative CAM-18 route between San Francisco and Chicago, Hubbard suggested that Boeing Airplane enter into the air mail business.

First, Hubbard approached Clairmont L. Egtvedt with the idea. Egtvedt, the designer in charge, was a young, round-faced, soft-spoken man originally from Stoughton, Wisconsin, who had come to work at Boeing straight from the University of Washington in 1927, when William Boeing had asked the university for young engineers. Earlier, the company had wisely donated funds to assist the university's aeronautics studies and produce new talent. The program paid off handsomely, as Egtvedt was to lead the company for decades and eventually become chairman of the Boeing Aircraft Company. Another Washington undergraduate, Philip G. Johnson, was also chosen and joined

Philip G. Johnson, president of the Boeing Airplane Company
and president of the United Air Lines, 1932 (Smithsonian,
SI# 2000-6124)

Boeing at this time. These two highly creative young engineers were to figure
prominently in the future of the company.

Hubbard and Egtvedt discussed the details at length; Hubbard examined
the operational aspects of the proposal while Egtvedt worked on producing a
suitable aircraft for the role. When they had jointly concluded that such a plan
was feasible, the two presented their case to Bill Boeing. After some hesitation,
Boeing realized the possibilities presented by the project and agreed to gamble
and finance the new airline.[41]

Promptly, Hubbard was assigned the task of creating Boeing Air Trans-
port (BAT) with Philip Johnson as first president. Hubbard immediately hired
Duard B. Colyer, an ex-Army pilot and former superintendent of the Central
Division of the government's transcontinental route, as superintendent of

operations. Colyer in turn hired many veteran air mail pilots he had known while with the Post Office and thus rapidly established a reliable system with experienced personnel.[42]

Boeing Air Transport's success was based on Egtvedt's trump card, the Model 40-A aircraft. This remarkably efficient mail plane was the logical outgrowth of Boeing's experience in building sturdy, metal-fuselage, wooden-winged biplane fighters. The first Model 40 was designed in 1925 in response to a Post Office request for new aircraft to replace its aging DH-4s. This version was powered by a single 400-horsepower, water-cooled, V-12 Liberty engine of World War I vintage as required by the Post Office, and incorporated a fuselage of mixed wood and metal construction. Despite the soundness of its design, only one Model 40 was purchased.[43] In 1927, Egtvedt resurrected the aircraft, incorporating several significant improvements in the process.

First, he redesigned the fuselage with an all-welded steel tube frame, which improved the aircraft's strength. Of greatest importance to BAT's future success as a commercial carrier, the 40-A was built to include two passengers as well as a payload of twelve hundred pounds of mail. Although the pilot sat exposed to the elements in an open cockpit well behind the trailing edge of the wings, the two passengers could ride in reasonable comfort in an enclosed cabin immediately behind the engine. This arrangement, although not ideal, was certainly an improvement over competing designs, which paid little if any attention to the needs of the few courageous early passengers. This inclusion of adequate extra space for passengers was meant to ensure BAT a source of additional income. Finally, the incorporation of a major technological breakthrough in powerplant design, the air-cooled radial engine, made the 40-A an outstanding success.[44] The inclusion of a 420-horsepower Pratt & Whitney Wasp was a result of Boeing's close relationship with the navy while building fighters and William Boeing's friendship with Pratt & Whitney founder Frederick B. Rentschler.

A determined man of stern appearance and disposition, Rentschler learned metal working firsthand at his family's successful foundry in Hamilton, Ohio. He was a formal man who guarded his privacy and whose modesty and shyness could often be interpreted as coldness toward others. Standing six feet two inches in height, the broad-shouldered Rentschler acquired his obsession with engines while working with his father's abortive experiments in automobile manufacturing. Educated at Princeton, the young Rentschler took these lessons with him when he entered the army as a captain in World War I. Assigned to the New York district, he was given the task of supervising the production of aircraft engines. After the war ended, Rentschler joined the Wright Aeronautical Corporation, where he actively pursued his new interest in aircraft powerplants.[45]

During the early 1920s, the U.S. Navy became increasingly interested in the air-cooled engines produced by the tiny Lawrance Aero-Engine Corporation of New York City. In the immediate postwar years, the only engines producing enough horsepower for high performance aircraft were bulky water-cooled types. With the rise of the aircraft carrier as an important weapon, the navy had to find an engine that could produce sufficient power without the weight and maintenance problems of the water-cooled motors. The Lawrance J series of engines seemed ideal for the task because they had no troublesome and heavy radiators, water pumps, or vulnerable cooling lines.

Wishing to find a large company with enough resources to produce and develop this engine, the navy threatened and cajoled Fred Rentschler, then president of the Wright Aeronautical Company, into purchasing the Lawrance Company in 1923. By 1924, the Wright J-3 and J-4 engines, better known as Whirlwinds, were in service. Incorporating Englishman Samuel D. Heron's revolutionary sodium-cooled valves, which virtually eliminated the chronic problem of burned exhaust valves, the improved J-5 series was the first to offer power and great dependability.[46] This powerplant, the world's first truly reliable aero-engine, made possible Charles Lindbergh's nonstop flight from New York to Paris in thirty-three and a half hours with no problems. With such proof of its technical experience, Wright was producing vast numbers of Whirlwinds for the navy and civilian interests.

In 1924, frustrated with banker-dominated management, Rentschler left Wright after a dispute over the future development of the air-cooled engine, disagreeing with the director, who he felt did not appreciate the engineering problems of aircraft engine production. Rentschler brought with him two of his colleagues, Chief Designer George Mead and Assistant Engineer in Charge of Design A.V.D. Willgoos. After securing the necessary financial backing through the good offices of Rentschler's brother George of the National City Bank, they formed the Pratt & Whitney Company in 1925, assuming the name of an idle tool factory in Hartford, Connecticut.[47]

The trio immediately gathered information and began the development of a new, higher-horsepowered engine. Incorporating numerous changes, their new Wasp engine could generate 400 horsepower from nine cylinders at 1,900 rpm, a vast improvement over the latest engines from Wright. By May 1925, the Wasp was undergoing flight tests. The navy was so enthusiastic over the results that two hundred engines were soon ordered for its new series of combat aircraft.[48]

From Seattle, William Boeing followed these developments closely. He had worked with Rentschler before and had formed a close working relationship. Boeing realized that, with the Wasp engine, the extraneous weight of water and the cooling system could be exchanged for payload. Unfortunately, he was frustrated in his efforts to acquire the engine because all of the production Wasps for 1927 were earmarked for the navy. Keenly aware that the fate of his new commercial enterprise hung in the balance, Boeing approached his old acquaintance Rentschler to see if any of the batch of two hundred Wasps could be allocated to BAT. Rentschler, acting on his friend's request, persuaded the navy to delay acceptance of some of the Wasps, allowing Boeing to receive a sufficient number on the assurance that Pratt & Whitney could step up production sufficiently to complete the navy contract on time.[49] Once in service, the twenty-five Wasp-powered Boeing 40-As fulfilled their potential and made BAT an important carrier almost overnight. This collaboration was to prove central to the subsequent development of commercial aviation.

On January 16, 1927, Bill Boeing and his wife Bertha boarded Great Northern Railway's *Oriental Limited Number 2* eastbound to attend the opening of air mail bids in Washington, D.C. Traveling across the northern transcontinental route rail to St. Paul, the couple nervously anticipated the impending competition with numerous scotch highballs. They arrived at Union Station at nine o'clock on Saturday morning, January 22, and were taken by Boeing representatives to their room at the Carlton Hotel. For a week they waited while accepting visits from numerous government, military, and industry leaders, including the MacCrackens and Ralph Williams, the vice chairman of the Republican National Committee.[50]

On Saturday, the Boeings returned to their hotel room following visits with Senator Jones of Washington and lunch with Assistant Secretary of the Navy Trubee Davison. They were greeted on their arrival with the telephone message they were hoping for:

> Ten minutes after we returned to our rooms at the Carlton, the 'phone rang and George [Tidmarsh, the Boeing D.C. representative] answered it. After the first few words his expression changed—and he fairly yelled into the 'phone, "You don't mean to say we got it?" The man who 'phoned was the U.S. Fidelity and Guarantee Company representative. George then 'phoned the Post Office Department and Mr. Glover confirmed the good news, our bid was accepted. . . . Many wires and 'phone calls of congratulations poured in, and many callers came.
>
> Sunday January 30 was a day of rest and relaxation. Monday—more callers, among them a Mr. Rentschler of the Pratt & Whitney "Wasp" Engine Company arrived to have a business talk with Bill. Mr. Rentschler is delighted to get an order for 25 "Wasp" engines that are to go in the mail planes. Bill says it is the biggest single commercial order that has been given in this country.[51]

Indeed, Boeing and Rentschler had a business talk. Their discussion in Washington presaged many other conversations over the next several years.

Air mail is loaded on an NAT Douglas M-2 at Cleveland Airport, c. 1927. Note the armed guard. (Smithsonian, SI# A5314A)

Boeing and Rentschler were about to change the face of American commercial aviation.

In the meantime, on January 29, 1927, Boeing Air Transport won the contract from an incredulous Western Air Express. Western, well established as an airline presence in the region, felt it had a lock on the bidding. Its sturdy, water-cooled, Liberty-engined Douglas M-2/4 mail planes had pioneered the air route from Los Angeles to Salt Lake City. Based on its substantial experience, Western bid a reasonable $2.24 per pound for the first one thousand miles and 24 cents per pound for each additional one hundred miles. In contrast, BAT's bid of $1.50 per pound for the first one thousand miles and 15 cents per pound for each additional one hundred miles, half of the maximum allowed by law, seemed ridiculously low. Nevertheless, BAT opened service as agreed on July 1.[52] The transcontinental route was now complete.

Chapter 3

The Aviation Industry Comes of Age

Six weeks before Boeing Air Transport opened service, a courageous twenty-five-year-old air mail pilot sharply focused the nation's attention on the potential of commercial aviation. On May 20, 1927, Charles A. Lindbergh took off from Long Island's rain-soaked Roosevelt Field, wrestling his overladen Ryan NYP *Spirit of St. Louis* into the air and toward Paris, 3,610 miles away.

With his single but reliable Wright J-5 Whirlwind droning faithfully onward through the night and into the next day, the young Lindbergh fought fatigue and worsening weather as he struggled across the dangerous North Atlantic. When he landed at Le Bourget Field outside Paris thirty-three and a half hours later on the evening of the twenty-first, Lindbergh ignited an explosion of public interest in the possibilities of aviation.

Lindbergh was a quiet, almost stoic individual of unremarkable accomplishments before his flight. The son of a Minnesota congressman, Lindbergh attended the University of Wisconsin but never graduated. He learned to fly after a few lessons in Lincoln, Nebraska, and embarked on an aviation career after purchasing a Curtiss Jenny in April 1923. He barnstormed around the country, enlisting in the Army Air Service Reserve and winning his wings in March 1925. One year later, he found a more permanent position as an air mail pilot for the Robertson Aircraft Corporation in St. Louis.

As chief pilot, Lindbergh opened Robertson's air mail route on April 15, 1926. Together with two other pilots, he flew the mail in de Havilland DH-4s between Chicago and St. Louis along CAM-2 and twice was forced to bail out with his load of mail when trapped by fog. During this time he became enamored with the idea of uniting America with Europe and winning the twenty-five-thousand-dollar prize offered in 1919 by hotelier Raymond Orteig for the first successful nonstop flight from New York to Paris.

Methodically, Lindbergh undertook this task, first gaining the financial support of Major Robertson and other St. Louis business leaders. He approached several aircraft manufacturers before settling on a modified M-2 mail plane built by Ryan Airlines of San Diego, California. With dogged determination, Lindbergh precisely calculated his requirements and those of his aircraft, producing his Ryan NYP (New York–Paris) and naming it in honor of his St. Louis backers.

Lindbergh, though stunned by the incessant public attention he received, nonetheless understood the effect of his flight across the Atlantic and his subsequent twenty-two-thousand-mile tour of the United States advocating aviation. In messages he delivered in person or through notes dropped above towns he flew over, Lindbergh underscored the promising future of passenger air travel.[1] During a press conference in Hartford, Connecticut, reported by the *New York Times* on July 21, 1927, Lindbergh described his vision for air transportation. "Passenger service will follow the mail service," he said. "The time when there will be an air service available for all who want to use it depends upon what use you make of the present air facilities. We now have a mail service that is struggling for existence and with 50 percent more cooperation and assistance from the public it would be a great success."[2]

Lindbergh suddenly became the quintessential hero in an age of American heroes, all the more so because of his quiet, unassuming manner. To millions of citizens, his flight represented a breakthrough in their conception of aviation. No longer was aviation the purview of the crackpot. The effect, coming at the beginning of the boom of Wall Street, cannot be underestimated. Suddenly, as part of the public feeding frenzy in the stock market, the stocks of the tiny aircraft manufacturers and airline operators attracted buyers in droves.[3] In fact, aviation stocks would prove a barometer of the state of the market, outperforming a number of more mainstream industries, until the collapse in late 1929. In the meantime, the possibilities for growth in the aviation industry seemed endless. Wall Street had discovered the airplane.

As before, the leader in the aviation financial world was Clement Keys. His Curtiss Aeroplane was a leading aircraft manufacturer and National Air Transport the preeminent airline. Now he was getting serious company; not only were enthusiasts investing in aviation but mainstream Wall Street investment houses were turning their attention to aviation for the first time. The possibilities for rapid growth seemed limitless, but he was aware of the serious financial pitfalls.[4]

Nineteen twenty seven marked the beginning of an enormous expansion of the aviation industry in general and air transportation in particular. The Post Office continued to effect changes to improve the delivery of mail and streamline the method of payment. For the first time, it willingly began to run an air mail deficit. On February 1, the Post Office abandoned its cumbersome zone system of payment, replacing it with a standard rate of ten cents per half-ounce anywhere in the United States. Although the new payment method greatly increased the simplicity, it did so at the cost of deficit expenditures estimated to be almost 25 percent.[5] The decision markedly increased the volume of air mail sent, as was its intention, but the new flat rate had its pitfalls. Despite the increased tonnage, most of the operators, with the notable exception of Western Air Express on its Los Angeles–Salt Lake City route, and Clifford Ball in Pennsylvania, all were losing substantial sums of money, as Clement Keys had predicted.

Following his retirement from active control of his business interests in the early 1920s, mining magnate Daniel Guggenheim was actively engaged in the philanthropical support of aviation, particularly following his creation of the Daniel Guggenheim Fund for the Promotion of Aeronautics on January 16, 1926. He and his foundation spent considerable sums to advance the science of aeronautics. The fund sponsored aeronautical research and education and, under the auspices of Daniel's son Harry, supported Lindbergh on his 1927 tour promoting commercial aviation around the United States.[6]

Daniel fervently pressed for improvements in commercial air transportation and, to this end, encouraged Harry to provide loans to airlines for the purchase of new equipment. The Guggenheims were aware that air mail aircraft were generally unsuitable for passengers, but comfortable passenger-carrying aircraft were much more expensive to acquire and operate. On May 27, 1927, Harry called a conference of airline operators in New York; attending were all of the preeminent names, including Harris Hanshue of WAE. Because of its huge profits along CAM-4, Western had been able to open regularly scheduled passenger service almost exactly one year earlier. In fact, only they and Pacific Air Transport were carrying passengers to any significant degree, all other airlines were comfortable flying air mail and express and did not wish to carry people, who had to be treated much more carefully than mail.[7]

The decision was made to award no more than $400,000 in low-interest loans to Western Air Express based on its excellent record of safety and reliability. Harris Hanshue gladly accepted and turned his attention to finding a suitable large aircraft. After much deliberation, Western decided to purchase the Dutch Fokker F-10, an improved version of its successful F.VII/3m, now built in the United States by Atlantic Aviation, a Fokker subsidiary. The F-10, with its fabric-covered steel-tube fuselage and an all-wood cantilevered wing, was conventional in every way and was noted for its mild handling characteristics and superior safety features.[8]

On October 2, 1927, WAE and the Guggenheim Fund announced that

Western Air Express flew Fokker F-10 airliners on the Model Air Line as well as on its later routes in the West. (Smithsonian, SI# 95-8033)

Western would begin operation of the Model Air Line, flying between Los Angeles and San Francisco. The fund lent $155,000 at 5 percent interest for two years, enough to purchase three of the plushly equipped Fokkers. On May 28, 1928, Western opened its new passenger service up the California coast amid much fanfare and publicity and was soon operating with great regularity and reliability with a dispatch rate of 99 percent.[9] So pleased was Western that it formed a holding company, Western Air Express Inc., with $5 million in financing and in 1929 bought control of the manufacturer, by then known as the Fokker Aircraft Corporation. Western unfortunately lost money on the Model Air Line. Although ticket prices were as high as $50 per person, the ten-seat F-10s were so inefficient that they could not cover the operating costs.

Despite Western's difficulties, other investors remained undaunted. The dream of carrying passengers by air drove Clement Keys to risk his personal fortune on an experiment that he knew was filled with risk but promised to reap long-term rewards. In order to benefit the country the most, it was important that regularly scheduled, long-distance passenger travel begin as soon as possible. The initiative came from an unexpected source—the railroads.

Initially, U.S. railroads saw the nascent aviation industry as both an investment opportunity and a potential rival that should be controlled from the outset to prevent ruinous competition. In fact, in order to curtail the government's successful air mail operation, the railroads, through their congressional representative, former Progressive Republican Clyde Kelly, were directly responsible for the Contract Air Mail Act of 1925. The implementation of the law removed the threat of government competition and gave the railroads an opportunity to invest in a new and potentially profitable industry.

Because of Keys's close ties to the New York investment houses and his known support of the railroads from his days at *World's Work* and the *Wall Street Journal,* he was the obvious choice as an aviation executive with whom the railroads felt they could do business. As early as 1926, the Pennsylvania Railroad approached Keys and National Air Transport with a novel air-rail proposal to link New York City and Los Angeles[10]

It was felt that flying passengers at night over the treacherous Allegheny Mountains of western Pennsylvania with the current generation of aircraft was too risky a venture for passengers.[11] The Pennsylvania Railroad's offer removed the problem by carrying passengers by train at night from New York to a central terminus at Columbus, Ohio, where passengers would transfer to a waiting aircraft, fly during the day to Oklahoma, transfer again to an overnight train to New Mexico, and again take an airplane over the last leg to Los Angeles. Total travel time was estimated at forty-eight hours, cutting at least one full day from the normal transcontinental crossing.

Beginning in April 1928, Keys's ideas began to take shape:

> The plan is to form a company the general purpose of which shall be to establish passenger transportation by aircraft as a supplement to the railroad systems, to this end that passengers desiring very rapid transportation over great distances will be afforded facilities giving the maximum safety and comfort as well as speed.
>
> As the first link in a proposed nation-wide system of this combination plane and rail service it is proposed to establish a service from New York to Los Angeles in cooperation with the Pennsylvania Railroad and the Atchison, Topeka, & Santa Fe Railroad.[12]

Keys was methodical in his approach. His tentative plan outlined all of the financial and operational problems and their alternatives he expected to encounter. He detailed the known factors. First, Pennsylvania Railroad was to be responsible for the New York–Columbus stage. In discussions, it was agreed that the Pennsylvania reserved the exclusive rights to sell "through" tickets from New York to points west, thus reserving any available space on the aircraft out of Columbus. In return, the Pennsylvania Railroad Board of Directors was expected to vote $200,000 for the route to St. Louis and $500,000 in total for development costs for the entire transcontinental route. The board was eager to begin and receive the publicity value for being the first eastern railroad to initiate such a route. National Air Transport, in turn, was willing to subscribe $2 million and operate the route in order to protect its position. It was equally willing to cooperate with Western Air Express and divide the flying portion of the route with NAT operating from Columbus to Wichita and Western from Los Angeles to Clovis, New Mexico. Ford Motor Company was amenable to the deal and wished to exchange its aircraft for an equal value of stock in the new enterprise.

In St. Louis, Keys hoped for $500,000 to $750,000 in financial support to be sold in the Columbus, St. Louis, and Tulsa areas. With the backing of banker Harry Knight, Harold Bixby, and others, Keys wanted Lindbergh to enter the equation to help St. Louis become the center of the new operation and provide additional public promotion. Keys envisioned WAE as the sole operator of the new airline's western division. Although Keys had sought to broach the subject with Harris Hanshue, he was confident that Knight and, especially, Lindbergh could convince WAE to join Keys.

Lining up Curtiss Aeroplane to provide financing and equipment would be a simple task because Keys controlled the company. The Boeing Company, however, would pose a problem. Keys correctly felt that Boeing was the most ambitious of the aircraft builders and one of the few airline operators to carry air mail and passengers successfully.[13]

Keys's plan was straightforward. He and his group from NAT and the Pennsylvania Railroad were to organize an operating airline using the latest three-engined passenger aircraft available from Fokker, Ford, or Boeing, the decision to be made independently by a technical committee. The route would be administered by three divisions, each responsible for raising $500,000 from local investors subscribed in nonvoting, Class B stock. To ensure efficient management, something notably lacking in many aviation enterprises, the president of each operating division would receive a salary for operating his office while "doing nothing else." The eastern division would have its headquarters in St. Louis and would control the route from Columbus to Wichita by way of Indianapolis and St. Louis, capitalized at $1.5 million. With headquarters in Los Angeles, the western division would control the route from Clovis, New Mexico, to Los Angeles through El Paso and Yuma, also capitalized at $1.5 million. The northern division, which flew feeder routes, would link St. Paul to Columbus by way of Chicago.[14]

Once his plans were completed, Keys would create his "Transcontinental Airways" as a holding company to buy $1 million of Class A voting stock in the eastern and western division. In turn, he planned to issue $4 million worth of Transcontinental stock: $3 million to acquire the three divisions and $1 million for a cash reserve for future expansion and as a hedge against expected startup losses. A wise and responsible investor with a keen awareness of the increasing problems of stock speculation, Keys wanted the Transcontinental stock issued to the public in small amounts with the full understanding that this was a pioneering enterprise "rather than an established business" and therefore possessed great risk.[15]

This point was central to Keys's behavior and beliefs. He was adamant that aviation be controlled by responsible individuals willing to assume great risks on the behalf of the public in developing a potentially lucrative new form of transportation. Because of this, Keys insisted the "Board of Directors and officers *must be strong,* because their character is the only thing that would justify offering and buying these shares. The Board must include: character, experience, public reputation, (and possess) financial standing beyond reproach." In addition, all policies, accounting practices, rules of discipline, and operations would be controlled by the board of the holding company to promote uniformity.[16]

The complicated arrangement of separate operating companies was designed to appeal to western interests in WAE and Southern Pacific Railroad. It was crucial from the outset to determine the degree, if any, of western participation in Transcontinental. Initial conversations looked promising. Keys had discussed the proposition with WAE representative Herbert Fleishacker, who, as the largest stockholder, also spoke for Southern Pacific and several banks. Fleishacker recommended an even larger investment but seemed to possess ulterior motives. "These people are full of energy and big ideas," Keys said. "They think that the company should be a $5 million company instead of a $3 million company. They think it should be financed to run connections with all railroads, both east and west wanting to run connections and also have some ideas that would make it uncomfortable for Boeing."[17]

It was generally agreed thereafter to raise $5 million in order to lay a substantial foundation and establish Transcontinental as the predominant line. Writing to St. Louis investor stockbroker Thomas N. Dysart, Keys stated, "There seems to be a general feeling, in which I think your group shares thoroughly, that this job should not be done piecemeal because if it is we shall have confusion and competition in every part of the country. That is the reason for the slowness in moving in the matter, which requires an awful lot of thinking and hard work."[18] Dysart agreed with Keys's assessment and his deliberateness. "I can quite appreciate the difficulty in setting up properly the transcontinental deal," he commented.[19]

Keys was still concerned about western participation. He reiterated his tentative plan to Dysart, especially the idea of three operating companies. According to Keys, this curious plan was evolved in order to give the West Coast people a chance to buy the actual stock of the operating company if they preferred, to the extent of $500,000, rather than the stock of the holding company, and to let the banking operation be purely in holding company stock, with the holding company owning all of the voting shares of the operating companies.[20] Keys wanted to spread the stock in such a way as to prevent one group or individual from gaining control, allowing each group the option of purchasing $500,000 in either operating stock or holding company stock.[21]

Despite Keys's best efforts, Southern Pacific was not interested. Getting Western's concurrence was seen as vital before the Pennsylvania Railroad would agree to the deal.[22] That concurrence did not come. On April 24, Harris Hanshue politely but firmly declined to participate. More to the point, Western had its own vision of the future and wanted to control its own transcontinental line.[23]

Colonel Henderson was concerned about the possibility of competition from Western and Hanshue. Western was already one of the few air mail operators making a substantial profit and now was showing definite signs of expansion into NAT's territory. He reminded Keys that Hanshue possessed a war chest of more than $1 million for future projects. Because of this and WAE's lack of nighttime flying experience, Henderson perceived Western as "perhaps less timid about a plan . . . than we might be with our varied experiences in that sort of work."[24] Henderson specifically expressed his concern that WAE was a direct and growing threat. "I have a growing conviction that Western Air Express has a reasonably well matured plan for the operation of multi-engine ships for passengers (and mail if they can get a contract) from Los Angeles through to Kansas City, St. Louis, or Chicago," he declared. "In declining to come into the larger plan, Hanshue has said that he would be willing to meet up with our eastern operation at some point to be determined upon."[25] Keys understood that Hanshue's tactics would give Western a transcontinental service at virtually no cost. All they had to do was extend their existing route some six hundred miles east to meet eastern railroad and airline connections without spending a penny for the development of the eastern portion. According to Keys, "The result of this plan would, therefore, be that the WAE, operating the Western line alone and owning it outright would be the direct beneficiary of all the development cost and effort of the Eastern lines and would undoubtedly be much the more profitable division of the whole enterprise."[26]

Keys was also aware that several Western stockholders had complained to their New York bankers that the proposed transcontinental line would interfere with WAE's expansion plans and that Western's actions placed two air mail lines at risk. "I think it may be taken for granted," Keys asserted, "that if that plan went forward this new line [Western's] would constitute sharp mail competition for Boeing and N.A.T. and a complete breaking up of the situation as it exists at present."[27]

For the time being, no more would be heard from Western. Three years hence, however, the story would change dramatically, and with the direct help of the Post Office.

Keys pressed on. On May 14, 1928, Transcontinental Air Transport (TAT) was born under the laws of the state of Delaware. It authorized one million shares of capital stock at no par value with Keys as president and Henderson as vice president. A banking syndicate headed by J. Cheever Cowdin of Blair and

Company sold five hundred thousand shares at $10 per share to members of the syndicate, thus raising the required $5 million.[28]

Under the terms of the sale, no stock could be sold to the public and any stock resold to members of the syndicate had to be sold at no less than $12.50 per share.[29] Along with Blair and Company and Keys's personal fortune, other substantial financial interests backed TAT, including Hemphill Noyes and Company, Howard Coffin, William Mayo, Jeremiah Millbank, Richard Hoyt of Hayden Stone and Company, and Charles Lawrance of Wright Aeronautical.[30] This was clearly not a "fly by night" organization but a powerfully financed, serious operation that would soon attract the interest of the Post Office.

Within three days stock was exchanging hands at $28 per share. Keys promptly began organizing TAT with the goal of opening service in one year. It was a prodigious undertaking, but one he was more than capable of handling. As part of his methodical organization, Keys established a technical committee to make objective decisions on aircraft and equipment purchases. To this end, Keys approached Charles Lindbergh through the Daniel Guggenheim Fund for the Promotion of Aeronautics. Lindbergh had completed his promotional tour of the United States and Central America and donated his *Spirit of St. Louis* to the Smithsonian Institution.

Lindbergh, who was extremely careful in his business dealings, agreed to join Transcontinental Air Transport. Keys offered him twenty-five thousand shares at $10 per share, for which Keys would pay Lindbergh $250,000. In addition, TAT would pay Lindbergh an annual salary of $10,000. For this sizable sum, Lindbergh would head the technical development of the new corporation, acquire the equipment, and develop the route system.[31]

Lindbergh was free to pursue other activities so long as they did not compete with TAT. This was a serious offer. Lindbergh was not merely "window dressing"; he was expected to take a leading role in the creation of this new airline and did so. In return, Keys received his expertise and the right to call his airline the "Lindbergh Line." Keys was also aware that the association of this famous airman with TAT could lead to unwise stock speculation. He suggested that Lindbergh put only a small portion of stock in his name: "When you sell it—and I hope that you will sell part of it on the first favorable opportunity—either the delivery of the stock in your own name or the transfer of it on the books, would excite a lot of attention which is quite unnecessary."[32] This advice would later be recalled under much different circumstances in wrongful efforts to embarrass and discredit Lindbergh.

Following TAT's well-publicized activities, other companies began to show interest in aviation in 1928. Although an effort by New York Central failed, the formation of Universal Airlines on July 30, 1928, posed a real threat. Investment bankers in Minneapolis, St. Louis, and Chicago pooled their resources to open the inaugural leg of an ambitious transcontinental operation, flying first from Chicago to Cleveland. Universal's backers quickly exercised their expansionist tendencies, purchasing Continental Air Lines, along with its mail contract from Louisville to Cleveland (CAM-16), and the Robertson Aircraft Corporation, with its air mail contract from St. Louis to Chicago, Lindbergh's former route. Led by John A. Love of St. Louis, the new organization had visions of overnight growth and of forming a holding company to coordinate its activities, ostensibly buying into Fokker Aircraft and Mid Plane Sales and Transit Company of Minneapolis.

Western was also expanding aggressively, making plans to extend passenger service throughout the Southwest and into Kansas City while acquiring large blocks of Fokker Aircraft stock as they consolidated their interests. Western was serious, and Colonel Henderson nervously noticed their efforts:

> It is my personal opinion, however, that they intend to fly from Los Angeles to some point like Fort Worth, then up our lighted airway to perhaps Oklahoma City, maybe Wichita, then maybe east to St. Louis for their eastern terminal, where the Robertson company could take their passengers to Chicago, with the Universal company connecting with them east out of Chicago.
>
> Unquestionably, there is some very definite hook-up between Hanshue and this Robertson—Universal hook-up.[33]

Nevertheless, Keys stressed the industry-wide need for cooperation in order to advance aviation. Writing to Western board member and major stockholder J.A. Talbot, he reiterated his desire for mutual assistance rather than destructive competition, particularly on technical matters, including two-way radio communications systems. "This is only an example which could be multiplied many times," he noted. "It seems to me that in all these matters where the air industry is dealing with much bigger, older and rather ponderous outside industries, the weight of our united force would get results more quickly and probably better results than any of us could acting alone." Keys understood that eventually there would come an accommodation. Although TAT stockholders refused to let WAE operate the western part of the line, Keys reassured his supporters that Talbot "and Hanshue promised full cooperation in matters like terminals, traffic development, etc." Of crucial importance to the future, Keys strongly felt that "both these men believe that ultimately there will be [a] merger with us."[34] These were very prophetic words indeed.

This gentleman's agreement to avoid competition and promote cooperation held fast, leaving only one major player unaccounted for—William Boeing. Boeing's enterprises were efficient and well managed, reflecting the keen managerial instincts of its founder. It also reflected his personality, which made the company appear somewhat insular and mysterious to its competitors. But as with Hanshue and Keys, Boeing was a serious investor.[35]

Keys had no desire to antagonize Boeing and was careful in explaining his plans to his peers in Seattle, even though BAT declined to invest in TAT. Keys carefully analyzed Boeing's position in the sincere effort to avoid irritating a potentially powerful opponent. Boeing, like Keys, was seen to have a sophisticated vision of the future of aviation, having invested substantial personal capital on CAM-18 from San Francisco to Chicago and developed a nascent passenger business along that route. Keys stressed the advantages of cooperation where NAT and TAT met Boeing Air Transport as he had spent considerably capital developing eastern lines, something Boeing chose not to do, at least at this time. "On this view," Keys stated, "I think that we can meet Boeing people squarely, taking the attitude that while his existing line will be fed by the Eastern development, the Eastern development will also be fed by his present capital outlays and all his efforts in development."[36]

Keys was willing to cooperate on developing complementary schedules and wished to let the market determine whether a new transcontinental line could be created from St. Paul to Seattle.[37] As for Keys's expansion westward to Los Angeles, he was hopeful that William Boeing would not take offense. "I do not see that it has any bearing on our plans for Los Angeles," Keys remarked, "although he might remotely consider that line a competitor with his line. Frankly, I want to cooperate with Boeing in every way and I think that he will see that even if we do run a Los Angeles line in cooperation with his passenger line to Chicago it will be more helpful to him than harmful."[38] Keys had no real intention of encroaching on Boeing's territory in the Pacific Northwest, only of countering local speculators, Universal in particular, between Chicago and St. Paul.[39]

In any future TAT plan to extend to San Francisco, Keys wished for Boeing's assistance. "My idea is," he said, "there are two air links in any air-rail line across the continent, and, since you are already established, I should certainly prefer to see you operate the Western line, if any line at all is to be operated."[40] While Boeing graciously declined to enter into Keys's securities company as well as TAT, he reciprocated Keys's desire for cooperation, much to Keys's relief. "As you already know, we are shortly going to start operations with 12-passenger planes," Boeing replied. "We are most anxious to cooperate with all other lines and do not look upon our colleagues in the transport game as competitors, as it is now our intention to devote our entire efforts to the building up of our own project and staying on our own lines, taking such traffic as the other lines might give us and reciprocating by turning our passengers over to the other lines at the terminals. . . . We are desirous of hearty cooperation with all other lines."[41]

Still, Keys was concerned about the rumored joint effort of New York Central, Boeing, and the Union Pacific. Such a link would force TAT to complete a line from Columbus to Chicago originally intended to extend to St. Paul. If this three-way link were completed, Keys said, "we shall have to run an intermediate line between the Union Pacific and New York Central or Boeing will run it and this would bring him into Eastern territory and would not be very good business from anybody's point of view." Keys asked Cuthell to find out if the stories were indeed true. "I think the Bankers Trust Company, or the Morgan Partners can and will check up on the New York Central," he suggested, "if you have any difficulty in getting this information from Mr. Harriman of the Union Pacific Board."[42] Harriman would soon show his interest in aviation in a different and unexpected manner.

Cooperation was indeed paramount for both Boeing and Keys. As their attention refocused on organizational and financial matters concerning their vast enterprises, the political and economic climate of the nation was rapidly changing.

Chapter 4

Consolidation

*F*ollowing Lindbergh's dramatic transatlantic flight, the public's interest in aviation as transportation and as an investment grew exponentially. Until March 1928, however, only Curtiss Aeroplane and Wright Aeronautical had issued public securities.[1] All other stock was privately owned or unissued. With the market booming in other stocks, the temptation had now become too great, and most of the aircraft companies went public in successful attempts to raise new capital and satiate the public's newfound craving. Most stocks were highly speculative common shares of no par value, and, as a result, countless individuals entered the fray to make a fast dollar. It was against these "wildcatters" that serious aviation backers, such as Keys and Boeing, fought so hard. Poorly managed, highly speculative enterprises such as Universal gave aviation a poor reputation, which hurt legitimate companies. But for eighteen months, there was fast money to be made by all. Aviation securities would prove a barometer for the entire stock market, rising faster than any other stocks and crashing sooner.

The Post Office Department unintentionally encouraged the aviation stock boom. Its activities to this point, though beneficial, were indeed haphazard, as aviation grew too quickly and without constraints. In 1928, before the advent of direct leadership from the department central to the industry's future development, the Post Office rode the tide as well, paying ever increasing public monies unevenly to an increasingly disorganized airline industry.

Once again, former Progressive Republican Clyde Kelly stepped in, this time sponsoring the Second Amendment to the Air Mail Act of 1926 in an attempt to increase the volume of air mail. It would also lead to the beginning of massive, unevenly distributed overpayments amounting to a subsidy for many of the airlines. Introduced on January 4, 1928, the amendment reduced the minimum rate per ounce of an air mail stamp from 10 to 5 cents. Although mail loads were steadily increasing, most flights departed with mail compartments less than half full. Also, though payments were steadily increasing, averaging 73.6 cents per mile by late 1927, this still was generally less than half the operating expenses for most of the air mail carriers. It was hoped that the expected increase in mail volume would more than offset the losses from the rate decrease.[2]

The second part of the amendment was an attempt to address a potentially destructive problem while concurrently providing a stabilizing measure for the airline industry. Kelly and industry leaders realized that the original four-year term of the air mail contracts would expire soon. It was generally agreed that it would be grossly unfair to those pioneering companies that had invested millions of dollars in aircraft, equipment, and development costs to risk forfeiture of their contracts to a lower bidder after they had done all of the trailblazing work. To this end, Kelly sponsored a provision calling for the exchange of the four-year contract for a ten-year route certificate, providing the contractor had performed according to Post Office standards for at least two years. It was hoped that this provision would encourage long-term capital investment, thereby promoting development and consequently reducing operating costs while improving service. As part of the arrangement, the postmaster general was now empowered to modify the rate of payment for each carrier after consultation, though not above the amount originally contracted.[3] After some debate concerning the term length of the route certificates and a preliminary discussion of similar rate determination by the Interstate Commerce Commission (ICC) for the railroads, (a point Colonel Henderson argued for), the measure passed Congress and became law on May 17, 1928. As economist Paul David noted, the amendment also changed the rules for subsequent contracts, setting a precedent for the removal of competitive bidding with the awarding of long-term route certificates.[4]

The changes wrought by the modified law allowed investment to increase, it was hoped in the public interest, thus marking an important change in public policy, for now the airline industry, at least that which carried the mail, could operate under a long-term set of rules. Surprisingly, Postmaster General New refrained from issuing route certificates for the remainder of his term in office. The reason would soon become clear. With the expansion of the nation's economy, the promise held by the Second Amendment to the Air Mail Act of 1925 enabled the aviation industry to enter a new stage—consolidation. Before making the routes essentially permanent, the Post Office adopted a wait-and-see attitude to determine how it and the taxpayer could benefit from the dramatic changes now taking place in the industry.

When William Boeing and Frederick Rentschler met the previous year in Washington, D.C., following the awarding of CAM-18, their discussion touched on many aspects of aviation. With the stock market boom capturing the attention of investors across the country, the time appeared right for major changes in the industry, now that capital was becoming readily available. To this end, Boeing and Rentschler continued their conversations. Boeing, a very successful businessman in his own right before he became involved in aviation, understood the potential savings and efficiencies possible through the vertical integration of capital intensive industries. Although the barriers to entry in aviation were low for the moment, they were growing, and with breakthroughs in aircraft technology on the horizon, development costs were certain to increase exponentially. A large, consolidated, efficient organization encompassing every aspect of the aviation industry appeared to be the answer. Boeing took the first step.

In the late summer of 1928, Boeing realized that even his substantial personal resources were insufficient to finance such a merger. He had already backed the creation of the Boeing Airplane Company and Boeing Air Transport with his own money. In addition, he personally underwrote the surety bond required by the Post Office. Although he had access to additional local sources of capital through his control over the Pacific National Bank in Seattle, the bank's resources were also inadequate for the task at hand.

Through Dietrich Schmitz, president of the Pacific National Bank, Boeing contacted Joseph P. Ripley, vice president of the National City Bank in New York with his proposal.[5] Boeing required $5 million but realized that the separate public offering of the stock in these companies would not raise sufficient capital. To solve the problem, Ripley suggested the merger of the three companies into Boeing Aircraft and Transport Corporation (BATC), a holding company. While in Seattle, Ripley examined both Boeing and Pacific National and found them solid organizations. Pacific at first wanted one million shares of the new corporation but National City was reluctant because of the Seattle bank's relatively small size. A compromise was reached at five hundred thousand. Ripley's primary concern was with the Post Office Department. He was desirous of making their plans clear to the authorities in Washington and receiving their blessing before National City would proceed with the merger.[6] Second Assistant Warren Glover voiced no objection, though he and the postmaster general had the power to prevent the merger simply by invoking clauses in the air mail contracts that gave power to the department to control the financial activities of the contractors.

As for the question of a public offering, Boeing and National City were cautious, given the speculative environment of Wall Street at that time. They wished to ensure that BATC stock not fall into the hands of speculators and attempted to keep the negotiations as quiet as possible.[7] The newspapers learned about the discussions, but not before the deal was nearing completion.

On October 30, 1928, the Boeing Airplane and Transport Corporation was officially formed in Delaware. The corporation was created with an authorized capital stock of 650,000 shares of no-par common voting stock and an authorized $10 million of preferred stock of a par value of $50 each. National City agreed to purchase 90,000 shares of the preferred stock, series A, for $4.5 million and 90,000 shares of no-par common stock for $500,000, thus raising the $5 million in cash that William Boeing needed for his development plans.[8] For its efforts, Pacific National Bank received 10 percent.

National City was pleased and immediately offered this new stock to its "special friends" and industry insiders. The combination of these solid companies, with the blessing of the Post Office and Department of Commerce, promised great profits for the future. On October 31 the stock was offered on the curb market, before approval from the New York Stock Exchange. National City attempted to restrict the trading to a degree, but to no avail, as enthusiastic investors rushed to buy the new offering.[9] Immediately the offered shares were in high demand. Common stock prices soared, opening at 57 and ranging from 55 to 70. Preferred stock prices opened at 60 and fluctuated from 57 to 70 1/4 almost overnight.[10]

The overwhelming success of the BATC issue prompted William Boeing to expand his horizons. Recalling the excellent working relationship he had developed with Frederick Rentschler of Pratt & Whitney, Boeing took the next logical step and recommended the merger of their complementary organizations. Rentschler readily agreed that joining the diverse companies of BATC with one of the nation's premier engine manufacturers made an ideal vertical combination. Together they would form the strongest aviation organization in the country. Negotiations began in earnest in December and quickly included the Chance Vought Company, a builder of outstanding naval aircraft. By the middle of the month, the details had been completed and a new company, United Aircraft and Transport Corporation (UATC) was formed.[11]

More specifically, BATC purchased all of the shares of Pratt & Whitney with 868,000 shares of its own stock as well as all of the shares of Chance Vought for 90,000 shares of BATC. Because the investment firm of Niles Bement Pond owned half of Pratt & Whitney, they received 434,000 shares of BATC at a rate of 2 1/8 of UATC to one of Niles Bement Pond. National City then purchased $7.5 million of UATC, 6 percent preferred at $50 par value of each share. This resulted in United Aircraft having $12 million of preferred stock outstanding, the market value of which was estimated at a prodigious $150 million, a phenomenal amount.[12] According to the *New York Times,* the new holding company was to have an authorized capitalization of 1 million shares of 6 percent preferred stock valued at $50 per share and 2.5 million shares of common stock of no par value.[13]

The new holding company would allow William Boeing to proceed with his aviation plans and greatly expand his development of passenger air travel and the carriage of air mail and express. Boeing was to serve as chairman of the board, typical of his managerial style, leaving the day-to-day operations to others. Rentschler assumed the duties of president and in essence ran the new corporation. The vice president was Chance Vought; Charles W. Deeds was secretary and treasurer. Eleven other individuals completed the board, including Deed's father, Col. Edward A. Deeds, director of National City Bank and chairman of the board of Niles Bement Pond; Philip G. Johnson, president of Boeing Air Transport and the Boeing Airplane Company; Gordon S. Rentschler, assistant to the president of National City Bank and the brother of Frederick; and Joseph P. Ripley, vice president of National City.[14]

Immediately after the formation of UATC an attempt was made to acquire Western Air Express. Borrowing 150,000 shares of stock from William Boeing, National City approached WAE in the hope of completing a stock switch as the market for UATC stock had reached $72 per share and was still climbing. Desirous of maintaining their relative independence, even in the face of great temptation, Western and its stockholders declined.[15] Despite this setback, United Aircraft and Transport comprised the most formidable aviation organization in the United States. But they were not alone.

In October, Clement Keys wired Boeing to congratulate him, offering to purchase shares of BATC. Boeing politely deferred the request to the National City, but in so doing underscored the industry-wide drive toward consolidation following the growth of the economy and the changes in the postal laws. Keys was genuinely pleased with these events, as such moves were seen as greatly benefiting the industry as a whole. Writing to Western stockholder Harry Chandler, publisher of the *Los Angeles Times,* Keys expressed his approval. "I have myself purchased the small amount that was available of the Boeing Company," he stated, "and hope to do the same thing when the Western Air Express financing comes into the market, if it does come. I believe that, while passenger transportation is still purely experimental and cannot be regarded as anything but that, it will arrive in time."[16]

That time was approaching rapidly, and Keys was taking steps to take advantage of it. After three years of operation, National Air Transport appeared on the verge of profitability and had become a valuable commodity on the market, especially after the passage of the Second Amendment to the Air Mail Act of 1926.[17]

Like Boeing, Keys sought to make rational his diverse aviation holdings. Although TAT was still many months from opening service, by December, most of the organizational work was complete. Leaving the details to subordinates, Keys also sought to streamline his many operations and improve efficiency, thereby improving profits. In addition to NAT, TAT, and his interests in Curtiss Aeroplane and Wright Aeronautical, Clement Keys was anxious to find ways to raise money for future investments in aviation. For this he arranged the formation of North American Aviation, a Delaware company, on December 6, 1928, with an authorized capitalization of six million shares of no par value. According to Keys, NAA was organized for the purpose "of holding, buying, selling, and trading in the securities of aviation companies." But the company, he continued, "will not confine its operations to purchasing and selling securities, as it plans to take a part in furthering the expansion of aviation, especially in the commercial field."[18] Working with Blair and Company, Keys sold two million shares of the new company at 12 1/2 per share, thus raising $25 million. It was offered to the public at no less than 15.[19]

North American immediately began to reinvest its capital throughout the industry, particularly, but not exclusively, in Keys's airline holdings. This holding company was more loosely organized than United Aircraft; Keys thought that in the early stage of the industry it was important to preserve the relative independence of numerous small companies, which would create a larger pool of creative individuals for future leadership when the industry settled down.[20]

North American also purchased large blocks of stock in UATC, Western Air Express, Douglas Aircraft, Sperry Gyroscope, and Berliner Joyce Aircraft. The company's executive committee and board of directors contained most of the members of the boards of NAT and TAT, including Keys as president and his executive committee, which included J. Cheever Cowdin and Chester W. Cuthell. Fifty-three directors were appointed to the board. Keys himself financed a great deal of the North American formation as well as his other aviation acquisitions through his own firm, C.M. Keys and Company. This company handled the transactions of North American and carried the larger portion of NAA's cash in a call loan account, which Keys himself controlled.[21] Although this arrangement allowed Keys a great deal of freedom to acquire new companies for North American, it later would prove his undoing.

The Aviation Corporation was the third and last of the large holding companies to emerge. A product of the machinations of some of the greatest financial minds on Wall Street, it was nevertheless the most convoluted and poorly run of the companies.

The company's beginnings were conventional. Sherman Mills Fairchild was a thirty-one year old Harvard graduate who was denied enlistment in the U.S. Army during the Great War because of poor health. Moving to the dryer climes of Arizona, this brilliant engineer began to study the art of photography. His remarkable ability to take clear, sharp, long-range photographs attracted the attention of the U.S. Army Air Service, for which he rapidly developed cameras for use in aerial reconnaissance. He translated this ability

Sherman M. Fairchild
(Smithsonian, SI# 95-8033)

to the commercial and civilian market in the early 1920s, becoming a pioneer in his field.

Fairchild developed better and smaller cameras for his Fairchild Aerial Surveys Company, but he always felt that the current state of aircraft design limited his productivity. Never one to wait for others, Fairchild designed and built his own aircraft to fit his special needs and created a line of small, high-powered aero engines. In November 1927, he formed the Fairchild Aviation Corporation, which sold aircraft, engines, and cameras as well as aviation services throughout the United States, Latin America, and Europe.[22]

Fairchild Aviation profited from the wave of public and private investment interest in aviation at the time. As early as 1924, Sherman Fairchild had hoped to interest Robert Lehman of Lehman Brothers in investing in his fledgling organization, but without success. Four years later, the economic climate had improved dramatically, and Fairchild took advantage of the situation through the same Wall Street contacts he had wisely maintained. As a result, Fairchild was able to find adequate financing to form his company in 1927. On September 13, 1928, Fairchild and his business partner, Graham Grosvenor, a former president of Otis Elevator, completed an exclusive contract with noted aeronautical engineer Virginius E. Clark. The purpose of the new Superplane Corporation was to design and build a huge flying boat for commercial uses in hopes of opening transatlantic air service in the near future.

Gathered at a meeting at the Post Office headquarters in Washington, D.C., in the summer of 1927 are (left to right) Harris M. Hanshue, president and general manager, Western Air Express; William B. Robertson, president, Robertson Aircraft Corporation; Walter T. Varney, owner, Varney Airlines; Col. Paul Henderson, Second Assistant Postmaster General; Mr. Varney Sr.; E.P. Lott, manager of operations, National Air Transport; G.A. Parsons, Colonial Air Lines; and Donald Bartlett, assistant to the general manager, National Air Transport. (Smithsonian, SI# 89-12165)

Concurrently, Sherman Fairchild had made other important contacts. Pittsburgh attorney and investor George R. Hann had thoroughly investigated Fairchild's holdings in 1927 before enthusiastically becoming a major investor and a director after arranging financing on several occasions. An honest and forthright individual, Hann would soon become a major player in the expansion of commercial aviation. Hann was also successfully attempting to foster interest in aviation at home. He had seen the results of civic boosterism in New York, St. Louis, Chicago, Los Angeles, and, especially, Cleveland, his city's rival, and feared that Pittsburgh would fall behind without prompt action by civic leaders from the financial and political community. Through great effort in overcoming civic inertia, Hann, Richard W. Robbins, and C. Bedell Monro formed the Pittsburgh Aviation Industries Corporation (PAIC) on November 15, 1928.[23]

By the end of December, Hann and his associates had raised $6.25 million through the subscription of 250,000 shares of stock in their new holding company "to control, manage, and develop in the Pittsburgh district the various phases of aviation." PAIC would serve as an investment trust to promote general transportation, aerial surveys, air taxi service, express delivery, and, most important, the transportation of air mail.[24] The corporation stood ready to participate in the rush to consolidate and to help anyone who could benefit Pittsburgh's growth.

At this time Sherman Fairchild was becoming increasingly concerned that one of his distributors was being courted by Clement Keys and Curtiss Aircraft. In 1927, entrepreneurs T. Higbee Embry and John Paul Riddle had formed the Embry-Riddle Aviation Corporation to operate a flying school, an air taxi business, an airport, and sell aircraft—particularly Fairchild aircraft. In July 1927, the Post Office advertised for bidders for CAM-24, the route from Cincinnati to Chicago. Embry-Riddle bid and won, opening mail, passenger, and express service on December 17, the twenty-fourth anniversary of the Wright brothers' first powered flight. The company had raised almost $100,000 for the effort but soon realized that this amount would be insufficient if capital improvements were to be made.

During the search for additional capital, Keys and company made their offer to provide additional financing, provided that Embry-Riddle forfeit their Fairchild connection and sell only Curtiss products. An alarmed Sherman Fairchild approached his board, one member of which was George Hann, and recommended that they step in to prevent the Curtiss incursion. With great enthusiasm, the board went one better and quickly raised $500,000 to make Embry-Riddle a subsidiary of Fairchild and search for similar air mail operators to acquire.[25]

Fairchild and Hann realized that the success of such an enterprise required a serious injection of capital and, therefore, approached their connections on Wall Street. Their request fell on receptive ears. Earlier, in July 1928, Fairchild and Hann had helped arrange for the acquisition of West Indian Aerial Express, a small U.S.-owned airline operating over the Dominican Republic that possessed a tempting and profitable foreign air mail contract from the U.S. Post Office. Included in the formation were Fairchild directors Graham Grosvenor and Col. Thurman Bane, the latter an expert in aviation; Arthur and Robert Lehman, two prominent financiers who formed Lehman Brothers; and Roland Palmedo of Lehman Brothers.

After lengthy negotiations, Fairchild and company sold the airline on December 15, 1928, to a covetous Pan American Airways at a considerable profit. In so doing, Fairchild and his associates gained entry to Pan American's holding company, the Aviation Corporation of the Americas, headed by financier

Richard Hoyt of Hayden, Stone. More important, the deal had whetted their appetites for more such deals.[26]

Promptly, Robert Lehman contacted W. Averell Harriman, son of Union Pacific Railroad entrepreneur E.H. Harriman and president of Harriman and Brown, a New York investment house. Intrigued with the possibility of creating what they called the "General Motors of the Air," Fairchild's group sat down with Lehman Brothers and Harriman to forge a new company to consolidate the remaining domestic airlines holding air mail contracts with Fairchild's aviation interests and hopefully repeat their earlier success on a much greater scale.[27]

This new proposal suited all parties. In January 1929, after preliminary discussions were completed, Fairchild sought to bring his Superplane Company into the fold. Superplane was in need of a factory building, and Harriman possessed the empty Cramp Shipyard in Philadelphia. The arrangement seemed perfect and obviated Colonel Clark's need for new financing to build his huge flying boat. Telegraphing Clark, Fairchild informed him, "Our attorneys [are] having a meeting with W.A. Harriman in an effort to have them put all of their banking and financing with you."[28]

By February, George Hann was drafting a proposal to Grosvenor for the holding company formation and to determine the proper valuation for the issuance of stock. Hann's primary concern was to keep the price of the stock in line with the actual value of the new corporation as much as possible. Because these enterprises were still very much in the early, entrepreneurial stage, despite the sudden input of outside capital, much of the value of the consolidated companies rested in the intangible worth of their dominant personalities, such as Sherman Fairchild. Hann understood very well the importance of individuals at this early stage of industry development and recommended that the Fairchild Company consider insuring its key decision makers.

Hann further recommended that the investment group immediately undertake the consolidation of their interests along his proposed lines with an exchange of stock and supply any additional funds that might be necessary from their own pockets. This plan, he felt, had little risk, as he expected the stock to rise rapidly in value, as had the stock in UATC and North American. "Upon the announcement of such consolidation," Hann prophesied, "the securities of these consolidated companies would immediately enhance in market value and would permit the issuance by the bankers of stock in the holding company at a much higher figure than would otherwise be warranted if the larger financing is done hand in hand with the corporation."[29]

The investors agreed. Two weeks later, the plans for the new corporation were taking shape. It was agreed to issue two grades of stock: A, or preferred, stock would be used for purchasing tangible assets with a par value of twenty dollars, the B, or common, stock was designated for purchasing intangibles

Originally a Fairchild design, the obsolescent American Pilgrim 100A was the only airliner produced by the AVCO combine. All sixteen were flown by American Airways. (Smithsonian, SI# 91-9172)

such as good will, with no par value.[30] The corporation authorized ten million shares of common stock of no par value, of which two million were offered to the public on the curb market at twenty dollars per share.[31]

On March 2, 1929, a contract was signed between the Fairchild interests and Lehman Brothers and W.A. Harriman and Company creating the Aviation Corporation of Delaware. Among a wide variety of tasks, AVCO, as the company was popularly known, was authorized to trade in aviation securities, manufacture and distribute aircraft, and acquire aircraft and other transportation vehicles, aviation equipment, and landing fields. More important, AVCO was created to "transport in intrastate, interstate, and/or foreign commerce by aircraft, motor and/or other means of transportation, passengers, freight, securities, and articles of merchandise of every nature and description." Of greatest significance, the new corporation was explicitly authorized "to carry mail under contract with the United States Government."[32]

Other backers quickly evinced interest in AVCO. In Pittsburgh, George Hann encouraged one of his associates to push his father to buy AVCO stock immediately. To Richard Mellon, Hann telegraphed, "[I] understand your father cabled you he is favorably inclined—(it is) absolutely necessary to tie in Pittsburgh situation with this group. Humphries of Westinghouse has accepted, please cable me today. Your Aviation Corporation of America stock [is] selling at 90." Richard's father was Secretary of the Treasury Andrew Mellon.[33]

Heading the new corporation was W. Averell Harriman as chairman of the board of directors, Graham Grosvenor as president, Robert Lehman as chairman of the executive committee, and George Hann as vice chairman of the executive committee. In addition to Lehman and Hann, the executive committee also included Harriman, S.W. Walker, Harvey L. Williams, Frederick C. Coburn, corporate attorney William Dewey Louckes, and Louis Piper. The board of directors included prominent names from business and government from all over the country and eventually reached some sixty-four in number. Of the 2 million shares offered, 1.6 million were reserved as options for AVCO's original investors. Lehman Brothers held 381,250; W.A. Harriman and Company, 288,250; Charles D. Barney and Company, 80,000; E.F. Hutton, 25,000; and Pittsburgh Aviation Securities, 17,700. Each director was offered an option for 1,000 shares at twenty dollars a share.[34]

The immense size of the board was a portent of future organizational problems, but this was not seen at the time. George Hann also was concerned about the heavy burden of operational leadership assumed by Graham Grosvenor. AVCO was quickly becoming a huge organization and was negotiating with both Colonial Airlines and Universal Airlines interests for imminent acquisition. Grosvenor, whose personality was convivial but prone to micromanagement, was expected to perform well as president, if he could delegate his responsibilities.

Grosvenor had worked his way up the corporate ladder, starting as an office boy at Otis Elevator. By the time he was thirty-three, he had reached the vice presidency. Grosvenor then left Otis, serving briefly as a consultant before accepting the presidency of Fairchild Airplane Manufacturing Company. His self-reliant nature led him to concentrate his hard-won authority, which unfortunately prevented him from sharing responsibility with others. Hann strongly felt that no one man could handle the difficult tasks involved the birth pangs of an infant industry, and urged the company to take steps to delegate and decentralize enough so that AVCO would have a chance to prosper under enlightened management. Hann had expressed his concerns to Grosvenor and received his grudging concurrence.[35] Three days later, a meeting of the AVCO organizers agreed to find an understudy for Grosvenor.[36]

The following week, Hann and Grosvenor interviewed candidates. They were particularly desirous of finding individuals with aviation backgrounds who understood the industry and the inherent problems of flight. "A splendid business executive, no matter how keen," Hann wrote Lehman, "might well be a liability to Graham during these coming months, because it would take both time and a great deal of coaching to supply for such a man the aviation background and knowledge which is so essential in order to be of any real assistance at this critical time to Graham."[37] These were indeed prescient words, for AVCO's future difficulties were inextricably intertwined with cumbersome management knowledgeable in finance but inexperienced in aviation. It would take the leadership of the Post Office and of outside challengers to forge an efficient company from AVCO's diverse holdings.

George Hann was perhaps the most dynamic and clear-thinking individual involved with AVCO. His reflections on proper management and the incipient difficulties faced presaged the problems AVCO was to face. He also was keenly aware of the inherent benefits of such an organization and pushed hard for more consolidations after the corporation came into being. His first target was the Colonial system.[38]

Colonial had come under increasing pressure from its stockholders to cement a merger in order to avoid being subsumed by the wave of consolidations sweeping the economy. Since mid-1928, Colonial president John O'Ryan had attempted, without success, to forge an alliance with Stout Air Services. Stout was more interested in a lucrative offer from United Aircraft, which therefore left Colonial without access to the Chicago-Buffalo route and threatened to open the door to an unwanted incursion by United into New York and New England.[39] Colonial had to act quickly but ran into resistance from the numerous stockholders of the Colonial component companies, each wanting to improve his financial position. In addition to Colonial, which operated CAM-1, O'Ryan and company had also formed Colonial Western, to fly the mail from Cleveland to Buffalo and eventually to Albany along CAM-20, and Canadian Colonial to carry the U.S. mail north across the border. These three companies were now operating at cross-purposes, to the dismay of O'Ryan.[40]

O'Ryan was leery, however, of combining with any holding company that manufactured aircraft on a large scale and therefore rejected Stout Air Services's last minute attempts to draw the Colonial interests in with Boeing and United Aircraft. As a result, O'Ryan turned toward his New York connections, particularly Sherman Fairchild, who was a major stockholder. O'Ryan did not favor any one investment house, feeling that any of the major firms was solid.[41]

In fact, Colonial was being courted by all of the major holding companies. Writing to Sen. James Wadsworth, a Colonial director, O'Ryan outlined a telegram he sent him to explain the situation: "Great pressure from National City Company to get me and Colonial into their picture. Similar pressure from Keys, Curtiss and Blair & Co. . . . Much pressure from Lehman & Company to have me go on their Aviation Corporation Board. Said I could not consider it without conferring with my associates. . . . None of us seem so keen about Stout Airways. They ought to play ball or get off the diamond."[42]

On April 1, 1929, Colonial and Stout mutually agreed to break off negotiations, releasing each other "from any obligation whatever because of prior oral or written negotiations between officers or agents of either said parties."[43] Now Colonial turned to AVCO, and within days an agreement was forged, although not without some pointed questions from stockholders. To John H. Baker, O'Ryan's eagerness to merge with AVCO and its small manufacturing companies instead of the strong aircraft and engine companies of United was perplexing. "I remember very clearly you stating verbally, objections to any merger set-up which would involve Colonial stockholders in the manufacturing risks of other companies," Baker wrote. "You now propose to enter into a merger which consists only of weak units. I do not quite follow you."[44] Baker was also concerned that, unlike United's and North American's stock, AVCO's recently issued shares had not immediately appreciated and, in fact, had declined from their twenty-dollar par value.

Unfortunately, Baker's suspicions were to prove well founded. The boom in aviation stocks was coming to an end, and despite the support of two of the strongest investment banks in the nation, the Aviation Corporation had no coordinated plan for air transportation. The declining value of the corporation's stock posed an immediate problem as it was becoming increasingly difficult to purchase the outstanding shares of Colonial.[45]

The situation grew worse, compounded by the ever-increasing value of United Aircraft's stock, which had risen from $80 to $120 a share during the time of the Colonial negotiations with AVCO. Colonial stockholders were aware of this fact and were increasingly anxious. "It would be regrettable if our consolidation agreement were not consummated by reason of failure to secure the required stock," O'Ryan wrote Robert Lehman. "Such an outcome is not unlikely should dissatisfied stockholders coordinate their views and decide upon affirmative opposition. . . . The market advance in the stock of United Aircraft does not simplify our difficulties."[46]

O'Ryan was also distressed at the apparent laxity of Lehman Brothers. "I am very much concerned about the apparent apathetic attitude of Lehman Brothers in relation to the market value of the Aviation Corporation stock," he complained. "There has been no material change during the past several weeks. The result is that our Colonial stock is not coming in for exchange for the Aviation Corporation stock in a satisfactory manner. Our stockholders can hardly be blamed for their apparent unwillingness to exchange their stock which cost them $125 for stock which instead of netting them a profit nets them a loss of over $5 a unit."[47]

Gradually, after much effort, enough stockholders exchanged their shares, and on May 20, a sufficient number of shares were acquired for the Aviation Corporation to gain control over Colonial, Colonial Western, and Canadian Colonial Airways.[48] Colonial and AVCO had made less tangible arguments to persuade the reluctant stockholders. Replying to an inquisitive reporter asking about the price differential, James Walsh, the assistant treasurer of Colonial Airways, reiterated that the board of directors felt that price alone should not be the exclusive factor. The deal allowed for the exchange of nonvoting preferred stock for voting common shares, and that unmarketable stock was being exchanged for marketable and diversified stock that had an unlimited earning power. The presence of ten Colonial members on AVCO's board of directors was stressed as adequate insurance to protect their interests.

Of greatest importance, the merger presented an opportunity for tremendous future profit. For months, the talk in the industry was the coming decision by the Post Office to establish additional transcontinental routes. Although no formal discussion was underway, the decision seemed to many a foregone conclusion. Unless Colonial merged, it would be in a poor position to bid because the routes were expected to be in the South, not the North.[49]

In fact, the Post Office was entering a new activist phase, unprecedented in its scope. In May, the Post Office Department called the first of many conferences bringing together industry leaders and the administration to reach workable solutions to the problems of the aviation business. These meetings would touch off a new, highly productive yet politically charged period in the relationship between government and industry. This associative approach, so typical of the former commerce secretary and now president Herbert Hoover, would forever change the face of commercial aviation, struggling to come to grips with the changing economy and the rapidly growing industry. The meeting, the first of many that were to alter permanently the shape of American air transportation, was called by Hoover's chief political lieutenant and new postmaster general, Walter Folger Brown.

Chapter 5

1929: The Calm before the Storm

Industry leaders were cautiously optimistic concerning the incoming administration and its new air mail chief. Immediately before the election, Clement Keys and Col. Paul Henderson attempted to predict the Post Office's course of action under the incoming leadership, and in so doing outlined with remarkable clarity the issues facing the industry and the department. Henderson spent a considerable amount of time at the main Post Office headquarters at Eleventh and Pennsylvania Avenue, NW. He was primarily interested in the department's plans for implementing the new Second Amendment to the Air Mail Act.

In discussions with Deputy Second Assistant Postmaster General Chase Gove, Henderson was able to determine that there were no plans extant to extend the air mail contracts, most of which were coming to an end in 1929, past their expiration date. This was an obvious point of contention as the industry was rapidly consolidating, in large part because of the promise of these contract extensions, which would protect investors' extensive capital investments in the airlines. A uniform system of payment was also necessary to streamline the overly complicated and inefficient system of payments to the contractors. Despite improvements in the law, difficulties remained. Post Office officials, Henderson told Keys, "have no plan yet for negotiating extensions to our contracts under the new law. Mr. Gove, who I think is after all the strongest man and the straightest thinker in the Post Office, believes these contracts should be based on some sliding scale, not unlike our New York–Chicago contract. I don't think we need expect any action along this line for several weeks to come."[1] In fact, action was not forthcoming at all, as the department was waiting to see the results of the industry-wide consolidations before acting. Henderson also voiced concern over the Post Office budget as a whole, noting that an appropriation of $15 million was requested, but the

Bureau of the Budget authorized only $13 million. With monthly payments to the contractors increasing as a result of the postage rate decrease, a shortfall was imminent.

Of greatest concern to Henderson and indeed the entire airline industry were the department's plans for the creation of new routes. By the end of 1928, the Post Office had expanded service throughout the country, but had done so in a way that lacked coherence and was marked by a surfeit of short and intermediate lines, often operating against one another. The sole advantage promised by air mail was speed—effectively demonstrated only on long routes. Consequently, talk among the airlines centered on the establishment of new transcontinental routes. Henderson found Gove's position reassuring. "Relative the route proposed from Los Angeles east, there is an agitation for a route from Atlanta to Los Angeles," reported the colonel. "Gove believes that it should run from Atlanta to Birmingham, Shreveport, Dallas and Fort Worth, and from there to Los Angeles." Gove was well respected by the industry and was expected to soldier on in the new administration, as were Glover and most of the second-level administrators.

Profitable lines such as NAT were not eager for any rate revision, but clearly they expected it would happen. For sister airline TAT, both Henderson and Keys were hoping for a friendly administration that would eventually reward their pioneering efforts with an air mail contract over their ambitious transcontinental line once it opened in 1929. Keys was only concerned about the present economic conditions and the frenzy of consolidations that were transforming the industry. "I am not afraid of Western Air or Universal or Boeing," he declared. "The only thing I am afraid of is the results of the general clean up of stock selling companies, which must come before very long and which will undoubtedly make our task more difficult than it now is, but it won't be bad provided we have obtained the money we need and use it honestly."[2]

All of these points would prove central issues in the coming months. In the meantime, Henderson was correct in stating that nothing would change until the coming of spring—and with it a new postmaster general. He hoped that President-elect Hoover's choice would be a wise one, for much lay in the balance.[3]

Walter Folger Brown, the incoming postmaster general, was an individual of great intelligence, unassuming in appearance, who avoided publicity, preferring to work quietly and effectively behind the scenes. Several historians have described him simply as "a Toledo attorney." Indeed he was, but he was also much more. Walter Brown was a political animal of great influence in the Republican Party of Ohio, whom President Hoover referred to as having "a greater knowledge of the federal mechanism and its duties than any other man in the United States."[4] Brown brought to the government the vintage

Walter Folger Brown, Postmaster General,
1929–1933 (Smithsonian, SI# 75-8646)

Progessivism of Theodore Roosevelt's New Nationalism with regard to busi-ness. Monopoly operating in the public interest was efficient, beneficial, and worthy of support. Unbridled monopoly operating against the public interest was intolerable.

Brown came of age politically at the beginning of the Progressive era. He campaigned on behalf of William McKinley's successful gubernatorial cam-paign before entering Harvard Law School. After his graduation in 1894, Brown joined his father's law firm and quickly reentered politics. By 1897, he was elected chairman of the Republican central committee of Toledo. His political acumen ensured the election of noted Progressive reformist Samuel M. "Golden Rule" Jones as mayor of Toledo, from whom he eventually broke. Brown allied himself with the very powerful camp of Sen. Marcus Hanna and continued to exert his growing influence first by controlling Toledo through his strength in the Republican Party and later, from 1906 to 1912, as chairman of the Ohio Republican Central Committee.[5]

A friend of Theodore Roosevelt, Brown bolted the Republican Party in 1912 to support Roosevelt's Bull Moose bid for the White House as chairman of the newly formed Progressive Party. Brown, a supporter of Roosevelt's New Nationalism, had broken with Taft because he felt the president was overly zealous in antitrust prosecution, particularly of the steel industry.[6]

Following Roosevelt's defeat, it took Brown several years to regain his power base after he rejoined the Republican ranks. His power remained prodigious. Through his careful work, Brown helped secure the nomination of dark-horse senator Warren G. Harding at the 1920 Republican National Convention. Despite losing his only bid for elected office that year, Brown declined Harding's offer of the ambassadorship to Japan but accepted a presidential appointment as chairman of a joint congressional committee on the reorganization of the executive branch of the government. The committee sought to rearrange government along principles of business management to improve efficiency. Harding's untimely death coupled with bureaucratic intrigues stymied any attempts at change.[7]

During this time in Washington, Brown forged a friendship with then–Secretary of Commerce Herbert Hoover. In 1927, Brown accepted an offer from Hoover to become assistant secretary of commerce, a move widely seen as Hoover's unofficial announcement of his candidacy for the upcoming 1928 Republican presidential nomination. Once again Brown excelled in his role as president-maker as Hoover won the election easily, rewarding his campaign manager Brown with the top patronage position of postmaster general.[8]

Assuming office in 1929, Brown, charged with the task of promoting commercial aviation as well as efficiency in the Post Office, wished to bring reason to the rapidly growing yet still fledgling industry. Many small airlines had been created overnight and flew haphazard, disorganized routes in many areas of the country. Passenger traffic in particular was confused and sporadic. The existing situation, similar to that of the railroads in the nineteenth century, with which Brown was familiar, offered little chance for improvement if left uncontrolled.

Brown was expected to move slowly, as he had no experience in aviation matters. Universal Airlines' Washington representative Hainer Hinshaw, the brother of top Republican David Hinshaw, commented, "Of course, the inauguration killed everything in Washington for about five days and then the incoming administration made it necessary to go out and make over all the contacts we had established prior to the old administration going out. I am not saying this officially, but it is my belief that Walter Brown is going to be very cautious about future air mail contracts and I am afraid our Dallas line is yet some distance off."[9]

This assumption proved incorrect. Brown's quick mind immediately grasped the problems facing air mail and the airline industry and sought solutions through cooperative meetings between government and industry. Brown was a believer in Hoover's associative state and hoped to apply this effective methodology of cooperative informal regulation to this new industry, setting it on a course to efficiency in the public interest. Most important, Brown fully understood the impact of the mergers and consolidations affecting the industry and knew that if he acted with dispatch, the government could reap the benefits of the industry's new, inherent efficiencies. With the airlines completely dependent upon the Post Office for their primary source of revenue, the department had a unique opportunity to control this new oligopoly from its inception, protecting the public interest without the need for a formal regulatory agency. This was Brown's goal and the perfect model of Theodore Roosevelt's New Nationalism with regard to the question of monopoly. Monopolies acting in the public interest were seen as good and deserved encouragement. This latter-day embodiment of Theodore Roosevelt's Progressive Republicanism was never more clearly demonstrated. It was the sole driving force behind Walter Folger Brown's actions for the next four years.

Brown studied the air mail situation with regard to the newly emerging aviation holding companies, and within weeks of taking office, began to take action. At this stage the new postmaster general felt it was his duty to reduce the payments made to the contractors and bring the growing postal budget deficit under control. It was a daunting task. One of the original purposes of the Second Amendment to the Air Mail Act of 1926 was to reduce both air mail expenditures and postage rates. Determining the actual costs of the service to the contractors was virtually impossible due to the plethora of accounting methods used. Compounding the problem was the fact that every air mail contractor had an individual contract and was paid a separate rate, ranging from nine cents per pound to the maximum three dollars per pound allowed by law.[10] Such payments were confusing in the least.

With operating costs averaging more than one dollar per pound, some carriers were reaping huge profits and others were going bankrupt. The new postal rates were to have reduced the maximum payment to two dollars per pound in exchange for a long-term route certificate, but Brown's predecessor, Harry New, had refused to act, delaying his decision six months to see the effect of the postage cut on the amount of mail sent. This effectively left the difficult job up to Brown. In addition, while the postage was halved, the contracts remained unaltered, presenting a highly profitable, and legal, opportunity to the few unscrupulous operators. These individuals would mail heavy packages to themselves at the new lower postal rate while in return receiving a much higher payment for their service from the Post Office. Stories of airlines mailing bricks, engine parts, and other heavy equipment were rife throughout the industry.[11]

To deal with the mounting chaos, Brown worked with industry and government to find solutions. He called all of the air mail contractors to meet in Washington on May 27 to discuss new certificates and rates.[12] In his typically blunt manner, the postmaster general made his opinions clear at the meeting. "Many contractors are now making money in their transactions with the government," he stated, "and I am glad they are because a bankrupt is a poor person to do business with. Some negotiations, however, must be made in the near future looking to a readjustment in the pay rate. The government is spending a very large sum for air mail in excess of its return."

This disparity brought up an important point. Hitherto, the air mail contractors had received only that which was necessary for their survival. With the changes in the law and subsequent problems, the government was overpaying to an extent that could only be defined as a subsidy. At this stage, at least, a subsidy was unthinkable and went against all that the Republican leadership had argued several years earlier. "There is not, in air mail," said Brown, "the fundamental reason for subsidy that exists in shipping where foreign competition in ship construction and cost of operation are essential factors. The air mail lines, under consideration, are wholly within the United States and are without foreign competition. However, I am not disposed to drive a hard bargain with you men who have put your money and skill into the flying game. We want you to prosper and the service to grow. I want to give the air mail every encouragement consistent with sound business."

Brown wanted to change the method of payment from the current poundage basis to a mileage or distance system, which he felt would more equitably distribute the air mail funds. Together with the operators, it was decided to study the matter, the Post Office first preparing a detailed questionnaire that would gather all relevant information on operating costs and other expenses facing the contractors. Only after this data was digested would the department, working in conjunction with the operators, devise an improved payment method.[13]

Part of this questionnaire contained a new uniform accounting system, which was desperately needed if the department were to compare real costs among the contractors. The new system was devised by the Post Office based on the uniform accounting practices in use by the Interstate Commerce Commission for determining revenues and expenses of common carriers. The system was designed to factor in all of the economic information concerning the air mail revenues of the contractors and the monies collected from passenger service, aerial sightseeing, and express and freight delivery. The system also made provisions for determining expenditures and, especially, losses in actual operations. Uniform depreciation rates were incorporated, with the understanding that with the rapidly evolving state of aeronautics, improvements in design and construction made aircraft, engines, and instruments obsolete often within two to three years. "It is expected," the Post Office summarized, "that the application of this system will serve not only in the determination of fair rates for carrying mail by air but will also provide for comparison of results of different companies looking for economy of operation."[14]

To President Hoover this last point was key. He convened a meeting with the Post Office leadership on July 8 to discuss methods by which all postal expenditures could be cut. As part of his campaign to balance the budget and economize government operations across the board, Hoover sought reduction in railroad, marine, and air mail contracts. Second Assistant W. Irving Glover announced that a reduction from $1.5 to $2 million was in the works and that the operators could expect this to be reflected in their negotiations when their contracts come up for discussion beginning in October, when the original four-year term of the first awards came up for review.[15]

To Brown and the department, the application of the uniform accounting system was a practical part of the solution of rational rate revision and clearly indicated his attitude toward the airlines as common carriers. He realized the need for some form of regulation in the public interest at this early stage, but only without the bureaucracy of a regulatory agency and its inherent, and possibly detrimental, interference during the industry's formative stages. The operators left Washington to return home and mull over Brown's proposition until summoned again in the fall.

Rumors began circulating in the halls of the Post Office Department about the formation of another committee, this one to determine future air mail routes. The department had been inundated with requests from all over the country for the extension of air mail service into virtually every city and town. Such overwhelming and contradictory petitioning resulted in much lobbying in Congress and the department but few practical solutions. Representatives, particularly from the South, hounded the Post Office for the creation of a southern transcontinental route. Explaining the Post Office's position on such a route, an exasperated Glover made clear his support for rational growth and abandonment of the haphazard methods of the former administration: "We have already in operation a two-a-day transcontinental service between New York and San Francisco and with the railroads entering into the passenger carrying business by air, it would seem to me that we should await the results of this experiment before attempting to establish another transcontinental line."[16]

Postmaster General Brown sought to apply more rational means in planning new transcontinental routes. At the suggestion of President Hoover, Brown announced the formation of the Interdepartmental Committee on Airways. Composed of officials from the Post Office and Department of Commerce, its task was to "hear and determine questions relating to the extension of the civil airways system of the United States." It was the intention of the committee to hold public hearings with members of the airlines, private citizens, and representatives from federal, state, and local governments.[17]

The six members of the committee were W. Irving Glover, second assistant postmaster general; Chase C. Gove, deputy second assistant postmaster general; Earl B. Wadsworth, superintendent, Air Mail Service; William P. MacCracken, assistant secretary of Commerce for Aeronautics; F.C. Hinsburg, chief, Airways Division, and Harry H. Blee, chief, Airports Division.

It was announced that on May 22 the committee would hear petitions concerning the creation of a possible airway between Pittsburgh and Norfolk by way of Washington, D.C. On May 23, a hearing was scheduled for discussion of an East Coast route from Richmond to Charleston, South Carolina. The third gathering would hear arguments for establishing a route from Pasco, Washington, to Seattle, Spokane, Portland, and Tacoma.[18]

In California, the former secretary of the treasury under President Woodrow Wilson saw the announcement of the formation of the Interdepartmental Committee in his morning edition of the *Los Angeles Times*. William Gibbs McAdoo was deeply interested in starting his own airline and saw this announcement as an opportunity to present his case and find financial supporters. He also accurately perceived the motivations behind the creation of the committee. He enclosed the *Times* clipping in a letter to his son-in-law and law partner Brice Clagett, explaining that the committee was a form of nascent regulation that would protect the existing large enterprises:

> The Interdepartmental committees have no legal authority to restrain or to approve airway lines . . . but they can, of course, exercise considerable influence upon public confidence in them by expressing their approval or disapproval. I doubt if it is the intention of this Interdepartmental Committee to go this far, but it may go so far as to express a preference in favor of certain lines for air mail contracts; that, in itself, would accomplish much in favor of existing quasi-monopolies in air mail transportation, and I have no doubt that the big companies are doing their utmost to secure, through this committee, what they would like to have enacted into law. It is analogous to the power confirmed by the Transportation Act on I.C.C. in reference to railroad construction, either original or by way of extension of existing lines.[19]

As scheduled, the Interdepartmental Committee met in May and heard the arguments put forth by the representatives of local governments along several possible routes. On June 12, the committee met once again, this time to hear testimony on the proposed line from Louisville to Dallas and Fort Worth and, most important, to discuss the creation of the first leg of a southern transcontinental line from Atlanta to Fort Worth. For the time being, these meetings were called only to gather information and were not a call for bids.[20]

Numerous representatives from Congress attended the June 12 gathering. Among those present who were to later prove of great importance were Democratic representative Joseph P. Byrns of Tennessee, a member of the House Appropriations Committee, who urged a connection from Nashville to Memphis to join the line from Louisville to Fort Worth. The loudest proponent of a Nashville-Memphis line was Sen. Kenneth McKellar, a longtime southern Democrat and staunch Progressive who would later prove to be a large thorn in the side of the Post Office. A Memphis resident, McKellar insisted that the route run through his hometown and forcefully reminded the committee that it was he who wrote the amendment granting the Post Office permission to inaugurate service between Washington and New York in 1918. His position on the Senate Appropriations Committee also placed him in a powerful position to influence future legislation and funding.[21] He was not to be trifled with.

The numerous delegations expressed their concerns, anxious that they receive the full benefit of air mail services to their respective communities. They were also deeply worried that if service were not granted, their towns would fall by the wayside, as had so many communities when the railroads bypassed them. These concerns were real and still fresh in the memories of the representatives present.[22]

The initial meetings accomplished a great deal in helping the Post Office sort out the numerous claims and representations. In Washington, D.C., James Edgerton, one of the original U.S. Air Mail pilots, had joined with McAdoo in his efforts to create a new airline. As part of the planning, Edgerton attended the meetings and aptly summarized the events:

> The Interdepartmental Committee charged with investigating new air mail routes has favorably reported on a route from Richmond to Jacksonville with stops at Raleigh, Charleston, and Savannah, with a feeder to the present New York–Atlanta route from Augusta through Columbus to Charlotte.... The Interdepartmental Committee is understood to have reported favorably on a route from Birmingham to Fort Worth and from Norfolk to Cleveland, with stops at Washington and Pittsburgh....
>
> The Interdepartmental Committee is understood to be still considering a route to Dallas–Fort Worth, the choice lying between the Louisville–Dallas, and a route from St. Louis via Tulsa to Fort Worth–Dallas. It is understood that the committee will hold hearings on this subject about the 27th of this month.[23]

The routes from New York to St. Louis and from St. Louis to Dallas and Fort Worth were of interest to many parties, but none more so than Col. Paul Henderson. After months of planning and expenditures of more than $3 million to create the infrastructure along its route, Transcontinental Air Transport opened its passenger service on July 7 amid great celebration. The next day eastbound service was started by none other than TAT's technical advisor, Charles Lindbergh, who was at the controls of a new Ford 5-AT-B Tri-Motor, the *City of Los Angeles*. With one-way ticket prices ranging from $337 to $403,

Charles Lindbergh warms up the Ford 5-AT Tri-Motor "City of Los Angeles" before taking off on Transcontinental Air Transport inaugural eastbound flight from Los Angeles, California, on July 8, 1929. (Courtesy of TWA)

the service was plush and expensive.[24] The threat of competition was real as well. Western Air Express had already opened service from Los Angeles to Kansas City and was poised to move farther east, particularly through its association with the Universal organization. Of equal importance, such a new air mail route would also parallel National Air Transport's operation along CAM-17 from New York to Chicago. It also could jeopardize their CAM-3 route from Chicago to Fort Worth. Much was at stake. These two proposed routes would inevitably drain mail loads from this route and harm NAT's bottom line, which was beginning to show a profit. Now, with the specter of a new air mail route paralleling the eastern half of their transcontinental route, NAT and TAT fought back.

The president of the St. Louis Chamber of Commerce, Walter B. Weisenburger, appealed to J.V. Magee, the local representative of TAT, for that line's cooperation in placing St. Louis more solidly on the air mail map. The Robertson route from St. Louis to Chicago was adequate to some degree, but a direct link to New York promised much greater returns.[25]

Immediately, Magee contacted Henderson, who told him not to respond to Weisenburger's request. Stated Magee, "I have not answered this letter and as a matter of fact, I have been steering clear of any definite attitude one way or the other regarding air mail for St. Louis."[26] Henderson, in turn, emphatically expressed his concern to TAT director Chester Cuthell. "This is the line which we are most anxious to avoid being installed," he remarked. "Consequently, I am returning to Washington in plenty of time to prepare a statement setting forth N.A.T.'s position with respect to this new route."[27]

On August 1, the Interdepartmental Committee met to hear arguments for the New York–St. Louis and St. Louis–Fort Worth lines. With Walter Brown presiding, more than one hundred individuals attended the meeting and heard numerous well-prepared and professionally presented presentations. Surprisingly, no decision from the Post Office was forthcoming, largely due to the efforts of Henderson and company. Particular attention was paid to Clifford Ball. Ball, the brother-in-law of Clyde Kelly and possessor of one of the most lucrative and least important mail contracts, realized his airline was located strategically in western Pennsylvania, across the proposed line from New York to St. Louis. He let it be known that his small line was available for purchase but wanted the department's opinion. Officials from the Post Office made it clear to Ball that the New York–St. Louis route would not be offered for bids until the rate revision question was settled. They strongly suggested that he sell now to Pittsburgh Aviation Industries Corporation at a reasonable price or face ruination, for his contract and those of the other air mail carriers flying at the maximum three-dollars-per-pound rate were soon to be cut drastically, perhaps by as much as 50 percent, when the rate hearings reopened in the autumn.[28]

In the meantime the Post Office called for bids following the earlier decision of the committee for extending the Salt Lake City–Pasco route to Spokane and Seattle. Not surprisingly, after the call for bids was answered, Varney Air Lines won with an astonishingly low offer of nine cents per mile. This was not as absurdly low as it would seem. Varney was a well-established company with a proven record, unlike other petitioners on other routes, and already possessed the contract from Salt Lake City. The extension would cost Varney little extra in developmental expenses. Boeing Air Transport offered $1.19 per pound and lost.[29] Varney now controlled the most direct access to the Northwest, but within a year this would be a moot point. Although no one perceived the stock market crash about to strike the nation's economy, the aviation industry was undergoing sudden, unexpected paroxysms that presaged the impending crisis. Money was becoming scarce during this time of plenty.

Clement Keys took the opportunity to enhance his holdings by consolidating his properties even more during the summer of 1929. Working closely with Richard F. Hoyt of Hayden Stone and the president of Wright Aeronautical, Keys forged the merger between two of the industry's leading manufacturers, creating the Curtiss-Wright Corporation. This union joined Curtiss' aircraft manufacturing companies with Wright, one of the nation's preeminent aircraft engine builders, thus creating a powerful industrial rival to the well-diversified United Aircraft and Transport Corporation. Curtiss-Wright authorized twelve million shares and had an estimated value of $70 million. This new corporation greatly improved the efficiency of production and opened new avenues for research and development. It did not, however, include airlines. Keys wished to keep these holdings separate, though they would work closely in improving commercial air travel. To this end, under the aegis of his other holding company, North American Aviation, Keys completed his air transportation consolidation.

At the same time the Curtiss-Wright negotiations were being completed, Clement Keys personally purchased all of the capital stock of Pitcairn Aviation, which held CAM-19 from New York to Atlanta and CAM-25 from Atlanta to Miami. These routes had been heavily patronized since their inception. Harold Pitcairn, one of the original investors in National Air Transport and a friend of Keys, was losing interest in air transportation and wished to concentrate his efforts on manufacturing. He sold his airline for $2.5 million.[30]

On June 12, the deal was completed. Immediately Keys offered the line to North American. Personal profit was not his motive. Keys wished to open passenger service to complement Pitcairn's profitable air mail operation and thereby feed passengers to his recently opened Transcontinental Air Transport and to passenger service recently proposed by National Air Transport.[31]

Two weeks later, Keys offered all of the stock of Pitcairn to North American Aviation at cost of $2.5 million. It was accepted on June 27. To reflect the change in ownership and the expanded vision for the new acquisition, the corporation decided to change the name of Pitcairn to Eastern Air Transport. Keys, J. Cheever Cowdin, and Chester Cuthell were to serve on the board of directors.[32]

While these negotiations were underway, Keys purchased a substantial interest in Varney, which was expanding to Seattle, and, more important, acquired total control of an influential Southern California company, Maddux Air Lines. Maddux had been formed by a Los Angeles automobile dealer, Jack L. Maddux, who became fascinated with the possibilities shown by the Ford Tri-Motor during a demonstration in 1927. On July 21 of that year, he opened regularly scheduled passenger service between Los Angeles and San Diego, and on April 14, 1928, he extended the service to San Francisco. Using the ubiquitous Fords, Maddux Air Lines spread throughout the Southwest, eventually reaching Phoenix.[33]

This company was a natural rival to Western Air Express. In late 1928, Western was so concerned with Maddux and the rumored entry of Boeing Air Transport into southern California that Harris Hanshue attempted through legal means to halt the expansion. Using the threat of state regulation, Western tried to restrict competition and protect its interests by introducing legislation giving the California Railroad Commission power to control intrastate air travel.[34] Fortunately for TAT, the legislation was forestalled. Taking no chances of a recurrence, however, TAT decided to solidify its position in California by purchasing Maddux and thus obtaining an excellent network to feed its transcontinental service and directly face Western's challenge.[35]

Western did not sit idly by. Already in May 1929 Hanshue had opened direct service between Los Angeles and Kansas City by way of Albuquerque and Amarillo, Texas. This was Western's part in its own transcontinental air-rail scheme, connecting with several different rail companies at Kansas City for the trip east. With the direct challenge of the TAT-Maddux acquisition, the complete merger of which was completed in November, Western purchased Union Air Lines of Sacramento and its subsidiary, West Coast Air Transport. West Coast, based in Portland, Oregon, operated a purely passenger line from San Francisco to Seattle, in direct competition with UATC's Pacific Air Transport. This acquisition gave Western a route system along the entire Pacific Coast.

United Aircraft and Transport Corporation, while basically complete, made other important additions to round out its holdings. As previously noted, the Stout Air Services had rebuffed Colonial's advances and had cast its lot with UATC earlier in the year. This move gave UATC access to markets as far east as Cleveland with the hope of eventually reaching into New York. Earlier, in July 1928, Henry Ford had decided suddenly to abandon his interests in aviation and concentrate on his automotive empire. William Stout was left in control of the air mail lines out of Detroit as he had acquired the assets and the air mail contracts of Ford's two routes, CAM-6 and CAM-7, in addition to his own route, CAM-14 from Detroit to Grand Rapids, which he had operated since August 1926. Ironically, Stout willingly relinquished the mail contracts because of light loads and concentrated on carrying passengers and high-value freight between Detroit and the auto suppliers around the Great Lakes. The purchase was completed on June 30, 1929.[36]

At this time United also acquired control of three prominent aircraft manufacturers. Russian-born Igor Sikorsky was the world's preeminent designer of large aircraft, having built the first four-engined aircraft, the "Grand," in 1913 and a series of successful heavy bombers for Tsar Nicholas II before coming to the United States after the Russian Revolution. United outbid Curtiss for control of Sikorsky Aviation Corporation, the world's foremost manufacturer of large flying boats and amphibians in July.[37] In August UATC purchased the Avian Corporation. Avian was the creation of perhaps the greatest aircraft designer in the United States, John K. "Jack" Northrop, a pioneer in structures and, particularly, metal aircraft designs. The company was renamed the Northrop Aviation Corporation.[38] Completing the diverse product line was the acquisition of the Stearman Aircraft Corporation, a noted builder of light general and smaller commercial aircraft.[39] UATC now possessed a varied and highly complementary product line.

The Aviation Corporation, consisting almost entirely of airlines, used this time to complete the acquisition of a dizzying variety of large and small carriers in anticipation of new rates and postal policies expected from Washington. Southern Air Transport (SAT) was an important acquisition that brought AVCO into the huge, untapped market in the Southwest. SAT had been recently formed itself, combining the interests of Texas Air Transport with the former St. Tammany–Gulf Coast Airways. Texas Air Transport was the creation of Fort Worth bus line owner Temple Bowen and other local investors who formed the company in October 1927 to operate the mail contract, originally awarded to Seth Barwise, along CAM-21 from Dallas to Galveston via Fort Worth, Waco, and Houston. After receiving permission from the Post Office to start flying the mail on February 6, 1928, Bowen began service along CAM-21 and inaugurated CAM-22 operations between Brownsville and Dallas through San Antonio.[40]

In November 1928, Alva Pearl "A.P." Barrett, a prominent Fort Worth businessman, bought controlling interest in Texas Air Transport along with other investors, including Amon Carter, prominent newspaper magnate and publisher of the *Fort Worth Star-Telegram*. He owned interest in the Dixie Motor Coach Company, radio station KTAT, and several real estate properties. When he acquired control of Texas Air Transport from Temple and Chester Bowen, A.P. Barrett immediately reorganized the company, promoting an accountant, Cyrus R. Smith, to run the enterprise.[41] Barrett invested considerable sums of money into this profitable enterprise before merging his company with Gulf Air Lines to form Southern Air Transport on March 1, 1929.[42]

By early 1929, Texas Air Transport had also extended mail and passenger service to San Antonio and El Paso.[43] During the merger wave sweeping the industry, Clement Keys evinced considerable interest in acquiring Texas Air Transport in order to extend NAT's route southward from Dallas–Fort Worth. After a detailed financial investigation that revealed some inconsistencies with the mail contract between Seth Barwise, the original holder, and Texas Air, Keys decided to bow out of the negotiations.[44]

St. Tammany–Gulf Coast Airways operated CAM-23 from New Orleans to Atlanta through Mobile and Birmingham beginning on May 1, 1928. After an infusion of additional capital to restructure the company following heavy losses, in October 1928 the company was reorganized as Gulf Coast Airways, operating as part of a holding company known as Gulf Air Lines. On January 23, 1929, Gulf Air opened CAM-29 linking New Orleans with Houston.[45]

After the creation of Southern Air Transport, A.P. Barrett, who served the new airline as president, placed C.R. Smith in de facto control as vice president and treasurer. The airline then was separated into three parts: Division 1, encompassing the mail operations of Texas Air Transport; Division 2, controlling the air mail activities of Gulf Coast; and Division 3, handling all passenger service through the Texas Flying Service. By the summer of 1929, AVCO had acquired control of the assets of SAT, providing direct connections with their eastern holdings and the promise of a national network of routes.

For months, complicated negotiations had taken place with the backers of the Universal Aviation Corporation. This rapidly organized company possessed a voracious appetite and, in a remarkably short period of time, swallowed numerous airlines, both with and without air mail contracts, in its drive for a transcontinental route. Universal had rapidly become a thorn in the side of National Air Transport and TAT, and was suspected of having a shaky financial and organizational base. Despite Clement Keys's hope that Universal's expansion had been temporarily blunted in late 1928, Universal kept spreading.

After Robertson, Universal's most important acquisition was Braniff Airlines, which carried passengers throughout Oklahoma and into Kansas and Texas, roughly paralleling National Air Transport's service. Braniff was the creation of brothers Thomas and Paul Braniff of Oklahoma City. Thomas, the elder of the two, had made his fortune selling insurance and became interested in aviation through his brother in 1928, establishing the Paul Braniff Air Transportation Taxi Company of Oklahoma. The first route was between Oklahoma City and Tulsa, two major oil-production centers, and by February 1929 their line had extended to Dallas and Fort Worth. Paul served as company president; Tom's substantial financial interests meant that although he held no post, he was an active participant in all major company decisions.[46] In addition, Universal purchased another small company, Central Airlines, which flew between Wichita and Tulsa, with an extension to Kansas City.

It was in early 1929 that Louis H. Piper, the president of Universal, sought the consolidation of his company with AVCO. Negotiations between Piper and the Aviation Corporation went much more smoothly than they had with Colonial. George Hann, as early as March 1929, was calling for the integration of AVCO's airline holding with that of Universal and Embry-Riddle to ensure a smooth transition to a national route system.[47] Problems did arise, however,

Thomas E. Braniff
(Smithsonian, SI# 2000-6137)

and for the same reason they had with Colonial: many stockholders were leery of exchanging their holdings for shares in AVCO, as its stock was not gaining on the market as expected. Several stockholders correctly believed that too many shares of AVCO were outstanding and that this was depressing its value. One investor wrote AVCO's accounting firm of Hitt, Farwell and Company, voicing his concerns:

> The Universal stock at today's price shows actual assets of about $9 of $10 per share, with an excellent chance of earning the other half after the company gets going on a good commercial basis. But what way is there of knowing when the Aviation Corporation could pay a profit with twenty times the capitalization?
> Of course, the Aviation Corporation has absorbed two or three other valuable properties and may absorb more, but to us it looks like we are asked to exchange stock with 50% assets and 50% water, for stock which may ultimately represent a much larger percentage of water, with future appreciation discounted, that many extra years.[48]

The firm attempted to calm the investor's fears by stating that asset value of AVCO's stock value was actually 90 percent of the present market price. They also reminded the investor that AVCO earned $215,000 in March, whereas Universal had lost $60,000 in 1928. Most important, AVCO possessed a large cash reserve almost thirty times the total capital held by Universal with which to support its stock.[49] As with Colonial stockholders before, these arguments on behalf of AVCO were sufficient to sway enough shareholders to exchange their holdings for AVCO stock. By July, the merger was complete.

During the summer of 1929, AVCO continued its acquisition program, eventually gaining control of eleven of the twenty-five outstanding contract air mail routes. In addition to Colonial and Universal's holdings, AVCO finalized the acquisition of Embry-Riddle and purchased Interstate Airlines, which owned the rights to CAM-30 from Chicago to Atlanta.[50]

With the consummation of the deal with SAT, Universal, and Interstate, AVCO turned its attention to a new battery of problems. But first it had reason to celebrate. On June 14, just three weeks ahead of the well-planned opening of Transcontinental Air Transport, Universal beat its arch-rival to the punch by opening its version of air-rail transcontinental service. Universal's route took sixty-seven hours rather than the forty-eight hours by TAT and involved only one leg by air. Less sophisticated and involving much less planning, Universal's system involved a lengthy train trip along the New York Central to Cleveland, where passengers transferred to an awaiting Fokker F-XA tri-motor for the flight to Garden City, Kansas, after which the passengers once again transferred to the Santa Fe for the trip to Los Angeles.

On board the Fokker on the inaugural flight was George Hann, who enthusiastically wired W.A. Harriman en route: "This has been a great trip. Left this morning early from Cleveland over Universal system with two other twelve passenger Fokkers. All seats taken. Breakfast at Chicago. Lunch Kansas City and will soon be at Garden City for dinner. Total 8,870 miles and right on schedule. Beautiful sight other ships with us in formation. Jones, Dunwoody, Eison and other Universal officials deserving heartiest congratulations and Mrs. Willebrandt has been a splendid representative. Big crowds at both ports and very broad publicity. I only wish that poor old Louis Piper could have witnessed the splendid result of his handiwork."[51] Piper had died of pneumonia in late March, just after the negotiations for the merger with AVCO were concluding.

Carrying a thermos filled with water from the Atlantic Ocean on this trip was AVCO's new corporate counsel and lobbyist, Mabel Walker Willebrandt. President Hoover had just amicably ousted her, the former assistant attorney general and chief enforcement official of Prohibition in the Department of Justice, from her post, in part because of her overzealousness.[52] On June 7, she accepted Grosvenor's invitation to join AVCO.[53] Her presence underscored the seriousness with which AVCO, as well as the other major airlines holding companies, considered their political and economic positions and their willingness to use every tool available to protect their interests. It was hoped that Willebrandt's political connections and Universal's representative in Washington, Hainer Hinshaw, would bring considerable influence on behalf of their struggling corporation. Such help would soon be needed.

Financial problems continued to dog AVCO throughout the summer of 1929, despite the general national prosperity. Its newly acquired companies were diverse, often competing lines operating under considerably different managerial styles and efficiencies. With a few exceptions, such as Southern Air Transport, most of AVCO's airlines were losing money. This, coupled with the considerable amount of stock authorized and on the market, combined to continue to depress the value of AVCO's stock. The problem was affecting the corporation's ability to raise cash and continue their consolidation plans.

In June, Roland Palmedo set in motion AVCO's attempt to secure a listing on the New York Stock Exchange. Heretofore, AVCO had been listed only on the curb market and was thus eager for acceptance on the big board to make its stock more attractive to investors. Because of AVCO's weak performance since March, when its shares had first been issued, Palmedo was surprised at the warm reception AVCO received from the Stock Exchange—especially considering that the general speculation endemic to the market that summer was heating up to crisis proportions.[54] On June 26, Palmedo sent the official request to the exchange, and on August 2, AVCO won a place on the big board.[55]

Harriman was ecstatic. Now, after months in the doldrums, AVCO's stock would finally rise. Unfortunately, the honeymoon was over before it started. Almost immediately, the value of the stock dropped back below twenty dollars a share, thereby negating all of the AVCO's hard work and affecting the company's ability to borrow capital. Though not a financier, William Dewey Loucks, AVCO's general counsel, understood the situation all too well. "I personally am greatly disturbed over the action of Aviation stock on the Big Board since it has been listed," he wrote Harriman. "The unanimous thought of everybody was that if we could accomplish what seemed an almost unsurmountable task, of getting this stock upon the Big Board so that it would have a borrowing power and all brokers would trade in it, it not being a Curb stock, that the stock could be maintained at least around $20 a share. It struck 20 for a few minutes, and has constantly sagged to 16 1/2 with no support whatsoever, and with very little stock changing hands."[56] Loucks pleaded for the immediate creation of a syndicate to buy up shares and bolster the price before the value declined further. A meeting was called but little was done: AVCO's stock remained below its initial offering price.

AVCO's directors continued to cast about for additional ties to improve the company's weak position. Links with Western Air Express were forged following discussions in April leading to the acquisition of 10 percent of Fokker Aircraft's stock by Universal, in which Western had control. This led to negotiations whereby Western sold five hundred of its shares at fifty dollars per share to AVCO and Western purchased eighteen hundred shares of Universal at fourteen dollars, in effect an even swap and a promise for more cooperation and the placement of a representative on each other's board of directors.[57]

Western's control of Fokker had led General Motors into the aviation business as GM was beginning to look toward investing in this new industry. Desirous of forming a bond with this industrial power, AVCO hoped that some arrangement could be reached through its growing ties with Western and Fokker. It was hoped that General Motors' expertise in manufacturing could be employed to improve the poor performance of AVCO's Fairchild and Kreider Reisner aircraft companies, which were struggling with poor products and inefficient management and construction techniques. Access to GM's vast supply of capital was tempting as well.[58]

General Motors was indeed interested but wished to move slowly. Its executives wanted in the aviation game but apparently were cautious as to with whom they would play. Although AVCO's numerous liabilities were hurting its chances to attract large investors such as GM, Loucks and George Hann pressed harder to forge alliances that could improve the corporation's position prior to the Post Office Department's forthcoming meetings. Loucks had been in conversation with officials at United Aircraft who were contemplating acquiring AVCO's airline holdings—but only without Graham Grosvenor. Loucks telegraphed George Hann concerning the matter: "Harriman and Walker very anxious you to attend luncheon Monday to discuss proposal of United on acquisition transport lines. At present time they do not want to discuss with Grosvenor and want it kept confidential from him. Try and be here. My present attitude negotiations premature but should be kept alive."[59]

George Hann agreed, and although he could not attend the meeting, strongly felt that an association with the powerful United Aircraft, with its diverse, well-run, and profitable companies, would greatly benefit AVCO. As United's airlines were primarily in the West, such a merger would complement AVCO's holdings and result in the elimination of a great deal of overhead and administrative duplication.

What was really hurting AVCO's chances at further mergers was the poor performance of its stock, despite the success of other aviation stock. Hann blamed the investment banks themselves for this predicament, allowing too many inside investors to purchase too many shares, thus preventing a wide distribution throughout the country while creating too much speculation.[60]

Talk of additional consolidations raised the issue of antitrust actions by the Justice Department and consequent regulation by law or court action added to AVCO's mounting concerns. Loucks believed the corporation was safe from any prosecution but wanted the company to stay on guard just the same. Writing to board member Alexander Royce, Loucks stated, "Being such a large entity I have felt from the outset that we must guard ourselves most carefully so that any investigation that might take place, Federal or otherwise, we would be thoroughly protected on. We have done nothing so far, as far as I can see, that brings us under the Clayton Act; but from now on we may get into situations in which we might purchase controlling interests which might lessen competition between companies interested."[61]

Hainer Hinshaw expressed his concerns to Willebrandt, stressing his position that the Aviation Corporation was probably exempt from any action because of its close relationship with the government as a Post Office contractor.[62] Willebrandt's reply is not known, but she and AVCO were aware that the industry was making rapid advances and could no longer be seen as a purely private operation. At a conference on aviation legislation held at New York's Hotel Roosevelt on June 27, 1929, AVCO's top executives were brought together to discuss the future.

The participants, Loucks, Willebrandt, Hann, Hinshaw, Cletus Keating, and Talbot Freeman, understood that their industry was rapidly maturing and that its perception by the public was changing as swiftly, now that transcontinental service had begun. Despite their reluctance to admit it, these AVCO board members knew that their air transportation companies were now viewed as common carriers and subject to eventual public control beyond that of the Post Office and the Department of Commerce. Already the Post Office Department was discussing the exchange of their contracts for certificates of public convenience and necessity.[63]

Although regulatory legislation was not encouraged, the participants agreed that federal rather than state control would be the lesser of two evils. "I am quite clear in my own mind that if Congress did occupy the field, a great many legislative troubles would be ended," said Cletus Keating. "First of all, we would have one legislature instead of forty-eight, and . . . if jurisdiction is exclusively in the Federal courts, you would have a very speedy and uniform law. . . . There are very few directions where you can fly without crossing the state line; therefore, it seems to me that it is the kind of thing that the Commerce clause is designed to deal with, and is something that Congress ought to deal with" (15).

The question of the regulation of rates proved contentious. Responding to Loucks's suggestion that increased regulation inevitably led to rate control, Willebrandt put the matter before Keating. "I have been through a good many fights on the regulation of rates," she said. "I was always opposed. . . . I have come to the conclusion that what we need is a fair, reasonable rate, enforced by a policeman, and the only policeman I know is the United States Government" (16). Arguing against Loucks's assertion that such an act would harm an infant industry such as aviation and that the time was not ripe, Keating responded,

"One thing is certain: we are going to have regulation of rates, so wouldn't you rather have regulation of rates by the Federal Government than by forty-eight states? State Rate Commissions are pretty dubious bodies; they are the lowest type of political adventurers." Keating reminded Loucks that the airline industry was a public utility. "You may put off the regulation of rates for a few years, but everything of that character is regulated sooner or later," he declared (9–11).

Loucks saw the matter differently. He understood that often the regulatory agency involved was slow or unwilling to provide rates that provided a reasonable return and was therefore injurious to the industry, such as the ICC was to the railroads. "The difficulty is that the rate will be made on present conditions, not taking into consideration the fact that any line loses money when first started," Loucks said. "For two years it runs at a substantial loss. The Post Office Department is, incidentally recognizing that in the readjustment of rates." Regulation, he continued, "is bound to come, but I have been hoping that it would be deferred for several years. (11)

Organized under the auspices of the Aeronautical Chamber of Commerce, the national trade association for the aviation industry, the First National Air Traffic Conference opened in Kansas City, Missouri, on September 16, 1929. ACC president Frederick Rentschler, the head of United Aircraft and Transport Corporation, opened the three-day event, which centered on the common problems of the airline industry and was attended by 150 representatives of 30 air transport lines.

General agreement was reached on most topics, but one remained a point of contention. T.B. Clement, the general traffic manager of TAT, stressed that with greater passenger traffic would come increased pressure for the airlines to be considered common carriers. AVCO had already begun to address the question, but Clements placed it before the entire industry, recommending that the industry declare itself a common carrier in order to head off unwanted outside interference.[64]

Common carriers, of course, could be offered protection by the government as they were operating in the public interest, but this in turn raised the specter of regulation. This tendentious issue was raised by independent airline owner and operator Erle P. Halliburton, the founder of Southwest Air Fast Express, which flew passengers throughout Texas and Oklahoma and did not have a mail contract. Halliburton was a quarrelsome individual, possessing a knack for infuriating most people he met, but he was equally determined in his well-founded opinions and felt that regulation by the Interstate Commerce Commission was the solution to the industry's financial problems.

As with the railroads, Halliburton contended, the ICC determined rates based on the return against the property investment. For airlines a similar method, based on a return against the capital stock would insure steady and profitable rates. The rate determination methods of the ICC, he felt, would guarantee that the industry could charge rates that would guarantee a profit while not being too high to scare off traffic. These rates must consist of passenger fares, express delivery, and, particularly, air mail, which "is quite an important source of revenue in the development of commercial aviation."[65] Halliburton called for an equitable distribution of the air mail traffic and a flat-rate payment system to encourage development across the country. Under the present system, only those lines that carried heavy loads received large, weight-based payments, to the disadvantage of the smaller lines. Federal regulation would accomplish this end.

Speaking at the conference on behalf of Halliburton was his assistant, W.J. Winn:

> The airlines have reached that stage where they should be regulated and protected by an institution similar to that of the Interstate Commerce Commission if not by the Commission itself. Thus the public would derive the full benefits of fast transit afforded by air and the inventor's money secured by building up traffic and elimination of the transportation wastes that are existent amongst certain air lines today. If regulation is had aside from the great benefits derived by mail traffic there would be no wasting of the public's money in the establishment of non-essential lines in duplication of service and the like.
>
> ... It seems appropriate at this time now since so many other air lines have come into the scheme of things to enact some laws protective alike to the air lines, their patrons present and potential and to the investing public.[66]

Winn called for a resolution from the Conference supporting Halliburton's views that would then be forwarded to Congress for appropriate action. Assistant Secretary of Commerce for Aeronautics William P. MacCracken responded on behalf of the industry in rejecting direct rate regulation by the ICC. His statements reflected as well the ambivalence of business in general toward government intervention:

> It has been my experience the last three or four years that just as soon as anybody gets well started in commercial aviation their first thought is they want Government regulation of their business for them. After they have been in it for about two or three years they are pretty well satisfied that they are running their own business and not having the Government run it for them. ... Let me point out that the railroads weren't regulated until after they had been running about 75 years ... before there was any real regulation. In that time they did develop some very pernicious habits. If the aircraft industry follows in the footsteps of the railroads they will get the same type of regulation that the railroads have. It will be difficult at first. It will work out all right in the long run. But if the air transportation industry can avoid the pitfalls that the railroads put themselves

into, I think they can avoid this type of regulation on the part of the Federal Government to the benefit of all concerned, and certainly in the early stages of the industry, when it is changing so rapidly, you cannot expect any Governmental organization to keep pace with it.

I want to cite just one example. . . . That was the famous bid the Boeing Company, at $1.50 a pound made on the Chicago–San Francisco air mail. There wasn't a single government official that thought it was possible for that line to make money to that rate, and yet we all know from practical experience that they have made money.

Now an industry that is changing as rapidly as this one . . . can't afford to have the thing run by any set of government officers, I don't care how wise or intelligent they may be. Keep it in your own hands and if you can keep it clean, you will never need Government regulations. If you don't, you will get it.[67]

After much discussion, MacCracken's persuasive arguments prevailed. In the forthcoming months, the matter of equitable rates and the protection of the industry by an individual or an instrument of the federal government would consume the Post Office as it focused its attentions on the questions of air mail payments and new routes.

Chapter 6

The Post Office Takes Charge

Aviation Corporation's financial woes were reflective of the growing problems in the economy: the hyperactive stock market, the problems of overproduction, and the growing uneasiness with the overvaluation of the airlines and other industries. By the early autumn of 1929, most of the nation's airlines had been consumed by the three major holding companies. It was clear to the industry's leaders that aviation was rapidly coming of age technologically and financially and that mergers were a logical step in the growth of air transportation. These consolidations promised greater efficiencies, lower overhead costs, and greater productivity as, it was hoped, a more rational airline system emerged.

Unfortunately, without external direction, this growth was haphazard and uneven. The first rumblings for state or federal regulations were heard, which added increased pressure for changes in the present system. Postmaster General Brown had begun to address these problems with the Interdepartmental Committee on Airways and during the rate revision meetings with the airlines earlier in the year. Now, the Post Office was to take serious steps to bring reason to the airline industry by increasing its attention to the establishment of crucial routes and by creating a rational and fair system of air mail payments. This was done in order to improve mail service and ward off the threats of formal governmental rate intervention. Brown sought to regulate without regulations.

Slated for November, the most important meeting of the Interdepartmental Committee on Airways would determine the route for the forthcoming southern transcontinental line. The promise held forth by the department was a lucrative air mail contract to the winning contractors once the route was determined and advertised. With United Aircraft involved in the Northwest and North American flying primarily in the East and Midwest, the southern route was open to the few independents that were left as well as the fractious lines of the Aviation Corporation that operated in the South. The competition was expected to be fierce.

Into the fray came former secretary of the treasury William Gibbs McAdoo with his proposed Southern Sky-Lines. Born in Georgia, raised in Tennessee, trained in New York, and now living in southern California, McAdoo was a forward-looking Wilsonian Democrat aware of the efficiencies inherent in large enterprises but wary as well of their potential for detrimental behavior. This Progressive southern Democrat, who shared Louis Brandeis's aversion to monopolies, fervently embraced Woodrow Wilson's concept of New Freedom policies regarding the evils of concentrated wealth and power.

McAdoo, Wilson's son-in-law, had become aware of the problems and opportunities inherent in transportation from the earliest days of his career. He invested twenty-five thousand dollars in a Knoxville mule-powered streetcar line and immediately recognized the need for capital to upgrade the system. His search for money led him to New York, where his pleas fell on deaf ears because northern investors cared little about struggling southern enterprises. By the time a Philadelphia investor was found, the money was too little and too late to convert the system to electricity and save the line. Undaunted, McAdoo moved to New York, where he quickly proved his mettle as an attorney and financier, becoming involved with the successful reorganization of failed railroads.

In 1901, at the age of thirty-eight, he joined with corporation attorney John R. Dos Passos and acquired the rights to the corporation that had attempted but failed to build a tunnel under the Hudson River. McAdoo ably found new sources of capital, and, under his leadership, the Hudson Tubes, the first tunnels connecting Manhattan with New Jersey, was opened in 1907, solidifying McAdoo's reputation as a highly respected railroad entrepreneur.[1]

As biographer Jordan Schwartz points out, McAdoo understood that railroads, finance, and politics were interconnected. This in turn led him into the political sphere, following fellow southern Presbyterian Woodrow Wilson's New Freedom tenets, which favored the small businessman over the powers of entrenched wealth. The New Freedom appealed to capital-hungry entrepreneurs such as McAdoo, who had earlier been denied access to Wall Street. In 1912, Wilson asked this prominent southern financier and recent widower to enter his cabinet as secretary of the treasury. McAdoo's marriage to the president's daughter in 1914 raised eyebrows in Washington as Eleanor was twenty-six years his junior. As secretary, McAdoo proved successful, leading the fight for the Federal Reserve banking system, centered in Washington rather than New York, thus breaking the hold of Wall Street over investments in other regions of the country.

Under his stewardship, the government took on a new, active role in providing state funds for worthy projects in which conventional sources of capital were leery of investing. This form of state capitalism was, in fact, reflected by Hoover's policies toward the aviation industry. McAdoo took the lead again in mobilizing the nation for war and actively fought against monopolies in shipping. His greatest success came with the nationalization of the railroads in 1917. McAdoo correctly perceived that the railroads were in a sorry state because of a lack of capital and did not have the ability to coordinate their actions on behalf of the war effort. Under his direct leadership of the Railroad Administration, the nation's rail system developed a well-integrated national infrastructure, operating in the public interest.[2]

After losing his bid for the Democratic presidential nomination in 1924, McAdoo moved to California to take up his law practice and invested heavily in oil and real estate, adding considerably to his wealth. When he renewed his interest in transportation in 1929—first by buying his own aircraft, a modern high-speed Lockheed Vega—and then elicited the aid of former air mail pilot James Edgerton to form their ambitious Southern Sky-Lines transcontinental airline, McAdoo well understood the financial and political situation surrounding aviation, the newest transportation industry.

In April 1929, following the widely publicized creation of the Aviation Corporation, McAdoo first expressed his interest in aviation and in the possibility of acquiring the southern transcontinental route from the Post Office. Writing to fellow entrepreneur H.P. Wilson, he explained that this undertaking had great potential for profit, either from operating the route under contract or from the profit entailed through merger and acquisition. McAdoo reasoned that the route from Atlanta to Los Angeles was the only one "not yet occupied," and that, because of the better climate in the South, the probability for success was greater. "My idea is that you and I and a few other acceptable friends should form a corporation and submit a bid," he wrote. "We could then finance it on whatever seems to be the most desirable set-up." Aviation stocks were hot, he declared. "There seems to be no difficulty whatsoever in financing any well-conceived and sponsored aircraft organization, leaving our group, which will do the initial work, in control of the common stock or equity at nominal cost, or perhaps merely for service rendered."[3]

McAdoo, ever cautious, wanted to secure the mail contract before organizing his airline, despite the Post Office's known desire to give awards only to companies with operating experience; it would be a major mistake.[4]

Throughout the spring, McAdoo attempted to interest other airlines in joining his plan. Unfortunately, St. Tammany–Gulf Coast and Robertson, though interested, cast their lot with AVCO. McAdoo was growing wary, fearful that all the existing airlines were being snapped up by the holding companies, making it "extremely difficult to successfully compete for any mail contract."[5] He feared that the growing oligopolies would force out the independents before they had a chance to enter the business:

> The activity in the aviation field is so great and the consolidations that are going on are so numerous that they foreshadow, in my opinion, an early grouping of the various sections of the United States into strong companies which will preempt the entire field and have a tremendous advantage over later entries because they will be in possession of some desirable mail contracts and in position to bid to better advantage on the new ones that are offered than any new company.
>
> . . . I am inclined to think that it might be well to get together immediately a small group, with a limited amount of capital, say $100,000, . . . and organize a company for the specific purpose of operating a line between Atlanta and Los Angeles, via Dallas, Fort Worth and El Paso, and another line between Chicago and New Orleans. . . . It might be well to start this going immediately. We will then be in a position to bid on the mail contracts when they are offered. . . . Since [Frank] Robertson has severed his connection with his old company, I wonder . . . if he would be willing to join the new enterprise.[6]

Robertson was not willing, having decided to reenter the field on his own. Edgerton, to whom McAdoo entrusted all technical details, urged him to form the airline as soon as possible and was willing to devote all his attention to this project if McAdoo decided to proceed. Still cautious, the former treasury secretary was willing to make all of the necessary arrangements just short of operating and decided to call the new enterprise Southern Skylines. McAdoo was anxious to form a syndicate to raise the necessary two hundred thousand dollars. Aware of the importance of political expediency, he would ask prominent Republicans to be among the subscribers.[7]

Raising money was not as easy as McAdoo had hoped. His friend H.P. Wilson had subscribed to twenty thousand dollars, but no other money was forthcoming. He pressed on regardless, but was becoming increasingly aware that his competition was from Wall Street, not in the air. "The big aviation investment trusts seen to be corralling everything in sight," he stated. "Perhaps they may be able to make it impossible for the small fry to get into the game."[8] Investors were also not completely confident that Southern Sky-Lines was sufficiently well organized and were fearful that the airline's cost estimates were far too rosy. By late spring, investors were growing increasingly wary of aviation stocks, which, as in the case of AVCO, were not performing as well as advertised. McAdoo's good friend Bernard Baruch forwarded a negative report prepared by an anonymous acquaintance that criticized Southern Sky-Lines' initial prospectus as too enthusiastic and based on incomplete research.[9]

McAdoo was appreciative of the comments but rejected the substance of

Earl P. Halliburton, owner of S.A.F.E. Way standing in front of his personal Lockheed Vega (Smithsonian, SI# 88-12862)

the remarks, firmly believing that he and Edgerton had correctly assessed the market and the costs of entry. In the meantime Edgerton and McAdoo began an intensive survey of their proposed route and contacted potential investors in every city along the way. Though interest was fleeting, McAdoo was undeterred. As part of his efforts, he traveled on TAT's new transcontinental service and was deeply impressed with the operation. "We had a wonderful trip," he declared. "Made Los Angeles in two days. . . . Without mail contracts, I don't think these propositions will pay immediately, but eventually they will be wonderful investments."[10] He hoped that the commencement of TAT's line would renew interest in his plan among potential investors. "The opening of the T.A.T. has enormously increased the general interest in commercial air transportation," he stated, "and it seems to me that it makes sense for any banking house of standing to raise the capital needed for our Southern Sky-Lines. . . . I think it is a good time to strike."[11]

McAdoo was slowly listening to Edgerton's insistent advice to open an operating company to prove Southern's qualifications to the Post Office. The quickest way was to either merge or forge an operating agreement with a current airline. McAdoo had just the airline in mind. Erle P. Halliburton, owner of Southwest Air Fast Express, which had been flying since early April, was his neighbor in Beverly Hills. In fact, Halliburton owned a home down the street and the two men's daughters were classmates. Halliburton had assisted McAdoo in arranging for the purchase of McAdoo's private Lockheed Vega, named *The Blue Streak,* and now he was being approached to join Southern Sky-Lines. Halliburton gave a qualified positive reply to McAdoo's suggestion. "I would be glad to know more about your organization and the method you intend to use in raising capital before I would commit myself in connection with a consolidation," he wrote. "The SAFE Airline has raised all of its money without the use of a banking group, and as a result nothing but earnest money has been used to finance the organization. If you would care to purchase some stock in the SAFE Airline on the same basis that all the rest of us have come in, that is $25.00 per share, we would be glad to have you participate with us."[12]

McAdoo knew Halliburton was interested in expanding and was desirous as well of obtaining a mail contract. Writing to Edgerton, McAdoo commented, "A friend of mine, Mr. Halliburton, is operating an air service over this route and I know he is keen for a mail contract. I talked to him once about hooking up with me, but I haven't had a chance to discuss it with him since my return home."[13] McAdoo had been slowed by a troublesome impacted wisdom tooth that had caused him a painful distraction throughout the summer, and only by August was he sufficiently fit to return to business. He replied to Halliburton with a qualified answer of his own: "I thank you for the offer of taking a participation in your company but I think I had better wait until we meet before doing anything in that direction." These words would later come back to haunt him. In the meantime, McAdoo was sure that the current sorry state of the air mail could not last. "I have no doubt that that policy will be radically changed in the near future," he stated.[14]

Edgerton had attended the Interdepartmental Committee on Airways meetings throughout the summer and reported enthusiastically about the prospects. With the determination of the Louisville to Dallas line completed, the Post Office had promised a November meeting to establish the final route, the southern transcontinental. This was now McAdoo's and Edgerton's objective: to organize Southern Sky-Lines and present their application for this essential route. McAdoo had finally listened to Clagett and Edgerton's pleadings and understood that the Post Office was sincere in its firm decision to contract only with experienced operators, not pretenders. "Until a company actually goes into operation somewhere, its backers are looked upon as 'promoters' and are viewed with more or less suspicion in all quarters, and are not taken seriously by the companies themselves," stated Clagett. "The companies which are operating are building up a trained personnel and gaining valuable experience on all sorts of problems and inevitably governmental agencies and business people are much more inclined to do business with established companies than with those which exists only on paper. . . . The requirements at the Post Office Department for mail bids include the fact that the bidders must be 'responsible.' Being 'responsible' means more than mere financial responsibility and includes experience in operation."[15]

Clagett had examined all of the proposed routes and concluded that the southern transcontinental was an excellent opportunity if they acted immediately and showed their good faith by opening service somewhere along the proposed route from Washington to Los Angeles by way of Atlanta and Dallas, or from Chicago to New Orleans. "I doubt that if at this stage of the game a company which has no operating mileage will secure any contracts," warned Clagett. "It seems to me there are two possible methods of procedure. Either (1) to complete the syndicate of $500,000 and proceed to map and begin operations on a route . . . or (2) to enter into a combination with an existing company like Standard Air Ways or 'Great Southern Air Ways' which you mention as belonging to California interests and being in process of projecting a line over our southern route."[16] They hoped that Halliburton would provide the practical operating experience required by the Post Office, and by September, this, they thought, had been arranged. On September 20, 1929, McAdoo confirmed to Brice Clagett that Halliburton had decided to "go on board" and join with Southern Sky-Lines in their joint offer to the Post Office for the southern transcontinental route.[17]

Efforts continued in the hope of putting together the airline in time for the Post Office and Interdepartmental Committee. McAdoo's difficulties in raising capital were mounting. His constant delays because of his caution and health problems meant that they were running out of time as the state of the stock market continued to deteriorate. McAdoo was also anxious for some action from the department and was hoping that a statement made by Second Assistant Postmaster General Glover would allow the Post Office to place first-class mail on the airlines at the postmaster general's discretion. An anxious McAdoo was willing to submit a proposal to the Post Office for Southern Sky-Lines to carry first-class mail between New York and Los Angeles in an attempt to force Brown's hand. "If you think well of it," wrote McAdoo to Clagett, "we could proceed with the permanent organization of the Sky-Lines board and officers and make a serious effort to get the business."[18]

An operations staff was needed. McAdoo approached William MacCracken to head the airline, now that the assistant secretary had announced he was leaving government service. The offer was graciously declined as MacCracken wished to enter private practice and represent numerous airlines before the government. McAdoo was beginning to feel the pressure from a worsening economy and the growing presence of the large operators consuming most of the extant capital and qualified personnel. He was aware that the meeting between the department and the contractors was to reopen soon and that this could be a bad omen for the small independents. "I hope that you will attend the conference which the Postmaster General is going to hold with air mail contractors, beginning September 30th, if it is permissible," stated McAdoo. "I hope that new lines and independent lines are not going to be swept aside in order to strengthen the position and monopoly of a few large companies now in the field."[19]

McAdoo now focused his attention on the Interdepartmental Committee meeting scheduled for November 25 to make his pitch to the Post Office. Edgerton reported that the time was ripe, for with "the Post Office negotiation underway for the reduction of [the] air mail deficit, it is the opinion at the Department that new routes . . . will soon be advertised. We cannot afford to waste the long months occupied by all new and large organizations in growing pains, as we are now in position to start actual work."[20]

To get a head start on the potential competition, McAdoo and Halliburton submitted an unsolicited offer to the postmaster general offering to carry the transcontinental air mail for seventy cents per pound for the first thousand miles and seven cents per mile for each additional one hundred miles, approximately half of what Boeing Air Transport was currently being paid. In addition, they offered to carry first-class mail for sixty cents for the first thousand miles and six cents per hundred miles thereafter. McAdoo and Halliburton were hoping that the postmaster general could award them this route without the cumbersome necessity of competitive bidding, which usually drove the bidding prices so low that no contractor could make a profit. This they consciously did, even though such an arrangement could be interpreted as an unfair practice that favored insiders and the large holding companies. According to McAdoo and Halliburton, both Democrats, "We are familiar of course with the opinion of the Comptroller General, dated March 1, 1927, . . . to the effect that under the Air Mail Act there appears no reason why advertising for bids 'is not incumbent or is not contemplated by the law.' While we realize that up to the present time you have followed this opinion of the Comptroller General in making air mail contracts, we are not sure that such advertising for bids is mandatory. We do not believe that it is mandatory."[21]

Halliburton and McAdoo printed their two proposals and, attaching a cover letter, mailed their offer to the chambers of commerce, merchants' associations, and trade organizations in all of the major cities along the proposed route to garner local support for their effort. This was a wise move because it was expected that these same local representatives would attend the forthcoming Interdepartmental conference and their support for Southern Sky-Lines and Southwest Air Fast Express was crucial.[22]

Second Assistant Postmaster General Glover gave a lukewarm response to the offer, referring Halliburton and McAdoo to the Interdepartmental meeting. "Air mail routes are only established after the most careful consideration has been given to every factor surrounding such matters," he wrote. As to the offer to receive a contract without competitive bidding, Glover reminded them that, at present, their offer "could not be accepted under law, even if the Department was so inclined."[23]

Brice Clagett wrote to his father-in-law and told him not to worry about Glover's reply. He felt that the department was looking favorably upon their proposal but was being cautious pending the outcome of the conference and was concerned about angering the comptroller general, John McCarl, who by law passed on the validity of all government contracts before they could be executed. "In view of the Comptroller General's opinion, which I sent you," stated Clagett, "there is a decided tendency at the Department not to let any mail contracts without bids."[24]

Clagett was emphatic that it was essential to complete as much preliminary work as possible to impress the department. This would include determining schedules, equipment, landing fields, and financing to demonstrate that they were, in the department's terms, a "responsible bidder." Clagett suggested that Southern Sky-Lines bid under Halliburton's name alone because he had operating experience and, despite his irascible nature, which offended some people in the Post Office, his record was sound.[25]

McAdoo took this suggestion seriously. He and Halliburton had tentatively agreed to a merger of their two operations, on November 22, 1929, with McAdoo as chairman of the board and Halliburton as president. The airline was to be named the Southern Air Fast Express and was to be advertised as the "Southern Sky-Lines route" if, and only if, they won the contract.[26]

As scheduled, on November 25, 1929, more than two hundred representatives from dozens of communities in the South and Southwest together with their members of Congress gathered in Washington before the Interdepartmental Committee on Airways. Chairing the session was Postmaster General Brown. The only airline representative present was McAdoo. Brown opened the proceedings by stating that numerous routes had been suggested over the past year and that those in attendance must maintain an open mind about the decisions made that day. He emphasized that at present, the South was the only region of the country without adequate air mail service, and he felt it his duty to address this problem, but in a rational manner without favoritism and bound by the limits of congressional appropriations. "It is a matter of small importance whether or not any particular city be located on a direct air mail line," Brown said. "Cities can be supplied feeder lines for a distance of two or three hundred miles." As for money, the postmaster general stressed, "We have no control over appropriations and cannot pay for any service for which we have no money. The only reservation is that Congress must furnish us the money to establish additional air mail lines throughout the country."[27]

When his turn came, McAdoo did not disappoint. He formally presented his offer to the Post Office to carry the mail and air mail as he had outlined earlier, only this time providing even more detail and persuasion. McAdoo left the hearings exuberant, firmly believing that he had made a convincing case, taking full credit for the success of the event.

While the committee was deliberating, Halliburton was in Michigan attempting to interest investors, particularly the Detroit Aircraft Corporation, the holding company that now controlled Lockheed Aircraft, to join with him and McAdoo.[28] Merger negotiations were put on hold, however, pending the decision of the committee.

McAdoo was beginning to express some concern about the loyalty of his volatile partner. He was growing increasingly wary that, after all of his work in seeking a contract for the southern transcontinental line, Halliburton was going to abandon their partnership, take the contract, and leave Southern Skylines to wither on the vine. McAdoo expressed his worries in a letter to Clagett:

> Halliburton is on the train and I am reviewing the entire situation with him, but I don't see any particular light, at the moment, although he feels quite confident that he will ultimately get a mail contract since he is actually operating an airways system. I have reemphasized to him that since we started out to do the job together, we must stick together, which says he is going to do, and I think he will. Since the idea of the present campaign originated with me and has been given great impetus because of my work, it does seem that we ought to get some benefit from it, but Halliburton, having the only operation portion of the joint system, stands to get everything and my end nothing. This will be the irony of fate if it happens because I don't think he would have gotten far, if anywhere, for a long time but for our effective work and strategy.[29]

McAdoo's fears were well founded.

The Post Office released the committee's decision on December 11, the same day McAdoo wrote Clagett about Halliburton. After the completion of almost a year's worth of work, the Interdepartmental Committee on Airways decided that three routes should be pursued in the coming months. All would be delayed pending appropriations and the completion of the lighting of the airways for night flight by the Department of Commerce. The committee officially confirmed that an airway between Louisville and Dallas was approved, a line from New York to St. Louis via Philadelphia and Pittsburgh was granted, and, most important, the southern transcontinental was authorized from Atlanta to Los Angeles by way of Birmingham, Jackson, Mississippi, Shreveport, Dallas, Fort Worth, El Paso, and San Diego. To McAdoo's dismay, no decision was reached on when the contracts would be advertised. A subsequent letter from W. Irving Glover drove the point home that Southern Sky-Lines would have to wait pending new legislation proposed by the postmaster general.

McAdoo begrudgingly understood the situation but had faith that he would still win the contract, although he was growing increasingly aware of the strength of the competition. He expected strong opposition from Clement Keys, particularly as his holdings controlled National Air Transport, which operated the routes from New York to Chicago and Chicago to Dallas and Fort Worth, as well as Eastern Air Transport, which flew from New York to Miami through Washington and Atlanta along the eastern seaboard. "If they enter into a spirited competition with us for this business," McAdoo warned, "the bids may be so low that nobody can make any money out of it."[30]

He also expected pressure from Western Air Express through its recently acquired Standard Air Lines division, which operated passenger service from Los Angeles to El Paso. "It would be greatly to their advantage," stated McAdoo, "to have a good air mail contract between Los Angeles and El Paso and extend it to Dallas and Atlanta." McAdoo was less concerned with United Aircraft and Boeing Air Transport as they were occupied in the Northwest and with their route from San Francisco to Chicago.[31]

The former secretary of the treasury was astute in his predictions of strong competition for the southern route. He did not know the extent of the involvement of the Post Office in forging a new, rational transcontinental airways system, however, for within the year, great changes were to be wrought in the industry through the iron hand of Walter Brown.

The legislation that Glover spoke of was to have a profound effect on the industry and was the culmination of months of difficult negotiations concerning Brown's determination to bring efficiency and productivity to the air mail service through a revision of the rate system of the contract air mail carriers. A change in the law was essential if the airlines were to survive, now that the boom on Wall Street had just come to an abrupt end.

The air mail operators waited in nervous anticipation throughout the late summer for the postmaster general's new rate revision plan. They had expected some action from the Post Office for some time. In a letter to Harold Emmons, Col. Louis Brittin of Northwest Airways, who had earlier spoken with Superintendent Wadsworth concerning the postal deficit and the air mail rate problems, noted,

From my discussion with Mr. Wadsworth, the Department evidently has in mind a plan by which the operators will submit a sworn statement of their operations once a year and accept from the Postmaster General a rate that will give then a "reasonable return." This of course will require the operators to also include in their statements their program for new equipment, hangars, machinery, etc. The Department would naturally take all of this into consideration in fixing new rates.

Mr. Wadsworth stated very frankly that whatever the Department did in the way of adjusting rates, would be done in such a way as to protect and foster the air mail service. As he expresses it, no one "will get hurt." He, however, frankly says that the profits earned by Western Air Express and one or two others are entirely out of reason and cannot be continued without injuring the entire service.[32]

Although many were resistant to change, some understood that the present system was flawed and that the responsibility for making profits lay in the hands of the operators. "Now, it is true that if the Government would wipe the slate clean and start all over again tomorrow, they would do the thing in a somewhat different way," stated Hainer Hinshaw of Universal and AVCO. "They admit that. But they are wholly powerless to do this and we simply must make the best of what we have because there is no way of changing it. If a line cannot make money; if the traffic force cannot sell air mail in the territory the route covers and if the operation personnel cannot cut their cost to a point below the income, then, it would seem the only thing to do would be to give the Post Office sixty days notice and cancel the contract."[33]

The operators realized that the revised law from 1928 allowed the Post Office to issue certificates as contract extensions, but that came with a provision allowing the government to modify the method of payment and the amount. Those making the maximum allowed by law were resistant to change; others, receiving much less per pound mile, wanted more money but were concerned about possible new restrictive provisions. In an editorial, *Aviation* voiced its concern on behalf of the contractors, stating that "any approximation of fairness among the contractors requires some adjustment in planning compensation for a long term of years, for at present absurd differences in the scales of payment exist. . . . The need for reconsideration is clear."[34]

Aviation understood that with the lowering of the air mail postage, the Post Office would soon attempt to restore some balance in its bookkeeping to overcome the postal air mail deficit. "Complete self-support must be the goal at the end of the air mail's road," stated editor Edward P. Warner, "and we must move steadily in that direction. The progress toward financial independence cannot, however, be pressed too rapidly." Warner supported President Hoover's belief that because aviation was in an experimental stage, temporary government assistance was appropriate to promote air mail and passenger air travel.

It was felt that air transportation would eventually become profitable on its own when the industry reached maturity. Warner was most concerned about Brown's insistence on a uniform system of accounting. He feared that this would lead to direct rate regulation, which "at this early stage of development would be paralyzing to initiative and to efficiency" because it restricted earnings. Warner was adamant that the percentage of profit made should have nothing to do with relative rates. Those rates should depend upon only three factors—the average mail load, the distance that it has to be carried, and the inherent difficulties of the route and administrative costs. "It is earnestly hoped," wrote Warner, "that in the rearrangement of rates no penalty will be laid upon the contractors whose accounts reveal them already to have obtained an exceptional degree of economy and efficiency of operation."[35]

The new rates were not going to be unilaterally imposed by Brown but would be the product of joint meetings between industry and government, with the postmaster general setting the guidelines. He was willing to work with industry provided they were willing to cooperate in this associative approach. He did not desire formal rate regulation but did want the government to receive a better return on its investment through a change in the payment process that would provide greater efficiencies for all involved.

The Post Office Department announced on September 11, 1929, that rate revision discussions were to resume on September 30 to effect reductions in the carrying charges paid by the government to the air mail contractors as well as adjusting the payment rates on a more sound basis. Operating under the authority of the Second Amendment to the Air Mail Act, passed on May 17, 1928, Brown wanted to open discussion on the contract extension plan, which would allow the air mail carriers to exchange their contracts, soon to expire (the first on October 7), for ten-year route certificates. The Post Office had also spent the summer analyzing the data collected from the questionnaires that the contractors had completed. Armed with this information, the department was anxious to find an equitable way to reduce its expenditures while increasing the effectiveness of the air mail service.

The problem facing the Post Office Department was considerable. Expenditures for fiscal year 1929 were expected to be $15 million. Unfortunately, the appropriation was for only $13.3 million. Brown and Glover had no intention of curtailing service; on the contrary, they hoped to expand air mail throughout the country as witnessed by the recent Interdepartmental Committee on Airways hearings. Greater efficiencies were seen as the way to overcome the $1.7 million shortfall, and, in fact, Glover was hoping to cut approximately $3 million from the department's air mail expenditures on the present routes to allow for expansion. "Looking at the situation from every standpoint," stated Glover, "there is no idea in the minds of the Post Office Department officials to curtail any of the routes now in operation, but, on the contrary, it is believed that there will be sufficient money available when the time comes to take care of any normal and reasonable expansion of the air mail service throughout the country."[36] This came as somewhat of a surprise to Superintendent Wadsworth, whose job it was to administer the contracts. According to Hinshaw, "He points out that they are three millions of dollars in the red and that we all know Postmaster General Brown well enough to know that he would not sanction further extensions until there had been some indication that could be made up without a great fight."[37]

In advance of the Post Office meetings, the operators formed a committee among themselves and met in Washington and Chicago to determine a joint course of action. The results were mixed. They could not decide what they wanted; they only knew what they did not want. They did agree that a system based on weight per mile flown was preferred, but details could not be worked out. A straight mileage system was not desired.[38]

Each airline was to confer individually as part of the rate revision conferences. According to Hinshaw, some of the rate cuts were going to be dramatic. "The Post Office will definitely indicate the rate we are to have on the certificate," he stated. "I am rather inclined to believe that the $3.00 boys will get a 50 percent reduction and Robertson will probably find himself somewhere between $1.50 and $1.75."[39]

Each operator met individually with Second Assistant Postmaster General W. Irving Glover and Superintendent Earl B. Wadsworth together with an accountant from the department. All of the contractors brought their financial records with them for a detailed, confidential review and analysis.[40] At the conclusion of the private sessions, Glover called the operators back to discuss the matter in a joint session on October 3 and asked that they formulate their own rate reduction plan. Despite their best efforts, the operators' committee, headed by Colonel Henderson, could not find enough common ground, leaving the hearings deadlocked.[41]

Harris Hanshue of WAE and Clifford Ball, two of the so-called "$3.00 boys," were understandably reluctant to relinquish their highly profitable routes, whereas Boeing and National Air Transport, which were operating profitably on not so generous a payment, realized that a revision would not hurt them nearly as much and were more willing to negotiate.

At the general conference, Walter Brown made it clear to the operators that he felt the airlines required no more assistance from the government than they were already receiving. An alarmed Mabel Walker Willebrandt, representing all of the airlines of AVCO, adamantly stressed that she believed it was the intention of Congress to provide an indirect subsidy. Brown was more concerned about balancing the department's budget at this point, but a problem raised its head to the consternation of all, for at this juncture, the specter of ICC regulation reappeared.

In Congress, Sen. Sam G. Bratton of New Mexico and Rep. John L. Cable of Ohio introduced bills calling for the removal of authority for aviation from the Commerce Department and its transfer to the Interstate Commerce Commission. In essence, Cable proposed exactly what Brown was attempting to do, only through an outside agency, the ICC.

William McAdoo wrote to Senator Bratton to voice his objections, believing that the bill was unnecessary and cumbersome: "I think that it would be easy to seriously impair the development of air commerce through unwise or unsatisfactory legislation. I am convinced that the Interstate Commerce Commission is already overloaded and that it would be a mistake to place this new transportation arm under its jurisdiction. While I am strongly opposed to the creation of unnecessary independent commissions, I feel that a new commission is the only way to deal with the subject." Part of the proposal, however, seemed good. The restrictions on new entrants through the use of certificates of convenience and necessity would allow solid companies to prosper. "The present policy of allowing the Postmaster General to lay out mail routes and seek competitive bids is having a very unfortunate effect upon the development of commercial aviation," McAdoo noted, "because it is throttling many excellent companies which must have the opportunity to carry the mails in order to sustain themselves."[42]

Despite the opposition by the large carriers, who objected to the known inefficiency of the ICC and the fear of direct government control limiting their profitability, Brice Clagett felt that the powerful airlines might support the bills because of their protectionist nature. McAdoo was of two minds concerning the legislation, seeing the benefits of the certificates but also fearing that the big companies would take advantage of the law and use it to exclude independents.[43]

The postmaster general indicated to the gathering that he would support neither the Cable nor Bratton bill, but warned the operators that if they did not reach an acceptable rate formula, some other agency might do so for them in the near future.[44] Lacking the support of the Post Office and meeting sufficient opposition on Capital Hill, both bills died in conference.

The Post Office was beginning to lose patience. The general meeting on October 7 adjourned without reaching a consensus; the operators requesting additional information from the Post Office. On October 15, a frustrated department took the initiative, issuing a new proposal and its own questionnaire for the air mail contractors to be answered within the week. Negotiations would begin anew during the first week in November.

In the meantime, Brown was going to approach Congress and seek legislation in the forthcoming session to permit the department more leeway in the interpretation of the existing law. He wanted the authority to extend the routes up to four hundred miles without submitting the action to open competitive bidding. This move, intended to streamline the routes, would benefit the existing carriers and permit the postmaster general greater flexibility in expanding and rationalizing the nation's air route structure. It would give Brown even more direct control over the airways while affording greater income to the existing carriers, thereby offsetting their expected losses from the coming rate reductions.[45] To this end Brown had the support of Rep. Clyde Kelly, who was willing to introduce the requested legislation on Brown's behalf with the understanding that some shorter routes would face elimination if extensions were not practical.[46]

The contractors were puzzled, however, by Brown's public remarks. Although clearly supporting the established air mail carriers, the postmaster general sent conflicting signals in his address to the Advertising Club of Washington. "The air mail," Brown said, "should be used when speed is of such importance as to justify the increased cost, and then only between points which are actually served by air transportation." His point was obvious: the present state of aviation was such that air mail did not reach into every city at this stage, so it was pointless for a customer to pay the extra expense of air mail to send a letter that would have to be delivered by conventional methods. "The Department does not recommend the promiscuous use of the air mail," he continued, "and does not approve ballyhoo campaigns designed to influence the public to make all mailings by plane."[47]

These remarks upset the airlines. "Tex" Marshall of Thompson Aeronautical Corporation, which held the air mail contract from Chicago to Pontiac, Michigan, expressed his concern to Henderson after reading an article on Brown's address in the *Detroit News*. Marshall interpreted Brown's remarks as not supporting air mail completely and noticed a new unwillingness to cooperate on the part of the Post Office in Michigan as a result.[48]

The postmaster general was already "sold" on the air mail, but not at any cost. He firmly believed in its importance and in the continued need for government assistance until the airlines could survive on their own in the near future. He proudly sent President Hoover an editorial from the *Boston Herald* that summarized his speech. "Until the people of the United States become more thoroughly convinced of the safety and utility of air transportation for themselves," he told the *Herald*, "it is the duty of the government to continue its support." More important, he stressed his belief of the future shape of air transportation in America. Together with the continuing regulation of safety and the technical control of aviation by the Department of Commerce, Brown's plan for air mail favored the concentration of federal efforts "on a few natural transportation routes which have been travelled by ox team, pony express, railroad, automobile, and airplane."[49]

The debate over the new rate system was causing consternation on Wall Street. In late September and early October all the aviation stocks were taking a beating as investors were anxious to sell off and take their profit before the new rates came into effect and lessened the perceived value of the air mail carriers. An agreement was urgently required to bolster sagging stock values by restoring order to the industry and untangling the rate conundrum. As expected, the hearings resumed in November, but with little progress because no one could agree on a suitable yardstick to measure costs. Other arguments ensued over the new question of rate "variables," which were offered as a sliding scale of bonuses for flying in difficult weather, at night, over dangerous terrain, and with certain types of aircraft.[50]

With the threat of expiring contracts looming in the background, Brown decided he would indeed impose his own order on the system. Fortunately, under law, the postmaster general had the right to extend contracts for up to six months, which Brown chose to do when the first contract, that of Colonial along CAM-1, expired on November 6.

To Brown it had become increasingly apparent that more drastic changes were necessary to affect the program he desired and that this required new legislation. He felt that the current air mail act did not give him enough power to exercise the needed revisions and implement the radical alterations that would make the air mail system more efficient and eventually a profitable means of public transportation.[51]

While Brown wrestled with the nagging rate revision problem, the arena shifted to the White House, where representatives of the industry asked to meet with the president to discuss the general situation of aviation. Every year, President Hoover called in representatives of the Aeronautical Chamber of Commerce for a report on the industry to aid in his annual message to Congress. This year, with the rate revision matter still up in the air and the collapse of the stock market present in everyone's mind, the presentation took on a new sense of urgency as the operators met in Washington. They assembled at the request of Julius Barnes, who, on orders from the president, initiated a series of conferences of all the major industries to decide upon a course of action to deal with the market crisis.

To prepare for the presidential meeting, the members of the ACC sat down with Clarence Young, the new assistant secretary of commerce for aeronautics, together with the industry's legal representatives and lobbyists. They engaged in a heated exchange over the rate revision situation, the postmaster general, and the state of the industry. An ad hoc committee that included Frederick Rentschler, Clement Keys, and Paul Henderson drafted a memorandum for the president critical of the postmaster general's handling of the air mail situation and pressing him to take immediate action. Hainer Hinshaw and William "Doc" Bishop of Western Air Express took vocal exception to the idea of openly criticizing Brown, as their two companies held fourteen of the twenty-four outstanding air mail contracts and had the most to lose from angering the Post Office.

At a breakfast in the Carlton Hotel, the issue came to a boil as Henderson desperately tried to force Brown's hand to grant a contract to his financially ailing Transcontinental Air Transport. Bishop, a new arrival in Washington and not one to mince his words, reported:

> You know that Henderson is about out on his can. He has only one chance and that is to get these mail contracts and I don't think he has much time to do it in. At this breakfast Keys openly ignored his suggestions, vigorously contradicted him and then Keys finally left the room.
>
> Immediately he started in talking about the mail contracts. Keys had gone. He said the only way we were going to get anywhere was to go to the Postmaster General and tell him that we had been trying for months to work this thing out between ourselves and that we had failed. Therefore, as a body we had decided to come to him, tell him to decide what he wanted and to call us in and tell us what we could have. These suggestions met with some approval, especially from Rentschler, Bell, . . . and Halliburton.
>
> Hainer and I kept still. . . . Following the meeting with the President, Hainer, Mr. Grosvenor and myself went into a huddle and determined immediately that to allow Henderson to get away with that idea might be fatal.
>
> . . . Not being able to reach you by phone to advise you of the move to force the contracts[,] . . . I called Mr. Hanshue. He said substantially as follows:
>
>> 'You tell them that when we left Washington it was with the understanding with the Postmaster General that he would call us back to Washington when he was ready to talk business with us and that until he does call us back we are not interested and will not be a party to any move to force him to take steps he is not ready to take.'
>
> Hainer called Mr. Brown's office after we had all determined upon our course and tipped Mac [William MacCracken, who now represented Western] off to what was coming. Brown immediately decided he had to attend a funeral somewhere in Ohio Friday . . . so that ended Mr. Henderson's swell idea.[52]

Later during an afternoon conference with Assistant Secretary Clarence Young, the question of a petition to the president outlining the dire condition of the industry was again brought forward and almost passed, but Bishop, Hinshaw, and Colonel Brittin of Northwest quashed it once more. Hinshaw related the events to Gilbert Grosvenor:

The meeting was called for 4:40 instead of 4 o'clock. This allowed Bishop and myself to have a few words with Clarence Young. Young indicated to us that it was against his wishes for the memorandum to be presented but that if it was the sense of the meeting he would present it to Mr. Lamont [the Secretary of Commerce]. Of course we could not indicate this to the rest of the meeting. Fortunately the memorandum contained what Bishop, Col. Brittin and myself thought was a severe rebuff to the Postmaster General. . . . Bishop made a vigorous fight on this point and Brittin and I supported him. We had the paragraph completely eliminated.[53]

"Making a long story short," Bishop concluded in his report to Wooley, "the argument continued for a half hour, with Hainer supporting me and Henderson leaving the room so damn mad he didn't dare stay for the finish. We stopped the whole thing."[54]

Henderson was persistent, however. He and Clement Keys had earlier made an appointment for December 12 at 11:30 A.M. to meet with the president to express their views on the aviation situation.[55] Henderson, with his old connections, knew Hoover's aide Walter Newton well and thanked him for "listening to my tale of woe."[56] At 11:30 A.M. on the appointed day, Hoover received the gentlemen from TAT and their personal report on the declining condition of aviation in the country. Keys reiterated his publicly stated belief that the present crisis in the stock market was just a seasonal lull and that the economy would rebound by spring. Henderson pointed out the difficulties the airlines were having developing a new rate system. He was moderate in his opinions, stating that such a delay was perhaps to be expected because it took several decades to work out a rate plan for the railroads.[57] Hainer Hinshaw, not knowing that Henderson had modified his views, at least for the moment, reacted strongly when he learned of the meeting, telephoning the White House directly and expressing his opinion that the two were not speaking for the industry.[58]

Bishop and Hinshaw were correct in their approach. The postmaster general was not one who took criticism lightly, and he would have been greatly offended if he had learned that any of the operators had gone over his head and criticized him to the president. Bishop and Hinshaw confirmed this when they spoke to Kenneth McPherson, Brown's personal secretary, following an attempt on December 10 by Henderson and others to speak privately with the postmaster general:

When Hainer and I got together, we called McPherson, who advised us not to allow any of them to press the Postmaster General or do anything to make it appear that we are not satisfied with the way he has been doing things.

When we got down there Henderson and Bing Seymour were the only ones there. Halliburton had been told by Henderson and Colonel Brittin too, that there would be no meeting held. When we walked in he just about turned those pyles he's crying about inside out.

In about five minutes he was ready to call the meeting off, which was done and he left the building. MacPherson called Hainer and told him that everything turned out fine. According to the dope, the Postmaster General is going to have something to offer in about a week. He also let it be known that he appreciates the attitude Hainer and I have assumed.[59]

While at the department, Bishop ran into Erle Halliburton, who had become a virtual denizen of the Post Office building that fall following his joint presentation with partner William McAdoo to the Interdepartmental Committee on Airways. When pressed, Halliburton revealed to Hinshaw he had spoken with Brown and learned that the postmaster general was leaning toward proposing a space-based method of payment similar to that used by the railroads during World War I. This method would ensure an equitable distribution of payments based on the space available on the aircraft, not on just the weight of the mail load. Thus airlines with thin routes would receive as much revenue as those airlines carrying much greater loads over a heavy route of the same length. A good lobbyist, Bishop knew how to extract information from Halliburton:

> Got him stiff last night and he told me of having been in a two-hour conference with Brown that afternoon. He claimed that Brown told him he wanted to put the operators on a space basis with a minimum guarantee.
> I told Wadsworth this when I saw him today and Earl said he's crazy. Have it doped out that Halliburton told Brown he thought the space idea was the best and after taking a lot of the PMG's time to convince him of the merits of it—the PMG then told him he thought he [Halliburton] had a swell idea.[60]

In the meantime, Erle Halliburton was actively campaigning for a contract to the point of irritating Brown and the department. "The damn fool is talking himself out of Washington," Bishop declared.[61]

Halliburton, like many of the independents operating without a mail contract, thought he could make money carrying passengers alone but soon realized his error. Without a mail contract, given the existing state of aeronautics, no airline could make money with the current generation of inefficient aircraft. Transcontinental Air Transport's grandiose air-rail experiment was hemorrhaging money, as was Halliburton's SAFE Way, despite the companies' excellent organization and preparation. Henderson was in Washington representing NAT, which had contracts, but also TAT, which did not, and desperately needed help. Halliburton, in his blunt way, stormed into D.C. and pressured anyone he could for a contract. Whether working with McAdoo or working alone, Halliburton would stop at nothing to snare a contract. He was even threatening Western Air Express with the establishment of competing service along their Los Angeles—Kansas City route, though Bishop was not very concerned. "[I] can't imagine him doing much damage with his Fords across that run," he said, "in spite of the fact that he claims he has netted 40 cents a flying mile and that his cost has only been 72 cents."[62]

Halliburton was getting desperate for a contract during the meetings in Washington, pressuring the other operators for support as well as pounding the halls of the Post Office. The ever-observant Bishop noted his competitor's tactics and underscored the cutthroat competition between the airlines:

> Halliburton was crying like a stuck hog because he couldn't get any sympathy for his line. He and Henderson had a nice battle, but the latter elected to ignore him as well as did everybody else.
>
> Halliburton nailed me in the lobby of the Carlton and threatened to raise hell unless the committee took some action on changing the mail situation so he could live. I filled him full of crap about having heard he was sitting pretty to get a big hunk of the southern route just to find out how well he did stand on it.
>
> That was funny. He hit the ceiling. "Hell," he said, "you're crazy. They're playing around with this thing so we never will get it." He sure convinced me that he thinks he is in a bad way as far as that deal is concerned and I've got an idea of making it no better fast.
>
> Hainer, Grosvenor, and I got together again and decided that this memorandum should contain only a general constructive mention of air mail and that any attempt by Halliburton should be blocked if he wanted to try to force the issue between the operators and the PMG. But he was playing a lone hand.[63]

Western Air Express and AVCO were interested in securing all or part of the southern transcontinental line offered by the Interdepartmental Committee on Airways and thought they had an inside track. Halliburton was lobbying actively because he sensed that the department did not take the Southern Sky Lines proposal seriously. "McAdoo is clear out of the picture as far as Wadsworth is concerned," stated Bishop. "He is down on them."[64]

The operators expected a decision from the postmaster general within a few days, but nothing was heard. Brown finally spoke in January, and when he did, all took notice.

Chapter 7

The Watres Act

While the operators anxiously awaited Postmaster General Brown's decision on the new rate plan, troubles were mounting in the airline industry. Aviation stocks in particular were taking a beating. By the end of 1929 the drop was catastrophic. North American Aviation fell from a high of 19 3/4 to a low of only 4. Its two major airlines, National Air Transport and Transcontinental Air Transport, fell from 48 1/4 to 10, and 33 5/8 to 6, respectively. The Aviation Corporation dropped from 20 to 4 1/2, and profitable Western Air Express sank from 78 1/4 to 15. Even solid United Aircraft was hard hit, falling from an astounding 162 to 31 of its common stock and 109 1/2 to 44 7/8 of its preferred.[1] Were it not for the fact that the industry had raised a large capital pool through stock sales rather than debt financing, the aviation industry could have failed entirely.

As it was, the companies managed to struggle on, buoyed only by their dwindling cash reserves. Most of the airlines, with the enviable exception of those of United Aircraft and Transport Corporation, were losing money at prodigious rates. National Air Transport, Western Air Express, and Clifford Ball managed to make money during the last months of 1929. None of the independents did. Transcontinental Air Transport reported a net deficit of $986,591 from July 8, when it opened service, until December 31, 1929. Of this total, TAT lost $746,519, and its new acquisition, Maddux Air Lines, lost $240,072. The actual loss was much greater. Transcontinental offset the deficit by adding miscellaneous income: the actual total operating losses for TAT-Maddux was an astounding $1,291,679.[2] The Aviation Corporation fared no better, and it had the majority of air mail contracts to offset its costs. Primarily an airline holding company, AVCO reported a net loss of $1,443,822 for 1929, most of which was attributed to losses in air transportation.[3] From July to

December, AVCO's losses averaged almost $300,000 per month—$10,000 per day—totaling a gross deficit of $1,795,600, with nothing done by management to stem the bleeding.[4]

After Black Thursday and Black Tuesday struck in late October, industry analysts turned to Clement Keys for his opinion of the recent events. Keys, a longtime player on Wall Street, saw the collapse only as a seasonal decline and a necessary readjustment in reaction to the perceived inflated values of all stocks that had occurred over the last two years. "After a very complete study of all phases of aviation, I have no hesitation in stating that the reaction in the trade is grossly exaggerated in the public mind," Keys told the *Wall Street Journal*. "Most of it is, in fact, a reaction from the hysterical estimates of a silly boom, which played no part in the plans or policies of the old companies in the business." Keys felt that the market shakeup was, on the contrary, beneficial. "In all branches of the trade there is a wholesome, but widespread, cleaning up of loose ends," he continued. "Dozens of little transport concerns that started in the boom because they could get easy money, and have operated planes at from half to three-quarters the true cost of operation, are going out of business for lack of new capital to pay operating expenses. Flying a big tri-motor plane at five or six cents a passenger mile may be fun while it lasts, but it won't last long." For Keys, this was a necessary and welcome reaction that would benefit the solid companies and remove the harmful speculators and below-cost operators.[5]

By December, Keys was beginning to comprehend the depth of the widening crisis, stating that the results of the manufacturers and, especially, the commercial airlines were "seriously disappointing," compounded by the problem in the negotiation for the air mail rate readjustments. The airlines were particularly vulnerable, he noted, as "the passenger business is still in the pioneering stage which requires a lot of courage, hard work, and patience."[6] In his opinion, the passenger business was in trouble because the traveling public was not educated enough to understand its great advantages, but, more important, costs were not being matched by revenue. According to Keys, "The tremendously rapid growth of passenger facilities brought about an unsound rate structure—in other words, that the service is being furnished at less than cost."[7] The problem of fare structures was only getting worse, however, as passenger traffic as well as mail poundage was decreasing, not increasing.

It was widely known and accepted that the independent airlines had experienced financial difficulties for some time. Despite charging fares well above the cost of first-class Pullman rates offered by the railroads, the passenger carriers could not cover their operating costs, much less make a profit. Now with the collapse of the stock market and the general precipitous decline of the economy, other airlines were beginning to feel pressure and were forced to cut their fares drastically to stimulate traffic in a losing battle to stay in business.

Transcontinental Air Transport made the most important of the fare cuts. Despite Keys's earlier correct assertion that the airlines could not make a profit at the current high ticket prices, TAT lowered its rates in late November by 25 percent, cutting the cost of a transcontinental ticket from $338 to $267. Western Air Express and Universal followed suit in the hope of increasing traffic during the slow winter months.[8] The editors of *Air Transportation* trumpeted the change as great news for the industry and the consumer. "As the traffic builds, the operating and overhead costs per passenger will decrease," they stated, "and soon profits will begin to come as a result of the lowered fares." Transcontinental's reputation as a well-financed and well-organized operation led *Air Transportation* to the incorrect conclusion that this was a studied move, not one bred from desperation.[9]

Desperation, however, was the driving force. Ridership increased while losses mounted. By the beginning of the new year, Keys was willing to try anything to increase traffic and profits even at the risk of destructive competition.[10] His solution was another fare cut, this time to as low as the "wild-cat speculator's" 5 cents per mile fare structure. Transcontinental dropped its prices an additional $107.51 to a mere $159.62, less than half of its original fare and now below the cost of a first-class train ticket with a Pullman surcharge.[11] Further, TAT instituted a cost-cutting policy consolidating its national offices in Los Angeles and moving its eastern offices from St. Louis to Columbus, Ohio, and the Pennsylvania Railroad increased its influence, placing its vice president in charge of traffic, Daniel M. Shaeffer, on the TAT Board as chairman of the executive committee. Other executives were let go and not replaced.[12]

Even Western Air Express, which operated the very profitable mail route from Los Angeles to Salt Lake City, lowered its fares and consolidated its organization. Between Los Angeles and Kansas City, Western dropped its fares to $120 to compete with TAT, despite the fact that the corporation reported a net profit for 1929 of $1,087,852, 80 percent of which came from mail contracts.[13] In the meantime, Harris Hanshue acquired the Aero Corporation of California on a one-for-twelve stock swap.[14] The deal netted Western control over Standard Air Lines, which operated a route from Los Angeles to El Paso, and thus positioned WAE well for the expected request for bids from the Post Office for one of the two transcontinental routes.

The Aviation Corporation was in the deepest trouble. The officers' valiant attempts to bolster the value of its stock had failed even before the market collapsed. Now, they were in desperate straits. This huge corporation, organized by some of the finest financial minds on Wall Street but overladen with sixty directors and a plethora of executives, was in danger of total collapse. For

AVCO, all depended on the outcome of the rate revision negotiations. The corporation anxiously supported the idea for a space payment as its haphazard routes were generally sparsely traveled with light mail loads. Of all the companies, it was in the most urgent need for reorganization to stave off extinction.

By late 1929 a small-scale revolt was brewing from within the ranks, manifested in pointed complaints to top management. Director J. Gates Williams of Francis, Brother and Company, a St. Louis securities firm, decried the poor performance of AVCO's stock and the bad morale within the company, placing the responsibility clearly upon leadership problems. "The collapse and shrinkage in the value of the stock of The Aviation Corporation, dominating the industry as it did at its inception," stated Williams, "can be chiefly credited to the fact of mismanagement." Williams analyzed the company and recommended that AVCO reorganize and replace the financial experts running the company with men with operations experience. The corporation was attempting to control its entire empire from New York with managers who had little practical experience. The results were chaotic. Williams reiterated that he and other investors had understood that AVCO was to be strictly a holding company to invest in aviation securities and acquire solid companies in an effort to effect economies of scale through efficient, well-coordinated operations. It was with this belief that he and others had agreed to invest and now were seeing their money wasted because of poor management.[15]

Williams recommended splitting the corporation into four divisions, separating the manufacturing companies from the airlines, with aviation schools and sales also separate. He felt strongly that each division should have an autonomous head, each directly responsible only to the president, rather than the current centralized control under Graham Grosvenor. Each division should be led by someone "thoroughly competent and experienced and charged with the full responsibility and accountability and with sufficient authority to accept that responsibility. The only man capable of such a charge is a man who has had experience in transport operation." An angry Williams pulled no punches: "In view of the time elapsed since its formation, it is inconceivable that so little has been accomplished in the way of coordination and that so few economies obvious to the least experienced have been effected."[16]

High overhead costs were crippling the company, and the need to husband vanishing resources was vitally necessary if AVCO were to survive. "I do know that the New York payroll is terrific, and it might be advisable for you to look into the matter," Williams stated. "As I said at the last meeting, it was absolutely necessary for this company to conserve all its cash. I understand that they are starting to cut down and revise all their budgets in their various subsidiary companies. It is my feeling that the interest on the twenty odd million the company has in cash or securities should carry the complete overhead, not only the losses in the operating unit, but also the overhead of the office in New York."[17]

Williams urged that Harriman seek out the advice of A.P. Barrett of their Southern Air Transport subsidiary, who possessed the knowledge and ability to operate an airline profitably. The necessity for this recommendation under-scored the friction between the eastern and southern operations of AVCO's airlines. The coordination between the two sections was poor, and generally only the southern operations were sufficiently well run to turn a profit.

Harriman, unfortunately, held a narrow view, possessing no practical avia-tion expertise and concerned only with the immediate problems of mollifying stockholders in the short run while ignoring long-term problems and solu-tions. This attitude was no more clearly evident than in his reaction to reason-able suggestions forwarded by George Hann for improvements in AVCO. Hann wrote AVCO president Graham Grosvenor, stressing how important it was for AVCO to expand its research and development planning in order to produce aircraft of sufficient efficiency to operate profitably. It was the only way the company could weather the financial storm that was upon it and remain pre-pared for the future. "I believe that we have been quite correct in cutting down on our passenger operations," stated Hann, "and these should be built up again only as they may prove economically worthwhile. Meanwhile we should de-vote the great majority of our attention to solving the problems of better plane construction." Hann further noted that "a few million dollars spent along proper lines, such as the development of more perfect flying apparatus with better visibility, slower landings, larger payloads, . . . will mean much more to The Aviation Corporation's future than would the same amount of money expended in trying to force air transportation upon a public which must be gradually educated. . . . Times have changed and I believe that our policy should also be changed."[18]

This logical and farsighted approach the myopic Harriman decried as "the ravings of a wild man." He was appalled that Hann would suggest risking the company's money on unproven research and development projects. "He sug-gests spending a few million in development of aviation equipment for the benefit of the industry and all concerned," Harriman remarked, "except the stockholders of the Aviation Corporation." Grosvenor's reply was equally vi-sionary: "I consider this real piffle—and dangerous."[19]

The Aviation Corporation's management was not totally oblivious to the growing crisis. Lehman Brothers hired Frederick G. Coburn of the engineer-ing consulting firm of Sanderson and Porter to analyze the company and make their own recommendations. Coburn agreed with Hann that the time had come to promote research and development, but, more important, it was time AVCO decide on its future policy. "The Aviation Corporation has done a good bit of floundering," stated Coburn, "and I think a number of false starts have been made. It is getting better all the while." Changes were underway in improving accounting and in streamlining the management of Fairchild and the airline holdings. Coburn aptly described AVCO as "a big corporation with a big opportunity, but with corresponding big responsibilities and perils; and I am strongly of the opinion that its management should have policies and programs and some information as to what it owns and what are the earning power prospects thereof."[20]

Coburn wanted the executive committee to decide whether AVCO was to be an investment company, as originally intended by some, or a holding and operating company (especially with regard to air transportation), or a combination of the two.[21] Unfortunately, no decision was forthcoming. Grosvenor had forwarded Hann's letter to Coburn expecting a sympathetic reply concerning aircraft development. Much to his surprise, Coburn supported Hann's approach and wanted to keep funding aircraft development, including Virginius Clark's Superplane project.[22]

The founder of AVCO, Sherman Fairchild, was also frustrated with the lack of progress in aircraft development and was deeply concerned about the fate of the company's airline holdings, quickly becoming the corporation's most vocal critic. To him changes were essential or AVCO would be forced to make some painful choices. He echoed to a large degree the criticism of Williams and suggested that the company be divided into more manageable sections: transportation, investment, and manufacture. Of this, transportation was the most important and the most troublesome. To Fairchild, in turn, the transportation question could be divided into five parts: passenger transportation, air mail, air express and air freight, schools, and airports. And of this, the two most important issues were air mail and passenger transportation.

Air mail, in his view, was the only salvation for the industry and for AVCO's woes. With this government support, Fairchild felt that the airlines could gain practical experience that eventually could be applied to passenger carrying. "I recommend," concluded Fairchild, "that we continue our air mail, that we get the best brains available working on possibilities of reducing the cost, possibilities of better operation through a study of blind flying and through the medium of air mail we establish our airport contacts which will be available if air passenger transportation is solved within the next five years."[23]

Fairchild was one of the few within AVCO to state openly that carrying passengers without subsidy was not possible given the current state of aeronautics. With passenger load factors averaging less than 50 percent, it was not possible to carry passengers for less than eighteen to twenty-five cents per mile. Despite expected increases in efficiencies in the next few years, Fairchild did not see the costs dropping to a point where passenger fares or reliability and safety of service could be competitive with the railroads. "My recommendation, with regard to air passenger lines," he threatened, "is, therefore, to cut them all out." Fairchild concluded that "the only possible hope is government subsidy and I feel that that will be brought about more quickly if we cut out our passenger lines than if we run them."[24]

Without help, the elimination of passenger service was a very real possibility, and one that the postmaster general wished to avoid. Planned changes in AVCO's air transportation following the investigation and recommendations of new AVCO president James Hamilton were expected to cut their losses dramatically but not entirely. The pending decision by the Post Office Department would alone determine AVCO's future course in air transportation. Without a federal subsidy, the company would be forced to shut down its passenger service completely to cut its mounting losses.[25]

The Aviation Corporation deferred this drastic step pending the outcome of a general reorganization and other cost-cutting measures. George Hann emphatically stressed the need for greater decentralization of the corporation, and by January 1930, management began to take his suggestions seriously.

The executive committee decided to follow the suggestions of Williams, Fairchild, and Hann and separate AVCO's air transportation holdings from its other interests, combining the management of these numerous small airlines under an umbrella organization devoted strictly to managing air transportation. The new company would have a small board of directors composed only of Harriman, Lehman, Grosvenor, Hann, Hamilton, Bane, and Loucks. All of AVCO's airlines would be joined together under a single management, although the original companies would remain in existence on paper as they held the air mail contracts, which by law could not be transferred.[26] Under the central headquarters, run by president James Hamilton and assisted by Tom Hardin, the airlines would be formed into three operating divisions: Colonial, based in New York; Universal, with offices in St. Louis; and Southern. Graham Grosvenor suggested that they name the new airline Universal Air Ways.[27] The executive committee, however, decided to choose a new name reflecting the national scope of the airline: American Airways.

The sudden market crash revealed glaring problems in the airline industry, even with the well-financed holding companies such as North American and AVCO. Following the October economic debacle, Postmaster General Brown became increasingly aware of the need for active governmental intervention to save not only the air mail carriers but also the entire air transportation industry. He saw a pressing need for a rational and equitable method of air mail payments designed to promote every aspect of the industry and intended to foster its growth—for both the short-term results of air mail delivery and the long-term encouragement of air transportation as a viable means of passenger travel. For Brown, the former Bull Moose Progressive, the best way to promote this infant industry was through the support of those enterprises best suited financially and organizationally to fulfill his desire to develop a national transportation network operating in the public interest under the control of the government. In so doing, Brown hoped to avoid the chaos of ruthless competition that hampered the railroad industry during the nineteenth century. Large oligopolies, dependent upon the government, would do the people's bidding in a manner exactly as the New Nationalist Walter Brown would expect.

The Aviation Corporation's representative, Hainer Hinshaw, worked actively with the postmaster general, as did other industry representatives, to hammer out a new rate plan. By early January the plan was beginning to take shape, and Hinshaw reported that Brown was leaning heavily toward a space system of payment, which had been rumored earlier. Writing to Colonel Brittin of Northwest Airways (in whose company AVCO held a 22 1/2 percent interest), Hinshaw reported that Brown was actively seeking this method as a way to place mail on the passenger carriers and thereby save those struggling airlines. "Confidentially," Hinshaw stated, "Mr. Brown is striving to work out some sort of basis for buying space in a ship that is a passenger ship in order that it will help the passenger lines and naturally if he does this, it will effect the rates on the regular air mail lines. . . . He stated he was willing to spend from seven to ten million dollars a year for mail on passenger ships in order that passenger transportation may become definitely established." Hinshaw even complimented himself and his fellow lobbyists on their successful efforts. "From this statement you can see that he is being carefully educated," he wrote.[28] Hinshaw was in fact one of Brown's teachers. He revealed that he had spoken with Brown and other department officials on numerous occasions and helped form the postmaster general's plans.

At long last, on January 14, 1930, Walter Brown revealed how much he had indeed learned. Before a gathering of the Cleveland Chamber of Commerce, Brown set forth his proposal for the overhaul of the nation's air transportation system in an address entitled "Commercial Aviation and the Air Mail." Problems began to emerge, Brown stated, when the enthusiasm of aviation advocates was not matched by that of the traveling public. Although millions of dollars were poured into the industry, millions of passengers did not materialize. "Aircraft factories sprang up all over the country and air passengers line inaugurated flying services east and west, north and south," said Brown. "Many of these lines were planned and equipped in accord with the best practice of the flying art; others were less well considered. With a paying load of only 16 to 40 percent of capacity, all closed the year with operating deficits so great that the very life of the passenger transport industry today is in the balance."

Brown blamed the well-intentioned organizers for the problem. "The men who were most ambitious for the industry and who with infinite pains planned the longer passenger routes," he said, "perhaps forgot their own experiences in the air, perhaps forgot that children creep before they walk, that they toddle from chair to chair before they engage in marathon races." The public was simply not ready to fly in sufficient numbers to justify the expense of air travel.

Air mail payments were unbalanced, allowing some lines to profit greatly and others to starve. Because of the strict rules of the Second Amendment to the Air Mail Act of 1925, the government was prevented from addressing the inequities and affording relief to struggling contractors, despite their pioneering efforts on the public's behalf. The severe economic problems in the industry required rectification or all of the money invested by the government and private capital would be lost.

Brown offered a solution. As expected, he recommended that the weight-based method or payment be abandoned in favor of a new space-based system:

> The system of paying by the pound is manifestly unsound. Such a system compels the contractor to gamble on the volume of mail he will carry and creates an inducement for him to swell his volume by unethical practices. He is obliged to make his flight whether the Post Office Department furnishes him one pound or a thousand pounds of mail and he should therefore be paid a just compensation for his readiness to serve, as well on his service performed.
>
> The Post Office Department recommends that the Act of June 3, 1926, as amended May 17, 1928, be amended so as to authorize the Postmaster General to contract for the transportation mail by aircraft between such points as he may designate at fixed rates per mile for definite weight spaces.

Carriers, Brown said, should receive incentive bonuses for hazardous flying—at night, over mountains, or in foggy conditions—and greatly increase mail service to the public by placing mail on passenger aircraft. "At the same time," Brown continued, "it would enable the Post Office Department to give immediate assistance to air passenger carriers on such routes that were deemed essential, by paying for carrying the mails a substantial sum, based upon a definite weight space preempted."

Most controversially, Brown also recommended that he be given authority to extend the existing contracts to a maximum period of ten years from the date of the original award, thus preserving continuity but also excluding new entrant carriers. He also wanted to ensure that only well-financed companies participated, thereby giving preference to the established lines belonging to the holding companies. His New Nationalism perspective regarding monopoly was clear. "With the passenger lines, as with the exclusively mail lines," Brown concluded, "preference if possible in the awarding of contract should be given to pioneers in the air transport industry of good character and financial responsibility."[29]

Second Assistant Postmaster General W. Irving Glover concurred with Brown's remarks, stating that if implemented, the new plan would establish the air mail system and the passenger lines on a solid foundation and would go far in reviving the industry. "Legislation will of course be needed to carry out successfully the plans which the Postmaster General has in mind," stated Glover, "and I am sure that the Congress, which has been ever ready to lend a helping hand to this new industry which has very quickly taken its place alongside some of its older brothers, will not fail in this instance to give its aid to the fullest extent and quickly too." Glover added, "The increase in cost to the Post Office Department will be but a few million dollars over the present estimated Budget figures and, when one thinks what this additional amount of money means to the industry in general, no one with the interest of the industry at heart will refuse to assist and get behind this most progressive and life-giving plan to the Commercial Aviation Industry of the country."[30]

Word of Brown's speech spread rapidly throughout the industry. Colonel Brittin wired Hainer Hinshaw from Minneapolis to ascertain the specifics of the remarks and to determine the expected effect on the airlines. Brittin was particularly interested in the postmaster general's position about placing mail on passenger ships, new entrants, and competitive bidding. Brittin, as with the other air mail contractors, wanted to extend his routes without fear of cut-throat competition and was concerned about the effect of this proposed legislation on the creation of competing routes. Hinshaw calmed Brittin's nerves. The department had no intention of taking seriously any bid to carry mail from any upstart airline that would spring into being as a result of Brown's address. "I pointed out to Brown that a number of mushroom lines will probably spring up," warned Hinshaw, "and he insisted he would deal only with those established pioneers who were still financially and physically able to operate." Most important, Hinshaw wrote, "he will do nothing towards giving lines that may be established this week or next week—but rather he will extend and re-align the present existing lines in the territories which they now serve."[31]

No better statement could be made concerning Brown's Progressive approach to the problems of the industry. Unsound companies would not be given routes, and those airlines that pioneered their service would not face unfair competition. The well-financed lines, held by the responsible holding companies, were clearly in a superior economic position to provide the public with the service it needed and expected. Commenting further on Brown's ideas, Hinshaw stated, "I will reiterate that the present air mail contractors will be enabled to enlarge and extend their lines without competitive bids and will be given preference and protected from competition" (1). In effect, the proposed air mail legislation would enable the postmaster general to act as a regulatory agency acting in the public interest by restricting competition.

Brown did, in fact, wish to protect solid, independent passengers lines as well as the passenger service provided by the holding companies. By this time, most of the little independents had either expired or joined one of the three combines. Some, such as Erle Halliburton's SAFE Way, were adequately financed and managed but were in deep trouble. Stout, Standard, and TAT were all struggling passenger-carrying lines owned by the holding companies. As for putting mail on TAT, Halliburton, Standard, and Stout, Hinshaw stated that Brown "will put mail on these ships but he will not go over 100 or 200 pounds" and hoped to put first-class and other mail on these lines, rather than just air mail. "He intends to keep the actual mail lines the same highly specialized type of transportation of this special mail service," Hinshaw declared. "That is, he does not intend to disturb air mail" (1).

Far from employing the dictatorial methods he was later accused of using, Brown sought the advice of industry in the formation of the actual legislation. "I have talked with Mr. Brown, Mr. Glover, and Mr. Wadsworth several times about this whole thing," stated Hinshaw. "As a matter of fact, Mr. Brown permitted me to read his speech a week before he delivered it and we had two discussions on the matter. I believe their intentions are good and I will state further, for your own confidential information, that this proposal is a balloon in order that he can get some definite reaction from the operators and the public" (2).

Brown was also an astute politician who sought to co-opt his opposition. He intended to call the operators to Washington to help him forge the legislation to their mutual satisfaction. In this way he could bring powerful pressure on virtually every member of Congress whose state or district was served by air mail. By passing strong legislation that would enable the survival of the airlines, Brown would also maintain control over the airlines themselves forcing them to act in the public's interest without the expensive bureaucratic framework of a formal regulatory agency (1).

Hinshaw was willing to follow Brown's plan, provided it was applied equitably. The proposed law would benefit the industry, even though it would give the postmaster general unprecedented power to determine new routes, award extensions, and even forge new consolidations of routes and companies. Hinshaw approved, as long as "where passenger lines compete with mail lines that the mail line should get the preference; that the variables he speaks of shall be added to the maximum price of $1.00 and not come underneath it; that the consolidations and extensions be worked out by negotiation with these companies now operating in that particular field and other phases that we have to face" (1).

The industry's trade journals lauded Brown's new approach. *Aviation* was now convinced that Brown was a friend of aviation with a visionary approach, not a near-sighted penny-pinching bureaucrat. "The suspicion that Postmaster General Brown is inherently unfriendly to aviation, and desirous of finding some secret means of stifling the air mail, cannot survive a careful reading of his recent address before the Cleveland Chamber of Commerce," the journal stated. "He has approached the problem as a business man and with the desire to get it onto a common sense business footing." They were comfortable that now the department could set fair rates and restore airline profitability and some sense of reason to the air mail system to the benefit of the tax-paying public. *Aviation* believed that the Post Office could now "produce a formula that would be fair to all the contractors and that would hold out to the Post Office Department the hope of ultimate financial equilibrium."[32]

Brown soon called a meeting of representatives of the operators to discuss the forthcoming legislation. To the department came Col. Paul Henderson of North American, Philip Johnson from United Aircraft, Harris Hanshue of Western Air Express, Col. Lewis H. Brittin from Northwest Airways, and Hainer Hinshaw, Frederick G. Coburn, Mabel Walker Willebrandt, Graham Grosvenor, and Gen. John O'Ryan of the Aviation Corporation.[33] By early February, the operators and Brown had agreed on the text of the proposed legislation and were anxious to proceed.

All but one. Much to the department's dismay, independent operator Erle Halliburton objected strenuously to the proposal. Earlier, rumors had circulated that his airline, SAFE Way, had been acquired by the Pennsylvania Railroad in an effort to prevent him from extending his line to Los Angeles in competition with TAT. "Halliburton is very clever and means to do things in a big way," remarked Brittin. "All of this adds up to the fact that Halliburton was a very desirable man to get rid of from the point of view of these operators." Although the rumors later proved false, the idea reflected the general antipathy felt by the air mail contractors toward the obstreperous Halliburton. Stated Brittin, "Halliburton has been a thorn in the side of some of the larger operators in the south west for a long time. He has started certain things in Washington that were very embarrassing to some of the larger groups. If his schemes had gone through it would have upset a load of apple carts."[34] Between his call for ICC regulation and his joint offer for the southern transcontinental route with William Gibbs McAdoo and their Southern Sky Lines, Halliburton had few friends in the industry. Now, he was attacking the Post Office as well, with the expressed intention of receiving a mail contract, regardless of the consequences.

Halliburton wrote to his partner McAdoo, expressing his view of the situation. He was adamant that he was expanding westward and that all depended on a contract. "The air mail situation seems to be in a muddle that will require some time to straighten out," stated Halliburton. "I have given one year's hard work to the industry and have personally invested approximately $1,750,000, and am confident that in the end this investment will be protected by an air mail contract."[35]

Halliburton expressed his objections in a telegram that was delivered to Irving Glover. He was extremely wary of the wide discretionary powers it gave the postmaster general, which he felt could be used against independents such as himself: "[The] Watres Bill gives to the Postmaster General powers that will make it possible for him to discriminate to the end that the development of commercial aviation might be retarded for a period of ten years. Such a measure might be all right if we knew Postmaster General Brown would hold office during [the] entire period and his administration was not influenced by special interests but if this bill is enacted into law it is my opinion that it will retard the development of commercial aviation rather than cure a situation that is pressing for satisfaction."[36]

Glover was both surprised and outraged by Halliburton's attack. When last in Washington, Halliburton had shown support for the bill but had now inexplicably changed, though this quixotic behavior was in keeping with his volatile character. The bill was specifically designed to aid independent passenger lines such as Halliburton's as well as foster aviation in general. An angry Glover fired back a telegram:

> Mr. Philip has just showed me your telegram regarding new Air Mail legislation and to say contents your telegram astonish me is putting it lightly. The Department can truthfully say that yours is the only operating line which has made any objection to proposed legislation. On the other hand we are in receipt of favorable comment from practically every independent operator. You will remember last time you were in my office you said you were heartily in favor of it and would do everything to support proposed legislation. Natural to suppose that your operation would benefit under this legislation. . . . If legislation of this character does not pass this session of Congress Commercial Aviation will be the sufferer.[37]

Halliburton's outburst was, in essence, an attempt to force the department to buy his silence in return for a contract. The department noted this problem for later action. Regardless of Halliburton's objections, work progressed steadily.

Brown had the bill, H.R. 9500, introduced into the House by Rep. Laurence H. Watres of Pennsylvania, a member of the House Committee on the Post Office and Post Roads. Pointedly, Brown did not choose to have his political rival Clyde Kelly introduce the measure. This was to prove a strategic and tactical error by the otherwise politically astute postmaster general and would have severe repercussions, as Kelly, for reasons of his past advocacy, felt he was the guiding force behind the air mail in Congress. Brown's study of the air mail situation had revealed numerous flaws. He wanted a clean slate in order to straighten out the department and the industry. By visibly snubbing Kelly, with whom Brown had personal differences and blamed in part for the chaos, he turned the Progressive Republican from Pennsylvania into a powerful enemy.

Hearings were scheduled for Wednesday, February 19. Immediately beforehand, Clifford Ball sought to preserve his endangered airline by visiting the Post Office to ask for clarification of the pending legislation and seek out his brother-in-law, Clyde Kelly, for help. At the department, Ball met with Glover and Wadsworth, who reassured him that his contract would be continued but insisted that the law would change.

After his meeting, Ball proceeded quickly to Capitol Hill, where he met with Kelly and engaged in a long conversation concerning the airlines and the proposed legislation. Kelly was adamantly opposed to Brown's desire to make the postmaster general so powerful and was particularly concerned about the question of Brown's desire essentially to suspend competitive bidding. Kelly had also proposed alternative legislation addressing his concerns. "It was his opinion," remarked Ball, "that too much power will be given to the Postmaster General in the bill proposed by himself." Furthermore, "Under Mr. Brown, who is eager for the expansion and extension of air mail, this might work out very good, but we have the danger of someone succeeding Mr. Brown that might not be of the same political party and a very chaotic condition would also be probable." Kelly was determined that the new bill would preserve his poundage payment system, which he thought encouraged healthful competition and kept Ball's coffers full.

Ball was reassured that his airline was safe regardless of future events. "Mr. Kelly assured me," he stated, "that the contract will be continued, as under his original bill it clearly states that certificates will be given, and in the case the Postmaster General should refuse we have good reason to ask him to show cause." The forthcoming hearing would determine the final structure of the bill, and Clifford Ball had every intention of attending to protect his interests and those of the other contractors.[38]

Brown received his formal invitation from committee chairman Rep. Archie D. Sanders (R-N.Y.) to appear as the first witness. In his opening remarks, the postmaster general recalled the history of the air mail service and reminded the committee that the purpose of all air mail legislation during the air mail's brief history was the encouragement of aviation and "to the end that the habit and practice of the people of the United States might be developed to use air transport in their ordinary affairs of life, in traveling and in sending their merchandise and communications."[39] His new law would clean up the present system, eliminate waste and "unethical practices" by removing the incentive for contractors to cheat, and install a space method of payment that would ensure and equitably distribute payments. This in turn would promote the development of not only the air mail but also passenger travel by air, thereby protecting and fostering the new air transportation industry.

Brown quickly focused his attention on the need to support the oligopolies. In typically Progressive Republican fashion, he underscored the necessity for legal changes that would enable the Post Office Department to reap the benefits of the recent consolidations that occurred in the industry. As the mergers absorbed the numerous little lines, the new holding companies held promise of great economies of scale in their operations. Up to this time, the Post Office could not benefit from these economic changes as the contracts were already set in place and could not be modified. A new system whereby four-year contracts would be exchanged for ten-year certificates would allow stability in the industry and permit the department to adjust the payment rates downward to reflect increased efficiencies from the airline holding companies. Other proposed incentives would encourage the development of more modern, efficient aircraft and equipment and a realignment of the route system in a coherent and rational manner while protecting the rights of the pioneer companies. His proposal would greatly strengthen the position of the postmaster general, placing almost total control of the airline industry in his hands. In return, he would protect and promote the industry while encouraging its rational growth.

Brown clearly stated his support for the holding companies that in his view operated in the public interest by providing a national service at the lowest reasonable cost by responsible operators. When he assumed office in 1929, he quickly learned that the route system was hardly that: lines were haphazardly drawn in an illogical web of routes across much of the country. Short routes were particularly uneconomic and failed to provide a faster service when compared with surface transportation. To Brown it was clear that the speed advantage of air mail could only be realized over longer distances and over certain, natural routes. "When we examined the certificate law with a view to making the extensions of the contracts for the 10-year period, we discovered that the air mail map of the United States had grown a little at a time and, like any map made in this fashion, was entirely illogical," Brown said. "There were short lines and there were long lines. There were some lines that had no real excuse for existence and others that could be very greatly improved by slight additions. If we put into effect the certificate feature of the law, it would be necessary to fasten that illogical air map on the United States for a further period of six years, or for a total of 10 years from the time that the first contract was issued. That we dislike to do" (5). Changes were necessary in order to make the route system more efficient while taking advantage of the recent airline consolidations sweeping the industry:

> It was obvious that the economic law was coming into play and that some of the short lines, and longer lines too, were passing under a single ownership. Holding companies were being formed and taking over the smaller lines. The result was, of course, that economies in operation of those lines were being effected, due to the cutting down of overhead and supervision, but the government could get none of the benefits of consolidation, because from our viewpoint, the viewpoint of the law, each of the original contracts was an entity and had to be dealt with by itself.
>
> So it was desirable that the air mail map, if possible, be revamped and made a logical map, like the railway map of the United States. That has been made by economic law, largely, through in recent years some control by the Interstate Commerce Commission. . . . However, up to this point economic law has put together railway systems, has combined little lines that were 50 or 100 miles long, until we have the great railroad systems as the result of natural law. The same thing has started with the airways. But under the present, inflexible air mail law, the department is able to take no advantage of the consolidations that economic laws are forcing. (5)

Brown felt obligated to protect the vested interests of capital and the so-called pioneer rights of the original contractors who had invested heavily, and at great cost, in the establishment of their route infrastructure and equipment. "It will be necessary to change the law," he said, "if any relief is to be given to these pioneers in the business who have been losing their money" (10). It was unfair that the contractors who had risked their capital on behalf of the government and the people also risk losing their contract to a lower bidder after four years of hard work, just when their efforts were about to pay off. Brown told the committee that he fervently believed that the only way to protect the rights of these courageous companies was to permit the postmaster general to make route extensions and let new contracts without resorting to potentially ruinous competitive bidding:

> Now, the proviso is the matter that you will want to consider the most carefully. This language permits the Postmaster General to make a contract when, in his opinion, public interest so requires, without advertising or considering bids, but by negotiation. That involves a departure from a time-honored policy of our country, and should have very careful consideration. . . .
> We recommend this proviso, not because I want any such responsibility—

personally I should be glad to have anybody else have it—but because we can think of no other way in which, in the present condition of the aviation industry and the art of flying, we can save to the United States the experience of the men who have done the flying for the last ten years, and in no other way to protect what we believe to be an equity, if not a right of the pioneers who are in this business. If we throw these matters all open to competitive bidding, you will find promoters coming in and wanting to bid off the contract, having no knowledge of costs. . . . They will come in and bid a price that will be lower than the experienced man who has had his fingers burned. . . . As I say, I can think of no other way to protect the rights of the public in the experience that has been gained at the expense of many, many lives; I can think of no other way to do it than by placing in the discretion of some official of the Government the power of negotiating these contracts directly, within certain maximum limits. If you gentlemen can think of any other way of doing it, we shall be very glad to have you do it. (24)

Brown was not averse to competitive bidding but felt that under these special circumstances, such a drastic measure was necessary. "We would use the proviso only where we were very clear that the public interest required it," he said. "I personally believe in competitive bidding as a fundamental principle." Representative Kelly agreed that the rights of the pioneers deserved protection, but without sacrificing an open competition. "I realize that you ought to have some power to go ahead for the protection of those who have risked their money and property and all that," said Kelly. "I am very much in favor of that, and I would like to see it on a certificate basis in some way or other, where you could protect them, instead of favoring new companies without any bids and making contracts which would bind the Government."

Brown stood firm in his support for this extraordinary measure, despite the pressure it placed on his shoulders because he felt it was vital for the very survival of the industry. "I am inclined to think, Mr. Kelly," he said, "that if you pass this bill, you will add about six years to my age by so doing. But somebody has got to try to solve this problem or we are going to have a collapse of the passenger carrying industry in this country" (25). In Brown's defense, Mabel Walker Willebrandt, speaking for AVCO, reminded the committee that precedent already existed within postal law for the awarding of contracts without competitive bidding. She reminded them that Section 571 of Title 39 of the United States Code permitted this, as it stated, "The Postmaster General may enter into contracts for carrying the mail with railway companies without advertising for bids thereof" (38).

Supporting the passenger-carrying business was one of Brown's primary objectives. He underscored the department's fundamental belief that the air mail was created to encourage aviation throughout the country, to encourage people to fly, and to make the public aware of the potential of aviation while forming a strategic reserve of trained pilots and mechanics in case of war. Brown reiterated that the present law did little to encourage aviation beyond that of the air mail and in so doing risked the collapse of this nascent industry at the moment when it was on the brink of success. "There is not anything in the present law," he said, "that encourages passenger flying in any way." Americans had yet to acquire the habit of flying, and as a result the nation had not "obtained the supremacy in the air that is necessary for national security." Through experience it was found that the aircraft developed to carry mail were not suitable for carrying passengers and so passenger traffic growth was hampered. Brown realized this inherent problem and was seeking to address it through his legislation, thereby protecting those airlines that were adequately financed but losing money carrying passengers:

> So the problem was to find some method of promoting passenger lines. Well, during the last calendar year passenger lines sprang up all over the country, some operated by people who had air mail contracts and many by those who had not. The impression seemed to get out that it was an industry that was coming very fast, and that there were opportunities for great profit in it. I think perhaps the speculative era that came to close in the Wall Street collapse had something to do with it. The public was very ready to subscribe to flotations of securities for aircraft factories and for air lines, and there was plenty of money, and for that reason it was possible for these lines to start up. Without exception they lost money. There was not a single passenger line in operation in 1929 that did not lose money. (10)

The discussions with the operators in late 1929 were conducted in part to address the difficulties of the passenger lines and to promote the development of larger, more efficient aircraft until such time as the passenger lines could become self-sufficient. "When we got to studying this problem in the autumn of last year, the problem of passenger operators," said Brown, "they were discouraged and about ready to give up. That perhaps stimulated us to try to formulate a plan which would give them some hope to carry on until the public should be educated to travel by air." The recent fare cuts and resultant increase in passenger loads showed that the public was indeed willing to fly, provided the price was within reason. Unfortunately, the current state of the aeronautical art was so inefficient that it was impossible to charge a competitive fare when the average cost per flying mile of an airline was more than one dollar. Stated the postmaster general, "The cost, apparently, can be reduced only by increasing the capacity of the planes." Of critical importance to the future technological development of American aviation, Brown reasoned that wisely placed incentives would encourage the development of newer, more profitable aircraft:

At a time when people were reluctant to travel at all and pay for this service, there was very little inducement for inventive genius to design, or for capital to produce the larger planes, which would naturally cut down transportation costs. In this transition period in the development of the art, we think it is necessary to give some aid to the passenger-carrying lines, particularly if by giving that aid we greatly increase the air mail facilities of the country. That is the principle motive, perhaps, back of the suggestion in this bill, which is to promote directly the major purpose of all the legislation of our country with respect to air transportation, to go right to the heart of the matter, to encourage the transportation of people by air, to get the people of the United States to fly themselves, so that we will have a great flying personnel and a great flying industry with efficient planes and efficient equipment. (11)

In answering Kelly's direct challenge to his position, Brown asserted that "in the evolution of this problem the suggestion is now made that we put some mail on the passenger ships on regular lines, enabling them to carry on until the flying public increases sufficiently to pay the costs of air transport and until those costs can be reduced by the development of larger planes and other improvements that are in contemplation" (12).

Brown did not intend to waste taxpayer's money on frivolous lines. It was his intention that the passenger carriers receiving aid would do so only along those routes most heavily traveled. "The purpose of this bill," he continued, "would be to enable the passenger-transport people to build up a passenger service on routes that appear to be essential, on routes where there is natural traffic back and forth: . . . I would not think of establishing a line where there never had been an actual route and where people are probably are never going to travel but we all know that there are routes in our country that have been traversed ever since the Indians used to traverse them, because they are natural routes for transportation" (14).

Instead of spending money to create lines all over the country, whether needed or not, Brown had a recommendation: "We think the right way to do it is to pick out some essential transportation routes that the public are using now and have been ever since we had a country, and to give all the Government encouragement we can to those lines. We want to see if we can not make these main lines self-sustaining and develop a habit of air travel which will then spread to all the other lines" (22). The department was already planning those routes, primarily the two transcontinental lines discussed and agreed upon during the meetings of the Interdepartmental Committee on Airways.

Those existing lines that followed natural transportation routes and that could be improved with judicious planning Brown hoped to support through the method of route extensions, without the burden of advertising the extension as a new route through competitive bidding. The proposed bill would allow the postmaster general to effect such changes at his discretion. "Section 6 authorizes extensions and consolidations when the public interest will be promoted thereby," stated Brown. "The purpose of that is to enable us to re-vamp the air mail plan of this country and make it a logical one, so far as we have the wisdom to do so" (27).

As expected, Brown hoped to change the payment scheme from the weight to a space system that would distribute the air mail largess equitably among the carriers. Kelly sharply questioned the postmaster general on this point, expressing his opinion that the contractors knew the risks when they bid and that although the present rates were not entirely fair, part of the airlines' re-sponsibility was to generate additional mail through promotion campaigns. That they failed to receive sufficient poundage was their problem, not the government's. To this argument Brown replied forcefully, "There is no fair-ness, there is no sound business in asking a mail contractor to gamble on the amount of mail he is going to get, but that is what he is required to do now. He must go on schedule. When 8:30 at night comes at Chicago, the contractor must start whether he has got 1 pound or 1,500 pounds, and to ask him to gamble on it, in my judgment, is immoral. I think it is unsound from every viewpoint" (14).

Although the exact rate of payment was yet to be determined by the de-partment, Brown felt that a base rate of ten cents per mile was probably ap-propriate but that variables should be applied depending on the size of aircraft and the type of equipment. In this way the department could pay the airlines enough to cover the difference between their costs and revenue but not ensure their profitability at government expense. Based on existing information pro-vided by the airlines and based on the new uniform system of accounting, the Post Office would be able to ascertain the correct amount to pay for the space available on the aircraft.

In responding to Chairman Sanders, Brown wanted to keep an open mind concerning the actual process of rate determination, as numerous technical and operational factors would influence the decision. "We do not know what the changes will be in the art," replied Brown, "and we think that the rate mat-ter should be made as flexible as possible" (23). The department was willing to provide enough money to allow the carriers to break even—any profit would be the responsibility of the airline by generating additional revenue through passenger or express service. "What we want to do," said Brown, "is to give to the passenger lines on essential routes enough money to keep them from go-ing out of business and making us lose all the money that we have put into the aviation business" (21). Thus, in the view of the postmaster general, the mail payments were not a direct subsidy in the strictest sense and would be steadily reduced as the airlines improved their efficiency until such time they required no assistance. The government would not buy more space than it required along each route. This method was precisely how the railroads were paid to carry mail (20).

Because the Post Office had a space system of payment for the rails, they also had a greater flexibility in directing the mail. The department could choose whatever line it thought best to carry the surface mail by train without interference. Although the rates were set by the Interstate Commerce Commission, "determining which roads shall carry the mail is a matter that rests solely within the discretion of the Post Office Department, because there is not any other practical way to work it out," stated Brown. "Now there is precedent all through the mail service for permitting us to choose the carrier, the compensation to be within certain limits" (26).

Brown had no illusions about the future of air transportation as an industry and as a public utility. Although he wished to control its development during its formative period, he understood completely that once aviation was able to stand on its own, it would naturally be subject to the normal forces of federal regulation based on the experience of the railroads. In fact, he expected it. "I am quite sure that some day or other the rates will be fixed by the Interstate Commerce Commission, in the natural evolution of things, and that this is merely one step in the development of the air mail service," he told the committee. "I think, in view of the present condition of the art, that we should carefully consider the unwisdom of junking the valuable experience, the invaluable experience, that had some to the pioneers in the art" (26).

For this new and expanded air mail system Brown requested an additional $3 million on top of the previous year's $15 million appropriation. "The air mail routes that have been recommended by the Interdepartmental Committee, the Post Office Department, and the Department of Commerce aggregating 224,953 miles a month," stated Brown, "would call for an additional cost under the plan of the bill of $230,733. The passenger routes that we have under consideration now, in addition to those which would form a part of the day service of the regular air mail operators, would call for $66,159 additional [per month]" (28–29). Concluded Brown, "We believe that the entire job can be done, that the industry can get its essential support from the Government at this time, and that the air mail service be greatly expanded for the public for a maximum of $18 million a year" (29).

Subsequent testimony from the department and from members of industry supported Walter Brown's plan to change the air mail system and directly assist passenger lines. Second Assistant Postmaster General W. Irving Glover, Mabel Willebrandt, and Col. Thomas Bane, vice president of AVCO, spoke in support of Brown's bill. Philip Johnson of United Aircraft and William

MacCracken, representing Western Air Express, underscored the need for immediate action to save the industry and promote passenger transportation.

Col. Paul Henderson, privately one of Brown's antagonists, publicly supported the postmaster general and his effort to save the airlines. Henderson approved of the plan to encourage mail lines to carry passengers and thought the idea to suspend competitive bidding wise under the circumstances. Most surprisingly, he openly stated his trust in the actions of Brown, affirming that "this bill places the responsibility for air mail and passenger lines of the United States, right on the desk of the Postmaster General. I have been acquainted with four Postmasters General, and I do not know one whom I would not trust with the job of making a good deal with my company." He openly supported the department and its air-mindedness. Asked if he had any question about the ultimate fairness of the postmaster general in dealing with contractors, Henderson replied, "No, sir. I think that the worst that could happen to those of us in the business would be to have some postal administration unsympathetic to air transport generally. The interest of the public in it is such that no matter what the personal feeling of any Postmaster General might be, the public interest in air transport would force the Postmaster General to do what this law gives him authority to do" (47).

James Edgerton was present during the day-long hearing and reported his observations back to his partner, William Gibbs McAdoo. In his opinion, the deliberations went well and the postmaster general presented his case forcefully. Some question remained in the minds of several of the congressmen regarding the request to abolish competitive bidding, but Edgerton felt that this would be easily overcome. Edgerton was more concerned with the question of new entrant carriers but was reassured by Glover that the department would not recognize the validity of any operation created simply to take advantage of the new law. According to Edgerton, Glover said that "where a new company announced or seemed to start operations between now and the time the bill is approved it would be considered by the Post Office Department as an obvious subterfuge which the Department would disregard." Edgerton recommended that McAdoo get Southern Sky-Lines flying as Glover was receptive to those companies that were already organized. "He did intimate, however," stated Edgerton, "that the Department would take a keen interest in the organization of the would-be contractor, his financial status, personnel employed, and other pertinent points. In other words, the thing the Department desires to avoid is the concern organized simply to secure a contract, which might have the objective of selling outright, or who would not show proper financial responsibility."[40]

Other contractors immediately began a letter-writing campaign to influ-

ence their respective representatives, particularly Pittsburgh Aviation Industries Corporation, which wanted a mail contract for a line to Washington, as
recommended by Brown. Despite the intensive campaigning, Clyde Kelly and
several holdouts refused to support what was now known as the McNary-Watres
Act, or, more simply, the Watres Act. As Laurence Watres introduced the bill in
the House, Senate Majority leader Charles McNary of Oregon introduced it in
the Senate. There it met no significant opposition. The House of Representatives was another matter, as the bill could not make it out of committee.

Kelly was obstinately fighting for the retention of competitive bidding with
an unexpected determination. Richard Robbins of PAIC wrote Postmaster
General Brown to relate to him his recent meeting with Kelly. "We are hopeful
that we made some progress in convincing him of the importance of this legislation at this time," Robbins remarked.[41] Nevertheless, he reported that "things
[are] going badly."[42] William "Doc" Bishop of Western Air Express was more
sanguine. "The President is confident the bill will get through okay," he wrote,
"and since I have been here I think, with the exception of two members of the
House, the attitude of those opposed to the several features of the bill has
changed for the better."[43]

Brown held a meeting with the full Steering Committee of the House Post
Office Committee on March 15 in hope of ironing out the differences concerning the bill. Rather unexpectedly, Kelly led off with a rancorous speech
condemning the unlimited power it seemed to give the postmaster general
over contracts and expenditures. Bishop was surprised at the attack, noting
that William MacCracken, Western's legal representative, had just concluded a
conversation with Kelly in which the congressman had toned down his objections. Instead, Bishop stated, "Kelly made a violent speech against the bill after
he had told Bill he thought it would be okay with a few changes. After making
his speech, he left the hearing and aroused the ire of every member of Congress in attendance by the disrespectful attitude he displayed. He seems to have
lost practically all of his standing."[44]

The rest of the Steering Committee supported the bill. Rep. Frederick P.
Lehlbach felt strongly that the government should aid the aviation industry to
the same degree that it supported the merchant marine and concluded that
competitive bidding was not workable under the special conditions of the airline industry and Brown should be given the right to negotiate directly.[45] "One
of the interesting features of the meeting," noted Bishop, "was two speeches by
two members of the steering committee in favor of the bill—both calling attention to the fact that if the government decided to help an industry that it
should do so to the best of their ability and that any attempt to curtail the
powers of the executive officer working with the industry would only hurt the
industry. Both urged passage of the bill with the provision to allow the post-

master general to negotiate contracts without throwing the routes open to competitive bids."[46]

Majority leader John Q. Tilson also lent his support and reassured Brown that he would report the bill favorably to the House and that any further difficulties could be worked out between the committee and the postmaster general. Brown was heartened. According to Glover, "Speaker Longworth brought the Postmaster General down in his car and said that he did not think there was any doubt but that it would be passed; said that some of the members thought that there was too wide a latitude given the Postmaster General but felt that this could be overcome. In any event, the Postmaster General was very much encouraged over the hearing."[47]

Brown was cautiously optimistic, for although it appeared he was near victory, time was running out not only for the industry in general but, more specifically, because several of the contracts were due to expire within the next two months. Recalled Glover, "The Postmaster General left with the Committee the parting word that—'bear in mind that some of these contracts are expiring on May 5, 1930, and, if no legislation is available, the situation will be serious.'"[48] The outspoken Bishop summarized the situation aptly to Jim Wooley after his meeting with President Hoover:

> There is this much about it, Jim. Neither the President, Brown, or the Republican Party can stand the public consequence of being responsible for the bankruptcy of commercial aviation. The seriousness of the national defense angle . . . ; not even to mention the loss of service to the nation as a public carrier of fast mail and rapid transit; are two factors we can depend upon to force the government to continue their support.
>
> As you know, all of the operators are in an extremely pessimistic frame of mind. Should they tell the truth publicly, were we to threaten operation cancellations on our systems, using the powerful publicity avenues available; I am confident the public would be or could be aroused to such a favorable fighting frame of mind Congress and the Administration would be convinced public acceptance of aviation is as commonplace and important as it had made radio and the railroads.
>
> This may sound like a wild dream, Jim, but damn it all Jim, let's not forget the good will we have developed through the banks, brokerage houses, manufacturers and others. If these fellows really knew that air mail operations over the nation may cease after May 17, then this bunch of baboons here would think Washington had been hit with a cyclone of condemning mail.[49]

Recalling his trip back from his visit with the president at Rapidan with Hoover's aide Lawrence Richey, Bishop stated that although he and the others had the utmost confidence in the postmaster general and his new air mail plan, "I let him know that all operators are keenly worried, that the saturation point had been reached and that unless the bill becomes a reality and is honestly and fairly applied, the commercial aviation structure will fall." Bishop was comforted by the knowledge that Brown had the full support of the president and that Hoover would back neither any plan in opposition nor any plan to place the industry under ICC control. It was rumored that Senator Bratton wanted to reintroduce his bill and Bishop and the other operators, with the exception of Colonel Henderson and Erle Halliburton, were strongly opposed. Ritchie, reported Bishop, reiterated that "the President would not let the industry fail and while he didn't say so in so many words, he made me feel sure the President would veto any bill placing us under the control of any agency other than the Department of Commerce."[50]

Despite the best efforts of Brown, the department, industry, and most of the committee, Kelly still refused to compromise. He had earlier introduced his own revised bill H.R. 9556, which would allow route extensions or consolidations provided that the Post Office not pay the carrier more than the rate previously determined by contract.[51] This small amendment was referred to the committee, where it was allowed to expire without action. Undaunted, Kelly continued his attack against the Watres bill.

Despite Speaker Longworth's assurances to Brown that the Watres bill was proceeding smoothly, the legislation was in trouble.[52] The longer some members thought about it, the less comfortable they were with extending virtual dictatorial power to the postmaster general over the entire air transportation industry. Both Colonel Henderson and William MacCracken were now voicing doubts that the bill as written would pass. Henderson appeared particularly pessimistic as his personal fortune was rapidly being devoured by TAT's huge losses. Edgerton feared that concentrating power in the hands of Brown would give him "a powerful club" that would favor the large oligopolies at the expense of the small independents. In Section Five of the bill the department would only deal with responsible contractors with two years' actual operating experience, thereby by definition excluding new entrants. Edgerton feared the worst. "The effect of this two year proviso," he noted, "would be to concentrate all air mail operations and in fact all air transport operations, in the hands of one or two very powerful holding corporations."[53] Edgerton had correctly judged the postmaster's intentions, though not his motives.

Brown did wish to concentrate the industry, but he did not wish to destroy healthy competition. He wanted to weed out the unfit and reward those companies that possessed sound financial and organizational backing. Despite McAdoo's best intentions, Southern Sky-Lines existed only on paper, and the department was not about to risk tax dollars on unproven enterprises, no matter how well intentioned they appeared to be.

Halliburton also feared the growing power of the postmaster general but was attempting to cut his own deal through direct pressure on the Post Office Department. Halliburton and Brice Clagett, McAdoo's law partner and son-in-law, were wary of the potential for monopolistic control of the industry, but Clagett could not shake the feeling that Halliburton was working behind his back.[54]

While McAdoo and company were hoping to head off action, the bill was faltering on its own. Chairman Sanders withdrew his support, forcing Brown to call a special conference on Friday, March 17. During this meeting with congressional leaders, it was decided to let the bill be reported and brought to the House floor for debate, where the supporters believed the measure would pass.[55]

In response to a request from Second Assistant Glover for help, William MacCracken lobbied the four dissident committee members, Republicans Clyde Kelly and David Hogg of Indiana and Democrats James Mead of New York and John H. Morehead of Nebraska. Although Kelly and Mead were unavailable, MacCracken thought he had made some headway with the others. "Saw Hogue [sic] and while he said he did not feel enthusiastic enough about the bill to speak for it," MacCracken wrote Richard Robbins, "he was going to vote for it, and if the Postmaster General had been willing to consider some amendments on the subject of competitive bidding, he would have been glad to speak for the Bill."[56] Writing to Harris Hanshue, MacCracken explained that even though Hogg disagreed with Brown, he did not wish to break party ranks.[57] Hogg was still concerned about the legality of the competitive bidding exemption, and although he agreed to vote for the bill, he also sought the legal opinion of the comptroller general, John McCarl. By the end of the month, McCarl had reviewed Hogg's request and rendered an unofficial opinion against the measure along similar lines to those of Kelly.[58]

MacCracken used his old political connections to contact the former Populist Democrat and Nebraska governor Morehead through Ruth Bryan Owen, the representative from the Miami district of the state and daughter of William Jennings Bryan. "I saw her and had a talk with her," stated MacCracken, "and she promised to see Morehead. She now advises that while he had signed the minority report before she reached him, he has promised to vote for the Bill, and stated that he did not think the minority report would carry much weight or have much effect."[59]

The report of the Committee on the Post Office and Post Roads was released on March 24, when the Watres bill was reported out of committee and sent to the floor of the House. They agreed with the arguments made by Postmaster General Brown and recommended its passage, stating, "Finally, it should be frankly stated that while aviation has unquestionably demonstrated its economic importance, it is not as yet on a self-supporting basis in the United States or any other country. The air mail at the present stage of development is necessarily the backbone of commercial aviation. The American people have shown enterprise, courage, and faith in their support of aviation. If private capital is to continue our national progress in this field, it must have some reasonable hope of at least a fair return on capital actually invested.... To fail to continue support at this critical time would possibly result in the loss of all the progress made."[60]

Representatives Kelly and Morehead filed their minority report condemning the legislation for its haste and for giving the postmaster general too much power. They were particularly concerned about Section 4, which gave Brown the authority to award contracts through negotiation alone. "This provision making the Postmaster General a law unto himself," the report noted, "eliminates competition, and is nothing more than a subsidy in the interest of the aircraft industry. While we favor, and have in the past voted for liberal appropriations and liberal legislation in the interest of the development of aeronautics, we believe this legislation is a step in the wrong direction and some limitations and safeguards should be written into the bill before it becomes law."[61]

Clyde Kelly remained adamant in his objections. "The Postmaster General's air mail bill is a most unprecedented grant of power to one man," stated Kelly to fellow representative Judge Robert Moore of Virginia. "The Postmaster General is anxious to assume this responsibility, but I am of the opinion that it will lead him into great difficulty in the future. Something should be done to help the air passenger lines, but I would like to see it hedged around with proper restrictions."[62]

By early April, it was clear that some form of the bill would pass, though perhaps with some compromising amendments. James Edgerton recommended to an increasingly skeptical William Gibbs McAdoo that they focus all their efforts on the pending legislation to secure their fair share. Edgerton thought that the current political situation might work in their behalf, as the Republicans were sure to lose much support in the upcoming fall congressional elections.[63] McAdoo remained in a pessimistic mood and on the brink of withdrawing entirely, correctly believing that the bill would favor the large oligopolies. Writing to Brice Clagett, he lamented, "Frankly, I am loath to have anything to do with it."[64]

With Brown and Glover working behind the scenes to twist arms to garner enough support, the industry's representatives were for a time left wondering about the fate of H.R. 9500. In a letter to James Wooley, William Bishop openly wondered about the effectiveness of the politically astute Brown in saving this bill. "Having watched the Hoover political machine rise and fall, with much of the credit given to Brown and knowing what I do about Glover, Henderson, Hainer, and Mabel," pondered Bishop, "I've been doing a lot of deep thinking—just trying to figure what there is to justify the confidence all of us seem to place in the political judgment of these men."[65] Bishop did not expect any action on the House floor until mid-April because primary elections called most of the members home until then.

In the meantime, the industry lobbyists were working hard to forge a compromise acceptable to both Brown and Kelly. It was difficult. Richard Robbins of PAIC met with Kelly to discuss the air mail bill and left with the hope of a breakthrough. Robbins was under the impression that Kelly was more concerned about what he called the "indefiniteness" of the bill and wanted the payment rates to be more specific. On the most tendentious issue, that of competitive bidding, Robbins believed Kelly could compromise. Robbins and William MacCracken had proposed a compromise based on the wording of the Air Corps Act of 1926, which allowed the issuance of negotiated contracts under certain specific circumstances and Kelly's own Foreign Air Mail Act of 1928, which in effect allowed the government to negotiate with one national flag carrier if it were deemed in the public interest, when faced with possible ruinous foreign competition. According to Robbins, if such changes were made, Kelly would agree to support H.R. 9500.[66]

Brown still wanted total control, which the compromise would not give him. Robbins attempted to convey the proposition to Brown but was rebuffed by an angry Glover. William Bishop observed this attitude with concern. "Brown has expressed deep hatred for Kelly and will not, under any condition, try to meet his demands, not even halfway," he remarked. Rumors were rampant that Kelly was willing to cut a deal to save his brother-in-law Clifford Ball, "but there is no truth to it." Bishop understood that these decisions were no longer rational but emotional. "It's a case of hurt pride, more than anything else," he concluded. "But I would tell you I think it's just as much a case of a political blunder on Brown's part as anything else."[67] James Edgerton agreed with this analysis. "Opposition has developed on this Bill which seriously threatens its passage," he wrote. "In the first place Brown, the so-called political expert of the Administration, has shown very poor judgment in handling this Bill through trading Watres for Kelly, the latter rather considering himself as the real father of air mail legislation. As a result Kelly has declared war on the Bill, and is a powerful enemy. In addition, as I anticipated, the Comptroller General has just answered an inquiry from a member of congress, which says that he considers it absolutely unnecessary and contrary to public policy to eliminate competitive bidding. The Bill will at least have a stormy passage, and may fail altogether."[68]

Bishop, Edgerton, and the rest of the industry were concerned about their fate should the Watres bill fail. Five routes were to expire on May 5, and pressure was on the department to find a solution through either legislation or a less suitable alternative.[69] Edgerton believed the postmaster general would be in an embarrassing position if the bill failed and the contracts lapsed. He thought that, if possible, Brown would use the opportunity to his advantage. "If the Bill fails of passage he will undoubtedly allow the short routes to die for the purpose of consolidating them in longer routes," he stated. "I have particularly in mind the route from Cleveland to Pittsburgh, which they desire to extend to Washington, and the Chicago–St. Louis, which should go through to New Orleans."[70]

It appeared that regardless of events, Clifford Ball's expensive line would soon disappear, but not without due process. In fact, as of April 26, Brown extended Ball's contract for six months to cover the possibility that H.R. 9500 would not pass in time.[71] Richard Robbins was most interested in an explanation for this action, as his PAIC was hoping to acquire the expected route from Pittsburgh to Washington, D.C., and Ball's reluctance to cooperate with them was causing great consternation. Brown was not showing favoritism but only following the letter of the present law until he could consolidate this costly line. William MacCracken checked with the department and was informed that this was indeed the case. "Glover tells me that they have already granted Cliff an extension of six months," MacCracken wrote Robbins. "This was done, I presume in order that there might not be any charge of discrimination between him and the other contractors."[72] In the meantime, the department asked for bids for temporary two-month contracts on the original five contract air mail routes while reserving the right to withdraw the advertisement or reject any bid should H.R. 9500 be passed.[73]

Despite his reluctance to cooperate with Kelly, by mid-April Brown was left with no choice. Hainer Hinshaw reported that "the war goes merrily on" and he now expected the removal of the clause, which would allow Brown to negotiate for space on aircraft. Hinshaw believed that the law could still be written to preserve the contractors pioneering rights. "I think that we can word it so that we would shut off anyone starting competition," he stated.[74]

After a tiring six-hour session in the House Rules Committee, Brown and Kelly forged a compromise that eliminated the postmaster general's power to negotiate contracts on routes but restricted bidders to those with six months of actual flying experience on routes of four hundred miles or more. This in effect confined the pool of prospective bidders to those large, well-financed airlines Brown favored but opened the door to some independents. Of greatest importance, the new space method of payment, the rate variables system, and the right to extend routes without bidding remained untouched.

Under Section 4, the postmaster general was authorized to pay a fixed amount per cubic foot of available space, not to exceed $1.25 per mile for purely air mail operations. Each cubic foot equated to 9 pounds of mail. A maximum of 225 pounds, which occupied 25 cubic feet, could be carried at no more than 40 cents per mile. This 40-cent payment was intended as a subsidy for passenger aircraft operation. The department was prohibited from entering any new contract from two points not previously served by air mail after July 1, 1931, that was not authorized or paid for by Congress.[75] Brown wanted a raise in the air mail postage rate to help pay for route growth, but no additional monies from the Treasury would be provided.[76] Section 2 gave the postmaster general the power to exchange contracts for route certificates, not to exceed ten years from the date of the original contract and provided that the airline had operated satisfactorily for two years. In return for the security of a long-term certificate, the postmaster general could revise the rate of payment at his discretion and at least annually in order to take advantage of "advances in the art of flying and passenger transportation." This gave him the power to lower the rate of payments at will. Under Section 7 the postmaster general was given the right to make extensions or consolidations of existing routes in the public interest.[77] On April 17, the new bill, H.R. 11704, was reported out of committee.

The bill was not exactly what the Post Office or industry wanted, but it was the best they were going to get. Richard Robbins of PAIC was not pleased by the compromise bill. He and others found the wording muddled and difficult to understand. "Speaking generally, the language of Section 4 is involved, and certain to be a source of grief to the Post Office Department and to the air mail contractors," stated Robbins. Regardless of Brown's interpretation, he felt that the comptroller general would dictate the terms of the bill and upset the department's plans for the industry. "It is of little consequence what the Postmaster General's intent is, or what the legislative intent is, or how the Post Office Department may wish to administer the law," complained Robbins, "the Comptroller General will hold that 'the language of the Act speaks for itself,' and that will be the end of it." Robbins would soon see firsthand the accuracy of his prediction.

Robbins wanted MacCracken to see what he could do to improve the bill before it was passed. "I think the thing to do is to get busy and see if something cannot be done about amending this bill from the floor of the House or, if it passes the House, in the Senate Committee," he stated. "The Postmaster General's plans are thrown in the discard by this bill, and I see little hope for any sound development of commercial aviation under its provisions."[78] He overstated the case, as events were to prove. The space/mileage payment system would provide a fair and widely distributed method of payment for all of the contractors while the passenger lines were now given a subsidy along important routes. The postmaster general could now alter the air mail map at will. But the law, as worded, was unclear on key issues and their interpretation.

Despite Robbins's objections, the bill quickly passed the House and was sent to the Post Office Committee of the Senate on April 22. Postmaster General Brown wanted no more modifications, even if the bill was not exactly what he wanted. According to MacCracken, "I talked with the Postmaster General after he had been before the Committee, and he said he hoped no amendments would be offered on the floor, as he was afraid it would only tend to complicate the situation, and he thought there was enough flexibility in the Bill to take care of almost any kind of situation."[79]

Sen. Lawrence Phipps of Colorado, chairman of the Senate's Post Office Committee, had discussed Robbins's concerns with Brown and assured Robbins that they would be eligible for any new contract:

> For your private information, I believe I am justified in stating that it is the desire of the Postmaster General to consider any bids which your company will be in a position to make; that he is anxious to have your company qualify as contractors and does not know of any reason why your bids should not be considered for any air mail route which it is proposed to establish or extend.
>
> The necessity for securing prompt passage of this Act is such that it was believed unwise to make any modifications of the bill in the form in which it has just passed the House, as this would necessitate a conference which might unduly delay the adoption of the measure. In the light of the explanations made by the Postmaster General it was thought unnecessary to modify the bill along the lines suggested by you.[80]

With this information, Robbins withdrew his effort to amend the bill. "We do not wish to be obstructionists," PAIC president George Hann wrote Brown, "and we appreciate that the best good for the whole aviation industry will certainly have its eventual compensations for Pennsylvania and for the Pittsburgh community."[81] Guided by Senators Charles McNary and Phipps, the McNary-Watres Act was approved without further difficulty on April 24. On April 30, President Hoover signed H.R. 11704 into law.

Chapter 8

Realignment

W hile the fight raged in Congress over the future of air transportation, industry was preparing for the expected changes in different ways. Some airlines fought desperately just to survive until the new legislation passed; others sought to position themselves to take advantage of the coming reforms. It was a time of turmoil. All the airlines and air mail contractors felt the pressure, but none more so than the Aviation Corporation.

Chaos still reigned in New York despite the recent reorganization and the creation of American Airways. The disparate operations and business philosophies of the numerous component parts of Aviation Corporation continued to work against efforts to streamline the corporation's activities. Embry-Riddle, over which the idea of AVCO was born one year earlier, refused to join with the other air mail carriers and submit to control by American until the minority interests of their stockholders were better protected. The continuing problem of integrating the various accounting systems plagued the company while losses mounted. A top-heavy organization with no clear-cut lines of communication or authority undermined attempts to improve the corporation's performance; management divided into competing cliques issuing conflicting orders, and top leaders micromanaged and refused to listen to constructive advice.

The crisis came to a head while AVCO's Washington representatives were working strenuously on behalf of the Post Office for passage of the Watres bill. A frustrated and distracted Hainer Hinshaw expressed his opinions to Interstate Airlines chief Col. William Schauffler. "There has been very little change in the New York situation as yet," stated Hinshaw. "There has been a great ado with orders to do this and that and the others and about what is going to be done, but as yet, the companies have not been dissolved, or the operating company legally formed, and I have expressions from the different companies to the effect that they are going to fight it as long as they can." Hinshaw expected the chaos to continue until, in desperation, significant improvements were made.[1]

Aviation Corporation director George Hann demanded immediate steps be taken to sort out the difficulties and find a solution before the company collapsed and their best efforts over the past year were wasted. He reiterated his complaint that Graham Grosvenor's management style was paralyzing the company. "Graham has been his own worst enemy," he declared. "His refusal to delegate authority enmeshed him in the constant petty bickerings and minor problems best left to middle managers to solve. He should have freed himself instead to apply his skills to the long range tasks required of a corporate president."[2]

Despite Hann's support for the new president of American, James Hamilton, he was concerned that the lack of aviation expertise in upper management was crippling the company. Grosvenor knew Otis Elevators well, and Hamilton was an experienced bus line operator, but neither of them understood the new business of aviation sufficiently to run an aviation holding company or an airline. They needed to travel to the field to acquire a better understanding of actual operations, not remain isolated from the industry's real problems while still issuing conflicting and inappropriate commands.[3]

Hann felt that these top-level problems were enervating the entire company and damaging its effectiveness and even the safety of operations. He strongly pressed Chairman W. Averell Harriman to make additional organizational reforms before time ran out.[4] Hann urged that the board immediately authorize creation of a special investigating committee to examine the worsening situation and make recommendations for changes. "The investigation should be a thorough one and, if properly accomplished, will require considerable time," stated Hann. "If necessary, the Aviation Corporation could consider this report as a professional service and make payment therefore. . . . They will be the cheapest dollars we have ever spent." Hann suggested that Roland Palmedo and Frederic Coburn of the engineering firm of Sanderson and Porter arrange for the special committee. "It is very apparent that a period of readjustment is confronting the industry at the present time," he concluded. "If we are to build wisely for the future, it is necessary that we now 'put our house in good order' and profit by our past experiences."[5]

Harriman and the board of directors agreed to form an executive advisory committee with members Roland Palmedo, R.H.M. Robinson, W.L. Campbell, Thurman Bane, and Frederic G. Coburn. Their first meeting, held on February 18, examined the organization of AVCO, the organization of American Airways, and the accounting systems used by AVCO and American. Seven meetings were held over the next two months. On March 7, the committee released an interim report so that AVCO could take immediate action on the most pressing issues.

The committee urgently requested that clear lines of authority be determined and that all presidents of the subsidiary companies report to the AVCO Executive Committee through the president of AVCO. At present, Hamilton, the president of American Airways, had a free hand and was not working with Grosvenor, the president of AVCO, or the executive committee. Hamilton's dictatorial management style during his brief tenure was clearly not working. Frederic Coburn shouldered the blame for the managerial failures. "I had a man in mind whom I hoped would be brought in with an idea of contributing something along the lines of organization and operating routine that air line operators up to date seem to have lacked," he stated, "but not at all the idea of letting a public utility man come in and attempt to run the whole works." Coburn concluded, "The czar idea is all wrong."[6]

This problem reflected other difficulties, as the leadership of American Airways was not coordinating its technical and engineering matters with the other branches of the corporation. Earlier, Coburn had noted that American Airways had a responsibility to AVCO to consider itself "a sales outlet for the manufacturing divisions of the parent company."[7] The report concluded that "a Technical Department, with personnel competent to exercise technical control over the operations of [American] Airways, be created and put into operation promptly" and "a competent technical control of all purchases be inaugurated."

In addition, the newly created treasury and accounting departments were discovered to have been working at crossed purposes, complicated by the fact that a third branch, a different accounting department, was operating in New York. The problem was so acute that American Airways had no way of knowing their true costs of operation. The cavalier methods of accounting had hidden the actual costs of running the airlines and were ruining the corporation. A careful audit prepared for the committee revealed that previous estimates were grossly inaccurate. Earlier, it was believed that it cost 40.5 cents per mile to fly a Wright J-5 powered, single-engine, open-cockpit mail plane and $1.33 per mile to fly a Ford Tri-Motor. Actual costs were 89.2 cents and $2.09 per mile, respectively.[8]

The advisory committee recommended that "the Treasury and Accounting Departments be combined under a Treasurer, he to be Treasurer in addition to all subsidiaries of Aviation [Corporation]." Two principal assistants would share the workload and report directly to the treasurer. This, it was hoped, would unify control and improve cooperation within AVCO.[9]

On March 24 and April 2, while the Post Office was battling for the Watres bill, the advisory committee released its final report. Along with making detailed recommendations concerning Fairchild and the manufacturing aspects of AVCO, the report made explicit recommendations concerning air mail and the fate of passenger operations. It was clear that without government help, AVCO should admit defeat and withdraw from the passenger-carrying business. The industry was too new and too volatile to risk further capital expenditures without some assurance of profitability at some time in the future. Committee members agreed that AVCO should continue in the mail transportation business "but that it remain in passenger transportation business only to such extent as may be necessary to retain mail contracts." They would recommend abandoning passenger service "if it should be found possible to retain mail contracts without continuing in the passenger transportation business," and suggested that in such a case, AVCO fly customers only on an experimental basis.[10]

The committee hoped that if AVCO were compelled to carry passengers, the Post Office would help them by consolidating existing unprofitable routes into a more rational and profitable network. The fate of American Airways and passenger air travel now lay completely in the hands of the Post Office. "Under the new law," the report continued, "the Post Office Department should have available funds and latitude of authority such as probably to make all of Aviation's mail contracts profitable, and also such as to make some contribution toward the cost of passenger transport; but the Committee understands that as one of the purposes of the mail contract law is to foster passenger transport, Aviation will be required to remain in the passenger transport business to some extent."[11]

To this end committee members recommended that AVCO's existing passenger lines, operated by Southern Air Transport from Dallas to El Paso, be retained to gather experience and, more important, "to not give up the present priority rights for a portion of the southern transcontinental mail contract." They also suggested that the passenger routes operated by Braniff and Robertson be continued between Chicago, St. Louis, and Tulsa in order to strengthen American Airways' bargaining position with the Post Office. Under the new law, they reasoned, Robertson's CAM-2 would be extended from St. Louis to Tulsa. All other passenger routes were to be abandoned.[12]

While the advisory committee was working on its report, a self-appointed committee composed of board members made its own recommendations concerning AVCO's management crisis, dealing specifically with operations. This committee, operating with the approval of the advisory committee, undertook a detailed field examination of AVCO's operations and reached similar, damning conclusions about the organization's lack of well-developed programs, poor coordination, and consequent huge losses. Specifically, this group examined AVCO's New York organization and transport operations. The pending changes in the postal laws pressed this committee to force a reorganization so that AVCO would be better positioned to take advantage of the expected changes wrought by the Watres Act and thereby give the corporation defined objectives and a chance for profitability in airline operations.

They, too, discovered confused lines of authority and responsibility between AVCO and American Airways. Local managements were over-organized and carried excessive overhead costs, often with overpaid and redundant executive staff. Although middle management was competent and actual operations proceeded well, overhaul, maintenance, and shop facilities were generally inadequate and the acquisition of aircraft and related equipment haphazard and uncoordinated. The poor coordination with the corporate leadership was found to produce "resentment, jealousy, and friction locally and between local executives and the New York office."[13]

This problem, which manifested itself through the rise of cliques in the New York organization, was largely responsible for the confusing state of AVCO's accounting practices. The committee agreed with the earlier findings that the existing three accounting systems were causing tremendous problems and that one standardized method, based on the model developed by the Post Office, should be agreed upon. In this way, accurate data, necessary for the computation of true costs with relationship to the Post Office Department's requirements, could be determined (4–5).

Equipment was found to be obsolete and inefficient, and the consequent economic losses were heavy. Although maintained properly, the aircraft were generally used incorrectly. Aircraft of too great a capacity were flown on thin routes, unnecessarily producing high operating costs. It was further learned that of the 289 aircraft in American's fleet, 132 were surplus to their needs but had not been written off or sold. There was apparently no attempt to standardize on any one type that could have reduced acquisition and operating costs as well (6). Although traffic had greatly improved because of the recent rate cuts, with load factors increasing from an average of 35 percent before the cuts to an average of 65 percent after, the new fares were too low to permit a profit without a government subsidy.

Attempts to cut costs through the suspension of subsidiary operations by Braniff Air Lines and Central Air Lines in Kansas, Oklahoma, and Texas were offset by the replacement of cheaper single-engined aircraft with more expensive tri-motor airliners. The committee laid the blame for this situation squarely at the feet of AVCO president Graham Grosvenor, just as George Hann had feared the year before (9–10).

The chaotic conditions in the field were reflective of the disorganization of the New York office. The committee discovered a very loosely knit, unorganized department run by a president unwilling to share authority or responsibility. The absence of any delegation of duties produced poor communications and resulted in the rise of competing cliques within headquarters. This in turn resulted in much wasteful duplication of efforts on the part of the operating companies when confronted with conflicting instructions and requests. As with the operating companies, AVCO was burdened with overhead, particularly in excessive personnel, exorbitant salaries, and the leasing of extraneous office space. The original plan, which was to operate with a decentralized management that would allow each subsidiary more freedom of action, had never been implemented. They found that the creation of American Airways was too hasty and the selection of James Hamilton as president a poor choice based on his subsequent performance. This resulted in a conflicting line of authority, as Hamilton was responsible not to the president of AVCO, which was the proper channel up the organizational chart, but only to the American Airways Board of Directors. Consequently, many important decisions were being made without the knowledge of AVCO's complete board (12).

The committee was astonished to discover that neither Grosvenor nor Hamilton had bothered to contact the Post Office Department to explain the new organization of American Airways. This was a crucial point, as postal contracts were essential to American's survival, yet American's management had "taken little interest in this important phase of the organization's activities" (4). Given the cooperative nature of the Post Office and the possibility of improving service through route consolidations, the committee expected American to take advantage of this opportunity. Unfortunately, they had not done so. The cavalier manner of management had, in fact, imperiled American's relations with the department (13).

Despite the tireless efforts of Hainer Hinshaw to fight for the Watres bill, the committee discovered that AVCO's board of directors had little knowledge or understanding of these critical negotiations because all contact with the Washington office had been through either Grosvenor or Loucks. Hinshaw had performed admirably for the company in representing AVCO's interests before the department, yet "it is lamentable that Mr. Hinshaw has not received greater support from New York" (14).

The pending legislation was seen as providing the necessary support for AVCO and American to stay in the air transportation business and even operate profitably, if management could take advantage of the changing situation. It was correctly seen that of all the contractors carrying the mail, those under AVCO's control would benefit greatest under the proposed mileage payment plan, as American had numerous routes with substantial distances but little poundage. Estimates made by the committee concluded that AVCO would reap an additional $100,000 per month under the Watres Act, essentially doubling their subsidy to $3 million and increasing AVCO's share of the postal subsidy from 11 to 22.5 percent.[14]

Unfortunately, management had taken no steps with the Post Office to prepare for the coming changes by determining new routes, consolidated routes, or cost-accounting measures. With limited government funding, the department would no longer support inefficient operations and routes of dubious utility. The committee stressed the importance of developing a trunk line, operating directly from coast to coast, which would interest the department to the exclusion of other competitors. The corporation was faced with two options concerning passenger transportation: it could eliminate all unprofitable routes and later acquire other profitable airlines or it could continue all of its operations, even at a loss, in order to maintain control and the rights over certain routes and "cut out competition." Committee members suggested acceptance of the first option, except where the Post Office could provide an adequate subsidy. Most critically for the future of the air transportation industry in the United States, if the Watres Act failed to become law, they recommended that "all passenger lines be suspended, with the exception of an experimental model line."[15]

Their research revealed that the Post Office Department was willing to cooperate if AVCO showed a willingness to improve its management. The department also expected in return to participate directly in determining policies within the contracting companies for the promotion of air mail and passenger operations. The committee concluded, "Prompt steps should be taken to impress the Department with the desire of the Aviation Corporation to operate along such lines in close cooperation with the Department."[16]

Drastic measures were required for American Airways to survive the current crisis. The large size of the board of directors and their lack of knowledge hampered efficient operations, but the committee felt that little could be done to reduce the number of members. Instead, it strongly urged that the executive committee redouble its efforts to inform all members of the board of AVCO's activities and that the executive committee itself reorganize and acquire more members with actual operational experience. Most important, the committee recommended a significant change at the top: the removal of Graham Grosvenor. Committee members also recommended that James Hamilton be relieved of his duties as president of American Airways and did not mince their words: "The Committee believes that Mr. Hamilton is not qualified for the position which he is occupying and that immediate steps should be taken to sever his connection with American Airways, Inc."[17]

If these changes were implemented and if the important pending postal legislation passed Congress, the committee felt that AVCO had a good chance to emerge from the crisis in good order. The corporation had substantial cash reserves that, if not depleted because of bad management and unprofitable operations, would eventually enable the company to take advantage of the opportunity presented by the Watres Act and future developments.

The AVCO Board of Directors agreed with the recommendations of both committees and acted promptly. Grosvenor was relieved of his duties and elevated to the ceremonial position of vice chairman of the board and replaced by Frederic Coburn.[18] Hamilton was fired.

Throughout AVCO's convulsions, the executives of United Aircraft and Transport did not sit idly by. With the Post Office Department busy with the fight for the Watres bill, Fred Rentschler and company sought to strengthen their position for the immediate future through astute maneuvering on Wall Street. Their target was National Air Transport.

With the clear understanding of Postmaster General Brown's plans for the future of air transportation and his desire to expand passenger service, UATC saw an opportunity to jump ahead of the competition while fulfilling the perceived program of the Post Office Department to create a system of long, transcontinental routes. The lengthy discussions in the Interdepartmental Committee on Airways during the past year clearly demonstrated the government's plan for a middle and a southern transcontinental route. Through Boeing Air Transport's control and operation of the air mail route from San Francisco to Chicago, United Aircraft was in a strong position to take control of the existing transcontinental route through to New York.

Already, United Aircraft had acquired Stout Air Service, which extended United's network to Cleveland through Detroit. This move, while gaining control of another mail contract, was not a direct line upon which to base transcontinental service. The creation of a new airline or an extension of Stout to New York was impractical and potentially disastrous economically. National Air Transport already controlled CAM-17 from New York to Chicago and was operating efficiently. A direct confrontation would only prove catastrophic to both parties. To Fred Rentschler, the answer was obvious: buy NAT.

Quietly and carefully, United began to purchase NAT stock in February 1930. By March, United had enough shares to approached Earle H. Reynolds, president of NAT, with a proposal to exchange a large block of United common shares for a controlling interest in National. The NAT Executive Committee received the proposal favorably. In anticipation of the conclusion of the deal, United deposited eighty thousand of its common shares in the City Bank Farmers Trust Company of New York on March 26 with the understanding that each share of UATC was to be swapped for four shares of NAT.[19] The proposed merger would result in the creation of the most powerful airline in the country with over $33 million in assets.[20]

Clement Keys was not initially opposed. He was becoming increasing overburdened with the operations of his vast empire and was primarily concerned with saving Transcontinental Air Transport. His overarching concern was the promotion of aviation and air transportation. National Air Transport was a going concern that did not require his attention. TAT did. William MacCracken, an interested industry observer, expressed his opinion of the pending merger to Harris Hanshue. "There is to be a special meeting of the Board of Directors on Thursday of next week (April 5) to consider the proposition and make a recommendation to the stockholders," he stated. "I do not know what C.M. Keys' attitude is on this particular proposal, but I do know that he is inclined to get his affairs in such shape that in the future they will not require as much of his personal attention as they have in the past, and I also happen to know that he thinks very well of the United organization's management."[21] Keys's confidence in the excellent management of UATC was well placed, so losing control of NAT was not a primary concern.

His health, however, was a concern. Keys's years of stress dealing with business and Wall Street had left his nerves frayed. The collapse of the market in October had wiped out his personal reserves and had left him vulnerable. Unknown to most in the industry, including those in his own companies, Keys had personally borrowed $14.5 million from North American in call loans before the crash. He used this money to invest in various other aviation and nonaviation stocks as he had done successfully for years. But now the securities were virtually worthless. At some point the board would recall the loans, but Keys had no money to repay them. The resulting stress was understandably considerable. Increasingly, Keys spent time away from New York recovering from nervous collapses at his Saint Catharine's Island vacation home off the Georgia coast. The board eventually did recall the loans, but Keys was unable to pay back all that he owed. An arrangement was made, but it cost him his job. By the end of 1931, Keys withdrew from aviation after he was forced to leave North American and Curtiss-Wright and repay what he could.[22]

The acquisition of NAT by United was at first endorsed by Clement Keys. He analyzed United's offer for his board of directors following a meeting of the NAT Executive Committee on March 26, 1930. Although direct comparisons were difficult because NAT was strictly an operating company and UATC was a much larger and complex holding company, Keys calculated that the offer was profitable to NAT stockholders. Based on their reported earnings per share for 1929, he estimated that one share of United returned $4.52, whereas four shares of National returned $4.12. Although Boeing Air Transport was expected to have a reduced income following poor weather and the expected lowering of the air mail rates, it was seen as a very solid component of a very solid corporation. Based on this analysis and a comparison of their respective assets, Keys recommended accepting the offer.[23]

But when the matter reached National's board of directors, many, though not all, opposed the arrangement, not willing to relinquish control of their profitable airline. Col. Paul Henderson of NAT raised the stakes, announcing that, for the first time, National was to inaugurate passenger service along its routes. The new service would follow the mail route exactly but employ a separate schedule designed for passenger convenience, not that of the Post Office. This was in direct challenge to Boeing Air Transport's earlier announcement that they were to expand their regular passenger service along CAM-18 to Chicago. After United reduced its bid to a 1 for 3 1/2 exchange, following a reconsideration by the UATC Board, the NAT Board of Directors promptly and unanimously rejected the lesser offer.[24]

Undaunted, Rentschler pressed harder and announced that United would attempt to gain control through the acquisition of controlling interest in National. On April 4, United announced that they would make their offer directly to NAT's stockholders during the annual meeting scheduled for April 10 in an attempt to circumvent the NAT Board while continuing to gain control through the market. By this time, Rentschler estimated, United was already the largest owner of NAT stock, controlling approximately 30 percent, or 200,000 of the 650,000 outstanding shares. "We are seeking control of N.A.T. because we believe that great economies may be effected through the formation of a single transcontinental line, carrying mail, passengers, and express," stated Rentschler. "If the N.A.T. lines were to be paralleled by a United line, one or the other might lose money. From an economic standpoint, the air between the two coasts is not big enough to be divided."[25] In preparation for this attempted coup, Rentschler sent a detailed letter to all NAT stockholders asking for their proxies and outlining what he felt were the advantages of such an affiliation.[26]

National was willing to fight. In order to head off a possible stockholder uprising and a proxy fight, the NAT Board attempted to rewrite their corporate bylaws. On April 7, the corporate constitution was amended allowing that board members could only be removed for cause and only by a two-thirds majority. Further, they arranged that future changes in the bylaws could only be made by a similar two-thirds majority of the stockholders, although the same laws could be amended by just a majority of the board. Finally, the size of a quorum was reduced from a majority of stockholders to one-third. On April 9, NAT, through a complicated arrangement with its parent corporation, North American, issued 300,000 additional shares, enough, it was hoped, to preserve control and prevent United's takeover bid during the impending stockholder's meeting.[27]

Clement Keys now rose to the challenge and appealed directly to NAT's wavering shareholders. He decried United's efforts as an attempt to destroy one of the nation's pioneer airlines and to create a destructive monopoly against the public's interest. Rather disingenuously, he also railed against Wall Street interests gaining control:

> We do not think that it is to the best interest of the public, of our stockholders, or of the Nation as a whole, that the main line from New York to Chicago should be controlled by United Aircraft & Transport Corporation. . . . No economic purpose can be served by such an economic consolidation and the very diversity of interest between the two has led, and will lead to a competition in quality of service to the public that would be eliminated by such a consolidation.
>
> The theory upon which this raid was based was, in effect, that it was time to eliminate from aviation the pioneer group who have created most of the things that have been created so far in the United States in this art, and to put them under a financial control centering in one of the largest banking groups in Wall Street.[28]

The creation of one large transcontinental holding company controlling the two best air mail routes raised fears in many circles. William Gibbs McAdoo and James Edgerton, who were anxiously following the course of the discussions concerning the Watres bill, saw the specter of monopoly in the merger. Growing increasingly pessimistic about the possibility of starting Southern Sky-Lines, McAdoo expressed the mounting fears of many independent operators. "The way things are shaping in the air transportation game leads me to believe that a few powerful companies are going to have such a hold on it that it will be impossible for a new company to get a chance," he declared. "I notice that Boeing had taken over, or is about to take over, the National Air Transport. This, of course, creates a very strong combination with which competition will be most difficult, especially when that company has mail contracts and will undoubtedly continue to receive the favor of the Department."[29]

It was rumored by Western Air Express that Postmaster General Brown himself was angry with United and threatened to withdraw Post Office support and turn the industry over to the Interstate Commerce Commission. Negotiations over the Watres bill had reached a critical phase in early April and Brown was worried that members of Congress would see this move by United as an unwarranted step toward monopoly and an expression of their worst fears. Although Brown clearly favored the large holding companies, he did so only under his terms. He had no desire to see a true monopoly control the entire industry. This merger was viewed an attempt to circumvent his carefully laid plans, and it risked fatally damaging his air mail program. The rumor, if true, noted William Bishop, might give his company an advantage:

> However, there is this angle, interesting as it is and certainly to our advantage. Brown is plenty on the war path over the United—N.A.T. merger negotia-

tions. He called someone at the National City Bank and told them that if the deal was made he would withdraw his support to aviation and put it under (the) I.C.C. He accused then of giving him the double cross, of making things embarrassing, and in general he let them have both barrels.

Hainer said that he gave Paul Henderson just as much hell as he raised over the telephone. I don't believe, however, Henderson ever knew such a deal was hanging fire until he saw it in print.[30]

By April 10, United Aircraft had acquired a substantial amount of stock, but not enough had been transferred in time for Rentschler to gain control and oust the current NAT Board. Without sufficient proxies, United attempted to postpone the meeting by voting only two shares and challenging the legality of the new rules for a quorum. This was overruled when the board declared that a sufficient number of stockholders and proxies were present under the recently amended lower requirements.[31] Howard Coffin, chairman of the Board of NAT, declared victory:

> Efforts of the United Aircraft & Transport Corporation to secure control of National Air Transport through a publicly announced policy of preventing a quorum at the annual meeting today in Wilmington were signally defeated when a majority of the proxies at the meeting were voted for the retention of the present management.
>
> Two directors of the United Corporation, both of whom were named in the proxies solicited by the United interests, were present at the meeting. They voted only two shares of stock and did not offer the proxies obtained by United during the last five weeks. This action is astonishing inasmuch as they solicited proxies from stockholders with the evident understanding that the stock would be voted at the meeting and then deliberately refused to vote and, in effect, threw a large block of other people's stock into the wastebasket.
>
> Failure to vote the stock was explained by a public statement read into the record of the meeting, which said that the United interests sought to prevent a quorum and thus invalidate the stockholder's meeting.[32]

Congratulations poured in to Keys and NAT from around the industry. Harold Pitcairn was "delighted to see in the paper today that the control of the National Air Transport remains in the old hands."[33] Graham Grosvenor extended his congratulations as well, with the hope that NAT and American would soon begin discussions concerning the acquisition of several of American's unprofitable lines. Neither Braniff, which paralleled CAM-3 between Dallas, Kansas City, and Chicago, nor Universal, which paralleled CAM-17 between Chicago and Cleveland, had air mail contracts and consequently were losing prodigious sums of money. National Air Transport, on the other hand, had announced that it wanted to open passenger service but did not yet have the equipment or infrastructure. The acquisition of these two American companies would allow NAT to buy two existing passengers lines. American had approached Clement Keys with the deal and was to present it to his board before the April 10 meeting. Stated the minutes of AVCO's board meeting of April 7, "It is evident that N.A.T. must sooner or later commence passenger operations and it seems reasonable that at the reduced cost to them of operating this passenger line that it would be advantageous to takeover a 'going concern' rather than to build from the ground up."[34]

Grosvenor and American would have to wait, for United had not given up the fight. Rentschler had already purchased control of NAT but had not enough time to execute their plan during the stockholders meeting. Responding to Grosvenor, Keys replied, "The change in the whole situation due to the purchase of the control of NAT by United, may alter this entire situation but it does not remove the fact that it would be good judgment for our interests to draw closely together whenever possible."[35]

In response to the sudden change in NAT's bylaws, United Aircraft went to the Chancery Court in Wilmington, Delaware, to ask for a restraining order, which was granted on April 14, on the grounds that the board had voted proxies it no longer controlled. This prevented National from executing its plan to issue three hundred thousand more shares of stock and exchange it with Eastern Air Transport to preserve control of NAT by Keys's group.[36]

Keys had no stomach for the fight, wisely recognizing that he could not win. He also sincerely felt that any further confrontation would be harmful to the entire industry, especially during the delicate negotiations that were continuing in Washington. After analyzing United's complaint, Keys decided that the "policies of the company should not be dictated by stock market considerations."[37] The arguments were moot now that United had acquired sufficient shares to control the company. Keys had more pressing concerns with TAT and his others aviation businesses. He expressed his opinion to Chester Cuthell in a telegram on April 19: "On further consideration, [of the] plan [for] holding N.A.T., the less I like it. If United has bought control we should let them have it without trying to make it hard for them, the other policy is not in line with our usual corporation policies because it will do no good to aviation as [a] whole, we have plenty to do protecting our other interests and even if we won it would only be for a little while [that] we could hold N.A.T."[38]

On April 23, Cuthell telegraphed back to Keys that he had settled the controversy by agreeing to a one-to-three stock swap. The board concurred.[39] United was notified of the decision, and immediately Rentschler issued his formal proposal to the Board of NAT. The arrangement was contingent upon the withdrawal of National's plan to issue the additional three hundred thousand shares and to reorganize the board according to United's wishes.[40] National agreed. Control of NAT passed amicably to United Aircraft, as both parties were intent on preventing further discord within the industry. Some observers nevertheless were surprised by the news. Observed James Edgerton,

> Two events of importance to us have occurred during the past few hours. The chief one is the passage of the amended Watres Bill by the Senate yesterday evening. It is expected to receive the signature of the President today.
>
> The second is the assumption of a stock control of National Air Transport by United Aviation. This came as quite a surprise here, especially the fact that this control is reported to be 56%. The reason I believe this affects us is that the Keys group have been outmaneuvered completely and will be looking to future openings to recoup.[41]

Now, United Aircraft and Transport Corporation was perfectly positioned to take advantage of the new changes to be wrought by the Watres Act. In one swift coup, they had created the nation's first transcontinental airline. This was unprecedented. Not even the powerful railroads had been able to establish sole ownership of a major transcontinental line. In just over one year, the company would grow so quickly that the four major air transport components, Boeing Air Transport, National Air Transport, Pacific Air Transport, and Varney Air Lines, would be reorganized under one management holding company. On July 1, 1931, United Air Lines was born. But before this could happen, Walter Brown had an industry to reorganize.

Chapter 9

Drawing a New Map

At long last, after the protracted struggle to revamp the air mail rate structure and to enact the necessary legislation, Walter Brown was ready to take direct action. Passage of the Watres Act left him in total control of the air mail situation and the virtual dictator of U.S. air transportation. Acting as a one-man regulatory agency, Brown now had the power to redraw the air mail map to his satisfaction.

He did so with deliberation. He totally controlled the establishment of new routes and the extension or consolidation of existing routes. The department had already created a unified system of accounting and required the contractors to use it. Now Brown controlled the amount of mail carried, greatly influenced the type of aircraft used, and directly encouraged the carrying of passengers to offset expected losses. He determined the compensation as well as the subsidy allowed.[1] The Watres Act did not give him all of the power he wanted; he was still encumbered by the requirement for competitive bidding on long routes, and the interpretation of his ability to extend routes into new territory had yet to be determined. Nevertheless, Brown felt he now had sufficient authority to act.

Immediately following passage of the Watres Act, Brown prevailed on the airlines with contracts nearing expiration to exchange their contracts for ten-year route certificates. This gave the original contractors an additional six years to fly the mail and would allow them to make long-term commitments to their investors with the expectation of a proper return. In exchange, they agreed to abide by the postmaster general's periodic wishes to reduce the rates they were paid. CAM routes 1 to 5, affecting Colonial, Robertson, National, Western Air Express, and Varney, all received certificates.[2]

Brown's new space system of payment alleviated the department of a complicated, inefficient weight system and distributed the government largess much more equitably among the contractors. Each route was now considered equally important and operating in the public interest and was, therefore, entitled to an equitable disbursement of the air mail payments. The department was now also able to contract for space on passenger aircraft that flew into areas not previously served by air mail. Payment was not to exceed $1.25 per mile. In addition, the postmaster general was authorized to award new contracts on routes where the mail load would not exceed 225 pounds, that is, twenty-five cubic feet of space or 9 pounds per cubic foot—the same rate authorized by the Interstate Commerce Commission for mail carried by the railroads—to the lowest responsible bidder at a rate not to exceed 40 cents per mile. In a direct effort to forestall unprincipled bidders from creating an airline overnight without proper financing or organization, all potential new entrants had to have owned and operated a regularly scheduled air service with a route of 250 miles or more at least six months in advance of the advertisement for bids.[3]

The new payment formula, which became effective on April 29, 1930, allowed for two classes of air mail: B for routes carrying less than one hundred pounds and A for all other routes carrying more than one hundred pounds. Class A payments started with a base rate of 40 cents per mile. Brown specifically encouraged the development of safer, more powerful aircraft through the use of variables (i.e., bonuses), which were added on a per mile basis to the base rate and included 2 cents for difficult terrain, 2.5 cents for operating in typically foggy conditions, 3 cents for carrying a one-way radio and 6 cents for a two-way radio, and 15 cents if the entire route was flown after dusk.

The postmaster general greatly preferred multi-engined aircraft for safety reasons, particularly if they were to carry passengers: in fact, he insisted on it. To encourage the use of these larger, more expensive but safer aircraft, he gave a bonus of 13 cents per mile for machines with multiple engines.

Of great importance in sparking the subsequent development of a new generation of airliners that would revolutionize air transportation worldwide, the Post Office also gave bonuses for carrying passengers. Aircraft carrying from 2 to 5 passengers were awarded 1.5 cents per miles; 6 to 9 passengers, 3 cents; 10 to 19, 4.5 cents; 20 to 29, 6 cents; and 30 or more passengers, 7.5 cents.[4] These rates were to remain in effect until the end of the year, when the department would review and possibly revise the payment scheme either upward or downward.

Although most of the contractors who had been living well off their previously high rates would see their payments reduced, they had the opportunity, through these generous incentives, to improve their technological and operational efficiency, which would help to offset their decreased postal revenues. The air mail carriers who had been forced to bid too low to earn any profit along their routes were now presented with an equitable method of payment that would increase their income to a profitable level.

Explicitly, Brown wanted the airlines to acquire better, more modern equipment and to promote passenger travel that, when operating in the public interest, provided citizens with a new and faster method of transportation. In turn, the increased revenue would help offset the postal payment and subsidy, thereby providing an improved mail service at lower cost to the taxpayer while promoting a new transportation system.[5]

Brown clearly understood his self-appointed role as a one-man public utility commission. All that was now needed was to assemble the contractors in Washington to discuss the impact of the new legislation and to take action to bolster the industry and save the passenger lines from imminent extinction. Brown instructed Second Assistant Postmaster General W. Irving Glover to call a meeting of all the contractors and a selected group of the larger passenger carriers to assemble in Washington on May 19, 1930, to work out a plan for implementation of the Watres Act. As in 1929, Brown was true to his Hooverian associative beliefs and wanted to discuss this legislation with the interested parties before taking action. While given virtual dictatorial power, Brown wished to cooperate fully with the airlines in order to make his vision for the future of the industry work. With the economy free falling again after a brief spring recovery, the need for action was pressing.

The postmaster general's overwhelming desire, contrary to the opinion of future critics, was to save the major passenger airlines. He had no need for the small, newly created companies and specifically wanted no part of any airline created after February 1930, for it was obvious to him that the only reason for their existence was to take advantage of his new legislation for their immediate speculative profit. His Progressive Republican vision involved an integrated national network of transcontinental lines operated by large, well-financed corporations in regulated competition with one another. He also wanted the airlines to help him determine which airlines would serve what area, always in the public interest.

Glover received explicit instructions from Brown for the forthcoming conference. He wanted prominent industry leaders present and ordered that they find a way to aid the passenger lines without resorting to potentially destructive competitive bidding. Glover conveyed this message to Earl B. Wadsworth, superintendant of the Air Mail Service:

> The Postmaster General is desirous of having a conference with representatives of Companies mentioned below; by this I mean a substantial representative like [George] Wheat for the United Aircraft; Hanshue, Western Air, and Maddux of T.A.T. He sees the feeling developing among the passenger carrying

lines who have no contract and have no way of getting into the picture unless it is by competitive bidding, and he wants to have a meeting with these representatives on next Monday, May 19, at two P.M. in his office, and desires to have a talk with them along the lines of just the best way for them to approach the question of giving aid to passenger lines. In other words, he wants them to come to some understanding so that it will not all be thrown into the pot and the passenger line operators left entirely outside due to the fact that the air mail operators would have the inside and would have the territory covered.[6]

Brown would later be accused of attempting to destroy the independent passenger lines through these allegedly collusive meetings, but as Glover's statement clearly shows, Brown's intentions were quite to the contrary. He wanted to save the passenger airlines, not destroy them. But he wanted this process done by his rules and according to his interpretations, to which subsequent new entrant airlines took self-interested exception. As events would show, his methods would involve consolidations, forcing the small, weakly financed companies into cooperative arrangements and even mergers with larger holding companies, all in the interest of preserving a strong air transportation industry but at the cost of the independence of many small, inefficient operators.

To this meeting were invited representative of United Aircraft, the Aviation Corporation, Western Air Express, Transcontinental Air Transport–Maddux, Eastern Air Transport, and Stout Air Services. No new certificates were to be issued until executives from these companies met with the postmaster general. Of these, TAT-Maddux was the largest purely passenger line, and Eastern and National were solely mail carriers. Brown wanted to save TAT-Maddux while encouraging the strictly air mail lines to start passenger service. Other smaller passenger lines were not directly represented, but Brown had every intention of providing them a share of the air mail pie, though on his own terms.

According to the official Post Office Department press release, the May 19 meeting was "the first time that operators of the large passenger lines have had an opportunity to talk with the Postmaster General and exchange views with him since the Watres measure became law." In his typical associative way, Brown intended that the operators and the department meet "in order to acquaint themselves with the provisions of the Watres bill recently made a law through the signature of President Hoover." In so doing, "representatives of every large passenger and air mail carrying concern throughout the country conferred today with Postmaster General Brown, Assistant Postmaster General Glover and other officials of the Department in charge of the Air Mail service."[7]

At two o'clock on the afternoon of May 19, twenty-six prominent individuals from Western Air Express, National Air Transport, United Aircraft, TAT-Maddux, Eastern Air Transport, SAFE Way, Thompson Aeronautical, Ford,

Pittsburgh Aviation Industries, U.S. Air Lines, Curtiss-Wright, and the Aviation Corporation assembled in the Gold Room, immediately adjacent to the postmaster general's office on the fifth floor of the Post Office building on Pennsylvania Avenue. Though still spring in Washington, the temperature was unseasonably hot, and the noise of riveting on the new Post Office building under construction next door added to the oppressive atmosphere.

Brown entered the room and proceeded to outline the Watres Act and his plan for its implementation. He encouraged the group to find ways to cooperate in assisting the struggling passenger lines and wanted the established companies to agree among themselves the equitable division of the country based on their current operations in their most important areas. In essence, Brown was giving the pioneer airlines the opportunity to stake their claims, after which the department would protect their interests against unwarranted intrusions from unfit airlines. This point was crucial to Brown, for as long as aviation was still in its infancy, he strongly felt that it needed such protection to survive, particularly against unprincipled competition. As with the ICC before him and the Civil Aeronautics Board created later in the decade, Brown's plan envisioned government-regulated cartels that protected the regional interests of the major, established airlines while permitting responsible competition. He wished to ensure the protection of the corporations from destructive competition but would encourage direct competition over the transcontinental routes, which of course the department controlled. To do so he requested that the airline representatives also determine among themselves the best airlines to operate the new central and southern transcontinental routes. To prevent the invasion of underfinanced, newly created airlines, Brown hoped to limit competitive bidding on these routes with the understanding that through the extension of existing lines from proven carriers, the transcontinental routes would be completed swiftly. Earl Wadsworth summarized the day's events:

> The Postmaster General opened the meeting by discussing the general provisions of the Watres Bill and invited suggestions from those present as to the ways and means of assisting the passenger operators, inasmuch as it is understood none of the so-called strictly passenger lines are breaking even and it is apparent that they will need some assistance if they are to continue. The PMG expressed the desire to know whether it is going to be possible for the so-called pioneers to agree among themselves as to the territory in which they shall have the paramount interest. He outlined certain prospective routes that were in contemplation somewhat as follows: a Southern Transcontinental route from Los Angeles to San Diego, thence to Fort Worth and Dallas; also a route from New York to St. Louis to Kansas City and Los Angeles; from St. Louis to Tulsa and Fort Worth; St. Paul to Winnipeg; possibly from St. Paul and Minneapolis to Omaha; possibly a route south from Cheyenne, and possibly one from Albany to Boston.[8]

The operators agreed with the plan. As his airline was going bankrupt, Jack Maddux of TAT-Maddux supported the idea. All were in agreement that it was wise to avoid competitive bidding if possible. Lou Holland, of tiny United States Airways, which flew from Denver to Kansas City, said, "I think it should be worked out by agreement as I am afraid that competitive bidding will result in wild promotions." Colonel Henderson and William Mayo seconded that opinion, as did Harris Hanshue. Remarked Hanshue, "We are willing to do anything within reason to work out the plan rather than to go into competitive bidding." The operators also agreed that they could cooperate in the public interest to implement Brown's ideas. "I believe there is a community of interests among the operators and the Department," stated Fred Coburn of AVCO, "and they are ready to cooperate and find out how to do it." United's George Wheat echoed that opinion: "I feel sure the entire group would be delighted to go into such a conference and work it out along the lines suggested."[9]

After Brown and his lieutenants withdrew, the group decided to form a subcommittee to thrash out the plan. William MacCracken, the former assistant secretary of commerce for aeronautics and now the representative of Western and PAIC, suggested that they split up according to region; Henderson, now representing United's interests, thought they should organize into air mail carriers and non–air-mail carriers. Eventually, with Brown's approval, one subcommittee composed of Henderson, Hanshue, Daniel Shaeffer, Richard Robbins, Richard "Tex" Marshall of Thompson Aeronautical, Lou Holland, William Mayo, Hainer Hinshaw, Thomas Doe, and Frank Russell of Curtiss-Wright reconvened in the Gold Room that afternoon. By unanimous consent, they elected MacCracken chairman of the subcommittee and began their deliberations to determine the new extensions of the present air mail routes.

After meeting in MacCracken's Washington office the following morning, the subcommittee reported to Glover at 2:00 P.M. and prepared a statement for a meeting with the postmaster general on May 23. Twelve routes were discussed but little action taken, much to Brown's frustration. For Route 1, the southern transcontinental from Los Angeles to Atlanta via San Diego, El Paso, and Dallas, United, AVCO, Eastern, Western, and Erle Halliburton elicited interest. All but United were operating to one or more points along that proposed route. Eastern was particularly anxious to acquire this potentially lucrative line. Captain Doe reported this possibility to the Eastern Board of Directors, which enthusiastically supported his claim.[10] Route 2, from Los Angeles to New York, through Albuquerque, Amarillo, Kansas City, St. Louis, Columbus, Pittsburgh, and Philadelphia, was contested by almost all of the participants. United, AVCO, Eastern, and Western, Erle Halliburton, Clifford Ball, Transcontinental Air Transport, and PAIC each claimed the route. The third route, from Omaha to St. Paul and Winnipeg, was basically the territory of Northwest Airways, although United and AVCO flew into Omaha. United claimed part of Route 4 from Albany to Boston, as Stout originally flew over part of that territory, but AVCO had a better claim because its Colonial and Colonial Western airlines operated throughout that region. As for Route 5 from Pittsburgh to Norfolk through Washington, Eastern, TAT, PAIC, and Clifford Ball all wanted their share. Eastern was already operating between Washington and Norfolk, and PAIC and Ball competed for traffic out of Pittsburgh.

United, AVCO, Western, Halliburton, and Curtiss Flying Service contended for Route 6 from Louisville to Memphis, Dallas, and Fort Worth. All agreed that Route 7 from Kansas City to Denver should go to U.S. Airways because Lou Holland's airline was already flying that line. Route 8 from Pueblo to Fort Worth and Dallas was argued over by United, AVCO, and Western, and Route 9 from Pueblo to El Paso was already being flown by Western without opposition. Route 10 was to link Amarillo with St. Louis through Dallas and Oklahoma City. United, AVCO, TAT, Western, and Halliburton's SAFE Way all covered parts of this proposed route. The last two routes went uncontested: Al Franks of National Parks wanted Route 11 from Great Falls, Montana, to Lethridge, and United was the only party interested in Route 12 from Seattle to Vancouver, British Columbia.[11] Hainer Hinshaw reassured the absent Colonel Brittin by telegram that Northwest Airways' interest were recognized and that despite a great deal of talk, little of consequence had been decided.[12]

Others were becoming uneasy with the method with which the postmaster general was dividing the air mail map. James Edgerton, who was desperately trying to pressure William Gibbs McAdoo into action in order to save a chance to build and fly Southern Sky-Lines, was not invited to attend the meetings but acquired the press releases nonetheless. Their erstwhile partner, Erle Halliburton, was represented, thus giving Edgerton a slim hope that Southern Sky-Lines might be saved from oblivion. Edgerton reported to McAdoo that Brown's plan for consolidations and extension were meeting significant legal obstacles. "I was not eligible to be present, due to the fact that we had no operations," he wrote. "I understand Halliburton was represented by Mr. Clark. The upshot of the meeting seems to have been that the Bill (Watres) made very poor provision for the forty-cent passenger mail contract. Brown presented some wild idea to take care of the situation. This plan was to issue these contracts on negotiation and without competitive bidding to existing air mail contractors under the clause permitting consolidations and extensions, who would then be supposed to sublet these contracts to the passenger lines. Of course, this is foolish and can be stopped by the Comptroller General."[13]

Foolish or not, this was precisely how Brown wanted to take care of the hard-pressed passenger lines without harming the existing pioneer air mail contractors. William Denning, a Fort Worth attorney based in Washington who represented Thompson Aeronautical and would later lead the fight against Brown's air mail plans, concurred with Edgerton's appraisal and his skepticism about Brown's plan, stating, "I am still more convinced that ever that the scheme proposed by the Postmaster General is not warranted by law."[14]

Brittin managed to arrive in Washington in time for the subsequent deliberations of the subcommittee and noted the problems developing between the passenger lines and the air mail contractors. Carriers such as Thompson and Halliburton were desperate for immediate help yet were in cutthroat competition with one another over the chance of acquiring a contract. This infighting was undermining Brown's careful strategy. Brown had hoped that these businessmen would agree to cooperate in his associative program for the industry and was surprised to find them squabbling among themselves. After witnessing the Monday, May 26 session, Brittin wrote:

> It appears that the Postmaster General was not able to get sufficient authorization in the recent Watres Bill to enable him to put air mail on Passenger Lines without competitive bids. In order to avoid putting up Air Mail Contracts over these routes, to competitive bidders, he has called the principle passenger operators together and advised them that if they could agree among themselves on an equitable apportionment of routes he would grant the Air Mail Contracts under the power given him to extend Air Mail Contracts of lines already carrying air mail. This created immediately a difficult situation as practically all of these passenger carrying lines are competitive and extremely jealous of each other. They realized, however, the seriousness of putting these lines up for bids and are anxious to work out an amicable agreement among themselves. They have been trying to do this for the past two weeks.[15]

Despite the growing parochial conflicts among the ranks of the airlines, Brittin correctly perceived the broad scope of Brown's national plan for air transportation. The postmaster general clearly wanted a logical network of powerful independent carriers competing against one another in a rational manner and in the public interest. "It is the expressed intention of the Postmaster General," Brittin stated, "to develop three competing trans-continental lines; each line distinctly independent of the other and each controlled by one or more of the strongest aviation groups. 'United' through its recent acquisition of the 'N.A.T.' already has a transcontinental air mail line. . . . The other two transcontinental lines to be awarded are route no. 1 (Los Angeles to Atlanta) and route no. 2 (Los Angeles to New York). It is also the intention of the Postmaster General to develop five cross lines, North and South."[16] Brittin understood Brown's plan but questioned its legality, concluding that the plan was conceived "probably in iniquity" and was causing the operators no end of difficulties.[17]

The conferences were rapidly degenerating into shouting matches between the rival claimants. "Thus far little progress has been made," complained Brittin to Northwest's other officers. "'United' which is the strongest group in the country since its recent acquisition of 'N.A.T.' is trying to defeat routes 1 and 2 east of their Dallas–Kansas City–Chicago lines on the plea that these routes will carry business now transported by their Chicago–New York line." United was attempting to acquire Route 10 from Amarillo to St. Louis in the hope that this would be the eastern terminus of one of the new transcontinental routes. As for the central line, Brittin wrote, "Transcontinental Air Transport has claimed route no. 2 and route no. 5 (from Pittsburgh to Norfolk via Washington) with the hope of securing a transcontinental line branching at Pittsburgh to New York and to Washington and Norfolk. This route is considered the best route in the country next to the present 'Boeing'-'N.A.T.' line . . . already in operation. Most of the conflict is centered around these three transcontinental lines." For Brittin, his efforts to secure Route 3 from Omaha to Winnipeg through Minneapolis–St. Paul were succeeding.[18]

The horse trading continued the following day, Tuesday, May 27, with more progress slowly taking place. Brittin noted that his Route 3 was again approved, Route 11 in Montana was given to National Parks, and Route 12 linking Seattle with Vancouver, British Columbia, was awarded to United without argument. No permanent decisions were reached concerning the two transcontinental routes, although the early front runners in the race for the prizes were emerging. Along the southern transcontinental route Eastern Air Transport appeared ready to capture the Atlanta-Dallas portion. The subcommittee agreed that Western Air Express should fly the route from Dallas to Los Angeles. Western's pioneer rights were also recognized along the central transcontinental. Hanshue was assigned the rights to the Los Angeles–Kansas City portion of Route 2, and the purely passenger TAT was assigned the rest of the route to New York. This in essence repeated what Clement Keys had tried to do during his fruitless negotiations with Harris Hanshue in 1928. Erle Halliburton, the vociferous independent, was assigned route 10 from St. Louis to Amarillo with a possible route from Kansas City to Dallas taken from NAT's CAM-3 route. Western also received Routes 8 and 9, Pueblo to Dallas and Pueblo to El Paso, respectively. United States Airways would continue to fly Route 7 from Kansas City to Denver, and United was given Route 4 from Albany to Boston despite the protests of AVCO. It was agreed that PAIC and Clifford Ball would jointly operate Route 5 between Pittsburgh and Norfolk.

These decisions were still preliminary and dependent upon the ultimate judgment of Brown. "There is still some difference of opinion in eastern and western division of Routes No. 1 & 2," Brittin stated. "These are to be negotiated during the next few days and a final report made to (the) Postmaster

General next Tuesday (June 3)."[19] Brittin was hopeful that Tuesday's session would be the last and that new contracts and certificates would be awarded presently with the two new transcontinental services opening around July 1, 1930.[20]

The Tuesday meeting was delayed until the following day, June 4. At 3:15 that afternoon, the representatives of the passenger airlines met with Postmaster General Brown to hear the conclusions presented by MacCracken's operators' committee and to see a map MacCracken had prepared for the occasion. The results of their work left the postmaster general unimpressed. MacCracken's subcommittee had made recommendations on seven of the previously suggested twelve routes but had failed to reach agreements on five, including the two critical transcontinental routes. Undecided was Route 5 from Pittsburgh to Norfolk; Routes 1 and 6, which were combined to form the southern transcontinental from Atlanta to Los Angeles; and Routes 2 and 10, which were linked to make the central transcontinental from New York to Los Angeles.

Brown, Glover, and Wadsworth withdrew to the postmaster general's office to discuss the proposals. Presently, Glover returned to the gathered representatives and "informed them that the Department was somewhat disappointed in their report, inasmuch as they had in effect 'taken all the meat and left the bones.'"[21] Brittin's recollection of the meeting was somewhat more vivid. In a telegram sent to Northwest's headquarters in St. Paul, he recounted, "The operators have been unable to compose their differences and have thrown [the] whole program of [the] assignment of contracts to [the] passenger lines in lap of Postmaster General with [the] request that he act as umpire and make final disposition. He is obviously much displeased at [the] lack of cooperation among operators and states that he is undecided whether to go further or put routes up for competitive bids."[22]

Unable to reach an agreement on the two primary transcontinental routes, the operators attempted to relinquish responsibility to Brown. Writing on behalf of the committee, Hainer Hinshaw addressed the postmaster general: "The Committee has instructed me to advise you that the representatives of all the parties involved in the controversies desire to submit these controversies to you as arbiter and agree to be bound by your decision."[23] They suggested that they present their cases individually to the department at Brown's discretion. It was then suggested that the operators prepare a supplemental report and produce some answers by the time Brown returned to Washington the following week.[24]

The reprise did little good. The squabbling continued as each company jockeyed for position at the expense of its competitors. Western Air Express and Eastern Air Transport were apparently sure they would receive a generous portion of the air mail pie. James Edgerton observed the tumultuous June 6 session. "The report contained five points of controversy," he explained to

McAdoo, "the chief one being the fight between the Aviation Corporation, Western Air Express, and T.A.T. over the route from New York to Los Angeles by way of Kansas City. Western Air apparently intends to settle this by taking over T.A.T. Western Air also expects to get the Southern Transcontinental from Los Angeles to Dallas, and several other routes in the West. It is understood that the report is unsatisfactory to the Postmaster General due to these points of difference. Another fight, by the way, is between Delta and Eastern Air Transport for the route from Birmingham to Dallas–Fort Worth. Eastern Air Transport seems to think it a foregone conclusion that they will get this route."[25]

The major operators were most distressed with Brown's apparent anger with their inability to come to an agreement among themselves. Despite his dislike of competitive bidding, he seemed to favor such action, at least in Brittin's opinion, as the simplest way out of this dilemma. That possibility greatly disturbed TAT, Western, Eastern, and even the contentious Erle Halliburton.[26]

In large part because of the committee's failure to agree on the salient issue presented to them by the postmaster general, Brown was growing increasing wary of his ability to implement his plan as originally envisioned. According to Edgerton, "There is a belief here that the Postmaster General, following his return to the City Thursday, may throw out the report and proceed to settle matters himself."[27] The infighting over the proposed transcontinental route extensions underscored the potential problems of using this method to avoid opening the new routes to competitive bidding and additional appropriations.

Brown decided then that a ruling from the comptroller general was necessary before he could proceed. He selected the proposed extension of Route 3 from Omaha to Winnipeg, allotted to Northwest, as a test case and submitted it to John R. McCarl of the General Accounting Office. "In the meantime, the Postmaster General is having difficulty from another source," Brittin noted in a letter to Northwest's other officers. "The Comptroller General—the sole authority for government disbursements—interprets the extension clauses in the Watres Bill in a rather conservative way. He holds that the Bill gives him no authority to approve disbursements for transcontinental extensions to relatively short air mail contract lines and the only way to settle the question is to submit all transcontinental lines to competitive bidding. He is willing, however, to approve reasonable extensions to existing air mail lines where the new mileage will not exceed the original mileage. This embarrasses the Postmaster General and makes it appear that all these conferences with the operators have been to no purpose whatever. If the situation were not so serious it might be rather amusing."[28]

While Brown awaited the decision, the operators continued to plot. Edgerton was growing increasingly worried that not only were the contracts

going to be awarded to existing powerful carriers but that their supposed partner Erle Halliburton was cutting his own deal. Halliburton's invitation to the
conferences was a clear indication that Brown wished to incorporate Southwest Air Fast Express into its reorganization plans. Nevertheless, Halliburton,
in his blustering way, was bullying the Post Office to ensure that result. Impatient, he threatened to withdraw his support of Brown's plan and openly call
for competitive bidding, despite his personal aversion to this method, even to
the point of threatening legal action to overturn the Watres Act. "Unless
[Brown] takes immediate action under the Watres bill and grants to the air
passenger line air mail contracts in accordance with the provisions thereof,"
Halliburton warned MacCracken, "then I shall be compelled to withdraw my
consent to the Postmaster General to arbitrate the air mail route and demand
not only the privilege of bidding on any additional route but shall take the
necessary legal action to require a cancellation of any extension or route certificate that has been granted under the Watres bill."[29]

A frustrated MacCracken attempted to calm the obstreperous Halliburton
and urged patience until Brown could sort out the various conflicting requests
and determine the impact of the comptroller general's forthcoming decision.[30]
Others saw Halliburton's actions through different eyes. Brice Clagett doubted
the probity of the entire affair, stating, "Halliburton thinks he is inside with
others to get contracts without bidding which I consider illegal."[31]

Halliburton's machinations were also infuriating his supposed partners in
the stillborn Southern Sky-Lines. A resigned and bitter McAdoo saw his careful plans slowly disappearing. "There is no use trying to do anything with this
aviation business unless we can get a chance, and it is on a basis which will
enable us to raise capital," he declared. "I don't see any chance to do that, especially since Halliburton has thrown in his lot with the monopolists[,] . . . but
Halliburton's defection has hurt us badly."[32] Edgerton agreed: "With regard to
Halliburton, your assumptions regarding him are entirely correct. He is the closest
example of an individualist I have run across in some time, and he is certainly
out for Mr. Halliburton. At present, he considers himself one of the 'ins' on this
division of air mail spoils, and as long as he is satisfied that he will be taken care
of, he will play along with the existing companies without giving us a thought."[33]

An angry McAdoo contacted Halliburton, after considerable difficulty, and
reproached him for his apparent duplicity. Countering Halliburton's contention that he had offered McAdoo an opportunity to buy into his company,
McAdoo rejected that claim as irrelevant because it had nothing to do with
Southern Sky-Lines:

> I recall no offer you ever made to me to "come in" except in the very begin-
> ning of operation of your company. . . . I did not take this offer, which had

nothing whatever to do with our subsequent agreement, made here in Los Angeles, to jointly fight for the southern transcontinental route and to *cooperate with each other* until action had been secured.

You did cooperate until the hearing before the Post Office Department last fall. Since that time, however, I have had no evidences whatever of cooperation from you but, on the contrary, you have been playing your own game. I have felt that this was not acting in good faith, in view of our original understanding. . . .

I feel strongly that if you had stood with us and made the fight as we set out to make it, that the outcome eventually would have been very much better for you and all concerned than if you throw your fortunes with the companies which are now dominating the air mail situation of the country.[34]

Halliburton's reply was to renew the offer to purchase into his airline, but no mention was made of Southern Sky-Lines or their previous arrangements. McAdoo reluctantly realized that Halliburton was desperately fighting for the survival of his own airline, no matter what the cost. "Naturally," he stated, "I don't want to stand in the way of your doing what is necessary to save your enterprise because I realize that you have a very large investment and that it ought to be protected. I have felt, however, that if you were going to act independently of me, you ought to have told me so long ago, so that I would have known what course to take, because I would have realized that I must proceed independently of you." McAdoo concluded by saying that there were no hard feelings on his part. "I simply don't want to be put in a false position or to be misunderstood, so go ahead with your own plans, regardless of me."[35] With that, Southern Sky-Lines was laid to rest.

Edgerton urged McAdoo to pursue merger agreements with other independents, such as Delta Air Service, which was sporadically flying passengers from Birmingham to Dallas, as well as completing arrangements with Detroit Aviation, the manufacturing holding company that now controlled Lockheed.[36] Brice Clagett encouraged his father-in-law to pursue Delta as well for they had a legitimate claim for part of the southern transcontinental.[37]

Despite Eastern Air Transport's presumption that they were the line of choice between Atlanta, Birmingham, and Dallas, Delta's vice president and general manager, C.E. Woolman, had heard about the operators' conferences and made a hasty trip to Washington to stake his claim. Unlike Southern Sky-Lines, which had yet to begin operations, or other passenger lines, such as Robertson and Braniff, that had garnered air mail contracts then sold their assets to the holding companies before reentering the airline business, Delta Air Service of Monroe, Louisiana, had been carrying passengers on regular schedule between Birmingham and Dallas–Fort Worth since August 1929 in addition to their profitable crop dusting operations along the lower Mississippi River.[38] Although the conferences were announced in the press, they were by invitation only, so Delta had not heard of the discussions until MacCracken's committee had its preliminary report. Undaunted and desirous of acquiring a contract to keep Delta's nascent passenger service in operation, Woolman came to Washington and presented his case to the postmaster general:

> Like all passenger operations over the entire country, this Company in pioneering commercial aviation in the Central Southern States has lost money. But with faith in the future of aviation, and abundant confidence in the section over which it operates, it has continued operation in the firm belief it would eventually carry mail as well as passengers and thereby promote rapid communication between the two great sections of the South. . . .
>
> In no sense of seeking preferential treatment did we join this conference. Since the passage of the recent amendments to the Air Mail Act we had sought nothing more from the Post Office Department than the right to bid on this service. The present plan of the Post Office Department to extend the Air Mail System by negotiation only came to our attention a week ago, and in the interest of efficient and economical expansion of air transport communication, both mail and passenger, we submit most respectfully to the Postmaster General our claims, along with the other passenger operators represented at this hearing.[39]

In suggesting a merger with Delta, Clagett mentioned to McAdoo that he had discussed the Delta situation with Woolman at some length and was confident that Delta had a solid case. "I believe their claim to this route is very strong," stated Clagett, "and that if they fight hard enough they will get the contract over this route, which would make a very valuable addition to a transcontinental service." He discussed the possibility of either a merger or a cooperative arrangement involving an exchange of stock. "They are to consider this and discuss it further," he concluded.[40]

McAdoo thought either of these two options best to salvage his airline aspirations, or at least derail the proceedings on behalf of the small independents. McAdoo, a prominent attorney, offered the services of his firm to fight for Delta's case if need be. He held out little hope that Southern Sky-Lines alone could win against the large corporation, especially since it had yet to fly. "I don't see that we can do anything else," wrote McAdoo. "I am quite sure that a fight by Southern Sky-Lines alone against the powerfully entrenched interests now in control of the air mail situation, would be futile."[41] These old Progressive, New Freedom sentiments concerning monopoly echoed his father-in-law President Woodrow Wilson and would grow in intensity from other Democratic sources in the months to come.

McAdoo felt that some good could come of the struggle on Delta's behalf if only it forced the recognition of the rights of the small independents.[42] But Delta could not wait for McAdoo's help. Its sudden appearance caught the

Post Office Department unprepared. Delta's service was inconsequential compared with the operations of its rival Eastern Air Transport and had been overlooked. Much to the department's surprise, Delta had a legitimate claim to the pioneer rights along the Atlanta–Dallas route. The company was not well financed and its operations were minuscule in comparison with the major carriers. In fact, its primary source of income was from crop dusting in Louisiana, particularly along the Mississippi delta (hence their name). Delta flew single-engine Travel Air 6000 aircraft capable of carrying four passengers but little more.[43] They were not what Brown had in mind for an airline, but they were qualified.

Brown did not want a plethora of little airlines covering the nation as had happened before the mergers the previous year. With the Depression deepening, there was no room for ill-prepared carriers operating inefficiently and not contributing to the public's welfare. Brown could not build a national air transportation network around little companies. His solution was both practical and controversial. As had happened in 1929, the numerous inefficient airlines were swept up in the general consolidations then sweeping the aviation industry. This made the industry more rational and promoted much greater economies of scale while building airlines of national scope. The postmaster general wished to repeat this scenario once again, this time with Delta.

With this in mind, Brown approached the Aviation Corporation with the suggestion that they acquire Delta Air Service. This move would guarantee that Delta would receive its fair share of the forthcoming southern transcontinental route while preserving Brown's national plan. Despite AVCO's financial and managerial problems, the department still had confidence in its ultimate success, backed as it was by some of New York's largest investment houses. Delta was not enthusiastic about the prospect but understood that this was the only way the airline would survive as the route between Atlanta and Dallas alone was not open to competitive bidding, only extensions, provided the comptroller general agreed. Reluctantly, Delta acquiesced.[44]

On July 25, C.E. Woolman signed an agreement with Gilbert Grosvenor to sell 55 percent of Delta Air Service to AVCO. The Aviation Corporation acquired 16,805 shares for $143,000, approximately $8.50 per share, which was more than fair market value. Delta would operate their passenger service until October, when AVCO would disband the line and purchase the remaining capital assets. Afterward, Woolman and company reformed their crop dusting operation as Delta Air Corporation, flying only occasional passengers.[45]

Delta's timing was poor. On July 24, while Woolman was belatedly drafting the contract to sell out to the Aviation Corporation, Comptroller General McCarl rendered his long anticipated verdict. Brown had hoped that the decision would clarify the law and allow him to proceed unencumbered by the necessity to call for competitive bidding on all new transcontinental routes. The ruling left no one happy.

Brown had asked the comptroller general if the postmaster general had the authority to extend any existing route any distance he deemed necessary in the interest of the public. The test case was Brown's desired intention to extend Northwest Airways' existing route from Chicago and Minneapolis (a distance of 664 miles) north through Grand Forks to Winnipeg, Ontario (a distance of 445 miles) and south from Minneapolis to Omaha through Sioux Falls, South Dakota (a distance of 340 miles). Brown clearly stated that his purpose in issuing such extensions was to cut overhead costs and improve the efficiency of the contract air mail carriers. Short routes were clearly more expensive to operate than long ones. To Brown it made little sense to issue new contracts to competing airlines extending from existing routes because that would cause ruinous competition and inefficiencies in the entire system. In writing to McCarl, Brown underscored his philosophy for air transportation:

> In the administration of the air mail service it has become clearly apparent that short routes of, say 500 miles or 600 miles, established separately and operated by separate companies, do not fit into the general plan of air transportation development. If there ever was a transportation medium which called for long routes, it is that of the air. The cost of operating air mail planes is high and this cost apparently must be borne by the Department in a large measure. To keep an airplane in the air seven to eight hours a day on long routes it is necessary to meet its original cost, maintenance and operating expense, within the life of the plane; this is not possible on short routes, hence the increased cost. I cite this as only one factor in the reason for long routes and possibly fewer operators.
>
> A line north from Minneapolis to Winnipeg would carry by plane certain air mail which is now given to trains; and consequently, by an extension of an existing route into that territory the public would be better served. The proposed extension from Minneapolis to Omaha would provide a connection at Omaha to and from the transcontinental route, which connection is now received via Chicago. It would speed up the delivery of a portion of the air mail now carried on the Chicago–Minneapolis route and permit the same contractor to provide the haul. It would appear to the Department that in view of the representations made by the Department for the enactment of this legislation and in view of the benefits to be derived thereby, it would be in the interest of the public to authorize such extensions.[46]

McCarl's interpretation was different. While he agreed that the Watres Act gave Brown authority to issue contracts, grant certificates, and make extensions, he strictly interpreted the law. Brown had the power in essence to nullify competitive bidding on new contracts with the issuance of route certificates, but only on existing routes. Any extension must be a part of "an existing project of service, rather than itself a major project of service[,] . . . and the extension must necessarily have a subordinate relationship to the existing service, project or route sought to be extended." A small extension to improve the service along a given route was acceptable; a long extension that in essence created a completely new route was not, at least without competitive bidding. McCarl cited Brown's testimony in support of the Watres Act—that some lines "could be very greatly improved by slight additions"—as proof of the department's intention. The Winnipeg and Omaha extensions were not "slight" by McCarl's interpretation, as they involved expanding into new territory. The resulting new route from Omaha to Winnipeg was, by McCarl's definition, a major project that required competitive bidding on a new, separate route.

Confusing the situation even further, McCarl stated that the extension from Minneapolis to Winnipeg was legal if the department had no intention of creating a new route through to Omaha, and in no way could the extension to Omaha be considered an extension of the Chicago-to-Minneapolis route as it was obviously too circuitous and against the postmaster general's earlier testimony. In essence, the ruling was interpreted by the department to mean that no extensions could be made if the distance covered was more than half of the original route. Brown had hit a brick wall.[47]

Brown refused to accept defeat, however. If he could no longer complete his grand transcontinental plan by route extensions, he would do so by competitive bidding, but on his terms. Immediately, after McCarl's ruling, Brown and other Post Office Department officials met with industry leaders to discuss the changed scene. Opening the route to bidding could allow promoters hastily to form unfit airlines to underbid to win contracts. Their goal was to raise as much capital through public subscription to form the airline, win the contract, and then quickly sell off their assets at an enormous profit for themselves, as did many speculative railroads in the nineteenth century. They were not interested in actually running an airline, nor were they willing to absorb the huge startup expenses incurred by the legitimate air mail and passenger carriers. This, at least, was what Brown feared. To circumvent McCarl while staying within the law, Brown discussed the situation with MacCracken, the ad hoc head of the operators' committee. Their solution was simple: write the bidding requirements so restrictively that only legitimate carriers would qualify.

To this end, it was agreed that all potential bidders would have to post a $250,000 bond to ensure compliance with the contract and to demonstrate their good faith. All government contractors by law were required to do so; in fact, all the previous contracts were secured by bonds. The difference this time was the amount. Generally, the average amount required for an air mail route was $11,000 to $16,000. The longest route up to that time required a $100,000 bond. Brown's requirement for a quarter of a million dollars underscored the importance placed on the two new transcontinental routes and sent a clear message that only serious bidders need apply.

The second measure was the most controversial. Acting at Brown's request, William MacCracken analyzed the capabilities of the major airlines and determined that the inclusion of a night-flying requirement would separate the real bidders from the pretenders. The requirement was certainly reasonable if the needs of the Post Office were considered. Aviation's primary advantage over surface delivery is speed, but the speed advantage of aircraft is largely negated if transports are not permitted to fly at night, when the trains can continue to run. Although the Watres Act made no provision for night flying, the department and MacCracken felt that the requirement was justified to guarantee the best service possible. In MacCracken's notes he suggested entertaining bids from airlines whose total route mileage exceeded 2,000 miles, 250 of which were flown at night. He also recommended that the airlines be required to carry a minimum number of passengers and be qualified by the Department of Commerce to do so at night. Furthermore, he wanted to reward the successful bidders by giving generous allowances for the ability to fly at night, having two-way radio equipment installed, and for having passenger seats available in excess of that stipulated in the forthcoming advertisements.[48]

Of great importance, joint bids were to be permitted. In this way several airlines could be joined into one coherent structure over the transcontinental routes. This would allow the department to award one contract to several airlines, in this way giving contracts to deserving passenger lines in certain territories as well as rewarding the existing contractors. The department and the air mail carriers approved of the plan. On August 1, Hainer Hinshaw of American Airways telegraphed his agreement to Earl Wadsworth: "We are satisfied to have [the] advertisement published tomorrow."[49]

The next day, Second Assistant Postmaster General W. Irving Glover issued an announcement and the advertisement for Contract Air Mail Routes 33 and 34, the long-anticipated southern and central transcontinental lines. Reflecting the stipulations just worked out by MacCracken, the announcement stated that it was the intention of the department to encourage the development of passenger transportation by air. "With this end in view," declared Glover, "the advertisements sent out today carry a preference clause providing that the Department may award the contract to the lowest responsible bidder who has owned and operated an air transportation service on a fixed daily schedule over a distance of not less than 250 miles and for a period of not less than six months prior to the advertisement for bids." Night flying was a specific requirement: "In order for a bidder to qualify he must submit evidence indicating he has had at least six months actual experience in operating aircraft on regular night schedules over a route 250 miles or more in length. A bidder on that route must submit evidence with his bid indicating that he can meet the requirements of the Department of Commerce with reference to a Certificate of Authority to operate the route."[50] The department required the installation of advanced navigational and communications equipment and insisted that the schedule be flown at a minimum average speed of 100 miles per hour.

Two payment rates were possible, and all prospective contractors were expected to place two bids accordingly. If the mail load were smaller than twenty-five cubic feet (225 pounds), the contractors would receive no more than 40 cents per mile and would be required to operate aircraft that could carry a minimum of ten passengers. If they were approved to carry mail loads larger than twenty-five cubic feet, they would be paid no more than $1.25 per mile and would be required to have space available for no fewer than seven passengers. In this way, passenger travel was deliberately encouraged and it was hoped that it could also help offset the direct operating costs of the winning contractors. According to the advertisement, only conscientious bidders would be considered: "Air transportation is a serious business venture, requiring sound and conservative financing. The Department will not countenance the promiscuous sale of stock or any undue promotion of the same, where it is evident that such action is unwarranted."[51]

Brown's new plan was to guarantee that only those airlines approved by the department would qualify for the two lucrative contracts. In order to allow the incorporation of several smaller struggling passenger lines, he deliberately permitted joint bids provided at least one, but not all, of the prospective companies met all of the requirements. "In the event a bid is submitted jointly by two companies," stated the announcement, "the experience of either company, or both, will be acceptable insofar as the requirements of the advertisement are concerned." In essence, the two contracts would go only to those who attended the recent conferences. Tiny, underfinanced airlines need not apply.

The conference participants tacitly understood this plan. Brown attempted to distribute the largess as equitably as possible and sought to address the legitimate concerns of all involved as long as it was in the public interest. During the conferences several independent airlines sought and received entry into the proceedings. Though not invited, some, such as Delta Air Service, were clearly qualified and were therefore admitted into the discussions and a settlement reached. Brown was intent on placating all the bona fide carriers despite their contrary behavior, including Erle Halliburton and his Southwest Air Fast Express. Halliburton's methods were unorthodox and controversial, but the postmaster general's plan was as fair as humanly possible given the restrictions of the law, its interpretation by the comptroller general, and, most important, the restraints of the very limited federal budget during the deepening crisis of the Depression.

Armed with the new advertisement, and comfortable in the knowledge that they were the carrier designated by the conference to cover the southern transcontinental route, American Airways' representatives turned their attention to preparing their bid for CAM-33. Eastern Air Transport had earlier assumed that it would have the rights to the Atlanta to Dallas–Fort Worth section of the route. The unexpected arrival of Delta Air Service upset the company's plans, and the department agreed that Delta indeed had a fair claim. However, to conform to the postmaster general's plan, Delta merged with American in order to provide continuity and unified management along the entire route. Other problems emerged and were dealt with by the department.

While the airline operators were deliberating during their conferences with the Post Office, Thomas Hudson McKee, representing Wedell Williams Air Service of New Orleans, Louisiana, gained access to the meeting and presented his company's application for an air mail contract. Despite the Interdepartmental Committee on Airways' clear decision to route the southern transcontinental mail line from Birmingham to Dallas without diverting through New Orleans, McKee attempted to pressure the department to reverse the decision. He petitioned the Post Office on June 2, 1930, asking that Wedell Williams be considered, stating that his company had been flying for more than one year and, as of the day before, was operating a passenger line from New Orleans to Dallas and Fort Worth through Shreveport.[52]

Wedell Williams's two lengthy petitions were well argued but failed to sway the department into changing its planned route. Any such alteration would have skewed the direct route and left the department with the indirect and slow service it had been trying so hard to eliminate. The department felt it best not to alter its proposed route, despite receiving considerable political pressure to the contrary. Nevertheless, Brown and Glover quietly began negotiations with American Airways to do something on Wedell Williams's behalf—probably buy the airline out at a generous rate, as they had done with Delta. That nothing came of it was through a failure of American to cooperate, not from the department's unwillingness to address the small independent's needs. This failure would come back to haunt Brown.

Of greater immediate importance to the success of Brown's plans was the crescendo of complaints coming from Erle Halliburton. Throughout the summer Halliburton had cajoled or threatened the department for a contract as he had throughout the previous year. His ostensible partner, William Gibbs McAdoo, had correctly recognized that Halliburton was going to fight for his own selfish goals regardless of earlier promises and that Halliburton would let nothing stand in his way. Despite Halliburton's protestations to the contrary, he had every intention of abandoning McAdoo if the opportunity arose.

On March 3, while the department was fighting for the Watres Act, Halliburton wrote to the department requesting a route through his territory in Oklahoma and Texas and assumed for himself his earlier joint bid with Southern Sky-Lines. "I am ready and prepared with ample equipment and finances," he stated, "to begin the transportation of air mail in accordance with my proposal of October 15, as amended, at $2.10 per pound for mail moving between New York City and Los Angeles by way of either St. Louis or Atlanta."[53] McAdoo had no knowledge of this letter but was nonetheless convinced, correctly, that his partner had turned against him.

For more than a year, both the department and the air mail contractors had attempted to placate the persistent Oklahoman with little success. Representatives of the three large holding companies attempted to deal with Halliburton and remove his nettlesome presence from the scene. He refused to go quietly. National Air Transport, with Colonel Henderson now working for United, offered him part of CAM-2 between Kansas City and Dallas, but he refused, wanting a longer route. This upset the operators' plans because they had understood that once Halliburton had received a contract the Commerce Department and the Post Office would "absolutely forbid his flying over other mail contracts."[54]

To Daniel Shaeffer's request that Halliburton play ball with TAT and the other airlines, Halliburton tersely replied, "The Post Office Department should have acted in this manner more than a year ago and if I could have secured the cooperation of those parties who now want me to cooperate, this matter could have long since been adjusted." He threatened to upset Brown's entire scheme if he did not get his way, telling Schaeffer, "Unless I have definite assurance that there is to be an immediate adjustment I shall demand the right to bid on all extensions and new routes and am in a better position to do this than anyone else in the business."[55] Halliburton wanted no part of TAT: "I do not intend to merge with, become connected with, or associated with T.A.T. who prostituted [the] names of Lindbergh and Earhart to [the] general public and then asked tax payers to pay for such prostitution."[56]

Halliburton had no need for TAT because he was completing a deal with American Airways. At the instigation of the Post Office Department, Hainer Hinshaw and American approached Halliburton with a quiet offer to bid jointly with him for the southern transcontinental route. Both parties were aware that Halliburton's airline was not qualified to bid by itself, as it did not possess the requisite night-flying experience. Several secret meetings were conducted by Hinshaw with "Mr. Jones," as Halliburton was referred to in telegrams, at

SAFE Ways' headquarters in Tulsa in late June and early July. Immediately afterward, Halliburton sent his explosive telegram of July 9 to William MacCracken, just to remind all parties of his presence by threatening once again to demand competitive bidding.

Nevertheless, the petulant Halliburton was reaching an understanding with the department and American Airways. Brown made the situation clear to him that his airline was no different from the other small independent passenger airlines the Watres Act was designed to support and that method of support was not going to be any different for Halliburton. The department strongly suggested that he agree to a takeover of his line at generous terms, thus ensuring ample rewards for his efforts and for those of his stockholders while preserving the economies of scale inherent in the operation of the southern transcontinental line by one company. By late July, Halliburton had agreed and, in the words of McAdoo, had thrown in his lot with the "monopolists." Stated Hinshaw to AVCO president F.G. Coburn, "Halliburton just telephoned me that he would be in Washington in two or three days and that we would go to New York together and talk to you about a consolidation or merger."[57]

One month later, Halliburton completed his deal with the Aviation Corporation and agreed to file a joint bid for the southern transcontinental route with AVCO's Robertson Aircraft Corporation subsidiary. On August 23, two days before the bids were to be opened by the Post Office, American Airways signed a contract with Southwest Air Fast Express and Erle Halliburton. The deal for the joint bid involved the lending of $250,000 of Liberty bonds to Robertson and SAFE Way with the understanding that, should the two companies be the winning bidders, they would immediately assign the contract to a new company organized by American Airways to be known as Southern Air Fast Express. Ten thousand shares of stock were to be issued and divided into two equal lots of five thousand. American would pay $1.4 million in cash for SAFE Ways' five thousand shares and, at the end of three months, maintain an option for the remaining five thousand at a price of $569,000. This latter amount would serve to cover American's cost of the Liberty Bonds it lent to Robertson and to give the new company approximately $300,000 of working capital.[58] "Halliburton finally made a deal with Aviation Corporation by which a joint bid was made in the names of both companies," observed Colonel Brittin of Northwest, "but with a private understanding that if they secured the contract Halliburton would sell out to Aviation Corporation at a fixed figure."[59]

Indeed, the joint proposal from Robertson and Halliburton were the only bids received by the department when the bids were opened on August 25. As a result and as planned, they won the route award for CAM-33 at the 100 percent of the maximum rate of $1.25 per pound per mile allowed by the Watres Act.[60] Three weeks later Robertson Aircraft Corporation and Southwest Air Fast Express signed their contract with the Post Office Department immediately placing their earlier contract with AVCO into effect.[61] American Airways now had control of the new route through the newly formed Southern Air Fast Express. Just as important for the air mail contractors and the Post Office, Erle Halliburton was finally removed from the scene.

With the southern transcontinental route settled, all that remained was the awarding of the central transcontinental line. The operators and the department during their recent conferences had decided among themselves that both Transcontinental Air Transport and Western Air Express had prior claims to the territory. Daniel Shaeffer outlined the important aspects of the debate to TAT's Executive Committee: "For the central transcontinental . . . it was the desire of the Post Office Department that this be operated by one company, and as T.A.T. and the Western Air Express were the two important factors operating large mileage on this route, it was the Postmaster General's suggestion that, if possible, these two lines consolidate or in some manner work out an operating arrangement to that end."[62]

When the operators' conference opened in late May 1930, one of the first issues raised by the Post Office was the combination of these two lines into one long, transcontinental air carrier. Two years earlier, Clement Keys had actively pursued Harris Hanshue with this very proposition but was rejected because Western had its own plans for transcontinental service. Postmaster General Brown was not to be denied, however, as he sought to rescue the struggling TAT through a merger and a mail contract. Both companies were well run, and Western had grown rich through the largess of the department. Brown felt it was only proper that Western share the wealth. Western disagreed. The airline was one of the "$3 boys" and had profited greatly from its mail contracts. It had expanded from Los Angeles eastward to Kansas City on one route and to El Paso on another. Western had no desire to merge with anyone, unless it maintained control.

Reluctantly, Hanshue and company listened to the department's suggestion to forge a relationship with Transcontinental Air Transport, but they did not have to like it. Transcontinental was in dire straits, its stock value rapidly declining. Its proposal to sell out at book value was not well received. Just as the operators' conferences were opening, J.A. Talbot telegraphed his partner Hanshue on May 21 regarding the opinion of Western's board of directors:

Had [a] talk with [Harry] Chandler last night. . . . We are unwilling to deal on basis indicated by your talk with Shaeffer and think after full discussion of matter that basis of exchange in view of fact that we will have responsibility of management should be on five to one. Also that banker's options of 160,000 shares should be canceled leaving status as at present. Do not see how Shaeffer's associates can possibly figure on basis of book value as earning value and management must be taken into consideration. Chandler very strong in convictions and I agree we are willing to sit in on this situation but only on basis that Western and Western management shall control this being dictated by pure business reasons and also [the] fact that all interested have great pride in success [of] your company and will not surrender control to any other situation but would rather stay independent. Chandler and I leave matter in your hands.[63]

A concerned Hanshue petitioned Postmaster General Brown, arguing that Western Air Express had pioneer rights on both the central and southern transcontinental routes and that TAT's proposal to split the central route together with AVCO's assumption of all of the southern route would drastically cut into their profits. Hanshue reminded Brown of Western's well-earned interests in its territory and the risks the airline took in developing aviation in the West and Southwest and recited its excellent management and profitability. Not mentioned was the fact that the profits were made at an exorbitant payment rate Brown would no longer accept. Hanshue argued that Western was most profitable and efficient because it concentrated its operations form one central location, Los Angeles, and developed an interlocking, mutually supporting network of routes. For these pioneering efforts, "Western Air Express confidently expected to receive, and now requests that it be granted air mail haul on the Central Transcontinental route . . . and the Southern Transcontinental route. . . . This grant, we believe, is justified by our occupation and operation of these lines and the proof of our ability to maintain a schedule as yet unattempted by any other operator."[64]

Western Air Express, Hanshue continued, was willing to entertain reasonable proposals from other airlines provided the offers were based on the actual values of the companies involved. Discussions with TAT were under consideration but would remain in limbo until after the two transcontinental routes were awarded. Stated Hanshue, "We have gone so far as to tentatively agree to two suggested alternative compromises—neither of which we consider justifiable in the face of all the facts." Specifically, Western was reluctant to share the central route with TAT or sell out its portion of the southern route to AVCO.[65]

The operators during their conferences in Washington had recommended that only 340 of Western's 3,900 miles of passenger airways be left untouched. To this Hanshue took great exception. He wanted to maintain control of all of his routes and to preserve the operational control of his western regional airline. "We believe we have earned the right to air mail haul on every mile of airway we are flying," he declared. "We know that the great mass of people throughout the territory we serve are satisfied with the manner in which we have served them, and are eager to see this service perpetuated as a western enterprise, financed, controlled, developed, and operated in the west unhampered by the suzerainty of eastern capital."

Hanshue suggested that instead of dividing his company, TAT and AVCO be given additional routes or schedules in their own territories at profitable rates. Any other solution, Hanshue stated, would be hotly contested.[66]

Hanshue was most unhappy with the present course of events. Western was feeling great pressure from the Post Office Department, through the ministrations of TAT and AVCO, to hammer out a compromise solution. Hanshue had no desire to give up control of his routes or to sell off the assets of any of his routes. "For us to concede to these proposals," wrote Hanshue to Harry Chandler, "would so greatly restrict our operations and earning capacity as to reduce us to a very subordinate position in the industry." Unfortunately, he was running headlong into Brown's plan for a national airline network of strong, independent, competing lines. Brown wanted three strong national transcontinental lines; Hanshue wanted the nation served by strong regional lines, similar to the situation with the railroads. "The arguments against this sort of setup are the same that have operated to prevent transcontinental rail systems," reasoned Hanshue, "that is greater economy and more efficient operation can be had by concentration in a natural territory rather than elongated single tracks.[67]

Hanshue's argument, while stating what appeared to be obvious, overlooked the fact that the situation with the railroads was artificial, a product of much litigation and regulation stemming back to the late nineteenth century. Contrary to Hanshue's contention that regional concentration was more efficient, a national transcontinental scheme, with centralized management controlling the entire line without interruption was inherently more efficient. The railroads had earlier attempted to forge a national system but had been rebuked by federal actions, specifically the Northern Securities case of 1904. By employing the Sherman Antitrust Act of 1890, the court blocked the formation of a giant holding company between the Union Pacific, Burlington, Great Northern, and Northern Pacific, fearing that such a national combination would reduce competition. It would have been able to do so because of its inherent economies of scale and greater efficiency. This the opponents of monopoly successfully fought to prevent, thereby creating an artificial market. This Hanshue did not understand.

Transcontinental Air Transport was fighting hard for its very survival. Brown appreciated these efforts and saw the logic behind combining the expertise inherent in both organizations into one powerful force. It was he who pushed so hard behind the scenes for a merger during the operators' conferences in the spring of 1930.

Transcontinental, losing prodigious amounts of money each day while watching the value of its company steadily decline, was anxious to secure a life-saving air mail contract at almost any cost. Company officials were insistent that TAT's value was higher than Western was claiming and were pressing Western for a deal, as they correctly understood that the department was willing to accept a joint bid provided the winners formed a separate operating company.[68]

Western already had valuable contracts and were it not for the powerful presence of the postmaster general in forging the new legislation and dictating the terms of its implementation, they would have continued happily as one of the $3 boys. Brown was determined to forge three separate, independently owned transcontinental lines and was not about to allow Western's intransigent claims for sections of both routes to interfere with his grand scheme.

Following the initial collapse of talks, Brown persuaded all the interested parties to return to the bargaining table with the unwritten promise that they would secure the winning contract. Transcontinental agreed to transfer its appropriate tangible assets at their depreciated, not book, value. Any differences in values were to be made up in cash. The new company would consist of $2.15 million in assets from Western, $2 million in assets from TAT, plus a cash contribution of $144,000 from TAT. An estimated working capital of approximately $700,000 would be subscribed, bringing the total value of the new enterprise to $5 million.

After six weeks of intense sessions, Hanshue understood Brown's position and ultimate coercive power and reluctantly began efforts to form an arrangement with TAT and AVCO along the lines prescribed by the conferences. Of greatest significance, TAT and Western Air Express agreed to terms for the creation of a new company to bid on the central transcontinental. On July 15, 1930, Transcontinental and Western Air, better known as TWA, was formed.[69]

While the ink was drying on the contract, a third party laid claim to a part of the central transcontinental route. George Hann and the Pittsburgh Aviation Industries Corporation, which played such an important role in the affairs of the Aviation Corporation, were also desperate to participate in the forthcoming route awards. Pittsburgh Aviation had been instrumental in the construction of the Pittsburgh-Butler Airport and had successfully lobbied the Pennsylvania state legislature for funds to develop airways throughout the state. With their keen interest in aviation and the fact that Pennsylvania was astride the eastern terminus of the proposed central transcontinental, Hann and PAIC fought hard for inclusion. They had an argument. Although PAIC had yet to operate an airline, it conducted commercial operations from Pittsburgh. The company's claim was not strong, but it was in fact better than TAT's. Because TAT sent its passengers by train from New York City to Port Columbus, Ohio, it had no operating experience in Pennsylvania. George Hann made his position clear to Daniel Shaeffer of TAT and the Pennsylvania Railroad:

> As I very forcefully told you and Mr. Cuthell in Washington one afternoon, this Pittsburgh company is not a stepchild and we must insist upon working out our own problems, which means that in any final determination of this transcontinental line, T.A.T., Western Air Express, and ourselves have got to sit around the table and work it out.
>
> … The matter has been clearly presented on two occasions to our Executive Committee and I am but voicing our unanimous opinion when I say that we consider that P.A.I.C. had preempted more than anyone else the territory between Columbus and New York, and we are going to make every effort to protect our interests in this territory. Also we have kept the Post Office Department advised of our work since the very beginning, looking to the very situation which now exists.[70]

Hann's logic prevailed, particularly after direct meetings with Walter Brown. Transcontinental and Western signed an additional agreement on August 22, 1930, this time merging PAIC with TWA. The new company already had agreed to authorize 1 million shares at ten dollars per share. Half of this originally was to be divided between the two companies with the other half held in reserve. With the inclusion of PAIC, TAT and Western reduced their holdings to 237,500 shares each, extending 25,000 shares to PAIC in return for half ownership in the Pittsburgh-Butler Airport and a promise to promote aviation in Pittsburgh. The new company also acquired PAIC's rights to the Harrisburg airport.[71] After this, George Hann withdrew from the board of AVCO to concentrate his efforts on the new transcontinental line.

As had AVCO through Robertson and SAFE Way on the southern route, TAT and Western Air submitted their bid on the central transcontinental line after Second Assistant Postmaster General Glover called for bids on August 2, 1930. This fact did not please some people. A disgruntled William Gibbs McAdoo summarized the feelings of the few remaining small independents in his commentary to his friend W.M. Kiplinger:

> Recently the Postmaster General has advertised certain air mail routes to Los Angeles, routes for which I have vigorously contended. His advertisements restrict the bidding to favorites and absolutely shut out worthy competitors, in violation of the letter, as well as the spirit of the act. It is really quite raw and I am wondering if he can get away with it.
>
> … As a result, a few monopolists and pets of the Department will get the business unless someone should contest the Postmaster General's authority. The Western Air Express, in which Harry Chandler is largely interested and of which Hoover's son is a prominent officer, will undoubtedly, get most of the "bacon."[72]

McAdoo continued to refuse to acknowledge the fact that he never started his airline and the remaining independents were too underfinanced to undertake an enterprise of the magnitude requested by the department. These little companies could not raise sufficient funds to post the required $250,000 bond, much less develop and operate a national transportation system effectively. Nevertheless, he still objected. As for Harry Chandler, the powerful publisher of the *Los Angeles Times*, he was indeed an influential force in politics, but no more so than the illustrious McAdoo. Herbert Hoover Jr. was serving with Western, but not as a "prominent officer." Reflecting his father's interest in technology in general and radio in particular, Hoover had been hired not for his familial ties but for his acknowledged expertise in communications. In fact, he was in charge of radio development for all of Western Air Express. Despite this, he was eventually forced to resign.[73]

The protests mounted, however. After the call for bids was published, several of the small passenger lines not included in the recent operators' conferences threatened to take legal action, particularly over the recently imposed night-flying provision, which, they correctly felt, was designed to preclude them from bidding and would result in their eventual demise. The independents also hinted that they would ask for a Justice Department antitrust investigation or a congressional inquiry into the probity of the advertisements if their complaints were not heard. Of greatest importance, they threatened to ask for an injunction against Comptroller General McCarl to prevent the payment on the contracts if they were rejected solely because of the night-flying requirement.[74]

Much to the Post Office Department's displeasure, these independents submitted a bid. When Second Assistant Postmaster Glover opened the sealed bids in his office on August 25, he was surprised to find that TWA's bid of 97.5 percent of the maximum rate was bettered by a new company's offer to carry the mail for only 64 percent of the maximum rate. While TAT, Western Air Express, and the Aviation Corporation had been carefully working with the department in preparing offers tailored to Brown's requirements, a new corporation, known as United Avigation, had been quickly formed for the same purpose.

Unbeknown to PAIC, other aviation interests in Pittsburgh were anxious to acquire a mail contract, particularly Pittsburgh Airways, a small struggling passenger line that was operating a tenuous schedule to Philadelphia and New York with just three aircraft. Backed by wealthy businessman and company president Oliver Kaufman, Pittsburgh Airways leapt at the opportunity to save itself with a mail contract. Kaufman contacted another small local carrier, Ohio Air Transport of Youngstown, as well as W.A. Letson, the owner of United States Airways, a small passenger carrier operating between Kansas City and Denver. To complete this new holding company, Alfred D. Chandler, the sales manager at Bellanca Aircraft, and New York banker Sherman Adams agreed to participate in the new venture. On August 7, 1930, they met with the board of directors of United States Airways at the Athletic Club in Kansas City, where they first discussed the proposed merger and subsequent bid.[75]

On August 18, the executives of the respective companies formed United Avigation for the express purpose of securing the central transcontinental route. They approved the issuance of 490,000 out of an authorized issue of 2 million shares of common stock—enough, it was hoped, to raise $1 million to finance the new enterprise, all contingent upon winning the contract.[76] With this agreement in hand, United Avigation placed its bid with the Post Office Department.

The department was not happy with this unexpected bid. Letson had participated in the operators' conferences and knew the postmaster general's plan. He grew increasingly uneasy when he realized that his action had angered the department and could possibly threaten his existing contract, although no threats were made. Nevertheless, he took immediate steps to distance himself from the controversy, expecting only that his bid be fairly examined. When the *Baltimore Sun* published an article concerning the protests of the independent passenger lines, Letson immediately telegraphed, stating that he had no knowledge of the story nor the complainants.[77]

An angry Glover suspected duplicity and was anxious to ensure that all of the offers were fairly examined. He had several articles from the Pittsburgh press quoting United Avigation as willing to fight. "Am enclosing clipping from Pittsburgh paper," Glover wrote Chase Gove. "Looks as if they also wanted to be a second story man or men. Of course I know you would not accept any strengthening documents to the bids, but wanted to be sure." Glover wanted Gove and Earl Wadsworth to examine all of the bids and prepare them for examination by Brown "Have Earl go through the three bids and have their failings all lined up for the P.M.G. when he gets home," he stated. "Be sure to save clipping and telegram."[78]

The day following the opening of the bids, Glover departed Washington for a trip to Seattle. Brown had been out of town for several days as well. No more than one hour after Glover left, First Assistant Postmaster General Arch Coleman called Chase Gove and requested that all of the bids be turned over to him on the direction of an unnamed person at the White House for examination by the attorney general. Gove complied and was told by Coleman not to mention it to Glover. He wired Glover on the train anyway and informed the second assistant about the peculiar request. Glover placated an anxious Gove, telling him he had already discussed the matter with the White House and that, although the postmaster general would not be pleased "when he finds out that any action has been taken before he gets back and has a chance to see them . . . that's not our funeral."[79]

After examination by the attorney general's office, the files were returned later that afternoon. Immediately afterward, at 3:15, Chester Cuthell of TAT and William MacCracken representing Western Air Express called on Gove to examine the United Avigation bid, inquiring as to how much time they had to file a protest. Gove informed them that no decision would be made until Brown and Glover returned, which would give them sufficient time to file their brief. A suspicious Gove wondered whether there was any connection, stating, "Whether they had anything to do with the matter being handled as above indicated, I do not know and, of course, you can guess about that better than I can."[80]

Regardless of the source of the inquiry, MacCracken immediately went to work searching for flaws in the United Avigation bid. Just two days before the bids were opened MacCracken prepared a brief for the postmaster general reminding him of the superior position of the joint TAT–Western Air Express bid. He reminded Brown that the advertisement for bids allowed the postmaster general wide discretion in determining the fitness of a bidding company. Brown was empowered to award the contract to the lowest responsible bidder, and it was left to him to define "responsible."

The net worth of Transcontinental and Western was $9 million in excess of liabilities with cash assets in excess of $3.7 million, backed by the largest banks and most prominent financial minds in the country. The companies were certainly financially responsible and more than capable of developing and operating a transcontinental line based on the vast experience of their respective personnel who created and operated their large airlines. They also maintained their own airports, weather service, and radio communication departments, all developed at great expense in the interest of safety and efficiency. Transcontinental had night-flying experience, gained when it acquired Maddux while Western was operating 1,000 miles of its normal route at night, 660 miles of which were flown with the U.S. Mail. In addition, both airlines had the latest aircraft and equipment and a strong, well-trained staff. Such was the well-developed nature of the two companies that MacCracken boldly stated that if they received the contract, they could "within five days thereafter commence the carriage of mail over the entire route."[81]

Having established their strong economic and technological position with respect to the central transcontinental, MacCracken turned his attention to dissecting United Avigation. Among the seventeen objections, MacCracken stated that the bid itself was improperly addressed and not sealed in accordance with proper procedure. More important, although United proposed to start service with a fleet of twelve powerful tri-motored aircraft, the company did not own these aircraft or the infrastructure at that time. The existence of their company was completely dependent upon receiving the contract. Although TWA was also formed for that sole reason, its assets were to be drawn from two viable, nationally operating companies. MacCracken claimed that United Avigation's bond was defective because the insurers only guaranteed half of the required $250,000 and that it was incorrectly altered and witnessed. Of great significance, MacCracken claimed that United Avigation was not financially responsible, as it had no capital assets. The $1 million proposed for the company had yet to be raised because that sum was solely contingent upon winning the contract. The company did not even exist until after the announcement of bids was made, something the department abhorred. In essence, MacCracken claimed United was a paper company. Most important, the prospective bidder by its own admission had no night-flying experience. This, MacCracken hoped, would completely invalidate United Avigation's petition.[82]

After "a very satisfactory conference with Mr. Wadsworth," MacCracken filed the protest with the department on August 29, safe in the knowledge that he had the department's support. Both he and officials from TAT thought that now the road was clear.[83]

United Avigation did not give up. Through United States Airways, which flew into Denver, Letson and company approached Colorado senator Lawrence Phipps. Phipps, who had helped shepherd the Watres Act through the Senate, lent a sympathetic ear, insisting either that the transcontinental contract be given to United Avigation or that an arrangement be made on behalf of this Colorado airline.[84] Richard Robbins was already urging Phipps to continue to support the postmaster general and reminded him that TWA was the only responsible bidder and the only one on that central line that could start service immediately. United Avigation was a paper creation and would need many months to acquire the necessary aircraft and equipment before starting service.[85] These arguments were enough to temper Phipps's attacks.

George Hann, speaking for PAIC, was growing nervously impatient with the incessant delays from the Post Office Department. With Brown out of the office attending conferences and political affairs in this difficult election year, Hann was worried that even the large airlines might not survive the autumn. He suggested drastic action. Calling for Hanshue, MacCracken, Robbins, and others to pressure the administration, even suggesting going so far as petitioning the president, Hann urged his partners to force a decision:

> It is financial suicide to continue carrying passengers as we are going today, and, with winter coming along, there is going to be a very sorry picture for those companies which attempt to force this passenger carrying business throughout the next six months.
>
> I think it should be very strongly stated to Mr. Brown that he must take the responsibility of giving aviation a solar plexus blow, or else feed out a little nourishment at this time. I do not think that we should stop with Mr. Brown, but

that we should go also to President Hoover, and other members of the cabinet, and make this a real issue for cabinet discussion.

   . . . If this mid transcontinental air mail contract is not awarded on the present bid, and on a compensatory basis, I am going to recommend to my people that they withdraw entirely from this aviation development, salvage what cash they can and call it a day. . . . It is time to go to the mat, and we have nothing to lose but everything to gain.[86]

Brown listened. On October 1, 1930, Transcontinental and Western were awarded the central transcontinental route despite their higher bid of 97.5 percent of the maximum rate.[87] They promptly requested and were granted permission to sublet the route to their joint TWA subsidiary on October 24.[88]

While negotiations were continuing with the department, PAIC helped Brown solve another problem. For months, Clifford Ball had let it be known that his airline was for sale. He understood that Brown was not going to allow his little airline to continue with its lucrative but irrelevant air mail contract. Ball played AVCO off of TAT and PAIC until Brown made it clear to AVCO that a merger between Ball and Pittsburgh made more sense geographically.[89] After tense negotiations, with Ball's contract set to expire at midnight on October 25, a deal was struck with Postmaster General Brown's approval whereby Ball sold his airline to PAIC for $137,000. The following month the company's name was changed to Pennsylvania Air Lines.

Finally, on October 25, numerous officials gathered at Newark Airport just outside New York City for the inauguration of Transcontinental and Western Air's first regularly scheduled transcontinental air mail and passenger service along CAM-34. Among the passengers were Walter Brown, Irving Glover, Earl Wadsworth, Harris Hanshue, J. Cheever Cowdin, and Amelia Earhart. They boarded one of TWA's two Ford 5-AT Tri-Motors and one Fokker F-14. Almost thirty-six hours later, six passengers and six hundred pounds of mail reached Los Angeles.[90] Official opening of the route came just ten days after American Airways inaugurated its transcontinental line, through their Southern Air Fast Express subsidiary along CAM-33, and five weeks before Boeing Air Transport and National Air Transport followed suit with through passenger service.

Transcontinental, Western, and the Aviation Corporation had one more bit of business to attend to before Postmaster General Brown would settle the transcontinental route questions. Despite its stout arguments to the contrary, Western was forced to accede to the recommendations of the operators' committee and to the department and relinquish its claim to the southern route. Brown insisted that Western sell its property along the route that it had just recently acquired with the purchase of Standard Air Lines.

The original contract called for a payment to Western of $300,000 for these assets, an amount Western thought far too low. A clause permitted Western to request $500,000, provided the postmaster general made the final appraisal and decision.[91] This came as a surprise to Brown, who upon his return split the difference between the two parties and advised them that the price would be $400,000.

Believing it had invested at least $1 million, Western remained unhappy, but it was in no position to argue. An audit had set the value of the Standard properties at $290,000. Other details of the merger were equally contentious as Western was also forced to transfer its valuable in Alhambra airport in Los Angeles to TWA and was asked to cover additional unexpected expenses. Furthermore, in order to free Western and the future TWA from any problems of interlocking directorships, AVCO, the largest owner of Western stock, sold its holdings in Western to TWA. The department forced Western to spend $1,115,500 to reacquire these twenty thousand shares for TWA at $55 a share— $35 above the market price—thereby ensuring the independence of the new airline but at Western's considerable expense.[92] In all, Western was compelled to spend $1.4 million to complete the various transactions involved with the two transcontinental routes by the end of the year.[93]

By mid-December AVCO was demanding its money. The terms of its contract with TAT and Western required the latter parties to pay American Airways for Western stock immediately after winning the central transcontinental route and opening service. Transcontinental and Western Air was now flying. More than six weeks had passed, but TAT and Western had yet to pay. The reason was simple: the award had been challenged and there now existed the distinct possibility that it would be invalidated.

United Avigation had played one last card in the hope of snatching the award at the eleventh hour. On October 3, a dejected W.A. Letson wrote a terse letter to Walter Brown announcing the dissolution of United Avigation. Letson was "returning home disillusioned" after the trials of the past two months. Nevertheless, he and his partners had earlier threatened to challenge the legality of the night-flying clause and thereby the entire award process if they lost. This they now did.

They turned to Comptroller General John McCarl for a ruling on the legality of the bidding process. McCarl, the nemesis of Brown and the department's air mail plans, looked at the award for CAM-34 with a suspicious eye. On October 9, 1930, he asked Brown for information that would support awarding the central transcontinental route to the highest bidder rather than United Avigation.[94]

In a detailed report delivered on October 23, Brown outlined his reasons. Brown concentrated his argument on the fact that United Avigation did not have the requisite night-flying experience and was not a responsible bidder.

He also reiterated the numerous other points made by MacCracken in August, when Western challenged United's bid. McCarl was not persuaded. He ruled that the night-flying requirement was, in fact, illegal, because it existed nowhere in the law. McCarl quoted Brown's own Watres Act, which mentioned only that the prospective contractors be "responsible" and have "operated an air transportation service on a fixed daily schedule over a distance of not less than 250 miles prior to the advertisement for bids."

He concluded that the illegality of this clause acted to restrict competition and therefore any contract awarded under these conditions was invalid—unless there were mitigating circumstances. McCarl suggested that Brown provide additional corroborating evidence that United Avigation was not responsible. "Perhaps an enumeration of such defects," remarked McCarl, "will afford this office a better understanding of the matter."[95]

An exasperated Brown once again provided additional information to the comptroller general. This time he emphasized the numerous other deficiencies on the United Avigation bid while disingenuously stating that it was not his intention "to give the impression" that their bid was rejected only because they had failed "to show the night flying experience prescribed in the specifications." Brown explained in detail the numerous flaws in United Avigation's proposal, particularly pointing out that there was no evidence that the three operating companies of United were actually owned by United. Also, Brown stated that United Avigation could not legally bid because its existence was contingent upon receiving the contract, and then only if it could guarantee a profit. The three existing component companies did not bid and would not have been bound for the faithful performance of the contract. These factors, Brown argued, compelled the department to conclude that United Avigation was not qualified to bid:

> At the time its bid was submitted, the Avigation Company had a bare, naked corporate existence, its assets consisting solely of an executory contract for the exchange of stock with the three alleged subsidiaries. Not only would the Government have been exposed to the risk of immediate default of any contract entered into with this company in such circumstances, but, since the Company had no assets beyond conditional promises to subscribe to stock, it would have been left without recourse to recover for the default except against the Company's securities.
>
> The Department knows of no way to make it clearer that the United Avigation Company was not a responsible bidder within the meaning of the law.[96]

Brown also informed McCarl that a subsequent conversation with Letson of United States Airways revealed that United Avigation had no intention of operating the entire length of the route, only from New York to Kansas City. It hoped to sublet the remaining route to Western Air Express, though no discussions with Western had ever occurred. Western had performed the necessary financial analysis and had concluded that its own 97.5 percent bid with TAT was the lowest possible to still make a profit. Flying the route as a subcontractor at less than that amount was not economically feasible. "It is the Department's opinion, therefore," stated Brown, "that had an award been made to the United Avigation Company, that company would have been compelled to default on the contract from the beginning if for no other reason than that it could have made no arrangement for service over the western portion of the route."[97]

United had no tangible assets, no equipment, and no staff to operate such a complex operation. The planned financial arrangement to raise $1 million to provide for this and the entire route infrastructure was grossly inadequate for the task. The Watres Act was designed to prevent irresponsible operators from exploiting and wasting taxpayers' money and "to avert the discredit which would inevitably fall upon the entire aviation industry as a result of defaults and failures which would be bound to follow the award of contracts to irresponsible concerns." In the opinion of the department, concluded Brown, these additional facts "leave not the slightest doubt that the United Avigation Company was not a responsible bidder."[98] McCarl finally agreed.

On January 10, 1931, the comptroller general responded to Brown. "The facts now reported by you, together with those heretofore supplied by you, constituting the reasons for not accepting the low bidder . . . ," concluded McCarl, "appear such as to justify this office in not further questioning the administrative action in rejecting such a low bid."[99] The award was legal. In fact, this ruling validated all of Brown's actions in restructuring the nation's air transportation system. McCarl confirmed that the bids from the strong, responsible airlines were proper and within the law as interpreted by the independent Office of the Comptroller.

With the final approval of the contract award to TWA in hand, Walter Folger Brown was able to complete his reorganization of the nation's air transportation system. Brown's Progressive Republican vision had come to pass. After almost two years of unceasing effort on his part were forged three large, stable, financially powerful aviation holding companies, each formed around a solid core of air transportation companies, solely dependent upon the federal government for their support and thereby dedicated to operating in the public interest. America's airlines were rescued from the brink of extinction and given a clear vision for the future and a means to achieve that goal through the guidance of the Post Office Department. Brown determined the routes, the equipment, and the schedules to be flown. He determined the rates of pay and the amounts awarded, and, most important, gave direct incentives for the expansion of passenger air travel. By the beginning of 1931, the three holding companies were providing regularly scheduled air service for mail and travelers across the country along the nation's natural routes of communication. Brown's leadership provided the nation with a new, rational, efficient, and safe method of transportation for the benefit of every citizen. No clearer example of Progressive Republicanism can be seen.

Not everyone agreed with his version of Progressivism, however. As the country's economic crisis deepened, the political climate began to change. In the November 1930 elections, the Republicans lost control of the House of Representatives. Several small independents, most of which had just recently formed, saw an opportunity to exploit the changing situation and sought redress from the new, Democratically controlled House. Others sought to challenge the large airlines directly. Although Brown's vision for the future of air transportation had reached fruition, his problems were just beginning.

Chapter 10

Reaction

W ith the tribulations of the transcontinental route awards finally behind him, Postmaster General Brown moved to continue his carefully conceived efforts to promote the efficiency of the air mail carriers. The Watres Act had given him considerable power to make changes, particularly through the implementation of rate revisions on those lines operating under a route certificate. These certificates allowed the department to make periodic alterations of the air mail payment rates. Although the carriers disliked the ever-decreasing rates, they welcomed the ten-year protection the certificates gave them over their routes and clearly understood that the department had no intention of subsidizing the airlines forever. They knew to expect periodic rate reductions and therefore made conscious efforts to increase their passenger-carrying abilities and lower their overhead costs to promote greater economy —exactly the reaction the Progressive postmaster general wanted from this new industry.

Brown nevertheless was becoming increasingly exasperated. Although holding great promise, the newly realigned American Airways and the newly created Transcontinental and Western Air were still losing considerable sums of money. American was still burdened with large overhead and top-heavy management, and TWA was suffering through difficult birth pangs. Although Harris Hanshue was the new president of TWA, the merger had not proceeded smoothly. Incessant bickering and the perception of all parties that the others were using TWA as a dumping ground for their depreciating assets to increase the net worth of the component companies greatly harmed its early operations. Eventually, TWA sorted out its problems with the help of the department, but not before it too racked up considerable losses. Of the three transcontinental companies, only the airlines of United Aircraft and Transport Corporation, which received almost 50 percent of the air mail revenue, were operating profitably and efficiently.

Brown once again called the operators to Washington for a series of conferences starting February 16, 1931 to discuss the rate problem and to plan for the future. On May 6 the department and the airlines would complete their first year operating under the Watres Act.[1]

Brown pulled no punches. Despite the contractors' somewhat reluctant cooperation, the postmaster general lashed out at their inefficiencies. He made it clear that any continued government support was strictly dependent upon the continuing efforts of the air mail carriers to reduce costs and improve the quality and speed of service. The department was running a deficit of $150 million for all of its operations, with the domestic air mail consuming $20 million, two-thirds of which was subsidy. Brown warned the carriers that Congress would ultimately decide their fate, either by increasing taxes to cover the deficit, which was highly unlikely given the terrible economic climate, or by forcing a reduction in expenditures, the more likely scenario.[2] The airlines would have to improve their operations drastically in order to compensate for losses in expected postal revenue or face bankruptcy.

Furthermore, the airlines were not keeping to their published schedules. The Post Office determined the routes, the frequency of service, and the speed of service. Despite this, aircraft were late and slow, and they often missed connections for a variety of reasons, none of which the public would tolerate, no matter how valid. "These schedules are not being met," Brown declared. "Figures furnished me indicate that the highest percentage in a fifteen day period is but 14 percent. This is very low and a rather rare experience. If these schedules, as fixed, are too fast they should be modified. The average speed maintained by you operators is but 102 miles per hour. This is rather low and you ought to do better. Faster equipment may be necessary in order to maintain the schedules fixed by the Department. . . . While I realize that weather conditions are a prime factor in flying operations, there is no doubt that better time should be made, taking into consideration all the elements involved."[3]

Brown suggested that the operators consolidate their ticket sales offices in each city served and agree upon a uniform price for passenger tickets over routes of equivalent distance, as had the ICC before it with the railroads. "I am not suggesting any violation of the Sherman anti-trust law," Brown remarked, "but there are no parallel air lines of any consequence now operating throughout the country. There is a short service between Philadelphia and New York and one from Cleveland to Toledo but these are only incidental to the mail trunk lines at present in operation."[4] This last point was of great importance, as future events would prove. The air mail carriers were beginning to run into direct competition from a new crop of passenger-only lines that threatened the air mail carriers with their faster service. According to Colonel Brittin of Northwest, "Postmaster General Brown stated to the conference that he felt that the air mail operators should improve equipment and establish additional schedules sufficient to adequately serve their respective territories." Brown felt that newly formed passenger-only airlines were embarrassing the department because it appeared that the established air mail lines were not providing sufficient service. Brittin noted that "this was particularly the case where the New York, Philadelphia, and Washington line recently established 'on the hour, every hour' schedule in competition with the older Eastern Air Transport."[5] The department felt compelled to fight this threat.

These new carriers for the most part were unwittingly the products of the air mail carriers themselves. During the latter half of 1930, C. Townsend Ludington and his brother Nicholas established the New York, Philadelphia, and Washington Airway Corporation, better known as the Ludington Line. They, of course, were two of the original founders, with Clement Keys, of National Air Transport, and were now offering direct passenger competition to Keys's own Eastern Air Transport. In the Southwest, Thomas and Paul Braniff, who had originally sold their airline to the Aviation Corporation and served that corporation as executives, left to reform their company when AVCO closed down their operation in the summer of 1930 because of mounting losses. Also in Texas, Temple Bowen reentered the scene, forming Bowen Air Lines, which was now operating against his old Texas Air Transport, now also controlled by AVCO. In each case, these individuals took the money paid to them by the large holding companies and set up their new airlines in direct competition with the existing air mail lines.

They also deliberately used faster, though less safe, equipment. Their aircraft of choice was the streamlined Lockheed Vega, an all-wood, single-engined, high-winged monoplane. With a cruising speed of 150 miles per hour, it was 50 percent faster than the larger tri-motored Fords and Fokkers preferred by the Post Office and less expensive to operate. With a single engine, limited communications equipment, and, in some cases, poorly trained and poorly paid pilots and ground crew, however, Vegas were far more dangerous to fly. The new independents, ignoring their poor safety record, loudly advertised their superior speed of service, much to the embarrassment of the Post Office.

The Post Office Department saw the efforts of these new, so-called independents as no more than an unfair attempt by former air mail carriers, who had been bought out at more than a fair rate, to undermine the fragile network of Brown's elaborate national air mail and transportation plan for their own selfish ends. These former air mail carriers saw themselves as independent entrepreneurs challenging an unfair, oligopolistic system and immediately began to lobby for new contracts from the already apportioned air mail appropriation. Brown would have none of it, but the independents would have the last word.

Brown insisted that the air mail carriers join with the department to determine a new lower rate system to compensate for the expected shortfall in appropriations and revenue because of the worsening Depression. Passenger and air mail traffic was down throughout the country. Once again William MacCracken assumed the lead in organizing the air mail representatives at the postmaster general's request. He formed three committees to study Brown's several proposals. MacCracken was confident that a useful accord would be reached but that he would have to guard against any duplicity from the other operators. To Daniel Shaeffer, he wrote, "On the whole I think this conference ought to work out very well for the future of T & WA, but as you know it will necessitate our paying careful attention to see that the others do not slip anything over."[6]

After several days of discussion, the assembled airline executives agreed on a rate reduction plan. Generally, rates were reduced from 5 to 15 cents, depending on the weight-space bracket used.[7] No reductions in the variables were made, with the exception of a drop from 2.5 cents to 2 cents in the fog allowance. "The Department estimates that this will result in a saving of over $2 million," MacCracken stated, "which they claim they intend to spend with the operators who are doing the best job with the passenger service."[8]

Brittin was the outspoken representative for the smaller air mail lines. His Northwest Airways was fighting hard for survival and was desperately trying to expand westward from Minneapolis to complete a northern transcontinental route to Seattle. His initial efforts were constantly frustrated by the department, which cited insufficient mail and passenger volume to justify the expenditures on this long and hazardous route. Nevertheless, Brittin persisted in hopes that in time his lobbying would wear down the department's opposition. In the meantime, he fervently fought to maintain his position and protect Northwest's territorial rights against all threats, real and imaginary.

The savings effected by the rate revision, reported Brittin, were to be spent on route extensions, within the guidelines outlined last summer by the comptroller general. Brittin saw that the department was to extend lines from Pueblo, Colorado, to El Paso and Dallas; Kansas City to Denver; Louisville to Dallas; and from Pittsburgh to Washington and Norfolk. "Even with these lines established," stated Brittin, "the air mail structure is obviously incomplete. Further extensions are absolutely necessary in the opinion of the Department to care for the requirements of a nationwide air mail service. The question before the Department is how to do this without increasing the annual appropriation beyond $20 million."[9]

Brown stressed the matter of aircraft speed but only one company paid

The Boeing 247, the world's first modern airliner, was created for United Air Lines in response to a 1931 Post Office requirement for a new high-speed airliner. (Smithsonian, SI# 2000-6118)

heed. Philip Johnson of United Aircraft and Transport Corporation, representing Boeing Air Transport, National Air Transport, Pacific Air Transport, Varney, and Stout, was present at the conference, as was Col. Paul Henderson. Johnson's companies were operating primarily Boeing Model 80 tri-motor biplanes, capable of carrying up to eighteen passengers, and the Boeing Model 40 four-passenger, single-engine mail planes. Other aircraft in the fleet included Boeing 95 mail planes and Ford Tri-Motors inherited from NAT and Stout. These aircraft were perfectly serviceable, but none were what the Post Office now had in mind. Boeing, however, had an ace up its sleeve.

Under development for the U.S. Army Air Corps was the revolutionary Boeing B-9 bomber. This aircraft was all metal, was powered by two air-cooled engines, and possessed a fully cantilevered, that is, internally supported, wing of great strength and low drag. This was to be the world's first modern bomber and was capable of speeds up to two hundred miles per hour, as fast as contemporary high-speed fighters. Immediately after the conclusion of the conference, the Boeing Airplane Company began a competition to develop a commercial mail plane based on the revolutionary design characteristics of the B-9. Originally intended as a high-speed mail plane that could carry eight passengers as well as a two-thousand-pound mail load, the design evolved into the all-metal, cantilevered, midwing, twin-engine, ten-seat Model 247 with retractable landing gear—the world's first modern airliner—which was to enter service two years later, in 1933. This aircraft, with its cruising speed of 160 miles per hour, was destined to change the face of commercial aviation and was deliberately designed to take advantage of the incentives provided by the Post Office's variable payment scheme. Thus the Post Office was directly responsible for inspiring the creation of an entirely new generation of commercial aircraft, the design of which has changed little in the past sixty years.[10]

While this technological breakthrough was under development, the Post Office was more concerned with how to deal with unwanted competition. Ludington and proposed airlines operated by Errett Lobban Cord were now threatening Brown's carefully constructed airways system. Remarked Brittin in response to Brown's concerns, "In other words, the Postmaster General wants the air mail operators to be progressive and develop sufficient service to discourage successful competition."[11]

The development of new aircraft of sufficient speed and greater efficiency was the best way in the long run to handle the competition. In the short term, Brown decided he must stay the course despite growing problems. His program to improve the efficiency of the air mail carriers and wean them off subsidy was working. "The Post Office Department is gradually reducing rates and multiplying schedules," remarked Brittin. "This policy will shortly bring the operators to the point where air mail is not even paying the cost of their operations." Brittin understood that this was deliberate, as it would force the contractors to expand their passenger and express service to offset the declining air mail income. "It is more necessary right now to develop potential passenger schedules than it is to angle for relatively small increases in mail volume," he concluded. "We are paid by the mile, not by the pound and this pay is getting less and less."[12]

The Watres Act was working as planned, but the question remained whether Brown would have enough time to complete his program before the voices of reaction grew too loud to be ignored.

Brown's first point of contention was the new service between New York and Washington provided by the Ludington brothers. As they were in direct competition with their former partner, it naturally fell upon Clement Keys to deal with the new threat. The Ludingtons established their passenger shuttle service during the late summer of 1930 and immediately tapped a lucrative market of business travelers along the East Coast between New York and Washington through their base in Philadelphia. The brothers cautiously explained to Clement Keys that their service was intended as an experiment and was not designed as a threat to Eastern Air Transport. Keys tolerated the intrusion into his territory until the competition grew too intense. "The Ludington crowd," Keys told Shaeffer, "have invited sharp competition by coming in on an established air mail line, in exactly the same way that the Aviation Corporation invited destruction by putting a passenger route over the N.A.T. line from Chicago to Kansas City, which has cost them a very large sum of money and which is now abandoned." Keys was of course referring to Braniff, which AVCO had just shut down. "The same thing is almost certain to occur with respect to Ludington," Keys continued, "because with our air mail routes established as a main line, we will be able to operate passenger service at a minimum of overhead. In addition we will undoubtedly be able to obtain on some of our passenger runs between New York and Richmond the minimum air mail rate. Ludington could not obtain this rate."[13]

Keys was determined to take up this matter with the postmaster general. Brown insisted that the air mail lines carry passengers to offset their costs and had virtually demanded that they open such service. This Keys was preparing to do when he purchased Pitcairn and reorganized the all-air mail line into Eastern Air Transport. Unfortunately, the Ludingtons beat him to it.[14]

The Ludingtons opened service on Labor Day 1930. Two hundred and twenty three passengers flew with them that day, and passenger traffic was heavy thereafter. Eastern had opened service two weeks beforehand and reported good traffic as well. The fight was on.

By December, the competition had prompted Ludington to drop its already low fares to below the industry's goal of the cost of rail travel plus Pullman. A ticket from New York to Philadelphia was reduced 60 cents to $5.25, and a ticket from Philadelphia to Washington dropped 85 cents to $8.00. The Ludington brothers proudly reported that in four months of operation they had carried 17,139 passengers, and, more important, they claimed a year-end profit of $8,073, unheard of in the aviation industry.[15]

The numbers were deceiving. Despite the initial success, the competition with Eastern and a general decline in traffic once the market was saturated and the novelty had worn off eventually brought red ink to the operation. By the beginning of 1931, the Ludingtons were anxious for an air mail contract of some sort to stem their growing losses. Surprisingly, Brown was not unsympathetic to Ludington's enterprising adventure. He suggested the creation of a special high-speed air mail service between New York and Washington using the Ludington line. Special air mail offered at a higher 25-cent rate would speed between the cities providing remarkable same day service along the line.[16]

An enthusiastic Eugene Vidal, executive vice president of Ludington, jumped at the opportunity and wrote to Brown on January 16, 1931, offering the company's services for such a venture: "You will remember having informed us that you were considering for our operation, a deluxe airmail special delivery service between Washington and New York to include the other major cities on our route. We are anxious to learn at this time, the status of this plan; first, because we are now planning additional schedules and equipment for the spring, and secondly, since air passenger competition has appeared, we have been forced to add considerably to our traffic costs which is proving serious at this time."[17]

They were feeling the pressure from Eastern. In order to demonstrate their commitment to such a plan, Vidal offered to fly this special mail at or below cost. "We are equipped to carry special delivery mail any and all hours of the day at an exceedingly low rate," he stated, "and are willing to cooperate during an experimental period at cost to your department for say, one dollar per day."[18]

Although the department was thinking about such a scheme, it had made no definite plans. Following a meeting with Brown, Vidal raised the stakes, accusing the air mail operators of wasting taxpayers' money and profiting at government expense. In direct reference to Eastern, Vidal wrote Brown,

> Another company carrying the United States mail has gone in competition with us on the passenger business. It is our understanding that all the Government intends paying for the carrying of its mail is the actual cost which the carrier undergoes. However, the company in question reports a profit of $800,000 for the first 11 months of 1930 to its holding company. This cannot be all from passenger carrying.
>
> This money which obviously comes out of the United States Treasury is being used to support a passenger service in competition to ours.
>
> You told us that you would very much like us to succeed as you could cite us as an example in making other operators cut their costs and thus save the Post Office Department money. If this is to be possible, it is essential that the Government not help our competitors by giving them money on which to operate planes at rates cheaper than ours or to operate larger planes at the same rate. We are definitely not asking for mail, as we know we can stand on our own feet, providing another company does not have an unfair advantage over us in using profits from air mail to subsidize a passenger operation.[19]

Vidal failed to understand Brown's efforts in promoting his national air transportation plan, which, through the Watres Act, directly assisted the air mail carriers and the major independent passenger carriers operating at that time through subsidy payments, on Brown's terms. Vidal and Ludington, in fact, hoped for some sort of assistance in the form of a new air mail contract for the route or a special "de luxe" service.[20] Brown, however, was not going to pay for any new service out of the $20 million annual appropriation for domestic air mail. Such a measure would require a special appropriation from Congress, as would any new contract. Ludington would have to wait.

In the meantime, the competition between Eastern and Ludington was becoming personal. The two airlines shared the use of landing fields in Philadelphia and Washington. Tensions increased throughout the winter when rumors spread throughout both companies. Townsend Ludington had heard through unnamed but reliable sources that Eastern's Capt. Thomas Doe had sworn to a large gathering that they would drive Ludington out of Washington within six months. The owners of Washington Hoover Field wanted to sell out and tried to play the two airlines against each other. In so doing they promised Ludington, for the price of a loan, that they would not permit Eastern's competing shuttle flights to land at their field. Only their air mail flights were to be allowed.

When Clement Keys discovered this latest ploy, he took furious exception. He fired off an angry letter to Townsend Ludington, threatening cutthroat competition. "The proposition . . . looks like a pretty direct challenge to begin the kind of competition with which all students of railroad history are thoroughly familiar," he remarked. "I will try to hold down the natural desire of our organization to accept the invitation to a fight, but I cannot control the thoughts and ideas that have been engendered by this last episode."[21]

Ludington denied any wrongdoing while admitting that members of both organizations had made mistakes and ill-tempered statements. Even though his operations were a direct challenge to Eastern, Ludington urged cooperation, believing that their operations were complementary, though he felt that Eastern's new passenger service was the unfair competitor. "We fail to see why Eastern should want to erect something which might wreck both outfits, when the Company should save much money and undoubtedly increase profits by playing along," he wrote Keys. "The service Eastern Air gives seems to us to be essentially a deluxe through service, and ours it seems to us to be essentially a fast bus line. The two should complement each other. . . . If we should be forced into cut-throat competition, we would be forced to extend our activities into fields we are not now considering. In this case, I would be fearful that the result might be the upsetting of the whole air mail situation, which strikes me as being fairly delicate at the present time."[22]

This was no idle threat. Not everyone in Congress accepted the postmaster general's Progressive Republican vision of the airline oligopolies. Since November, rumblings had been heard from Congress, and the newly elected Democratic majority in the House was calling for an investigation of the air mail situation and Brown's handling of the contract awards. In the Senate the climate was also worsening. Although the Republicans maintained control, several outspoken Democrats had seized the reins and launched a preliminary attack on the Post Office. Sen. Clarence Dill of Washington, acting on behalf of Mamer Air Lines, a small independent passenger line in his state, decried the department's refusal to sponsor a northern transcontinental route from Seattle to Minneapolis. Despite clear evidence that such a route could not sustain the traffic necessary to justify the expenditures by the Post Office and the Department of Commerce at that time, Dill attacked United Aircraft and Transport Corporation for allegedly anticompetitive practices in forestalling the route. Heedless to the fact that Boeing was based in Seattle and already serving the Northwest well, Dill assailed UATC as a ravenous monopoly operating in connivance with the department to prevent competition. He demanded that the department provide pertinent data on the contracts and the contractors to support his claims and threatened an investigation.[23]

Sen. Kenneth McKellar echoed Dill's sentiments. McKellar, the flamboyant Democratic senator from Tennessee, was angered by the department's lack of progress in extending air mail service into his state, particularly his hometown of Memphis. An old southern Progressive, McKellar was a far more dangerous critic of the air mail than Dill and was motivated by his inherent dislike and distrust of monopolies to examine the workings of Brown's department. McKellar was the prototypical Wilsonian New Freedom Progressive who reacted almost instinctively against any economic concentration of power. In March 1931, along with Rep. Will P. Wood, he introduced an amendment to the deficiency bill calling for the complete investigation of mail contracts. This authorized a joint probe by members of the House and Senate appropriations committees.[24] Congress would not convene until the fall, however, giving Brown a temporary respite in the hope that the political climate might cool down.

Paul Henderson, ever the astute observer, was not encouraged by the changing political attitudes. "I am sorry to say," he remarked, "that I am afraid we are in a place where we are going to need the best possible handling of our affairs in order to avoid a smash-up":

> Commercial air transportation is costing the government now approximately 40 million dollars a year. This includes the domestic air mail at 20 million; the foreign air mail at 7 or 8 million; and the Department of Commerce expense at 12 or 13 million. This is more money than the government seems to be justified in investing in this sort of effort. There is no small amount of Congressional interest in the problem, a great deal of criticism of the situation has developed, and a general tendency toward a tightening up of government purse strings as far as commercial transport is concerned. The struggle will come with the opening of Congress in December, and unfortunately for us this next Congress is one which is so evenly divided, Democrats vs. Republicans, as to make it look as though it may be almost impossible to accomplish much with them.[25]

Clement Keys was keenly aware of the changing situation when he responded to Ludington's challenge. Air mail lines were supposed to start flying passengers despite Ludington's belief to the contrary. Ever since the Watres Act became law, stated Keys, "the Post Office Department, very wisely, I think, has recognized the same principle, namely, that no trunk line can be built up on air mail alone but that all systems must be complete systems operating every branch of transport aviation over the rights of way provided by the Department of Commerce from public funds." Far from encroaching on Ludington's passenger operations, Eastern Air Transport was obligated by the Post Office to start regular passenger service.[26]

Keys, ever prescient, envisioned the day when large aircraft carried passengers in inexpensive or deluxe service in the same aircraft, allowing travelers to decide on their level of service, as they could while traveling the railroads. He also envisioned the increase of government regulation, first on the state level and then the federal, just as happened with the railroads, which would greatly restrict competition. Although he did not look forward to that time, he fully expected that there would be formal national regulation of the airline industry, more restrictive than regulations currently handed down from the Post Office and Commerce Departments. "Interstate air traffic does not yet come under the Interstate Commerce Act, but it ultimately will," stated Keys, "and there will then be limitations upon the right of such institutions to duplicate one another's facilities to a destructive extent, but this is far off."

Keys suggested that there was enough room for both operations to fly between the financial and the political capitals of the nation, provided that both parties acted reasonably and not destructively.[27] Townsend Ludington agreed, at least for the time being. He wrote back to his former partner, stating, "Inasmuch as we are all people of sense, I fail to see why we cannot work this thing out in such as way as to avoid the kind of competition which would be destructive to both."[28] Eventually, through the good offices of William MacCracken, who had just become Ludington's representative in Washington as well as representative of Western Air Express and TWA, a mutually acceptable agreement was reached for the use of the Washington airport. Ludington's suggestion to Captain Doe to sublet the mail contract from Eastern between New York and Washington was rejected by Eastern's board.[29] Thus an unsteady truce temporarily quieted the growing tensions.

MacCracken had forged the compromise while observing the changing air mail situation in Washington. Not all of the other contractors were happy with Brown's recent rate reduction conference. As MacCracken wrote Townsend Ludington, "When I was over at the Post Office Department this morning, I came across Col. Brittin of Northwest Airways. Apparently he was feeling rather low, due to the cut in the air mail rates." MacCracken continued, "He suggested that he might be interested in selling out to Cord. I think that it was probably a bad cup of coffee that they gave him for breakfast that made him feel that way, but he promised to get in touch with me next week to talk further on the subject. Do not pass this on to any of your friends in the Cord organization, but I thought you might be interested in it yourself."[30]

"Cord" was none other than Errett Lobban Cord, the automobile mogul who had recently expanded his empire into aviation with the acquisition of the Stinson Aircraft Corporation and Lycoming Motors. The thirty-five-year-old Cord had gained prominence first as a race car driver before World War I and then as an automobile salesman in southern California in the early 1920s, from which he broadened his interests to include trucking and automobile service and rental. By 1925, Cord had acquired sufficient capital to form his own corporation and promptly purchased control of the Auburn Automobile Company, the manufacturer of some of America's finest luxury and touring cars. Despite the economic crisis following the market crash of 1929, Cord's empire grew as he acquired the pinnacle of automotive grandeur, the Duesenberg company, and bought Checker Cab and Yellow Cab.

In 1930, Cord entered the aviation field with the purchase of Stinson and Lycoming. Stinson was a manufacturer of a line of popular single-engined general-purpose aircraft. More important, the company also was producing an efficient ten-seat, high-wing, tri-motor that, though smaller than the standard Ford Tri-Motor, was significantly less expensive, costing only twenty-five thousand dollars as opposed to the fifty-thousand-dollar price tag for the Ford. Cord had Lycoming engines installed on these aircraft and marketed them to the smaller independent airlines just beginning to open service. One of these was Ludington.[31]

Unlike the newly reconstituted Braniff and Bowen Air Lines, which relied on the high speed, single-engined Lockheed Vegas that the Post Office disliked, Ludington deliberately chose the Stinson SM 6000B tri-motor because of the safety inherent in its three-engine redundancy. The aircraft was also fast enough to beat the larger Curtiss Condors flown by Eastern Air Transport and embarrass the Post Office in the process. The performance of this aircraft was, in fact, the catalyst behind the recent February operators conference.

So pleased was Cord with the successful relationship with Ludington that he entered into a marketing agreement with the Philadelphia firm. Cord, the two Ludington brothers, and Cord's attorney, Lucius B. Manning, were either directors or officers of the new company, Airlines Inc. Through this arrangement the Ludington Line acquired seven more Stinsons as their service expanded and Cord's taste for the airline business grew.[32]

Over the years, Cord had gained a well-earned reputation as an astute stock manipulator, an aggressive businessman, and a sworn enemy of organized labor. Having himself learned to fly, Cord was not impressed with the qualities needed for piloting an aircraft. He felt that pilots were no more than glorified bus drivers and would pay them accordingly.[33] Although not making for a happy work force, this would greatly reduce costs and enable Cord to compete directly against the major carriers—without an air mail contract.

On March 23, 1931, Cord opened service with his new Century Airlines between Chicago and Cleveland, in direct competition with American Airways. His pilots received $350 per month, half the pay required by the Post Office for air mail carriers. In July, he expanded his operations by creating Century Pacific, which flew out of Los Angeles to Arizona, again in direct competition with American. This time, his pilots received only $150 per month. Cord discovered a buyers' market for pilots and was more than willing to exploit their desperate economic situation to his advantage.[34]

Unlike most of the little independents, Cord's entry into the airline field was a serious threat to the existing air mail carriers. His unscrupulous business practices and well-known business acumen together with his political connections in the Democratic Party made Century and Century Pacific dangerous competitors for the air mail contractors and the Post Office. In Illinois, Cord was to prove exactly how dangerous.

Century Airlines was based in Chicago and was flying passengers on a regular schedule from its headquarters to Detroit, Toledo, and Cleveland charging rates that matched the railroads. These routes placed Cord in direct competition with both American and National Air Transport. Immediately, American and National reduced their fares to below cost in order to match the threat, which they could do secure in the knowledge that their air mail contracts provided a sufficient cushion against short term losses. Cord kept the pressure on, despite mounting losses, as he angled to secure an edge in the market. In a stroke of near genius, Cord and Vice President Lucius Manning devised a unique scheme to thwart their rivals along Century's other heavily traveled route from Chicago to East St. Louis, Illinois.

Using existing Illinois law, the first in the nation to regulate the railroads in 1886, Cord seized upon the idea of securing an exclusive certificate of convenience and necessity under the Illinois Commerce Commission and thus operate a legal monopoly within the state. If successful, this would prevent American from flying a competing route to St. Louis and force all of the passenger traffic onto his new airline.

Swiftly, however, the corporate counsels for AVCO and National Air Transport prepared the necessary briefs and outlined several possible courses of action to forestall Century. The Chicago law firm of West and Eckhart examined the existing state law and concluded that the commission did indeed have jurisdiction over the operations of American's subsidiary, Robertson Aircraft, the holders of the air mail contract, as long as they flew within the state. With that in mind, they recommended that American apply for a "certificate of convenience and necessity" in Illinois to counter Century's move so that both sides could be heard at the forthcoming April 29 hearing. This would enable American, through Robertson, to claim pioneer rights, as they had flown within the state since Charles Lindbergh began carrying the mail in 1926. If granted, American could outflank Century, receive the sole certificate, and push Cord out of the state entirely.[35]

National Air Transport rejected the notion that the Illinois Commission had jurisdiction, arguing that aviation was interstate transportation over which federal law prevailed. National's attorneys did not consider airlines a common carrier because they were not specifically mentioned in the state law. However, airlines could be considered public utilities over which the commission could exert regulatory control. Illinois could not interfere with carriage of the U.S. mail, but it might have authority over passenger traffic. Attorney Clarence Ross recommended that National move carefully so as not to anger the commission and prejudice their decision in favor of Cord. He also feared that, if Cord were successful, a rash of similar suits would be filed in every state. "It seems advisable," stated Ross, "that if there is to be regulation of air transportation it should properly be in the hands of the federal government owing to the close relationship of air transportation with national defense."[36]

Postmaster General Brown clearly understood the mechanisms of politics and was not about to allow a state commission or even the legislature to dictate federal air transportation policy. On April 21, Brown had Horace Donnelly, the department solicitor, appeal to the commission for a postponement until late May, which was granted.[37] Donnelly followed up this request with a detailed brief outlining the department's opinion that Illinois did not have jurisdiction in the matter and should cease any action. In the department's opinion, even though not specifically detailed in the law, an air mail contractor is a common carrier engaged in interstate commerce over which, by the Constitution, no state has control, even if that company is engaged in intrastate business.[38]

The federal government was spending millions of dollars annually to support the struggling airline industry under the direction of the Post Office Department. It was Brown's opinion that the actions of local or state governments should not impede these efforts. In so doing he also reiterated the department's position concerning its relationship with the promotion of passenger traffic. "Thus it will be seen that the carrying of the mails is linked closely with the transportation of passengers, and in fixing the rate of pay the Postmaster General must take into consideration the remuneration the contractor receives on account of passenger transportation," Brown declared. "It is apparent that if the State is to step in and give a competitor an exclusive right to operate another passenger line over a route established and maintained by the Federal government at high cost, such a kind of competition would make necessary either the abandonment of its major efforts to promote commercial aviation or the payment of a higher rate by the government and seriously hamper it in its endeavor to establish a network of airlines throughout the country and promote the cause of aeronautics."[39] Brown reminded the governor that most of the states were willing to cooperate with the Post Office and Commerce Departments and restrain from exercising any attempts at local regulation. They generally accepted federal preeminence and followed national guidelines concerning licensing at the state level. Brown expected Illinois to do the same.[40]

Charles Hadley, chairman of the Illinois Commerce Commission, responded through the governor to Brown's urgent letter, suggesting that all parties wait until the hearing to form a consensus.[41] Apparently, American's plan was having success, as its subsequent application forced the commission to examine the entire issue of jurisdiction as well as American's superior claim. Century's officials also recognized that they were no longer in a strong position and were running the risk of being excluded by American's claim. They decided to cooperate rather than fight. Lucius Manning wrote to Northwest Airways as well as National Air Transport and American, taking credit for the delay in the hearing schedule and requesting that all parties meet in Chicago to discuss the situation.[42]

After lengthy discussions with the commission in Century's Chicago office and hearings in Springfield in June, the airlines agreed to argue against the assumption of jurisdiction by the state. The commission reasserted its claim to jurisdiction but agreed not to interfere with the aviation industry.[43] With this decision, the question of Century's attempt to secure an exclusive certificate to operate in Illinois became moot. In late August the commission approved the applications of Century and their American rival.[44] No more was heard from Illinois, as promised. Postmaster General Brown and the air mail carriers carried the day; Cord was stymied—at least for now.

While the Post Office was waging its struggle to contain state regulation, it was completing Brown's national transportation plan by filling in the map with supplemental lines, intended to feed traffic to the primary trunk routes or to link primary routes together. Others were made for political purposes.

In April, Brown took care of past debts when he awarded American Airways an extension of its route from St. Louis to Kansas City, stretching it now across Kansas and Colorado to Denver. Scheduled to open in June, this route was flown by W.A. Letson and his United States Airways. During the operators' conferences in May and June 1930, it was agreed that Letson had the pioneering rights in this territory. Now, though American had gained the extra mileage, it, with the direct encouragement of the Post Office, sublet the Kansas City–Denver portion of the line to United States Airways. Not proven, though widely suspected, this was a reward for Letson not contesting too loudly his earlier bid attempt with United Avigation for CAM-34.[45]

The Pittsburgh Aviation Industries Corporation also received the benefit of the department's largess when Pennsylvania Airlines, the product of its acquisition of Clifford Ball's line, was awarded its long-desired route from Pittsburgh to Washington. George Hann and his PAIC compatriots had strongly backed the department's national plan and were instrumental in the creation of TWA, with the blessing of Postmaster General Brown. Brown repaid their efforts with a much-needed aerial connection between these important cities.

The department had received a great deal of pressure to expand its air mail operation along the Mississippi River Valley. To this end, powerful politicians, including Sen. Huey Long and Sen. Kenneth McKellar, pressured the Post Office for service into New Orleans and Memphis, respectively.[46] Brown did what he could to accommodate the requests, but the department had no money; the appropriations for the fiscal year had already been allocated.[47]

The route between St. Louis and New Orleans via Memphis promised great profits to the operators flying that line. The competition was intense, even though the Post Office did not offer this as an air mail route. From St. Louis, Frank and William Robertson, the former air mail contractors who had sold their operation to the Aviation Corporation, reentered the airline business in 1930 and were now operating a small passenger line to the Crescent City, serving numerous towns along the way. Having pioneered the first route between St. Louis and Chicago, the Robertsons hoped to provide service that would enable travelers flying from Chicago to transfer to their new line and complete their aerial journey to New Orleans. Flying a fleet of eight-passenger, single-engine Ryan Broughams, the Robertson Flying Service experienced initial success but found the traffic was not enough to offset an average monthly loss of three thousand dollars. With this in mind, on January 6, 1931, Frank Robertson appealed to Walter Brown for a mail contract[48] but was politely refused for lack of money.[49]

The excuse of a lack of appropriations to deny the Robertsons and other subsequent petitioners appeared unfair but was nonetheless valid. A new contract required the expenditures of additional federal funds, an extension did not. This important difference, overlooked in all previous interpretations of the air mail situation, is crucial in understanding the mechanisms of the Post Office's decisions. With no new appropriations available, the department could not legally award any new contracts. Only through extensions, which were paid out of existing funds that were reallocated at the expense of the existing contractors, could any additional service, at no additional cost to the taxpayer, be made in response to the public's demand for air mail. In fact, the contractors were often forced to fly schedules at reduced or even no pay, particularly toward the end of the fiscal year, to ensure that no postal appropriation deficiencies would exist. This did not endear Brown to the contractors, but they could only grumble, for it was the law. The Watres Act, which gave the department authority to issue route certificates and the subsequent rate revisions, was intended to expand service at no extra cost to the government. Whereas the contractors resented the additional burden of providing new service with no additional revenue, except for that generated by passenger and express traffic, the independents saw only that the "monopolies" were apparently receiving all of the money to which they felt entitled, no matter how weak their claims.

Few outside the department and the industry understood how Brown applied the Watres Act to expand the industry with a no-growth budget. Because of Brown's program, airlines expanded in a rational manner, with increasing frequencies of schedules and many more and longer routes—all on an annual budget of $20 million, a sum that remained constant throughout the Hoover years. Brown entered the Post Office in 1929 with a definite plan to hold down costs and to improve efficiency of the entire department. This he was determined to do.

From New Orleans, famed racing pilot Jimmy Wedell and Harry P. Williams of Wedell Williams, which had vainly petitioned the department for a contract the previous summer, were also flying a small passenger operation along routes to Baton Rouge, Shreveport, and on to Fort Worth and Houston. They, too, were losing money and were in dire need of a contract to keep themselves solvent. Politically well connected, Wedell Williams sought to influence Brown through the power of Assistant Secretary of the Navy Ernest Lee Jahncke, who appealed to the department on their behalf. This also was refused because of a lack of the necessary appropriations. Still, Brown did have a suggestion that Glover passed on to Jahncke: Wedell Williams should merge with the Aviation Corporation.[50]

Williams conferred with Gilbert Grosvenor, who frankly told him that AVCO was not in a position to help, despite the Post Office's wishes. The financial situation at AVCO was still precarious, and the corporation needed time to continue its reorganization while reaping the benefits of its new transcontinental system. The corporation could ill afford to spare the cash or time to absorb another bankrupt company. As Hainer Hinshaw explained to Grosvenor, "I told Mr. Glover that we were positively through with buying people out, and he said if that was our attitude then it looked like a hard winter for Wedell-Williams, as the Post Office was in no position whatsoever to give them relief."[51]

Brown, nevertheless, wanted to do what he could for these two struggling airlines. In May, he suggested that they themselves merge, after which, perhaps, the department could provide some assistance if the new company could serve as a subcontractor for American along the St. Louis–New Orleans route. Unfortunately, the merger discussions dragged through several months, as both bickering parties were reluctant to relinquish control. No agreement was reached in time; an exasperated Post Office awarded the route to American as an extension, not a subcontract.[52]

Much behind-the-scenes lobbying had been conducted by Hainer Hinshaw and, particularly, American's vice president of publicity, Silliman Evans. Evans, the dedicated disciple of powerful *Fort Worth Star Telegram* publisher Amon Carter, a director of AVCO, had persuaded the Post Office in American's favor by cleverly eliciting the support of powerful politicians in the region. To this end, Democratic senators McKellar and Joseph Robinson of Arkansas, as well as Huey Long, wrote in support of American, convinced that this airline would provide the best service to their constituency.[53] American was already serving Memphis, to the delight of McKellar, and was in the best position to extend air mail and passenger service immediately through the rest of the South. American's efforts carried the day with the department, convincing Brown that neither Robertson nor Wedell Williams, either separately or together, was capable of carrying the mail according to the high standards of safety and reliability required by the department. Hinshaw wired Evans, "Your good work decides the matter in our favor."[54]

Brown established the new route in an ingenious and controversial manner. He extended American's CAM-2 south from St. Louis to Memphis, where it merged with a northward extension from the new CAM-33 transcontinental line from Jackson, Mississippi. This line was then extended south from Jackson until it reached New Orleans. In essence, Brown extended CAM-33 in two directions, both ninety degrees from the direction of the original line. Not unexpectedly, Robertson took violent exception to this creative interpretation of the Watres Act.

On June 6, 1931, Robertson fired off an angry letter decrying the postmaster general's decision, claiming that it violated the spirit of the law.[55] In the postal officials' view, they had done what they could, but Robertson and Wedell Williams had been unable to work out their differences in time. Wedell Williams had at the last moment refused to complete the merger because even with the 49-to-49 split, the 2 percent held by a third party would still give the Robertsons effective control. Of even greater significance, Robertson began flying passengers only days before the passage of the Watres Act, as had most of the independents, and, therefore, was not qualified to bid on the contracts offered in 1930. Because of the restricted appropriations, only extensions, not new contracts, were possible.

Robertson persisted nonetheless. Through Republican state committeeman E.B. Clements and other influential Missourians, he took his case directly to President Hoover. Reminding the president that the situation was causing much unrest in some Republican circles, he appealed to Hoover's secretary, Walter Newton, "to ascertain the facts and let me know what I may expect if I continue to urge their claims."[56] A concerned Newton asked Brown to reply, reminding him that Harry Knight, Harold Bixby, and P.D.C. Ball were generous contributors to the party whose continued support was vital. Brown responded with an explanation and a vague promise:

> The Department gave careful consideration to the claims of the Robertson Company. I personally had several interviews with the Messrs. Robertson and their representatives. It was impossible to reconcile the kind of operation which they were conducting with the present air mail and passenger transport standards. For your information, they sold out their air transport business about two years ago to the Aviation Corporation for a large sum of money. Recently they have started a small operation south from St. Louis, one which fails wholly to meet the requirements of the Post Office Department. The Robertsons are excellent people and of course the men in whom Dr. Clements is interested are pioneers in the aviation industry. We hope at a subsequent time to find a place for them all on our air mail map. However, it was not in the public interest to meet their wishes with respect to the service between St. Louis and New Orleans.[57]

Brown later suggested to the Robertsons that if they could survive for a while longer, and if Congress would approve an additional appropriation, the department would look favorably upon issuing a contract for a route for them from Tulsa to Atlanta. Writing to Clement Keys, Frank Robertson expressed his optimism. "Evidently, Mr. Brown is sincere in his promises to us," he remarked, "and I conscientiously believe if we do start the route, we will eventually receive mail."[58] Unfortunately, neither the money nor the route materialized as Robertson was unwilling to take a route so far from his home base in St. Louis.

As politics played an important role in the St. Louis–New Orleans extension, so too did politics dominate the awarding of another, controversial extension.

South Dakota was feeling left out of the air mail picture. Although air mail routes criss-crossed the country, only South Dakota remained without service. Beginning in the summer of 1930, politicians and civic groups began to petition the Post Office Department but with no success. The focal point was the small city of Watertown, strategically situated between Omaha and Minneapolis–St. Paul, which saw itself as a natural stopping point on a route connecting these two larger cities. The Post Office saw it differently, remarking that the air mail traffic in that region was insufficient to justify the expenditure necessary to open service. Nevertheless, South Dakotans persisted.

By the summer of 1931, progress was being made. John H. Kelly, editor of the *Sioux City (Iowa) Tribune,* had pressured the members of the Iowa and

South Dakota congressional delegation as well as representatives from North Dakota and Oklahoma to appeal to the department. Stitz Way, a member of the Republican National Committee from Watertown, applied tremendous pressure on Walter Brown until the department finally acquiesced.[59] Through efficiencies found elsewhere in the system, Brown managed to reallocate enough funds to support an extension of Boeing Air Transport's CAM-18 from Omaha to Watertown, with a promise to Colonel Brittin that the line would be extended no farther, thereby keeping United out of Northwest's territory.[60]

Rapid Air Lines, Hanford's Tri-State Airlines, and Western Air Service (no relation to Western Air Express) were all small independents operating in the region, each desirous of an air mail contract. Boeing had no desire to operate this extraneous route and was willing to comply with the department's request to sublease it, provided Boeing would in no way be held legally responsible for the subcontractor's quality of service. Armed with this information, the three competing independents petitioned the Post Office for the subcontract.

John Kelly argued strenuously in favor of Hanford, stating that its airport in Sioux City was perfectly suited for this service and that BAT should consider purchasing Hanford in its entirety. Hanford, as with all passenger lines, was losing a great deal of money, especially under the poor management of Arthur Hanford Jr. Not mentioned was the fact that Kelly owned a significant part of the airport in Sioux City and wanted to protect his investment. Kelly admitted, however, that Rapid was the more suitable carrier, given their experience.

Rapid Air had also petitioned the department. Rapid's operation, despite its financial losses, was well managed and had been in operation for five years over the very route in question. It needed the money; Boeing did not. Rapid Air was willing to subcontract the route if necessary. "We are firmly convinced," stated Rapid's president W.F. Halley, "that the Boeing Air Transport would gladly sublease the operation of this route to the Rapid Air Lines Corporation if the Post Office would signify its approval of this course."[61] The Post Office did in fact approve, but Western Air Service did not and launched a successful campaign to forestall the arrangement. Western Air Service, like Braniff, operated from Oklahoma north into Kansas. Although the Watertown route extension was outside of the airline's immediate territory, it saw the extension as an opportunity to find a steady source of revenue for its struggling operation.

Faced with a deluge of letters and complaints, Brown backed down temporarily. Remarked Colonel Henderson to United president Philip G. Johnson, "Brown has decided to wait a few days on Omaha north extension believing that the atmosphere will clear with our help."[62] United was not particularly concerned, as it did not want the route, but was acquiescing to pressure from the department to address Brown's political problems. United expected to begin service on September 1, but this opening too was delayed, until January of the next year. First Assistant Postmaster General Arch Coleman expressed the department's opinion succinctly: "Mr. Glover advises me that the proposed extension from Omaha to Watertown brought on such a disturbing political war that the Postmaster General postponed the matter indefinitely before he left on his western tour. This is all that any of us know about it."[63] The delay pleased no one. Rapid Air Lines was left without the anticipated subcontract and Western Air Service, though successfully stopping the deal, was also left empty-handed after BAT opened service.

Oblivious or unconcerned with the Post Office Department's predicament concerning appropriations, extensions, and new routes, several of the independent passenger lines took exception to their perceived bad treatment at the hands of Brown. They did not share his Progressive Republican vision, instead favoring a Progressive Democratic antimonopoly view that abhorred all forms of economic concentration, whether or not operating in the public interest. Their mission now was to convince the rest of the country, and especially Congress, of the correctness of their views.

Tom and Paul Braniff had earlier established a new airline bearing their name, after taking the profits from the sale of their first airline to the Aviation Corporation. Temple Bowen did the same with the assets from his sale of Texas Air Transport. Bowen and the Braniff brothers worked closely in developing their new high-speed passenger air service, particularly in the oil-rich regions of Oklahoma and Texas. Both new airlines were created after the Watres Act became law, and both saw American Airways, built in no small measure from the assets of their earlier enterprises, expanding throughout the region. They in turn felt they possessed a right to some of the proceeds from the contracts and extensions, even though the contracts had already been awarded and no additional appropriations existed. Braniff and Bowen, as with Robertson, Wedell Williams, and Rapid Air, made unsolicited offers to the department to carry the mail for a fraction of the pay given the legal contractors. Though they possessed neither the equipment nor financial resources required by the Post Office to carry the mail and paid their employees at rates far less than required by the Post Office, they believed themselves qualified and took exception when their pleas went unheeded.

During the summer of 1931, Paul Braniff contacted Robertson, Wedell Williams, Rapid Air, Western Air Service, Bowen, and others suggesting a meeting to coordinate their efforts to break the air mail monopoly of the Big Three holding companies. Also attending as observers were representatives of E.L. Cord's interests. They were angry. Reacting to the perceived slights by Walter Brown, the independents met in Kansas City, Missouri, on July 10, 1931, to vent their frustrations and to plan a course of action. Their avowed purpose was to "discuss the organization of all non-subsidized lines into a group whose immediate objective will be the correction of unfair practices and discrimination in the administration of the Air Mail Act and in the distribution of the air mail subsidy." Of greater significance, "It was unanimously agreed that an association of independent lines should be formed without delay" in order to publicize the problem and lobby before Congress.[64] Their purpose was to find like-minded representatives, particularly former Progressive Democrats such as Senator McKellar, who shared their notions concerning the evils of monopoly and stir them to action.

In order to promote their parochial economic agendas, Braniff and the other independents sought to ally themselves with those in Congress who voiced similar antimonopoly sentiments by painting themselves as innocent victims. Although they were indeed at a serious disadvantage against the air mail contractors, the independents entered the industry with the full knowledge of the situation. Most of them had previously held contracts with companies they had later sold during the industry consolidations of 1929. The air mail contractors may have been part of large holding companies, but they were legally formed and had been operating legal contracts before most of these independents were created. The independent passenger lines understood this, but several, such as Braniff and the Robertsons, felt they had been unfairly forced to sell their operations, even at a large profit, and wanted back in the business they had helped to form.

The meeting's keynote speaker was E. V. Savage, an attorney for Ludington who formerly worked for Eastern Air Transport. He had compiled a detailed list of purported facts that, "if made public might prove very embarrassing to the present postal administration and most effective in obtaining satisfaction for the independent operators." With the help of publisher George Putnam, the promoter and husband of Ludington's vice president for publicity Amelia Earhart, Savage was preparing to launch a thorough campaign against Brown "to inform the public mind correctly as to the equities of the independent lines and as to the present inefficiency, waste, and favoritism being practiced in the air mail service."[65]

Savage made no attempt to interpret the Watres Act as it was originally intended. Brown had specifically worded the act to prevent upstart airlines, just like those assembled in the Hotel President, from exploiting the new law to their advantage, correctly fearing that they would offer cut-rate service at cut-rate prices that would not promote the logical development of a national air transportation network. Nevertheless, Savage incorrectly assumed that the Watres Act, which Brown wrote, was intended to benefit the new independents:

> I do not doubt that you have all laid awake nights trying to figure out some
> effective way to relieve the oppression and unfair discrimination which the non-

mail operators as a group have most certainly suffered. Perhaps you felt such relief had come when the Watres Act was passed last year. Most people in the industry with whom I talked at the time—excepting of course the air-mail operators themselves—were under the impression that the sole purpose of the Act was to distribute more widely the subsidy, giving especial consideration to passenger lines then in operation, which had no mail support.

Instead of an aid, then, the Act has really turned out to be a menace—an instrument with which the Post Office Department has sought to kill outright many of the worthwhile developments of passenger travel.

Money which was originally intended to come into your treasuries to lessen your losses or increase your earnings, is now being paid to your competitors so that they may fight you in prodigal style in the very territories where you have pioneered the development of passenger travel.[66]

Savage attacked the distribution of the air mail appropriation, correctly stating that virtually all of it went to the large holding companies. United Air Lines, the recently reorganized air transportation division of United Aircraft and Transport Corporation, did, in fact, receive more than 50 percent of the payment, but this was because they operated the primary transcontinental route from New York to San Francisco, which carried the most mail, legally and efficiently. This, Savage believed, was grossly unfair and proof that the system favored an unholy alliance of an aviation monopoly unjustly trying to destroy the small independent carrier. His skewed vision of the realities of the air mail situation further fanned the flames against the department. "From all this experience and these contracts I can only conclude that there exists a veritable ring of favored sons who are now sharing what amounts to a monopoly in the air mail appropriations," he said. "Even if we forget for the moment whatever reason there may be for this favoritism, we are still confronted with the fact that the ring does exist, and until it is broken, I am afraid that you gentlemen will not have a ghost of a chance of getting an even break."[67]

Savage concluded that the public had thus far been blinded by the exploits of aviation and were unaware of the alleged crisis, believing as they did the department's statements and reasoning. This perception the gathering of independents wanted to change, and Savage sought to do so through a national publicity campaign and an assault on Congress.

The independents voted unanimously at a subsequent meeting on July 17 to form an association to promote their goals and quickly sprang into action, using Ludington's facilities and publicity expertise in establishing an immediate presence in Washington. Northwest Airways' Colonel Brittin recognized the significance of the Scheduled Airline Operators Association and the threat it posed. "The air mail lines should not underestimate the possibilities of this move," he declared.[68] Brittin was prophetic.

Ludington immediately put this new machine into gear. Their negotiations with the Post Office to this point had been cordial. But this polite atmosphere changed in July and was reflected in the independents' Kansas City meeting. The reason was clear: a new route was given to Eastern without bidding.

Brown, master of the domestic air mail situation, also controlled the delivery of America's overseas mail. As he had with the three large holding companies, he promoted one strong line to serve the public interest in the face of powerful state airlines competing with U.S. interests overseas, particularly in Latin America.

Pan American Airways had been formed under the direction of former Colonial Air Transport executive Juan Terry Trippe in 1927 and had brilliantly extended its reach from Cuba and the Caribbean throughout South America with the blessing of the Post Office. As the operating subsidiary of the Aviation Corporation of the Americas (not to be confused with AVCO), it was well financed through several prominent New York banking houses, and its investors included Richard Hoyt and Sherman Fairchild. Brown logically saw no sense in the federal government supporting more than one airline internationally; such unnecessary competition would hurt the U.S. companies trying to compete directly with the well-organized state airlines of France and Germany operating in Latin America. In so doing he encouraged Pan American to expand and acquire, smaller, less-efficient U.S. lines such as West Indian Aerial Express and New York, Rio and Buenos Aires Line, better known as NYRBA.

North American Aviation also harbored interests in Latin America, despite the postmaster general's known preference for a single flag carrier. In Cuba, Eastern Air Transport had established a line in direct competition with Pan American. Meanwhile, Pan American had invested in a domestic line between New York and Atlantic City in hopes of eventually using this route to gain access across the Atlantic as it connected with the nearby U.S. Naval Base at Lakehurst, New Jersey, the center of dirigible activity on the East Coast.

As these actions encroached on another contractor's territory, the postmaster general was deeply concerned that the resulting cutthroat competition would harm the best interests of the industry. Brown made it clear to Eastern's officials that they should abandon their Cuban line and directed Pan American to stay out of all domestic activity. Interestingly, this proscription against Pan American remained in place until 1978. Brown instructed Pan American to abandon its Atlantic City route and then transferred control to Eastern as an extension.[69]

Brown reminded Captain Doe of Eastern that the department was assisting Eastern by giving it the Atlantic City extension in spite of Ludington's offer to carry all of Eastern's mail at a much lower rate. Their cooperation, therefore, was expected.[70] It was this act that infuriated the Ludingtons, for they felt they had a right to bid for this route, even though it was an extension without an authorized appropriation.

In Washington, the Ludingtons contacted the press on behalf of the newly organized association of independent airlines and themselves. Reporters Ray Tucker from Scripps-Howard and Fulton Lewis Jr. from Universal, William Randolph Hearst's organization, leapt at the opportunity to expose what seemed to be corruption in the Post Office and were fed tantalizing subjective information by the association to encourage further investigations. In a series of articles appearing in late August, both reporters repeated the association's earlier assertions concerning the present air mail system, claiming unfair practices and preferential treatment for the holding companies while reporting the plight specifically of Ludington and Robertson in their recent negotiations. They claimed that it was impossible for them to break the virtual monopoly held by big business on the contracts because no new routes had been awarded for almost a year. Extensions were viewed as an unethical way to prevent the independents from bidding on new routes while bolstering the incumbent carriers.[71]

It was assumed in their articles that the air mail carriers were getting more money because of the extensions. Neither Tucker nor Lewis understood the department's problem concerning the postal deficit and the need for additional appropriations for new routes. The carriers received no payments in excess of the authorized appropriation. The press reported that the offers by the independents to carry the mail at almost one-third the current price were deliberately ignored. On the surface this indeed looked peculiar, especially in light of the department's expressed intention to reduce costs across the board. Unfortunately for the independents, Brown had neither the desire nor, more important, the authority to cancel the existing legal contracts to satisfy later lower bids, some of questionable responsibility. All of the contracts awards were legal, as verified by the comptroller general. Brown had made attempts to mollify several of the independents, specifically Robertson and Rapid Air Lines, but problems with the independents themselves precluded immediate action.

Tucker and Lewis also failed to understand that the Watres Act had not been written with the new independents in mind. Brown had been very careful in 1930 to ensure that the viable passenger lines were taken care of either through a contract or by a profitable merger into a larger company. With little money available for the industry, Brown specifically wished to exclude speculators, which included those new passenger lines he knew were created during the negotiations over the Watres Act just to profit at the expense of the pioneering lines.[72]

The air mail contractors understood that the assault in the press was a direct result of a well-orchestrated effort by the independents to influence

Congress and public opinion. Clement Keys, an astute observer of the industry, thought the attacks had little actual effect. He saw that Ludington was the instigator of the reports. "Most of the information furnished to Scripps McRae has come from Mr. Paul Collins of the Ludington Lines," he noted. "So far as I have heard about it, most of the information furnished has been accurate as to the facts, however inaccurate it may seem as to implication. The first point of contact, I understand between Scripps McRae and the Ludington Lines was Miss Amelia Earhart."

More important, Keys believed that cooler heads were prevailing in the newspapers as reporters were beginning to understand the impetus behind the articles. "I think that another reason for the campaign not being quite so serious as it was at first," remarked Keys, "is the fact that at least one of the editorial counsel of Scripps McRae paper has come to the conclusion that it is largely a campaign on the part of one or two independent interests to obtain mail contracts, rather than a genuine criticism of the contracts that have been let."[73]

The contractors also suspected Hearst reporter Fulton Lewis Jr. of ulterior motives. They conducted their own investigation and learned that Lewis was the son-in-law of Claudius Huston, the former chairman of the Republican National Committee. They suspected, though without proof, that Lewis was settling old scores against the present Republican leadership on behalf of his father-in-law. Keys hoped to keep this information for future use if necessary. "Does it seem to you, from this fact, that the critical articles have a special meaning, as indicating possibly that Mr. Huston himself is trying to get even with some of his political enemies?" he asked Colonel Henderson. "Would this fact, if known to the Administration, be likely to make the Administration support Mr. Brown's policies more vigorously or otherwise? If so, what is the best method to use to get this fact generally known to the Administration?"[74]

Hainer Hinshaw thought they had little to fear, for once Lewis looked into the entire air mail story, he believed, the reporter would find that Brown's actions were legal. "Of course if he had good wit," Hinshaw remarked, "he would know that the Comptroller General has to approve all contracts before they are awarded, thereby making it impossible for the Post Office Department to show any favoritism to anybody." As for Tucker, "He is one of the aces of the Scripps-Howard staff, and I am rather surprised that Ray would travel in such company. I believed he was above such an association."[75]

Brittin understood the political significance of the articles, nonetheless. The bloodhounds of the press were searching for scandals. It was intended for this information "to be used politically in connection with the coming session of Congress and the work of the House committee investigating air mail."[76] Despite the inaccuracies of the reporting and the relative calm evinced by the air mail contractors, the lobbying efforts of the independents were effective.

One of the targeted congressmen was Rep. Clyde Kelly, the "Father of the Air Mail," who despite his party affiliation readily accepted the arguments of the independents. He had harbored deep resentment of the postmaster general ever since their fierce debates over the Watres Act, and not coincidentally, over Brown's treatment of Kelly's brother-in-law, Clifford Ball. Full in the knowledge of the personal animosity between the two Republican leaders, the independents wisely appealed to Kelly when voicing their complaints against the department. Kelly readily concurred with their opinion, citing, in particular, the recent example of the Ludingtons' rejected offer to carry the mail between Washington and New York at twenty-five cents per mile, which, they incorrectly estimated, would save the department four hundred thousand dollars.[77] Kelly and the independents blamed monopoly.

In a blistering attack on the air mail system, Clyde Kelly charged that Brown was "prostituting the Nation's air mail with monopolies" and promised that he would "force an absolute and uncompromising probe into the reasons for this the minute Congress convenes." Fulton Lewis Jr. took credit for exposing the alleged corruption of the Watres Act by reporting that the postmaster general had lied when he claimed that the act was intended to support small passenger lines and instead gave 90 percent of the appropriations to the holding companies. Unconcerned with Brown's real, stated intention to support only the financially strong and responsible passenger and mail lines, Kelly readily accepted Lewis's revelations as facts.

Recalling his fight with Brown over the clause in the Watres Act eliminating competitive bidding, which was ultimately removed, Kelly affirmed that "Mr. Brown now completely disregards the intent of the committee when it backed me in insisting upon the amendments and continues to carry out his intention of granting these contracts without bids."[78] Of course, Kelly misunderstood that; in fact, no contract had ever been awarded without bids—only extensions, which required no additional congressional appropriations. Regardless, the atmosphere in Congress was rapidly changing against the postmaster general. Although the contractors were not particularly concerned, given the highly partisan nature of the attacks, the very real threat of an investigation upset the department and interfered with the functioning of the air mail program.

Rep. Melvin J. Maas of Minnesota met with TWA's traffic manager, H.W. Beck, in early September to discuss the deteriorating situation. Maas was highly critical of the awarding of 90 percent of the air mail pay to the holding companies and was particularly suspicious when he learned that more than 50 percent of it went to United Air Lines. He remarked, confidentially to Beck, that "United Air Lines was growing fat off the bulk of air mail payments." Although disturbed that so much money was going into so few hands, he understood the practical reasons, as did most members of Congress. "Maas, however, expressed himself as favoring the financially strong, large, seasoned, and well-managed airlines," Beck related, "and we reminded him of the fact that many small lines had sprung up in this country after the passage of the Watres Bill."[79]

Regardless of Maas's better understanding of the air mail situation, his personal animosity toward Brown did not bode well for the future. Brown's abrupt, dictatorial manner had antagonized many in Congress, and even in his own party, undermining much valuable and increasingly needed support. Maas, noted Beck, "was not at all backward about expressing his personal dislike of the Postmaster General and frankly stated his belief that Mr. Brown's efforts to get a large number of planes in the air all over the country were merely for political purposes." Maas underscored the immediate future for the department. Kelly's bombast aside, enough members of Congress were sufficiently disturbed by the allegations to support an inquiry.[80]

With the coming of fall, the Post Office Department and its air mail contractors began to prepare for the worst. Congress was set to convene in December, and air mail was foremost on its agenda.

Chapter 11

Cord and Congress

W atching the evolving contract debate with great interest was Errett Lobban Cord. He, too, was anxious for a contract to offset his mounting losses, though his initial efforts in Illinois had been defeated. The growing controversy opened several new opportunities for him if given the chance. Cord was willing to attack the problem on several fronts: through the independents' association, through starting another competing airline, through congressional action, and through back-door political maneuvering.

He was persistent. In July 1931, Cord expanded his airline activities, creating Century Pacific to operate in California and Arizona, in direct competition with TWA, United, and, especially, American. Using his ubiquitous Stinson Trimotors, he opened service from Los Angeles (his home) north to San Francisco and south to San Diego, immediately precipitating a rate war with United's Pacific Air Transport and TWA.[1] It was Cord's intention to parallel all of the air mail contractors and undercut their rates. United vice president William A. Patterson informed Philip Johnson, his superior, of the situation, noting that Cord's activities were even threatening the railroads, and urged that United take direct action against Cord.[2]

Patterson suggested undercutting Century's rates, even to the point of suggesting collusion with TWA. "I pointed out to Mr. Robbins," stated Patterson, "that two or three dollars in my opinion would make quite a bit of difference to them and that we would be defeating the purpose of lowering our rates originally if we at this time decided to raise them."[3] Clearly, Cord's increasing presence disturbed the air mail carriers.

Cord's plans included expanding eastward through Arizona and New Mexico through to Fort Worth in the hope of reaching a connection there with his Century Airlines, which he planned to expand southwestward. In Arizona, Cord was expanding eastward from California, providing a direct challenge once again to American Airways, the existing air mail contractors along CAM-33. This time, taking a lesson from Cord, American managed to head off Century Pacific's ambitions by securing an exclusive certificate of public convenience and necessity just as Cord had tried to do in Illinois. Cord attempted to obtain an exclusive certificate, but when challenged by the Arizona Corporation Commission to produce the required passenger statistical reports, Century Pacific failed to do so and thus forfeited any claim. The fight in Arizona was long and arduous and only completed in American's favor in March 1932. Although American eventually won, the struggle reinforced the Aviation Corporation's fear of Cord.

Cord had his trusted associate Lucius Manning travel to Kansas City in July 1931 to attend the meeting of the independent operators called by Paul Braniff. Although an interested observer, Manning left the meeting unimpressed and determined upon another course of action to secure an air mail contract.[4] Lyndol Young, a Los Angeles-based attorney representing Cord's interests in California, strongly recommended applying direct political pressure on the administration to force an air mail contract out of the Post Office. Young was personally acquainted with Mark L. Requa, a member of the Republican National Committee for the state, a mining engineer, and a close friend of President Hoover. He telegraphed Manning, suggesting that they use Requa to further their goals: "Had very pleasant conversation with Requa today and he wants me to supply him with data with reference to our right to obtain share of mail contracts. . . . Requa is not tied in with any other interest, his connection with Hoover covers many years, he is a mining engineer and I personally know his influence in Washington is as strong as anybody's."[5]

Requa indeed traveled to Washington, where he met Hoover and Brown to discuss the present worsening air mail situation. Requa had requested and received a detailed report concerning Cord's operation and their version of the air mail history, which he then presented to Hoover. The president was not happy. According to Requa, Hoover was concerned with the rising chorus of criticism and the increasing embarrassment that this and his other crises were causing. In reviewing the course of events, Requa agreed with Cord that, at least on the surface, the awarding of the air mail contracts (he meant "extensions" but did not understand the difference) was unfair to Century and Century Pacific. "Day before yesterday, Requa was in Los Angeles with Vice President Curtis and dropped by the office to see me," Young wrote Manning. "He said that he had personally been looking into the air mail contract situation and was satisfied that Brown's present policy in awarding air mail contracts to a favored few to the exclusion of Century was not a fair practice and that it was embarrassing to the President and the national administration and that he was going to see to it that we received our share of the business, also that Mr. Brown would not continue to put the President in a bad position in connection with his campaign for re-election. Also Requa seemed piqued that Brown had not answered his telegram."[6]

The Republican National Committee was to meet in Washington on December 15. Requa had invited Young to attend to plead his case. Young was thrilled with the prospect. "Ed Thompson will probably go to Washington with us, and I think with the influence of these two gentlemen with Mr. Hoover and the administration, we are going to get some place," he stated.[7] Cord was as sanguine at the prospect: "Requa was very outspoken in saying that positively we were entitled to mail contracts and that as National Committeeman and in charge of Hoover's campaign he will see to it that we get them."[8]

Cord suggested an immediate course of action. Century must start planning to expand its operations throughout the country as soon as possible to take advantage of the expected change in the air mail situation. If Brown reacted to Requa's pressure in the manner expected, Century had to be ready to exploit the situation. Cord hoped to force the cancellation of all present contracts, along with their extensions, thus forcing a new competition for all of the routes. With their lower operating costs and growing route network, Cord hoped to be able to underbid the large airlines and thereby pick and choose those routes he wanted. "The important thing," Cord stated, "is to develop some plan which will give Requa and the National Committee a program upon which to base their argument to force Brown and Hoover into recognition of the situation and to have that program so low in cost that the competition cannot carry it out unless they deliberately donate plenty of money to it."[9]

By this time Brown had replied to Requa's telegram and turned him down, citing the usual reasons: the Post Office had no money and paying Cord for service paralleling the existing air mail contractors was not in the public interest. Brown was blunt in summarizing his policy, which directly reflected his belief in the associative state. "We believe the present task of the Post Office Department is to subsidize an infant industry until it can become self-sustaining," he declared. "This was done in the case of the railroads during their early years. Today the government pays no subsidy to the railroads but compensates them for the actual service which they perform in carrying the mail."[10]

Brown angrily decried the efforts of the newly formed independents seeking to exploit the situation to their benefit and strongly argued for his program. The contracts were never intended as a gift for anyone who desired to receive one. The department was charged with developing a coherent, nationwide system of air transportation operating in the public interest. The industry was too important to the nation to allow inexperienced operators of dubious financial or ethical standards to provide this valuable service.[11]

Hainer Hinshaw of American Airways angrily voiced industry's reaction to the rising tide of complaints from the independents. In arguing against Century Pacific's vain attempt to secure a certificate of convenience and necessity in Arizona, Hinshaw commented to International News Service reporter and former agent for Western Air Express William "Doc" Bishop that American had spent considerable capital in developing their routes while Cord had spent none. He openly challenged Century Pacific to find anything unsavory in the contract.[12]

Hinshaw welcomed the pending congressional hearings because he felt an investigation would completely exonerate the air mail contractors of any false charges and the truth behind the wild claims of the independents would thereby be exposed to the public. "Personally," he stated, "I hope that there will be a wide investigation. I would like for the world to know how these non-mail contractors operate. How they skimp maintenance; how they do not provide adequate communication; how they have no two-way radio, and how they fly only with God's arm around them, and some day God will forget to keep his arm around them and they will cash in accordingly. I think it would be most healthful for the world to know just how much it costs in order to provide for every possible safety factor in this business. I think the louder they cry the less they will help themselves and the more helpful it will be to us."[13]

Hinshaw reminded Bishop of the disingenuous arguments propounded by most of the independents—that they were poor, struggling operators trying to break into a closed system—when, in fact, many had already profited greatly from their previous involvement as air mail contractors. This, too, Hinshaw hoped would be exposed. "For instance," he wrote, "Ludington took around one million dollars out of N.A.T. and the old Pitcairn line. Universal paid the Robertson boys a cold million dollars for their three contracts. Universal bought out Braniff, and Temple Bowen made his out of the old Texas Air Transport. Personally, I think when these things are brought out it will show that the whole business is nothing other than blackmail on the part of most of the independents. They had their finger in the pie once and are now trying to chisel in and get another."[14]

Hinshaw and the rest of the industry appeared confident that they could deal with these independents. Cord was another matter. He had no skeletons in his closet, except for a well-deserved reputation for predatory stock manipulation; he was a dangerous competitor. Quietly, the contractors began to extend overtures in the hope of silencing his attacks. According to Stinson vice president William A. Mara, his sources within the industry reported that "the older airline operators would be favorable toward getting down to business and attempting to work out a trade and see that Century got some business, providing Century didn't upset the whole applecart." Mara suspected that

American was anxious to stave off Century's direct attacks. He reported that Reed Chambers, a World War I ace and now a leading executive in the aircraft insurance business, "seems to think that Coburn, the President of The Aviation Corporation, is the ring leader among the present holders of mail contracts."[15] Just how true this rumor was would soon be seen.

Fearing the threat of the independents' organized resistance, Brown instructed the air mail contractors to form an association of their own to foster their own agenda. As early as May 1931, industry leaders were discussing the necessity of such an organization, citing the need for unity. Gathered at Fred Rentschler's New York office, William MacCracken, Colonel Henderson, and UATC executives agreed that "the principal air mail contractors would have to work together, as otherwise the non-mail contractors would be cutting in on the available appropriations, and all lines would go broke."[16]

Following Brown's strong suggestion to form an association to counter the independents, all of the contractors met in Atlantic City on August 5, 1931.[17] In early October, the ten leading air mail operators formed the Pioneer Air Transport Operators' Association, which served as a clearing house for matters of common interest among the contractors and as a lightning rod for their activities in protecting their mutual interests. The association's first test came in December, when Brown once again summoned the contractors to Washington to discuss further rate revisions and reductions.

Brown was feeling the pressure of the impending congressional investigation prompted by the Braniff brothers and Errett Cord's efforts to force a contract out of the department. In private meetings with Brown, Cord's representatives proposed to carry all of the nation's air mail for just thirty cents a pound, an offer that created quite a stir when it was made public at the subsequent Post Office appropriations hearings.

Richard Robbins of TWA was perturbed by Cord's offer, rejecting it as a publicity stunt. It was not possible to fly the mail, under the department's strict guidelines, at such a low cost. "Any operator who makes a public statement that he can put on a performance comparable to ours, at 30 cents a mile," remarked Robbins, "is deliberately misleading the public: Nobody has yet been able to operate tri-motored Fords the year round for less than a dollar a mile." Robbins felt that Cord's efforts would prove futile because the courts and regulatory agencies had traditionally recognized the rights of pioneering companies in new industries. He didn't think Cord would "get far in attempting to tear down that which has been laboriously built up at great expense and from which the public is now deriving great benefit."[18]

Cord and Manning understood exactly what they were doing. These efforts were all part of Cord's earlier plan to force the department to accede to his wishes through either direct or indirect political pressure. Requa's work on

Cord's behalf was paying dividends. Brown agreed that no matter what the situation among the independents, Century and Century Pacific were well supported financially. Brown related Cord's offer to the contractors to remind them of their growing predicament. "This concern offers to take over the entire air mail system and conduct flights in the daytime," he stated. "There is no doubt about their financial responsibility, but I have not had an opportunity to give the proposition any serious consideration."[19]

Brown reaffirmed the immediate necessity for the air mail contractors to reduce costs, suggesting a 10 percent reduction in their base pay to help offset an expected deficit of six hundred thousand dollars. The new rate would become effective on January 1, 1932. Although the smaller operators were not pleased with another forced reduction, the contractors realized that they had no choice, especially with Congress looking over their shoulders.[20]

As feared, hearings into the conduct of the Post Office Department in the letting of air mail contracts were scheduled to begin in earnest in March 1932. In preparation for these investigations, the new Democratic majority prepared its case well. W. Jefferson Davis, a California attorney widely recognized for his pioneering work in aviation law and an associate of William Gibbs McAdoo, prepared a detailed report on behalf of the National Democratic Committee, outlining the issues presented and the possible courses of action. The Davis report especially concentrated on the growing call for formal federal regulation of all aspects of commercial aviation. Davis correctly reported that although most of the major carriers were still averse to direct government intervention, some, such as United Air Lines, realized that regulation would protect the air mail carriers who had pioneered their routes while excluding new entrants.

Davis correctly assumed that the recently formed Pioneer Air Transport Operators' Association of air mail carriers was created in part to influence the creation of favorable federal regulation and help deflect the attacks of the independents. Davis was reacting to reports that once again, Sen. Samuel G. Bratton of New Mexico was reintroducing legislation to bring aviation under the ICC. He saw this as "a smokescreen to conceal the real issues, which in the opinion of the independent air transport operators, call for a complete investigation of the air mail contract awards made under the Watres Act by Postmaster General Brown." Davis concluded that the problems of the industry were so great that a massive overhaul was almost inevitable.[21]

Cord sought to use the House appropriations hearings as a launching pad for his proposals to stir up support and set the stage for his total assault. Lyndol Young outlined Cord's scheme to Lucius Manning, who approved the plan. They were working strenuously to influence Rep. Joseph Byrns, Democrat from Tennessee and chairman of the Post Office subcommittee of the House Appropriations Committee, to cut the appropriation to $11 or $12 million or delay any decision until after the House Post Office and Post Roads Committee, led by Rep. James Mead, a Democrat from Buffalo, New York, opened its investigations. Young recommended directly lobbying the appropriate congressmen:

> When the hearing commences before the Post Office Committee, in fact a few days before, I think it would be a good plan to have both a tri-motor and a junior plane here and get each member of the committee to inspect the same and take a ride. There are twenty-two members. Mead likes to fly and I know it would be worthwhile to take him up. . . . You can rest assured that Coburn and the other mail operators will open the old sack for entertainment and campaign contributions and we might accomplish the same result with less money by impressing the members of the committee with our products, and at the same time entertaining them with a ride—some of them perhaps would take their families along. I gave Mr. Byrns a letter yesterday afternoon in which I emphatically stated that we believe the appropriation should be cut to 11 million. Mrs. Robertson, his secretary, and her husband are taking dinner with Mildred and myself tonight, so I will find out from her how Byrns took my letter.[22]

Cord was pleased with this plan. "It looks as though we will have a great party when the new air mail bills come up in Congress," he stated. "Incidentally, we have been asked to write the new bill under which two proposed air mail appropriations will be made. If we can get them through Congress, and it looks like as though we had a lot of supporters, we will give the boys a merry chase."[23]

In the early weeks of February, Lucius Manning appeared before the House Appropriations Subcommittee on the Post Office and formally set forth Cord's proposal to carry all of the nation's air mail for just 30 cents per pound per mile. During these hearings, Brown was grilled concerning the department's air mail expenditures and, while deftly deflecting the more direct attacks, was forced to concede that he envisioned increasing the air mail postage from the current 5 cents to 7 cents per ounce to offset the increasing deficit. This was the opportunity Manning was looking for. Instead of supporting the air mail operators' plea for an increase from $19 to $21 million, Manning presented his offer to carry all of the air mail for 30 cents a mile, some 70 cents less than the current average cost, and recommended an $11 million appropriation as planned. The offer created a great deal of interest and was widely reported in the press. Ironically, W. Irving Glover, speaking for the department, rebutted the offer on the grounds that such an offer, if accepted, would create a true monopoly in the transportation of air mail, which was unacceptable to the Post Office.[24]

Soon Cord was encountering unexpected difficulties. He could offer to fly the mail at such a low rate because he spent so little on overhead. Pilots were no more than glorified bus drivers, in his opinion, and he paid them accordingly. They disagreed. The average pay for pilots among the air mail carriers was $7 per flying hour, with the average pilot flying eighty hours a month. Cord had been paying his Century pilots a monthly retainer of $350. On February 1, just as the House Appropriations Committee began its deliberations, Cord suddenly cut the retainer to $150, the same he paid his Century Pacific pilots. The disgruntled Century pilots appealed for help to David Behncke, a United Air Lines pilot and head of the newly formed Air Line Pilots Association (ALPA). Cord refused to deal with Behncke but agreed to defer the pay reduction for ten days after meeting with a committee of Century pilots. No agreement was forthcoming, and when the pilots reported for duty, they were met by armed guards and Century management and presented with an ultimatum to resign and reapply for their jobs at the lower rate. The pilots refused and were promptly locked out.[25]

Jumping into the fray to support its members, ALPA organized an effective public campaign against Century. Cord responded by hiring replacement pilots, which was easy given the terrible shape of the economy and the large pool of unemployed pilots anxious to work at any price. When ALPA's efforts to dissuade the replacements fell on deaf ears, Behncke turned to the press and Congress for action.

Rep. Melvin Maas publicly denounced the lockout, as did Rep. Fiorello La Guardia, a former World War I pilot himself, who attacked Cord as an enemy of labor and promised to fight Cord's effort to secure a mail contract. Cord's attempts to paint the pilots and ALPA as bolsheviks and anarchists only further served to enrage key members of Congress.[26] Colonel Brittin of Northwest witnessed Manning's testimony for Cord and the repercussions of the Century strike firsthand:

> Century has been having a hard time here lately. Mr. Manning and Mr. Young secured a hearing before the Post Office sub-committee of the House Appropriations Committee.... Mr. Manning handled the negotiation for Century. A member of the Committee stated . . . that he (Manning) tried to high pressure the Committee with the result that he made a very unfavorable impression. The member stated that the Committee was rather favorably inclined toward Century originally and would undoubtedly have recommended that he be given an opportunity to demonstrate his ability to carry mail on one or two test routes, but that they had lost confidence in his plan at the conclusion of the session.
>
> On top of this, Mr. Manning and Mr. Cord precipitated a lock-out strike among their own pilots. This reached the floor of the House. Several of the members attacked Cord and his company openly for their treatment of the pilots and a number of Congressmen served notice on the Postmaster General

that they wanted to be heard whenever Century makes an application for an air mail contract. Even Will Rogers has commented unfavorably on Century and Cord in his column in the daily papers. The Washington papers carried considerable space on this situation and all of it was unfavorable to Cord.[27]

With La Guardia's denunciations still ringing in his ears, Cord approached Representative Mead's air mail hearings with trepidation. The other airlines were equally concerned. Northwest Airways' Colonel Brittin worried about pressure from politics and competition. "The air mail situation is rapidly becoming a political problem," he remarked. "The Postmaster General, as campaign manager for the next presidential campaign, is forcing political considerations into the affairs of the Air Mail carriers. It seems almost impossible to stay out of politics and hold our own with the other lines."[28]

Cord was fully aware of the game, and despite his stunning setback with the House Appropriations Committee was willing to proceed at almost any cost to win a contract. The plan was to induce Representatives Mead and Brunner to introduce new legislation following Mead's investigation and repair his tarnished image through intense lobbying efforts by Lyndol Young. Cord hoped to have Rep. William Brunner introduce legislation to lower air mail rates and cut the ten-year route certificates down to three years, thereby opening all routes to competitive bidding. Brittin, who had contacted both his connections in the Post Office Committee and Brunner, believed the legislation was to be used as "a vehicle for opening up a public hearing on the whole airmail situation." He learned that Lyndol Young was actually drafting Mead's proposed bill, preparing to present it as a less radical substitute that would "take a great deal of the power for extending lines and fixing rates out of the hands of the Postmaster General."[29]

Young's efforts had helped convince Mead that Brown's air mail system was seriously flawed, and he encouraged Mead to elicit support from Comptroller General McCarl, who had opposed the postmaster general's scheme. Young wanted to give McCarl final approval for all route extensions as well as contracts. This was something Brittin desperately fought, as Northwest was slowly moving westward on its determined drive to open a northern transcontinental route and was the prime recipient of route extensions. Brittin was concerned about Cord's efforts but puzzled by his apparent political clumsiness.[30]

Brittin learned of Mead's plan through his numerous Washington contacts and reported that Cord was the vanguard of the efforts of the other independents, particularly Braniff, Bowen, and Ludington. Mead was planning to take their testimony and then present his bill in lieu of the Brunner bill and have it endorsed by the independents. If this happened, Brittin was nervously fearful of the outcome in this election year:

If this new bill diminishing the power of the Postmaster General and increasing the power of the Comptroller General in air mail matters is favorably reported out of the Committee, everything indicates that it will become a party measure on the floor of the House. Mr. Mead is evidently actively canvassing the Democratic members of his Committee to insure favorable action. It is perfectly possible that his plan may go quite a way as it happens that the Postmaster General is in charge of Hoover's campaign and therefore is an ideal Democratic target for an attack of this kind.

Century's General Counsel Young has apparently stirred up Mr. Mead against monopolistic tendency in the air mail. At present his especial antagonism is centered on American Airways first and United second, with T.W.A. and Eastern a close third. Mr. Mead is looking for something special in the numerous extensions the American Airways has received from the Postmaster General during the past 18 months. He intends to show that these air mail extensions are purely political and essentially matters of political patronage in the State in which they have been granted. With the recent break between the Democratic Speaker of the House and the President, this situation may develop important proportions.[31]

Brittin was also concerned that Mead had powerful friends in the Republican Party as well, particularly Rep. Clyde Kelly. "It so happens," warned Brittin, "that Mr. Kelly is a bitter enemy of Mr. Brown's because the Postmaster General forced Mr. Clifford Ball, who is Mr. Kelly's brother-in-law, to sell the Clifford Ball Airlines . . . to the Pennsylvania Airlines, an ally of the Pennsylvania Railroad."[32]

On March 1, 1932, Rep. James M. Mead, chairman of the House Committee on the Post Office and Post Roads, opened his hearings into Walter Brown's air mail plan in the hope of recommending new legislation rewriting the current Watres Act and removing much authority from the postmaster general.

Opening testimony was provided by Second Assistant Postmaster General Glover, who vigorously defended the department's actions while calling attention to the success of the postmaster general's program to build a national transportation system. Glover criticized the two bills for undermining the present system and endangering the legal contracts now extant. The provision in the proposed Brunner bill, H.R. 8390, which would reduce mail pay from $1.25 to $1 per mile, was not objectionable, but the proposal to cut the length of the route certificates from ten years to three was, as it would jeopardize future investment in commercial aviation. As for the second bill, H.R. 9841, Glover rejected it outright.

H.R. 9841 called for the cancellation of all contracts awarded without public advertisement and competitive bidding. In a letter from First Assistant Postmaster General Arch Coleman read by Glover, the department rejected this legislation simply because all of the contracts had in fact been legally advertised and awarded, contrary to public statements made by the independents.[33]

Glover defended the use of extensions over new contracts because this allowed the department to extend routes at no cost to the government while preventing unqualified airlines from profiting at public expense. The provisions of the Watres Act allowed the postmaster general to extend routes without calling for bids, and that was exactly what he did within the law. Glover then challenged the committee to decide for the nation what it wanted for commercial aviation. "It is coming to the point where Congress must decide whether it desires just an air mail service or an air mail service with the highest efficiency of an air-passenger service," he said. "This flying game was just a new business. It was a new method of transportation; and go back, if you will, to the early days when railroads started out to pioneer their way; it took a long time before those railroads were on a basis, even with large government support, that they were able to operate such trains as the Twentieth Century Limited or the Broadway Limited."[34]

The postmaster general provided the same support to the airlines that the railroads received and did so with the approval of Congress. This support, in the form of temporary subsidies, encouraged the carrying of mail and, especially, of passengers to help defray costs and improve efficiency and safety. "The Postmaster General had a vision and that is best illustrated by the map that is being presented to your honorable body on the floor of the House today," Glover said. "That map is practically complete except for feeder lines. These extensions were made by the act which gave him that privilege of extension."[35]

The government was receiving excellent value from its expenditures on air mail, stated Glover. Despite Cord's offer to carry the mail for thirty cents a mile, "the character of passenger service which the Postmaster General is desirous of offering to the public at the present cost of operation cannot be given for much less than the rates which we are now being paid." Certainly if Congress were only concerned with the carrying of mail, payments could be significantly less. However, if Congress wanted to continue to encourage the growth of a new transportation system as it originally stated during the hearings for the Watres Act, they should understand that the department was fulfilling these obligations at the lowest possible cost to the government.[36]

The committee again raised the issue of extensions but was swiftly reminded by Glover that despite protests to the contrary, all of the extensions were legal and had been approved by the comptroller general, in spite of the latter's known antipathy toward Brown. "And furthermore," Glover said, "to my knowledge, the Comptroller General and the Postmaster General have twice been in conference on these very matters, and the Postmaster General explained to him what he had in mind regarding extensions and what he planned to do, and with what results." Concluded Glover, "All extensions granted by the Postmaster General have been approved by the payments for services rendered."

With that, the committee backed off its attack and tacitly acknowledged the competency of the department. Chairman Mead expressed, almost apologetically, his desire only to address the recent criticisms voiced by the independents and seemed satisfied that the department was willing to cooperate to smooth the troubled waters.[37]

Industry observers agreed that Glover had presented his case well. He had only to accede to the committee's request for assistance in modifying the proposed legislation, the effect of which would limit the distance of future extensions but not have a significant impact on the present system.[38]

Next to speak was Frank E. Ormsbee of the Air Line Pilots Association, who gave the existing air mail contractors a resounding vote of support while attacking the policies of the Cord operations. "I just want to call to the attention of the committee at this time that Mr. Cord can not carry the mail at 50 per cent less than it is carried to-day and do it safely, because the essential requirement in carrying air mail is cooperation between the pilots and the executives," he said. "This is a young industry. It is in the same stage railroads were in several years ago; and the pilots have been practically the heart of the industry all through its development. We are trying and hope to guide its future development along safe lines that will eventually lead to economy. Mr. Cord's offer is too radical."

Ormsbee believed Cord's assertions were not being thoroughly investigated by the committee. He challenged Cord to produce reliable data to support his claim that he could fly the mail for thirty cents a mile: "I think that if this committee will thoroughly investigate Mr. Cord's offer, his attitude with reference to his pilots, his equipment compared to other equipment, his methods of overhaul and upkeep, his salaries as compared to salaries of other operating companies, these will have a decided effect on the final decision of the committee."[39]

Lyndol Young did his best to repair the damage done by the strike but was unable to persuade the committee to his cause. Other independents presented their case, including Paul Braniff, Temple Bowen, and J.M. Eaton and Eugene Vidal of Ludington. All restated their previous positions, underscoring their need for a contract and their perceived mistreatment at the hands of the Post Office Department. Braniff argued for the immediate cancellation of all air mail contracts and the reannouncement of bids. He reasoned that because of the lower operating costs of the independents, obliquely referring to their much lower pay scale, far more pilots could be hired if the independents could fly the mail at the present air mail appropriation of $19 million. William MacCracken was an observer who thought Braniff's remarks were well stated but not completely accurate. "Braniff also made a good presentation of his case, and got away without having it brought out that he had been previously bought out by the Aviation Corporation of Delaware, and then gone back into competition with them," he stated.[40]

Two weeks after the testimony of the airlines, Postmaster General Brown appeared before the committee. Brown eloquently defended his carefully constructed system and stated unequivocally his Progressive Republican predilections concerning "good" monopoly and the public welfare. His antipathy toward destructive competitive bidding was never more clearly stated and his Progressive views never more apparent. Replying to direct questioning from Rep. Arthur P. Lamneck, an Ohio Democrat who asked Brown if competition in the airline business was possible, the postmaster general replied, "Probably not. I do not believe in competition in public service. I think competition in public service simply adds to the burdens borne by the public. Monopoly in public service under very definite regulation is my idea, and I think that is what will come here ultimately. We will have air systems knit together giving a competitive service." Brown continued by presenting the excellent service provided by United Air Lines along its transcontinental line as an example of his plan in action. "In the old days, when the mail got to Chicago from the West it might be late and the New York plane might have had to leave," he noted. "As the system is now, United feels to be under obligation to get that mail through and it gets it through. Unless you have the responsibility of moving the mail, gentlemen, you do not realize all the complications that arise. For instance, carrier A may be late in making his connection with carrier B, which latter carrier has a definite schedule to maintain and met, and that throws the whole system out of harmony. That is why these unified systems work so much better than a series of independent lines work."[41]

The large, well-financed, and well-managed companies were far better able to perform their duties than the poorly financed independents. Brown reminded the committee that United was able to provide a special airplane to catch up with the normal outbound flight if the inbound mail was late, something the smaller lines could never do, and United could do it safer as well. "Any day the air mail for New York is late in arriving in Chicago from the West, United has a special plane to pick it up immediately when the regular plane had to leave Chicago on time in order to make connections," he said. "These big organizations with spare equipment and a variety of equipment—passenger and mail planes, trimotor, bimotor, and single-motor planes—are much better able to do a job than a fellow with two or three planes and no money, with the sheriff just one leap behind him all the time."[42]

The postmaster general clearly understood the nature of business, government, and public policy. He was only interested in developing a new industry that would best serve the public. Although he felt that the current level of government involvement was sufficient to promote and protect the infant aviation industry, he completely understood the future necessity of formal federal regulation. "I think that the time will come when an airline operator will have to obtain a certificate of public necessity and convenience before he can operate," stated Brown, "because I do not believe that a multiplicity of operators, operating at a loss is going to help."[43]

In this as with many other observations concerning air transportation, Brown was prescient. In fact, this is exactly what happened. Between 1938 and 1978, America's airlines were regulated in precisely this manner, following Brown's script almost to the letter, long after he had disappeared from the scene.

Brown's testimony was sufficient to persuade the House Committee to drop further investigation. Mead asked for a proper study to be made of the industry by Harvard economist John Crane, to be completed by the end of the year, but, more important, no legislation was introduced. Because of the failure of the independents to sway the influential committee, the Senate investigation, prompted by the irascible Sen. Kenneth McKellar, proved anticlimactic. Although Democrats now controlled the House, they did not control the Senate, so further inquiries were blocked by loyal Republicans.

Brown's lucid, Progressive Republican defense of his air mail system convinced enough Democrats that the Post Office was acting correctly. Of even greater importance, however, was a significant practical change in the air mail situation: Errett Lobham Cord, the preeminent independent, sold out.

Throughout the winter of 1932, while American was desperately fending off the advances of Century Pacific in Arizona, negotiations were quietly underway between Cord and the AVCO Board. W. Averell Harriman, chairman and heir to the great Union Pacific fortune of his illustrious father, E.H. Harriman, was beginning to panic. Despite the reorganization of AVCO and the passage of the Watres Act giving American a reasonable transcontinental route system, the company was still losing money; for 1931 the total lost reached $3.2 million, half of that for 1930 but huge just the same.[44]

Although losses had indeed been cut because of the increased revenue from the air mail, which produced an across-the-board profit for all AVCO air mail companies of $123,831 from $5,505,808 in total revenue for 1931, the value of AVCO stock remained low, hovering around two dollars per share, while the existence of a huge board of directors underscored the corporation's continuing problems with high overhead costs and inexperienced leadership.[45] Cord's attacks on the industry in general and on AVCO in particular drew especial attention to American's weaknesses, causing Harriman many sleepless nights. According to Sherman Fairchild, who had left AVCO in 1931 because of its continuing difficulties, "Harriman was just scared to death of the whole thing and was afraid that . . . something would happen that would besmirch the Harriman name, and he was just ready to do anything to get out of this mess that he was in."[46]

Cord, a master of the financial world, understood AVCO's weak position and sought to exploit the situation if his public attempts to secure an air mail contract failed. By early 1932, as it became clear that Cord was losing his public fight, he turned his attention directly to AVCO, armed with the knowledge that the poor performance of that company was largely the result of bad management by the existing board of directors. In a subsequent interview, Roland Palmedo, one of AVCO's board members, recalled the situation distinctly: "I do remember that Manning and Cord had quite a club over The Aviation Corporation, which—oh, let's say a cause for blackmail—which rather scared Harriman, because by this time, in 1931 or '32, The Aviation Corporation really had a sorry record. . . . Cord had some pretty good ammunition, and used it effectively. [He] also pointed with scorn at this bunch of directors here including Harriman and Bobby [Lehman] and a lot of other bankers and people of that kind who supposedly didn't know anything about aviation."[47]

Serious merger discussions began in February, and by early March, AVCO and Cord were completing the details of the acquisition of Cord's airline properties. After delicate negotiations were completed on March 31, 1932, E.L. Cord agreed to sell his Century and Century Pacific airlines to the Aviation Corporation. In return, Cord received $621,000 worth of AVCO stock (approximately 138,000 shares) and two seats on the board of directors. In addition, Cord agreed to confine all of his future air transportation activities exclusively to AVCO, thus removing him as a direct competitor.[48]

The agreement came at a crucial time for AVCO. Since 1930, Frederick G. Coburn, of the engineering firm of Sanderson and Porter, had served temporarily as president in order to supervise the reorganization of the corporation. He succeeded in reducing losses and managed to force the company to agree to a plan for the reduction of the size of the board. He also recommended the consolidation of all of American Airways' operations in a central location, preferably St. Louis, while virtually eliminating AVCO's offices in New York City. Coburn also recommended the creation of an executive committee of American Airways, staffed with experts in air transportation and the strengthening of AVCO's board, separate from their own executive committee.[49] Though Robert Lehman believed Coburn had not gone far enough in reorganizing AVCO and American Airways, on March 17, 1932, Coburn felt his job complete and turned over the reins to La Motte Cohu.

These events caused great consternation within both the corporation and the Post Office Department. With Cord now on the board, Hainer Hinshaw resigned from American as their Washington representative and accepted a similar position with United Air Lines. Hinshaw was replaced by World War I ace Edward "Eddie" Rickenbacker.

Regardless of Hinshaw's objections, Harriman and AVCO felt that it was necessary to buy peace through the acquisition of Cord's airlines. Harriman had hoped that this would end the battles but soon discovered his error. After reviewing Century and Century Pacific's books, he discovered that their claim of profitability was in fact a lie. These two airlines had been losing money despite their much lower costs. Had it not been for their acquisition by AVCO, Century and Century Pacific would have gone out of business anyway.

An unnerved Harriman discovered that Cord had no intention of remaining quiet. With his acquisition of 138,000 AVCO shares plus the additional 100,000 he purchased on the open market, Cord was now the largest single holder of AVCO stock and, with two seats on the board of directors, aimed to gain control of the entire corporation. Board member and AVCO general counsel William Dewey Loucks sounded the alarm. "La Motte," he reported to Harriman, "has undoubtedly told you of the talk Mrs. Cord had with him at his dinner in which she said, in substance, that her husband had sold out his air operation, but of course, she supposed she should be satisfied as this only meant that he was running a larger enterprise."[50]

Cord was now pressing hard for AVCO to purchase his Stinson airliners, Auburn limousines, and other equipment his companies produced while denigrating the existing personnel of the corporation. Loucks suspected that Cord wanted to reduce the board to only four or five members, Cord among them. In such a position, Cord could quickly dominate the corporation. Loucks warned Harriman that steps should be taken immediately to control Cord before it was too late.[51]

Unfortunately, Loucks's worst fears were about to come true. Cord was determined to gain command over AVCO, thereby reentering the air transportation industry with well-financed airlines supported by government air mail contracts. Despite his reputation for stock manipulation, Cord was a shrewd manager who relied on capable lieutenants, such as Lucius Manning, for advice and expertise. Cord was indeed correct that AVCO was overladen with financiers and not enough aviation-oriented managers. In this complaint he had valuable allies, especially Sherman Fairchild, who had been stressing this very point from AVCO's inception three years earlier. Perhaps Cord's wisest move when he joined AVCO's board was pushing for the promotion of Southern Air Transport president Cyrus R. Smith as president of American Airways. C.R. Smith, a former accountant, brought order out of chaos and would soon lead American out of the doldrums and into a position of leadership for the next three decades. Under Smith, American's operations improved dramatically, helping to fulfill the promise held by the company from its earliest beginnings.

But Cord wanted more. Almost immediately, Cord attacked the existing management of AVCO as inefficient and pressed for dramatic changes in an effort to gain control. Already Loucks and company had agreed to reduce the number of board members from sixty-six to twenty-four, a decision that was confirmed unanimously during AVCO's annual meeting on April 29, but this was just the beginning for Cord.[52] Loucks was not a Cord supporter and, suddenly, along with George Hann, was removed from the AVCO Executive Committee after a disagreement with the new director.[53]

Sherman Fairchild was also dropped from the executive committee, even though he supported the installation of Cord and his associates on the board for their aviation expertise. This did not sit well with the AVCO founder, who demanded of Harriman his reinstatement. After some testy correspondence, he rejoined the committee.[54] George Hann resigned.

Tensions increased toward the end of the summer as Cord moved to consolidate his position. Throughout the year, Cord successfully attempted to impose his Stinson aircraft and Lycoming engines on American's fleet, despite the opposition of pilots and mechanics, who found this equipment inferior to that which they were already flying.[55] Cord's wildly optimistic claims for the future of AVCO's stock combined with the growing confrontation was having an adverse effect on morale.[56]

During the summer, Harriman assumed the presidency of Union Pacific, the railroad his father had led to greatness. He wanted out of aviation and hoped to forge a settlement of some kind that would protect his interests, salvage AVCO, and allow him to step aside into a business with which he was more familiar.[57] To this end, Harriman contacted Frank Vanderlip, a powerful financier, former chairman of National City Bank, and friend to both Harriman and Cord, who agreed to take the lead in resolving the brewing conflict. His initial efforts were overwhelmed by rapidly changing events.

Cord constantly pushed for reforms to the extent that Loucks and others who remained on AVCO's drastically reduced board sought ways to contain this dangerous upstart. Earlier in the year Loucks and Cohu became intrigued with the idea of purchasing Eastern Air Transport, which would give American Airways a direct connection with most of the major cities in the East Coast through their connection in Atlanta. Loucks hoped to acquire Eastern by gaining control of North American Aviation, its parent holding company, and eventually discarding those properties extraneous to AVCO's immediate needs. North American and Eastern were holding their own but, as with most aviation enterprises, they were just managing to get by because of their air mail and other government contracts. To many investors, the time was ripe for a merger on AVCO's terms.[58]

Following a contentious special meeting of the AVCO board in October, the differences erupted into a war. Cord and Cohu were vying for control of the Thompson Aeronautical Corporation, which operated Transamerican Airlines, a small air mail contractor flying in Michigan, Indiana, and Ohio. Cord owned 45 percent of Thompson and demanded that it not fall into the hands of Cohu, threatening legal action if need be. In a rather disingenuous statement, Cord warned that the sale of Thompson to AVCO would violate federal antitrust statutes and would never be approved by the Department of Justice. Furthermore, he stated, with the deteriorating position of the present air mail system in the eyes of the public, such action would not be favorably viewed by the Post Office.[59]

Robert Lehman informed Cord of what was happening in AVCO concerning Thompson. The corporation was prepared to exchange 1 7/8 to 2 shares of its stock for each Thompson share, provided that the North American deal was completed.[60] Now Cord had another reason to stop Cohu.

On November 1, 1932, AVCO made a formal offer to acquire North American Aviation. In return for 1,996,778 shares of AVCO capital stock North American would deliver all of North American's assets except for $1,175,000 in cash, the Ford Instrument Company, and other smaller holdings. AVCO would acquire Eastern Air Transport, 26 percent of TWA, and 26 percent of Douglas Aircraft.[61] This would increase AVCO's outstanding stock to 4,977,000 shares, thus reducing Cord's holdings from 30 percent to 17 percent.

In a move reminiscent of United Aircraft's takeover of National Air Transport two years earlier, Cord secured a court injunction blocking the merger offer and sought to win outright control of AVCO through a bitter, public proxy fight. Under Cord's direction, Raymond Pruitt outlined a campaign to gain proxies by outlining a detailed list of alleged misconduct by the AVCO Board. Particularly, Pruitt highlighted the incompetence and inexperience of AVCO and American management, which he believed led to vast losses as well as alleged corporate stock speculation by the investment committee. He further outlined the board's refusal to accept Cord's numerous suggestions to cut costs and improve efficiencies. Pruitt underscored Cord's greater experience in aircraft manufacture and airline operation as proof of their competency and ability to improve AVCO's poor financial position. Pruitt appealed to the uncommitted stockholders for their support in blocking the North American and Thompson takeover bids and turning over control of AVCO to the Cord interests.[62]

Immediately, in newspapers across the country, there appeared articles and advertisements bought by Cord in support of his plan, calling for proxies for the forthcoming special stockholders meeting planned for December 21. In the published broadsides, Cord decried the proposed North American acquisition as bad for AVCO. Cord felt that North American's stock was overvalued and that the cost was therefore too high for a gain of just 35 percent in air mail revenues. He also felt that AVCO should not acquire additional manufacturing companies, but should stay in the air transportation and air mail fields only.[63]

Cord became justifiably concerned when his lieutenants reported to him a conversation they had had with J.A. Talbot concerning the recent problems encountered by Clement Keys and his unsecured call loans. Talbot brought with him an auditor's report on North American. Apparently, as early as 1929, following the Wall Street debacle, North American directors had learned of Keys's inability to repay several million dollars worth of outstanding call loans. Keys had made it a practice for many years to borrow from his corporations for other investments, but he had always repaid the loans. Unfortunately, with the collapse of the stock market in October 1929, Keys was wiped out. Quietly, J. Cheever Cowdin and fellow directors allowed Keys to pay back as much as possible, seizing his remaining assets and writing off $766,997 in the hope that the unintentional embezzlement would not be discovered. In turn, Keys was forced to resign at the end of 1931. Armed with this knowledge, Cord was encouraged in his fight. He could use this information against Cowdin and company to force them and their accomplices into reneging on the sale of their North American stock.[64]

La Motte Cohu and the board vigorously defended their position in public, urging support for their plan that would give AVCO a direct connection to the East Coast and the prosperous northeast through the acquisition of Eastern Air Transport thus strengthening American Airways' transcontinental system. The merger would also reduce overhead costs while increasing revenue through additional passengers and air mail. Cohu strongly denied Cord's allegations and showed how his plans were reducing AVCO's losses. The merger would increase the current assets of AVCO by $3 million, increase the number of shares from 5 million to 6.5 million, and reduce the par value of AVCO stock from $5 to $4 per share, which would produce a return of $1 per share to each existing holders of stock.[65] Cohu claimed that far from attempting to improve AVCO, Cord's intervention actually prevented many planned reforms within the company and that his haste in attacking the proposed merger prevented a logical and reasoned analysis of the situation.[66] Neither side openly confessed to the actual reasons behind these maneuverings, as the stockholders would not have appreciated their investments being used as pawns in a personal power struggle.

As the battle escalated, cooler heads finally prevailed with the realization of the possible harm to everyone's sizable investment such a fight was producing. During the late evening of November 17, 1932, Cord and Cohu agreed to a compromise put forth by Frank Vanderlip that called for a new board of directors composed of fifteen members, five from the present directors, excluding Cord and Manning, five from Cord's interests, and five from independents. The newly constituted board would resolve all of the other matters at issue. In return, all litigation, advertisements, and other negative publicity was to cease. To this Lehman, Fairchild, Cohu, Harriman, Vanderlip, and Manning affixed their signatures, thus ending the dispute.[67]

The compromise was in fact a victory for Cord. His interests now controlled one-third of the board. The North American deal was permanently blocked, which ironically allowed another suitor, General Motors, to acquire North American in March 1933. Also, on March 15, 1933, Cord secured the resignations of Cohu, Harriman, Lehman, George Hann, and Richard Hoyt from the board, thus giving him complete control of AVCO. Cord was elected chairman of the board, Manning, president, and Lyndol Young, vice president.[68] They also assumed similar positions with American Airways, thus finally securing the airline and air mail contracts for which Cord had so desperately fought. In addition, Cord managed to acquire total control of Thompson Aeronautical by buying out Richard Hoyt and promptly selling it to AVCO, now that he had control of both corporations.

An independent had now become an air mail carrier. While Glover and the Post Office Department did not care for Cord, they had more serious problems: Hoover had just lost the presidential election to Gov. Franklin D. Roosevelt of New York. The Republican era was coming to a close, and with it its Progressive attitude toward business. In the air mail, the effect of this political change was not known but it was expected to be bad. Much depended on the attitude of the new president, his new postmaster general, and the new Democratic majority in both houses of Congress.

Chapter 12

The Democrats Take Control

Cord's successful takeover of AVCO and its American Airways subsidiary drastically changed the complexion of the air mail industry. The carefully crafted and well-protected system of awarding air mail contracts to the three large holding companies had been successfully circumvented by perhaps one of the most controversial stock manipulators in the country. Overnight, United Aircraft and North American Aviation found themselves confronted with a former enemy now on the inside.

They need not have worried. Cord was content with controlling AVCO and sought only to compete with the other holding companies, not undermine them. His vested interest now was in the preservation, not destruction, of the system, yet he was still feared. Under his leadership, American Airways greatly improved its efficiency and soon rose into a position of strength sufficient to rival TWA and United Air Lines. Smaller air mail carriers, such as Northwest, were concerned as Cord entered into their territory. The remaining independents felt betrayed.

Cord's sellout to AVCO in March 1932 nullified a pending agreement he had made with the Ludington brothers. Already a faithful operator of Stinson airliners, the Ludingtons had fought hard for recognition and an air mail contract, lending their strong voice in the recent congressional hearings. They had arranged a merger with Cord in the hope of forming a large, independent airline capable of competing directly with the air mail contractors, but it was not to be. After Cord sold Century and Century Pacific to AVCO, Ludington was left out in the cold. Sincere efforts by the Post Office to provide Ludington with a special express air mail service fell through when Congress would not authorize any additional expenditures. In 1933, Ludington, with William MacCracken as its corporate attorney, was sold to Eastern Air Transport.

Amon Carter, publisher of the *Fort Worth Star-Telegram* and major AVCO investor, confers with American Airways officials La Motte Cohu, Edward V. Rickenbacker, and C.R. Smith. Rickenbacker later became president of Eastern Airlines. Photo courtesy of American Airlines C.R. Smith Museum.

Cord was also in the early stages of negotiating a deal with Braniff when AVCO stepped in. Initially a supporter of the Braniff brothers and Temple Bowen in their strenuous efforts with the Scheduled Airline Operators Association to force the Post Office to supply contracts to the independents, Cord chose to fight alone in 1931 before his deal with AVCO, believing that he could accomplish more without the baggage of supporting the efforts of other, far weaker independents. This situation left Braniff and Bowen abandoned, at least for the moment.

Braniff and Bowen, serving the oil fields of Texas and Oklahoma and instilled with the intense fervor of the independent wildcatters, took their fight into the political arena of the Democratic Party. Both airlines served Fort Worth, the home of A.P. Barrett, the driving force behind Southern Air Transport, and powerful newspaper magnate Amon Carter, publisher of the *Fort Worth Star-Telegram*, an influential conservative Democratic paper. The Braniff brothers and Temple Bowen both maintained offices in that city and were friends with numerous influential oil men and cattlemen.

Carter was one of the original investors in Southern Air Transport and continued as a director of American Airways and the Aviation Corporation until Cord took over. He was a major force in the Democratic Party in Texas and one of the primary backers of the Speaker of the House, John Nance Garner. His faithful lieutenant, Silliman Evans, served him first as a reporter and then as vice president of publicity for American Airways.

All of these men possessed a sturdy independent streak and resented the mess they believed their eastern financial partners had created in AVCO. While not enthusiastic supporters of the upstart E.L. Cord, they sympathized with his efforts to clean up American while pursuing constant efforts to push United's National Air Transport out of Dallas and Fort Worth. American, along with Braniff and Bowen, wanted the CAM-3 route from Chicago through Oklahoma into Texas.[1] Braniff and Bowen traveled in the same social, political, and economic circles as the founders of American Airways and sought to use their connections to their advantage in the election year of 1932.

Their chance came during the Democratic Convention in Chicago. Earlier in the year, Gov. Franklin D. Roosevelt had seemed a shoo-in for the Democratic presidential nomination. His term as New York governor had produced critical reforms in the face of the escalating economic crisis, placing him in the forefront of national politics for the forthcoming election. Running against him were former New York governor Al Smith and Speaker of the House John Nance Garner, both of whom trailed Roosevelt by significant margins. By the time the Democratic Convention opened in Chicago on June 27, 1932, Roosevelt's position had changed. Despite his overwhelming lead in delegates, 666 1/4 to 201 3/4 over Smith, party rules required a two-thirds majority for nomination. This Roosevelt did not have. Campaign manager James Farley worked desperately for days to sway delegates to his candidate, but after three ballots little had changed. Sensing a growing harmful division within the party, Farley approached Garner for a deal.

Leading Garner's Texas delegation were Rep. Sam Rayburn, Amon Carter, and Silliman Evans. Throughout the day of July 1 the two opposing camps hammered out a solution to the impasse using Evans as the messenger. By evening a deal was struck: in return for Garner's ninety delegates, Roosevelt would place Garner on the ticket as vice presidential candidate. The arrangement was not favorably received by many of Garner's delegates, who disliked Roosevelt, but sufficient members, including Fort Worth attorney Karl Crowley, acceded to Garner's wishes and swung to Roosevelt. News of the switch reached the California delegation, which was led by the defeated 1924 Democratic aspirant, William Gibbs McAdoo. With his attempts at entering the airline business behind him, McAdoo had turned his attention completely to politics and, with the support of publisher William Randolph Hearst, had reentered the arena as a candidate for the U.S. Senate and the leader of the California delegation in support of Garner. McAdoo, with evident glee in blocking his former opponent Al Smith from the nomination, addressed the convention, announcing on the fourth ballot that he was releasing California's forty-four votes to Roosevelt. Thus began the avalanche of delegates that swung the balance in Roosevelt's favor.[2] After the successful campaign, Farley, Evans, and Crowley were among the faithful workers rewarded for their efforts.

Tradition required the new candidate to remain at home until informed of his party's decision. But Roosevelt, fond of impressive gestures and eager to break tired traditions, decided to accept the nomination in Chicago in person.

Chartering a Ford 5-AT Tri-Motor from the Colonial Western division of American Airways, Governor Roosevelt, together with his wife Eleanor, son John, and several others, climbed aboard the aircraft at Albany on July 2 and flew to Chicago. Roosevelt's flight helped to dispel malicious rumors about his health. He worked and slept during the flight. The others got airsick.

After a difficult flight, the entourage reached Chicago and was given a tumultuous reception by a throng clearly impressed with the new candidate's willingness to take risks. Roosevelt's invigorating speech to the convention, much of which he wrote while in flight, set the tone for his campaign. Speaking to the assembled delegates, he asserted, "I pledge you, I pledge myself to a new deal for the American people."[3] "New Deal" quickly became the rallying slogan and theme for his successful bid for the presidency.

Once again, President Hoover's campaign was run by Walter Folger Brown, this time with little success. With the Hoover campaign foundering along with the economy and the catastrophe of the Bonus Army debacle firmly in the public's mind, Brown had little time to attend to air mail matters.

That fall, as they reluctantly realized Hoover would lose the election, Brown and department officials slipped into a funk. The prospect of a Roosevelt presidency produced some gallows humor on the part of Superintendent E.B. Wadsworth. Post Office executives were keenly aware that despite their apparent victory during the recent Mead hearings, theirs was a losing battle as the independents gained strength with the rising Democratic tide. Wadsworth was concerned about the growing allegations of favoritism. In speaking with the superintendent about a particularly nasty attack in the press, Colonel Henderson reported, "Wadsworth was not a little concerned about the news item and told us that his future address would probably be Atlanta"—the location of the federal penitentiary.[4]

Even the contractors managed to find relief in humor. In late 1932, as the polls were showing an ever-widening lead for Roosevelt, the Pioneer Air Transport Operators arranged a gala dinner in celebration of their first anniversary and in honor of the postmaster general. Five hundred guests attended the festivities at the Newark Airport. When arranging the final details for the party, George Wheat of United Aircraft quipped to United Air Lines' Philip Johnson, "Both Brown and Glover insisted on flowers (probably sensing the November 8th results) so please add that to the bill sent you."[5]

The air mail carriers were concerned that a Republican defeat would greatly upset the existing air mail situation and were preparing for the worst. Capt. Thomas Doe of Eastern Air Transport underscored the industry's concerns. "It becomes more and more evident that aviation in general and air mail in particular are headed for a fight for existence," he remarked. He felt that the coming battle in Congress would obviously center on the economy, particularly the perceived inefficiency, apparent arbitrary route awards, and alleged corruption. The new leadership was particularly driven "to get at the bankers on the theory that these companies are all controlled by Wall Street," Doe believed. "It makes no difference whether there are any just grounds or not. Back of this fight will be some of the railroads–pacifists–taxpayers leagues–enemies of the Post Office Department and a lot of 'new brooms' out to change everything." Despite there being no basis for the attack, "attacking the air mail is going to be popular in the next Congress."[6] Doe's prediction was only too accurate.

Disliked by both business and Congress, Brown, in January 1933, incurred the wrath of the House when he attempted to extend more routes rather than award new contracts.[7] An angry House Post Office Committee drafted a resolution, H. Res. 359, urging Brown to cease making any further sweeping schedule changes that would benefit AVCO and North American. Hainer Hinshaw, now representing United Air Lines, speculated on Brown's reaction, stating, "He is a very strong minded man and had so often indicated his contempt for the gentlemen on 'the Hill' that he may go ahead and carry out his original plans."[8]

United hoped the effort would succeed, as it had not benefited from any extension, except the unwanted Watertown route. The airline had received all of its routes by competitive bidding well before Brown took office, and, therefore, wanted its name cleared before the coming investigations. "Congressman Maas is taking it wholly upon himself as the instigator of the resolutions, insisting that Brown does not move in the extension matters," stated Hinshaw. "This is most helpful for us because it removes us completely from suspicion that we might have been behind it."[9]

Brown responded to his critics with a thorough statement outlining his reasoning while refusing to cancel his latest extensions. The tardiness in making these route extensions was due not to political maneuvering, stated Brown, but to inevitable delays because of the recent rate revision he finally produced. This revision lowered the average pay to approximately forty-five cents per mile. In addition, since several of the extensions went to American and TWA, Brown wanted to wait until the two-year grace period on contracts for CAM-33 and CAM-34 had lapsed so that these airlines could exchange their contracts for longer-term route certificates for their respective transcontinental routes. This would allow the department to place substantially lower rates in effect on these two important routes.

Brown pointedly reminded the committee that any route or rate changes could only be made with airlines holding certificates, not contracts. Brown understood that new political pressures were being applied but managed to withstand the blast while delivering a none too subtle reminder of the partisan nature of the attacks and their ultimate source.[10] In summarizing his position to Chairman Mead, Brown took the opportunity to remind the committee of the purpose of his work. "In determining upon these changes the Department has been governed solely by the public interest," he declared. "Our objective has been, first, to promote the most complete, widespread and effective air mail service for postal patrons possible within the limit of the appropriation for air mail, and second, to enable air mail operators to build up non postal revenues and to effect economies in operation which would be reflected in reduced operating costs to the government."[11] Far from having received more money, the operators were furious at Brown's latest rate reduction, which cut their subsidy payments far more than they had originally thought.[12]

While Chairman Mead remarked that Brown was within the law, he and others warned that an even angrier Senate could hold up the appropriations for the next fiscal year.[13] Indeed, that was precisely the consequence when lame-duck Brown ignored the committee's warning and turned up the fire one last time in their often bitter feuding. Colonel Brittin observed the deteriorating situation with great trepidation:

> Postmaster General Brown has hopelessly antagonized the entire Progressive group in the Senate. He has also incurred the enmity of the entire Democratic Minority. Together Progressives and Democrats have formed an overwhelming majority against him. The sentiment is not only antagonistic to him but also against the extensions he has recently made. Some time ago chairman Mead of the House Post Office and Post Roads Committee asked the Postmaster General if he would defer making further extensions until the Committee report on Dr. Crane's investigation had been made. Mr. Brown replied that he

did not intend to make any last minute extensions. In spite of these assurances the Postmaster General recently made some very important changes in the air mail map and granted a number of extensions. This summary action ignoring the committee's recommendation altogether caused a great deal of unfavorable comment not only in the committee but throughout the whole Democratic majority of the House that had previously voted Mr. Brown his $19 million domestic air mail appropriation.

This general development prompted the Senate yesterday to report out favorably the Black Resolution calling for a sweeping investigation of the entire air mail situation. It was formulated by a coalition of Progressives and Democrats cooperating with the Post Office and Post Roads Committee of the House.[14]

Brown's effrontery infuriated Senate Democrats so much that they briefly struck out the $19 million air mail appropriation altogether and moved to open their own hearings. They had already agreed to cut the expenditure to $10 million before the postmaster general's actions. It was later restored to $15 million.[15]

Brown also replied to his Senate critics. He recalled the accomplishments of the last four years and the purpose behind the Watres Act:

Since the Department has been authorized by the McNary-Watres Act to exert pressure on air mail operators to carry passengers and express their revenues derived from non-postal sources, which were practically nil four years ago, have steadily increased until at the present time they are running at the rate of $6 million per annum and constantly increasing, notwithstanding the business stagnation. The increase in revenues from passenger and express traffic has enabled the Department to cut the average compensation per mile for air mail operators in successive stages from 82 cents in 1930 to an average of 45 cents effective November 1, 1932. With general business recovery I am confident the increased postal and other revenues that may reasonably be anticipated will justify further cuts to a level approximating the actual value of the service rendered, excluding any subsidy.[16]

In fact, the industry was about to be revolutionized. Following Brown's first rate revision conference in February 1931, he called on the airlines and aircraft manufacturers to build faster, larger, and more efficient aircraft, spurred by direct variables paid to the operators for such advancements as multiple engines, two-way radio, and larger carrying capacity.

United Aircraft and Transport Corporation listened. On February 8, 1933, in Seattle, Washington, the Boeing 247 first took flight, ushering in the modern age of aircraft design. The aircraft, with its all-metal construction, twin air-cooled, cowled engines, retractable landing gear, cantilevered wings, and seating for ten, possessed a remarkable cruising speed of 160 miles per hour,

50 percent faster than any other commercial airliner, thus rendering the competition obsolete overnight. By April, the 247 was in service with United Air Lines, and by June, it was operating United's transcontinental routes, at greatly reduced costs, cutting transcontinental travel time from twenty-four hours to nineteen and three-quarter hours. The one-way fare remained at $160 and the round trip at $260.[17] Compared to the 69.3-cents-per-mile operating cost of the Ford Tri-Motor it replaced, the Boeing 247 cost 51.9 cents per mile. The 247 cost per ton mile of payload was much lower at 37.2 cents per mile versus 43.3 cents per mile. This was even lower than the vaunted single-engine Lockheed Vega used by the independents. Its operating cost per mile was lower than the 247 at 38.1 cents per mile, but its cost per ton mile was higher at 56.5 cents.[18] The Boeing was a technological breakthrough, but far more important, it was more efficient to operate and therefore more profitable. It also led the way to the larger Douglas DC-2 and the classic DC-3, the first aircraft capable of making a profit by carrying only passengers—just as Brown had planned.

The first flight of the 247 received little notice in Congress. The renewed attack on Brown's extensions alarmed Brittin of Northwest Airways. Northwest, though one of the smallest carriers, had received the lion's share of the route extensions. This was due directly to Brittin's well-orchestrated plan, which mobilized the congressional delegations in the northern and western states his airline served for additional service. All of his requests, done carefully, were with the determined goal of extending a fourth transcontinental line, this time from Minneapolis to Seattle through the sparsely populated states of the Northwest.

Since 1929, the Post Office had constantly rebuffed Brittin's efforts, correctly stating that there was insufficient population to sustain a viable passenger and air mail base. Despite the clear logic of the Post Office's rebukes, Brittin persisted. Gradually, he persuaded the department to grant his airline numerous short extensions through North Dakota and into Montana, over the direct protests of Alfred Frank's National Parks Airline. Operating from Salt Lake City into Montana and Idaho, National Parks strenuously fought Northwest's advances and had the quiet, firm support of United Air Lines behind it. United was not overly concerned with the small Northwest Airways but had no desire for Brittin to enter Seattle, Boeing's home.

Northwest was particularly frightened by the sudden appearance of E.L. Cord in its back yard. During the merger mania in the airline industry in 1929, Northwest was subjected to heavy pressure from both Transcontinental Air Transport and Universal Airlines, both of which wanted to extend their routes into Minneapolis–St. Paul. Already TAT had purchased 45 percent of Northwest's stock as part of a deal to include Brittin's airline in Keys's transcontinental plan. This provided much additional capital but at the cost of some independence for the fiercely independent Northwest. When Universal began to invade Minnesota, a dangerous confrontation was averted when Universal agreed to withdraw from the territory in return for half of TAT's share in Northwest. Since that time, Brittin had tried to force TAT and AVCO to sell back their shares, even attempting to have the Post Office act in their behalf, but with no effect. For three years the point was academic, as neither TAT nor AVCO attempted to unduly influence Northwest's decision making. The seizure of AVCO by the ruthless Cord changed the situation dramatically for Brittin.

Now Cord controlled Universal's 22.5 percent in Northwest. More important, Cord also had just purchased Transamerican. This new arrangement directly threatened Northwest because it seemed to Brittin that Cord was planning to push into his territory either directly or indirectly. The climax to this struggle came over the question of control of Lake Michigan.

A small independent operator had been flying a regular passenger route from Milwaukee to Detroit across Lake Michigan since 1929. Founded by Frank and John Kohler, the Kohler Aviation Corporation, as with other independents, had desperately fought for an air mail contract to ensure its survival. Unlike the other independents, Kohler chose not to confront the Post Office Department openly but to work quietly and patiently behind the scenes with a tenacious letter-writing campaign and persistent political pressure. Even though Postmaster General Brown disliked overwater routes for his domestic air mail carriers and saw little need for the trans-lake service, Kohler finally prevailed in 1933, receiving a promise for help.

As with other passenger lines before, Brown provided the route through a subcontract to an existing carrier who received the route as an extension. This obviated the need for additional appropriations and competitive bidding for a new route while preserving direct responsibility of the smaller company by the financial resources of the larger airline holding the existing route certificate. When Brown decided to provide for Kohler, he did so by awarding the extension to Transamerican, which in turn was instructed to sublet the extension to Kohler.

For three years, Northwest had curtly rebuffed Kohler's numerous entreaties for a merger. Now, with the specter of E.L. Cord facing Northwest from across Lake Michigan, Brittin frantically leapt into action, anxiously trying to persuade the Post Office to give the extension to his airline. Brittin flooded the department with his desperate pleas to take the new route. He even called on Cord arguing that since AVCO owned 22.5 percent of Northwest, it would make sense to take the route and sublet it to Kohler, relieving Transamerican of the burden.

Surprisingly, his efforts worked. To the department's astonishment, Cord reversed his decision and declined to accept the trans-lake service, thereby giving the route to Brittin. Cord was not swayed by Brittin's arguments, nor was he overcome by a sudden wave of compassion for his competition: he simply felt that since he was a Democrat, unlike virtually all of the executives of the air mail contractors, he would receive a better deal directly from the incoming Roosevelt administration.[19] As events would show, he was correct.

Freed from this immediate concern, Brittin and the other contractors turned their attention to the pressing need to determine the attitude of the incoming Democratically controlled Congress and new administration. Thomas Doe's earlier assessment about the coming problems was astute: the question of monopoly in the airline industry was foremost on Congress' mind. The event that triggered this renewed interest was the release of Professor John B. Crane's report on December 5, 1932.

Crane, a professor of economics at Harvard University, was assigned the task of examining the nation's air mail system and reporting back to the House Committee on the Post Office and Post Roads. After nine months of gathering information from the department and the airlines, Crane released his report, much to the dismay of the air mail contractors.

Crane made six specific recommendations after completing his thorough examination. First, he suggested that "the air mail rates now being paid are higher than necessary, and that the air mail appropriations for the coming fiscal year could be reduced by $1,000,000 without seriously injuring the development of the air transportation industry, or defeating the fundamental objectives underlying the present governmental subsidy policy." Crane's second suggestion was that field audits be conducted on the contractors in order to determine accurately the actual costs upon which new rates could be determined.

Third, Crane suggested that a new "cost-balancing principle of rate making be required and that the administrative machinery in the Post Office be enlarged to enable this policy to be carried out." This system would balance the actual expenses incurred by an airline and supply a subsidy to balance out the difference to break even but no more. Crane gave tacit approval for Brown's 1930 decision to abandon Clyde Kelly's weight-based method of payment. Although paying a contractor for only the mail load actually carried made economic sense in a mature, profitable industry, air transportation was still in its infancy and required assistance to survive. "If this principle were rigidly followed," he stated, "from one-half to two-thirds of the present air mail route mileage would be eliminated at once, and several of the operators would go into bankruptcy in short order." Only those airlines operating mainline trunks, such as United and TWA, would prosper. Crane's fourth recommendation was to reduce the present maximum payment rate from $1.25 to $0.75 per mile if

Congress chose to continue the Watres Act. Crane did not consider the recently reduced rates imposed by Brown in November.

Crane's final two recommendations dealt with the contentious issue of route extensions. He strongly urged that greater limitations be placed on the postmaster general to prevent the apparent arbitrary extension of routes and revision of rates. In this, Crane overlooked the careful work both Brown and the department usually undertook before such decisions were made, even in the face of strong political pressure to the contrary.

More important, Crane argued that several of the present extensions were unnecessary and should be canceled. This latter point greatly upset those airlines most vulnerable, particularly American Airways and Northwest. American had its mileage increased by 63 percent and Northwest a remarkable 79 percent through Brown's extensions. In contrast, United grew only 6.37 percent and that was solely the unwanted Watertown extension. Crane's target was the expensive and unproductive "feeder" route that connected relatively unpopulated areas with the main line routes. This included Northwest's service from St. Paul to Duluth and United's Watertown line. The elimination of eight of these routes, he estimated, would save the department more than four hundred thousand dollars each year.

Surprisingly, while the report sought to streamline these apparently extraneous routes, Crane recommended the extension of Northwest's service westward into Montana in the hope of eventually opening up a northern transcontinental just as Brittin had wanted. Furthermore, Crane saw little need for National Parks' service, which he deemed extraneous in light of the fact that most of the actual traffic served by this airline would be better served by an east-west line such as Northwest. Against many of the department's critics, however, Crane recognized that larger companies were inherently more efficient. "The economics of the situation are such that in this way only can the operators hope to lower their costs to the point where ultimately a mail subsidy will not be needed," he stated. "Contrary to the opinions expressed by certain writers, transportation is clearly subject to decreasing cost as the scale of operations is enlarged."[20]

In fact, Crane determined that operating costs dropped by more than half if the route mileage were doubled. He recommended that airlines have their schedules increased to provide greater service and produce lower operating costs with the aim of reaching financial independence. Ironically, by so stating, Crane confirmed the wisdom of Brown's earlier plan, as this was precisely what Brown had wanted to do when he fought for the Watres Act. In fact, Crane drew the same conclusion as Brown about the oligopolistic nature of this new, capital intensive, vertically integrated industry: "The air transportation industry is one where neither complete monopoly nor pure competition is economically desirable. The ideal status is one of 'monopolistic competition' or balanced competition where a limited number of trunk lines compete evenly with each other in service at all important terminals."[21] Brown could not have described his program any better himself.

Crane argued for the eventual cessation of air mail subsidies and for allowing the airlines to compete on their own. Most important was the condemnation of the power of the three major holding companies, stating that despite their youth, the aviation combines were as complex and intricately developed as the railroads and utilities, and dominated 98 percent of the air mail system. Specifically, the report singled out the corporate infrastructures of UATC and AVCO for review:

> A closer examination of each company's corporate structure . . . reveals that United Air Lines controls four airmail operating companies through stock ownership, and is in turn owned 100 percent by United Aircraft and Transport, a holding company which controls airplane and airplane engine manufacturing companies as well as some propeller companies.
>
> American Airways controls numerous subsidiary companies, some of which have recently been liquidated, and is in turn owned 100 percent by the Aviation Corporation of Delaware, a holding corporation which is reported to have controlled in 1930 over 118 companies through stock ownership, many of which companies lay in the aviation field. Many of these corporations were acquired through mergers and have since been dissolved. The Aviation Corporation of Delaware also owns 22-1/2 percent of the stock of Northwest Airways.[22]

Crane nonetheless warned critics of the present air mail system that rash actions could irreparably damage a system that was functioning in the public interest even with its flaws. He noted that "extreme caution must be used in passing judgment upon the question of the excessiveness of air mail service. The motive responsible for the subsidy of the aviation industry by the government are shown to be four; the military, the economic, the political, and the social. The economic benefits or losses are readily measurable, but it is virtually impossible to measure accurately the military, political, and social importance of air transportation. In the final analysis, whether the volume of air mail service is excessive or not must be decided by Congress itself."[23]

Crane's report greatly upset the air mail contractors, even though his conclusions were mild, even complimentary, of the system. Nevertheless, the call for the elimination of several extensions and a lowering of the air mail appropriation and reduction of the rate system alarmed many in the industry. More important, the report laid the foundation for another investigation, this time by a Congress dominated by Democrats and insurgent Republicans.

On March 4, 1933, Franklin Roosevelt was sworn in as the nation's thirty-second president. As was customary, the new president quickly filled hundreds of positions with his supporters and specifically gave his former campaign manager, James Farley, the nation's premier patronage post of postmaster general. Serving alongside Farley were W.W. Howes of South Dakota as second assistant postmaster general, who was a backer of Rapid Air Lines' earlier attempt to garner a contract; former American Airways vice president of publicity Silliman Evans, as fourth assistant postmaster general; and Fort Worth attorney Karl Crowley as solicitor.

Brittin paid a visit to the Post Office Department and called on Howes and Evans to discuss the effect of the lower $15 million air mail appropriation facing the industry with the new fiscal year beginning on July 1. Brittin liked Howes but was deeply concerned about the latter's total lack of experience in air mail matters. In his favor, Howes was seen to be a studious and deliberate individual who would be easier to deal with than the autocratic Glover. As for Silliman Evans, Brittin was kinder. Evans wanted the post of second assistant because of his airline experience but was denied it by Farley because of possible conflicts of interest. Brittin had known Evans for years and was impressed with his work at American. Evans had supported LaMotte Cohu and had left AVCO after Cord took over. Brittin assumed correctly that Evans would be consulted by Farley and Howes on air mail matters.[24]

Brittin astutely ascertained the negative attitude of the new administration toward air mail matters and was not encouraged. "It appears that the new administration is thoroughly impressed with the idea that Mr. Brown's administration of the Post Office Department was marked by many irregular acts of favoritism," he remarked. He was concerned that the new administration in the Post Office thought that the Watres Act had been abused and that the system was in need of a good, housecleaning that could be politically explosive, however, if not handled well. "Mr. Farley," Brittin concluded, "wants to be relieved of the entire problem and has therefore given Mr. Howes complete authority and entire support."[25]

Air mail, however, was not the primary issue facing the new president. As Roosevelt took office, the nation was on the brink of economic collapse as the banking system was rapidly failing. Roosevelt quickly introduced a bank holiday to stem the tide of panic withdrawals, returning some stability to the weakened system while instituting his remarkable "100 Days" of emergency legislation to bring relief to the struggling country.

Roosevelt had no clearly defined public policy concerning air mail or the problem of monopoly. Though a former member of President Woodrow Wilson's administration, Roosevelt had yet to enunciate his views, thus leaving such matters, at least temporarily, in the hands of congressional Progres-

sive Democrats such as Tennessee senator Kenneth McKellar and Alabama senator Hugo Black. McKellar's record against the air mail "monopolies" was already well known in Congress and feared by the airlines.

Black's position was made just as clear when in February he introduced
legislation calling for a formal investigation of the alleged misconduct of the
former postmaster general. Reacting against Brown's last-minute attempt to
extend the eight routes, Black, suspecting massive corruption and malfeasance,
called for the Senate to delve deeply into the workings of the Post Office, particularly the machinations of the airlines and their holding companies. Black's
request was granted, and for most of 1933 he and his staff of investigators
undertook the time-consuming task of searching the books of all of the airlines while conducting a massive campaign of interrogations. Black's special
committee prepared for months in the hope of opening hearings in the fall. In
the meantime, the House and the president were to make their presence felt.

Republican representative Clyde Kelly, the sponsor seven years earlier of
the original Contract Air Mail Act, proposed a revision to his bill on March 3,
1933, that was intended as a protest of both Brown's actions and attitude. In
this he had the total support of Chairman Mead and the Democratic majority.
Kelly hated Brown and wanted to rearrange the air mail system completely
and restore the original pound-per-mile basis for payment. Under Kelly's proposal, no operator would be paid more than 2 mills per pound mile. This Kelly
did despite Crane's recommendations and the success of Brown's weight-based
method, which encouraged the development of larger aircraft but often resulted in the under-utilization of equipment. The bill was designed to cut costs
and waste and eliminate some forms of perceived corruption.[26] Stated Kelly
on the floor of the House, "During the past Congress the air mail service has
been under fire, due largely to the undue development of this new branch of
the service. . . . The United States air mail service has been a vital factor in
building the aviation industry of the United States. . . . The quantity of air mail
has steadily increased. A market has been furnished for planes and equipment
and a large number of pilots have been giving the opportunity for training.
However, the cost of these developments through subsidy payments has been
increasing and has gone further than was originally intended. This service can
and should be put on a self-sustaining basis."[27]

This speech set the tone for the forthcoming debate. Convinced that the
previous administration had managed the air mail system improperly and
with great wastage, congressional critics shortsightedly argued for immediate cost reductions rather than the gradual reduction plan with offsetting
encouragement for passenger revenue instituted by Brown. The obsession
with low-cost air mail service played into the hands of the independents,

who, without the requirement to carry passengers in safe aircraft, did indeed have lower operating costs.

Determined to cut federal spending no matter the consequences, Democrats and other air mail critics overlooked the long-range plan of Brown to develop a national air transportation system. In fact, Chairman Mead, in his final report on the 1932 hearings, recommended continuing much of Brown's work, particularly with regard to sponsoring the development of larger and safer aircraft, a continuation of the subsidy, and the return of the air mail postage of five cents per half ounce. This latter suggestion followed Brown's 1932 air mail postage increase to eight cents, which he thought would increase revenue. Unfortunately, the increase was offset by a corresponding decrease in letters sent. The industry was pleasantly surprised with the generally constructive nature of his report but was concerned with the chairman's interest in attacking the aviation holding companies.[28]

The recommendations of the Crane Report and the final report of the Mead committee moved Kelly to fight for another, more crucial provision in his bill. Under H.R. 3, he proposed that "no route warrant shall be issued to any air mail contractor who has any financial interest in or participates in the management of any line other than that covered in whole or in part by said route warrant."[29] This would effectively prohibit one airline from operating another airline (thus receiving additional indirect federal payments). The large operators were in general support of the provision of H.R. 3, except for this provision.[30]

With this, the question of monopoly in the airline industry was coming to the forefront. Progressive Democrats and renegade Republicans had been attacking Brown's deliberate favoritism of the large holding companies for years with little effect. Brown ably demonstrated his Progressive Republican reasoning for favoring these more efficient operations, which were certainly operating in the public interest as they were wholly dependent upon the government's largess for their very existence. Now, however, with Brown gone and the Democrats in power, the voices rising in opposition to the oligopolies became much louder.

The debate from this point onward revolved around the matter of monopoly. The discussion shifted from deliberations on the efficacy and legality of extensions and accusations of excessive air mail payments to increasingly demonstrative attacks on the very structure of the industry. Braniff and the other independents took advantage of the situation, which was largely their creation, and sought to portray themselves as honest small businessmen denied their right to a livelihood by the machinations of predatory monopoly. They carefully ignored mentioning their role in creating the very monopoly they attacked. The pictures painted by the independents and by Congressional Democrats recalled the worst predations of big business during the Gilded Age. Compounding this issue was the entry of one of America's largest holding companies into aviation.

In March 1933, General Motors officially completed its efforts to purchase control of North American Aviation, now that the battle between Cord and AVCO was settled. The company now gained control of Eastern Air Transport and TWA, as well as working control of Western Air Express, through a merger with its subsidiary, General Aviation Corporation, at a cost of $3,676,000.[31] The entry of GM clearly demonstrated that aviation was finally a serious, full-scale enterprise, capable of producing profits for the investor and operator alike. Significantly, it signaled the end of the speculative age in aviation trading.

A company as powerful and respected as General Motors would not enter a new field if the business conditions were not sound. Providing such a foundation for the industry was Walter Brown's primary intention during his time in office. Aviation in general and the airlines in particular were finally on a sound financial basis, and GM was ready to take part. Such a move caused great consternation, nonetheless, and initiated a Justice Department inquiry concerning any possible infringement of the Sherman or Clayton antitrust acts. The government found that all was in order, but the entry of GM into the airline and aircraft manufacturing business only fanned the fears of antimonopoly critics. They saw this move not as a benign turning point in the development of commercial aviation but as a strong confirmation of their worst fears that monopoly, with all of its supposed evils, was dominating this new industry. Brittin aptly summed up the situation: "It seems to me that the financial control of the big aviation holding companies have selected a most inopportune time to engineer their mergers and consolidations. They should at least have waited until the appropriation bill, upon which their very existence depends, had passed both Houses. I feel that their activities have seriously disturbed the present situation."[32]

The hearings on Kelly's new bill convened in April 1933 and revealed an unexpected maverick in the airline industry who urged that Congress bar interlocking directorates altogether. Col. Lewis H. Brittin of Northwest had no love of combines. Though his airline was owned in large part by AVCO, Brittin was energetically attempting to buy back the company. He correctly sensed the mood of Congress and sought to portray his airline as a small independent struggling to break free of the grasp of monopolies and thereby gain backing for his northern transcontinental route.

On April 20, Brittin broke ranks with the other air mail contractors and forcefully testified before Congress. "I feel that it would be distinctly detrimental to the development of this industry if we were to foster a monopolistic tendency," he said. "I think it is very important to keep alive this matter of independence among these air mail operators; and I do not think you could afford to encourage a situation where you will have in this country one, two, or three, perhaps, dominating systems of air mail. I think the public interest of this time would be promoted by your encouraging independent operations."[33] Specifically, Brittin recommended prohibiting holding companies from receiving any air mail payments whatsoever.

No other witness pleaded such a strong case. The other airline representatives argued against the specific payment provisions and agreed with Thomas B. Doe of Eastern Air Transport that "this discussion of interlocking directorates and ownerships is premature. I do not think it is nearly so serious as some of us have heard. . . . As this Air Mail service develops it is going to be regulated by the government. And it will make little difference who owns them."[34]

Surprisingly, H.R. 3 was generally well received by some air mail contractors. Especially supportive was United. The weight-based payment system would greatly benefit its service, as the airline carried the bulk of all transcontinental air mail. Stated Frederick Rentschler to Philip Johnson, "As I indicated to you over the 'phone this morning, I am convinced that we ought to get solidly behind the Kelly Bill." For Rentschler, the bill offered the opportunity to break free of the subsidy altogether, something the Watres Act had intended for the operators eventually to do, and thus free them from politically motivated attacks.[35]

American Airways officials felt differently. They feared that a return to the weight-based method of payment would drastically reduce their income, particularly over the lightly traveled southern transcontinental route. To prevent this from happening, Lucius Manning made a desperate appeal to the Illinois congressional delegation for support in heading off the Kelly bill. Cleverly employing the antimonopoly argument to his advantage, Manning told Rep. A.J. Sabath of Chicago, now that American had moved its headquarters to the shores of Lake Michigan, "We are strongly of the opinion that no emergency exists which would justify the adoption of the Kelly Bill at this time. . . . As far as our companies are concerned, we are willing to co-operate in any program which is in the interest of economy, and to take our share of the appropriation cut which has been made, but we shall oppose to the best of our ability a program which, as you can readily see, will give the air mail monopoly to our two competitors, destroy most of our company's investment in air transportation, and entirely remove competition from the field."[36]

Sabath responded quickly. Manning reported to Cord Corporation head R.S. Pruitt, "Congressman Sabath called me about 12:45 P.M. today and stated that he was leaving for Washington, also that he wanted us to know that he had called Jim Mead of the 'phone Sunday and arranged to have nothing further done about the hearings on the Kelly Bill until after he and Kelly reached Washington and had a chance to talk with Mr. Mead regarding the matter." Manning need not have worried; the bill never left committee.[37]

Any changes to the air mail legislation would have to wait until the forthcoming Senate investigation. In the meantime, the Post Office and Congress were trying to find ways to address the alleged problem of the extensions by way of cancellation.

One of the first efforts by Second Assistant Postmaster General W.W. Howes was to seek a way to annul the existing route extensions. Howes had approached Comptroller General John McCarl to ask if such a plan were possible. "Mr. Howes," stated Colonel Brittin, "takes the position that Mr. Brown granted these extensions in the face of an already created deficit against the express provisions of the Watres Act that no extensions should be granted unless the funds were available to pay for them." Brittin was worried that Howes was looking to both the new solicitor of the Post Office, Karl Crowley, and the comptroller general for an interpretation of the legality of the extensions.[38]

Brittin saw this action as evidence that the new second assistant did not comprehend the intricacies of the existing law. Brown never incurred a deficit; he always made up for shortfalls caused by a new extension by lowering the rate to all of the contractors, even forcing them to fly the mail for free at the end of the fiscal year. This was the expressed purpose behind having the airlines exchange their contracts for route certificates and showed the complete command of the air mail situation possessed by Brown. Howes was a neophyte compared to the former postmaster general and his second assistant. Brittin pointed out that although extensions had been granted in seeming violation of the Watres Act, "they have become legalized, so to speak, before the end of the year, due to the fact that the Post Office Department must inevitably balance their budgets. The Post Office Department had in some instances reduced schedules to accomplish this, but mainly it has been done thru the reduction of rates. The Comptroller General has heretofore always concurred in these matters with the Postmaster General and has held that a deficit did not exist. . . . In this way literally thousands of miles of extensions and extra schedules have been authorized and financed without increasing or overdrawing any domestic air mail appropriation."[39]

The Democrats, controlling the Post Office and Congress, now sought legislation to enable the government to cancel existing contracts. Known as the Independent Offices Appropriation bill, H.R. 5389 was reported out of committee in May and sent to the floor of the House for consideration. Section 6 would allow the president to nullify or cancel any existing contract if it were deemed that that service was no longer in the public interest.[40] While meeting strenuous opposition from most House Republicans, including Clyde Kelly, the measure passed the House by a large majority. Fortunately for the contract air mail carriers, Section 6 did not survive the Senate Appropriations Committee. Brittin was relieved; Second Assistant Howes was not.[41]

Unexpectedly, despite the recommendation of Sen. Carter Glass's Appropriations Committee, Section 6 was reinstated when it reached the Senate floor. Rumors spread that anti–air-mail senators McKellar and Black were behind the reinstatement as a result of the continuing work performed by Black's Special Investigative Committee on Ocean and Air Mail contracts in preparation for their forthcoming hearings.

Brittin felt more at ease having received the private assurances that his efforts to extend his line into Montana would not be blocked. Nevertheless, Brittin won the assurance from Sen. Gerald Nye that he would introduce an amendment to the bill stating that any such cancellation could occur only with sixty days' notice and would require a public hearing. This is, in fact, what happened, effectively removing the teeth from this legislation. Still, Brittin was concerned about the unexpected support Section 6 had from his competition at United. "Strange to relate, the cancellationists are being encouraged by Colonel Paul Henderson of United, Mr. Bruce Kremer, (of National Parks and United), and Mr. Sig Janus of American Airways," he remarked. "The General Motors group and ourselves are the only ones attempting to oppose or modify the cancellation provisions of the Act."[42]

Brittin had reason to be concerned. His strenuous efforts to extend his route westward into a northern transcontinental route to Seattle were meeting very powerful, though very quiet, opposition. Acting on behalf of National Parks, into whose territory Northwest was moving, and interested in preserving the integrity of its own service to the northwestern states, United was working behind the scenes to head off Brittin.

Henderson, never a strong supporter of Walter Brown's air mail policy, for years thought that Brown exceeded his authority with the Watres Act, particularly concerning the legality of his numerous route extensions, the majority of which went to Northwest. With the coming of a new administration, Henderson sought to sway the new officers in the Post Office Department to his position and thereby forestall Northwest. Henderson attempted to do so by supporting these public efforts to negate Brown's extensions. In so doing, he would in effect abruptly stop Northwest's encroachment.

Henderson felt that United and National Parks had nothing to hide because they were operating virtually the same routes they originally had been awarded through competitive bidding years before Brown had even taken office and had not benefitted from significant route extensions. Henderson did not perceive the mounting acrimony against United, the largest and most powerful of the air mail "monopolies." He only saw that their entire contractual history with the government had been above board and that any rational examination of the current system would validate that obvious assertion. Henderson spoke at length with the Post Office and also with Senator Black. It was a mistake.

Henderson also had another motive for arguing for the cancellation of the extensions. Throughout the summer, the air mail carriers were occupied drafting plans to accommodate the drastic reduction in air mail appropriations. Despite the comptroller general's long-awaited ruling in late June that extensions could be canceled, the airlines were no longer concerned as they realized that a significant body of law existed in their defense to the extent that the Post Office would not risk damaging suits if it canceled any route. They now could turn their attention to confronting the new reality of a 25 percent rate reduction for all of the carriers.

With appropriations cut from $20 million to $15 million, many hard choices were forced upon the department. Armed with the provisions of the Watres Act incorporated by Brown to modify the rate payment through route certificates, however, the department made equitable, though painful, reductions with a new rate of less than 42 cents per mile. As had Brown and Glover before them, Farley and Howes called the air mail contractors to Washington for an operators meeting in July to discuss the new provisions. Numerous delays ensued as Howes stalled the operators until the appropriations bill was passed. In mid-August the air mail contractors were given bad news directly from the White House: Roosevelt had cut an addition $1 million from the approved fiscal year 1934 budget of $15 million.[43]

After a lengthy wait, Howes finally convened his first operators' conference on August 24. This initial meeting produced little.[44] On September 5, the operators met with Post Office Department officials again in a marathon session. The discussions began in earnest when Superintendent Cisler decided to read aloud each company's proposal. All approved except a shocked Brittin. As newly elected United president William Patterson reported to Philip Johnson, the new president of the United Aircraft and Transport Corporation, Brittin "immediately jumped to his feet stating that there were some very confidential suggestions made in his communication. My assumption is that his recommendation was to eliminate all lines but Northwest Airways. Brittin then proceeded to suggest that the appropriation be distributed on a cost ascertainment basis. We all voiced our immediate objection to such a plan on the basis that it would be destructive and encourage extravagant operation."[45]

Chairman Mead was also present at the deliberations at the invitation of Second Assistant Howes. Mead stressed the importance of determining a new, weight-based payment method to help offset the negative opinions held by most of Congress toward the current air mail system and its large subsidy.

Patterson reported that Mead made the statement that "in the minds of every Congressman and Senator the air mail appropriation is considered 100 per cent subsidy. He then impressed us with the importance of establishing some method of pay . . . in order to clarify in the minds of the Congressmen and Senators the differential between actual revenue to the Post Office Department and actual subsidy." Mead was also expressing the concern of many in Congress with the allegedly secretive nature of Brown's operator's conferences and to the numerous route extensions. Patterson worried that the new Congress could not or would not discern the difference between the contracts awarded by competitive bidding and the similar looking but legally separate route extensions.[46]

Mead strongly suggested that the air mail carriers quickly decide on a two mills per pound mile even if that would exceed the $14 million budget. An offer to fly the mail for free under this new method of payment, similar to that which had been done at the end of every fiscal year since 1930, would greatly impress Congress with the sincerity of their efforts and would go far in heading off further troubles in Congress. Mead himself would then introduce legislation similar to the Kelly Act that would stabilize the industry and remove any possible stigma against the contractors.[47]

Patterson was delighted with what he heard. Such a plan fit United's requirements precisely. As had been Postmaster General Brown's original intentions as expressed in the Watres Act, United had been not only carefully building an excellent air mail service but also expanding its passenger and express operations to offset costs and wean themselves off the subsidy. These efforts were now bearing fruit: "Congressman Mead's statements were music to my ears. We could not have outlined our own attitude more clearly. I considered that he was speaking in identical terms the thoughts we have had for the past two years."[48]

The following day Patterson and company met again with the Post Office to voice their opinions about budget cuts and how different airlines reacted to them. United, he stated, took the yearly cuts without protest and turned toward expanding into other markets to compensate. Other, smaller airlines, particularly Northwest, did not. "I pointed out to Mr. Howes," stated Patterson, "that on each occasion when our air mail revenue had been reduced, we buckled up and went back to work to develop other sources of revenue; that we were enjoying as a result of this effort a very satisfactory passenger business," although this new business did not completely offset the cuts as was widely thought. Nevertheless, United, Eastern, and TWA were enjoying profits because of their efforts. Even long-suffering American, for the first time in its history, reported a first-quarter profit.

In fact, nationwide air traffic had risen dramatically over the past four years from virtually nothing to more than half a million passengers per year, just as Brown had hoped.[49] With the economic incentives in place and the direct encouragement of the government to build larger, faster, and safer aircraft, the populace was losing its fear of flying. While air travel was still the preserve of the businessman and the wealthy because of its high fares, more people each year were choosing to fly rather than take the train or bus.

Although subjected to vehement attacks from Progressive Democrats and other opponents of monopoly, the airlines were now effectively given the blessing of President Roosevelt to maintain their holding companies and their route monopolies. Among the many new laws and agencies Roosevelt created during his remarkable first one hundred days in office was the National Industrial Recovery Act (NIRA), signed into law on June 16, 1933, which was intended to lessen the impact of the Great Depression and correct perceived problems in the economy.

It was widely believed that overproduction brought on by destructive competition was the cause of the nation's economic woes. In order to address this perceived problem, Roosevelt sought to limit production artificially through industry-wide cooperation thereby preserving profits by fixing prices at voluntary minimum levels no lower than cost. Within each industry, the government would protect business from antitrust laws, in effect legalizing cartels and restricting competition in exchange for a set of industrial "codes of fair competition" containing mutually agreed-upon production limits. In return, labor would be protected by legalized collective bargaining, guaranteed minimum wages, and maximum hours with decent working conditions.[50] Led by Gen. Hugh Johnson and administered through the National Recovery Administration (NRA), the NIRA was seen as a cooperative plan uniting business, labor, government, and even consumers to extricate the nation from the economic doldrums.

This government-business cooperation was highly reminiscent of Hoover's associative activities and similar in practice to Postmaster General Brown's plan for the air transportation industry. Now the Roosevelt administration was in effect formally legalizing much of Brown's air mail scheme, protecting the air mail carriers from destructive competition from low-cost, independent airlines while protecting labor.

Although the contractors were never friends of labor, they were able to pay decent wages, unlike the independents, because of the generous subsidies they received and the clear understanding from the Post Office that they treat their employees fairly and pay them accordingly. As a result, unlike most industries, employment was not a problem as the air mail contractors were never forced to lay off any of their 5,461 workers or cut wages.[51]

In July, the Aeronautical Chamber of Commerce, the major airlines' trade association, was given the task of drafting the codes for the aviation industry: one set for manufacturing and the other for the air transport lines. The first task was to placate General Johnson. Because of the recent appropriations cuts, the contractors were reluctant to sign the NRA's blanket code before they had time to formulate their own. With the help of Edward T. Stettinius of General Motors, an emergency code was worked out with Johnson's approval, thereby allowing the air mail carriers to fly the distinctive NRA "blue eagle" to show their support for the president's recovery plan.[52]

The next order of business was to develop an industry-wide code through the normal practice of hearings. Brittin was ill at ease with this process because, quite naturally, the ACC was dominated by the "Big Three" aviation holding companies, whose practices and policies were at odds with Northwest's.[53] In addition, Brittin attacked the virtual monopoly held by members of the ACC on the proposed Code Authority, fearing that such an arrangement "would certainly tend to promote monopoly, especially if the Code Authority is to be given power to control competition."[54] In fact, Brittin had earlier withdrawn Northwest from the ACC in a demonstration of protest against the control of the "monopolists."

On August 31, in the ballroom of the Mayflower Hotel in Washington, D.C., Leighton Rogers, executive vice president of the ACC, and American Airways president Lester Seymour, chairman of the Air Transport Committee of the ACC, sat down with David Behneke of ALPA and Rep. Fiorello LaGuardia to open the hearings. Despite the generally high wages paid by the air mail contractors, the labor question dominated the code discussions as the American Federation of Labor and its ALPA affiliate sought to guarantee good pay for not only the flight crews but also the mechanics. Numerous witnesses appeared, including pilots, mechanics, and radio operators, along with independent airline operator Temple Bowen.

The hearings proved acrimonious and inconclusive. Rogers's handling of the testimony angered many in the audience and prompted direct criticism of the industry, exactly what the ACC did not want. At the last moment Rogers had substituted a revised code without notice or explanation, which was introduced piecemeal throughout the proceedings. According to Brittin, who was present, "The tactics of the Chamber especially irritated the American Federation of Labor and the Labor Board. They also brought forth an extremely bitter attack upon the policy of the Post Office Department in encouraging a monopoly through the long-established system of granting extensions to existing air mail lines."[55] The recommended wage and hour guidelines also met with stern opposition: "The high minimum hours and the low minimum wage for pilots and co-pilots brought forth a great deal of opposition. Most of the

Washington newspapers actively supported the cause of the pilots and criticized the operators. This sort of newspaper publicity at this time and in this place is anything but helpful to the cause of the air mail service."[56]

In late September the airlines relented and established new wage scales providing a substantial increase to the pilots with base pay ranging from $1,600 to $3,000 per year, depending on qualifications, with additional flying pay provided, from a low of $4.00 per hour for daytime flying in older, slower aircraft to $6.80 per mile for night flying in the latest generation machines.[57] William Patterson summed up the air mail contractors' position, stating, "Labor without question, is sitting in the driver's seat."[58]

United Air Lines and the other large carriers could live with this situation; Braniff, Bowen, and the other independent, non–air-mail-carrying members of the Scheduled Airline Operators Association could not. Thomas Braniff and Temple Bowen appealed directly to General Johnson, arguing that the code as formulated by the ACC did not represent their views and that they opposed several sections. They particularly disliked Article VII, which prevented the duplication of routes and service between two points already served by another airline. As stated in the draft code, "Members of the Code agree not to initiate service between cities already served by another member over an identical route."[59] This prohibition, which codified the Post Office Department's policy under Brown, would have forced the independents out of business entirely as they deliberately competed head-to-head with the air mail lines over many routes. This, they believed, was not what Roosevelt intended.

Ignoring the president's assumption that one of the primary causes of overproduction was destructive competition, Braniff went on to state that "the code is not designed to promote monopolies," when, in fact, it readily did so.[60] Braniff was correct in that the NRA was not intended to eliminate small businesses, but he rightly feared that the implementation of the code would do just that, as it addressed only those airlines possessing a treasured air mail contract. Braniff condemned the Post Office Department's policy of subsidy and extensions for squeezing out the small independents and blamed it for the creation of air transport monopolies.[61]

By the time the code for air transportation was approved and signed by the president on November 14, Article VII had been modified by the NRA. For Braniff and Bowen this was a reprieve rather than a relief. After discussions with the ACC, the NRA decided that the clause should not be the basis of law but could be worked out separately as a trade practice agreement. Under the new Article VII, according to the ACC, the Code Authority still had power "to call a meeting and agree on conditions which new air lines would have to meet before they could legally operate. Once agreed to by the Administrator of the Code, these new conditions would be binding on the entire industry."[62] With the Code Authority dominated by five members from the chamber and chaired by United's William Patterson, Braniff and the independents stood little chance of opening any new routes.

It was expected that the code agreements would be placed into effect by February. Barring any unforeseen circumstances, the existing oligopolistic state of the industry would now have the complete protection of the government against the non–air-mail carriers. But unforeseen circumstances would indeed occur, and with devastating effect. The independents fully realized the consequences if the trade practice agreement was codified in February as planned: they would be out of business. Braniff and its allies had to prevent that at any cost.

Chapter 13

Congress Assumes Command

Since February, Sen. Hugo Black had been calling for a sweeping investigation of all postal contracts. Black, a former police court judge, personal injury attorney, county prosecutor, and Ku Klux Klan member, and a future associate justice of the United States Supreme Court, was passionately predisposed against all concentrations of economic or political power. Growing up in poor east-central Clay County, Alabama, Black was raised in a Populist household. As a southern Progressive Democrat, Black vehemently opposed all monopolies and sought to expose their purported evil to the light of public scrutiny.[1]

Remarkably, the air mail operators failed to perceive Black as a dangerous opponent. When drafting their lobbying program for the forthcoming election of 1932, Eastern Air Transport thought Black "OK."[2] They were greatly mistaken. In February 1933, Black had been infuriated by Postmaster General Brown's last-minute route extensions before leaving office and won approval to initiate a detailed public investigation of Brown's entire operation. Senator Black assumed the worst and, provided with subjective information carefully prepared by the independents, read all they wanted him to read.

In particular, Fulton Lewis Jr., the conservative reporter who was provided information by Braniff and Ludington in 1931 to fuel their attacks against the department, gave Black a copy of his lengthy report detailing the alleged misdeeds of the department and the airlines. Lewis despised Brown on personal grounds because Brown had earlier successfully removed Lewis's father-in-law, Col. Claudius Huston, from the chairmanship of the Republican National Committee.

The document carefully pleaded the independents' position, exposing the alleged misappropriation of federal funds, waste, and fraud while ignoring the machinations of the independents' own deceptions, as most of them originally had air mail contracts and only wanted back in after selling off at large profit. The report especially ignored Brown's Progressive Republican vision concerning the financial stability and capability of the large companies to fund the development of this infant industry. Such a report, despite its flaws, played directly to Black's fears. He was already predisposed to believe the worst.

On the surface, without understanding Brown's plan, it did indeed look like deliberate favoritism of big business at the expense of small, struggling independents. Below the surface, it was much more complicated: the independents were not viable entities and the government had an obligation not to expend public funds on shaky, underfinanced, unreliable enterprises. The current independents had not existed when all of the contracts were originally let, so their claims of exclusion were invalid. Route extensions were the only way air mail service could be extended throughout the country without an increase in limited appropriation. This was overlooked.

Evoking the biblical vision of money changers in the temple, Black saw only greed and evil. To an enthralled national radio audience, Black displayed his unique interpretation of aviation history:

> Men who had flown over the battlefields of France pioneered in the aviation industry. Returning home with the spirit of flying controlling their thoughts and hopes, it was but a natural step for them to advance from the old barnstorming days to a regular passenger air traffic. Realizing the value of this new development in time of peace and war, the people were anxious to foster it. Legislation to aid this new industry was quickly passed and provided for the payment of money for the carriage of mail by air planes. It was at this stage that the money changers saw their golden opportunity. Interested, as always, in the exploitation of the invention and genius and efforts of some one else, alluring advertisements of prospective gains fascinated the gaze of millions. A wild scramble for the fruits of government subsidies began. As usual, the weak fell before the strong.
>
> At the directors tables there sat, not the pioneer air pilots, but the masters of American finance. The control of aviation had been ruthlessly taken away from men who could fly and bestowed upon bankers, brokers, promoters and politicians, sitting in their inner offices, allotting among themselves the taxpayers monies. Again fortunes were made overnight.[3]

A closer examination would have revealed that the major aviation holding companies, particularly United Aircraft, were in fact organized, managed, and financed by aviation pioneers. When they realized the need for additional capital to expand their industry, they logically approached "the masters of finance" and shared power. Even AVCO, with its terrible problems, was started by aviator Sherman Fairchild, and it required competent businessmen such as C.R. Smith, not pilots, to bring American Airways to profitability. Wall Street involvement was essential if the industry were to grow. Contrary to Black's claims, Walter Brown legally promoted the well-financed corporations over the under-capitalized, stock-promoting independents. Nevertheless, Black's intentions were honest; he genuinely believed that a terrible injustice had been committed.

Big business did triumph in aviation. To many, this fact alone was enough justification to fight for its elimination, especially at a time of breadlines and massive unemployment, when large aviation companies and their executives lived well off public subsidies while the general populace suffered immeasur-ably. To this end, Senator Black's Special Committee on Investigation of Air Mail and Ocean Mail Contracts earnestly initiated its investigation in the spring of 1933. In particular, Black demanded an inquiry into the organization and financial conditions of the contracting companies and their efforts to reap federal subsidies.[4] On June 10, the Senate adopted Black's resolution after quib-bling over its cost, setting the stage for one of the Senate's most controversial hearings.[5]

Heading the investigation was another Alabamian, Andrew G. Patterson, a former sheriff and now ICC investigator delegated to Black's committee. He too was a southern Progressive Democrat, harboring an intense dislike of monopoly, and did all in his power to uncover any evidence to prove his case. As the lead investigator, Patterson immediately went into the field, interview-ing all of the executives of the airlines while collecting data and copying their records. To the airlines, Patterson also revealed his biases.

On May 27 and 29, Hainer Hinshaw met alone with Patterson in room 317 of the Senate Office Building. Hinshaw, now with United, was one of the industry executives most intimately involved with the creation and implemen-tation of the 1930 Watres Act. Patterson started the interview by stating that he and Senator Black were only seeking to examine the industry and address the present criticisms in the hope that a new, conclusive government policy toward air mail could be determined for the benefit of all concerned. Patterson was particularly interested in learning about Brown's program of extensions, to which Hinshaw replied that all was legal, in order, and driven not by collu-sive forces of Wall Street but by legitimate local political concerns:

> Mr. Patterson then introduced the subject of American Airways extensions. He inquired if collusion had existed in obtaining them. His memory was re-freshed as to the wording of the seventh section of the Watres Act. His memory was again refreshed as to the numerous mass meetings held by the then Post-master General, who was hearing arguments of various sections of the country as to their crying need for air mail service—how Mr. Brown had yielded to pres-sure and had instituted in various sections of the country—how he had made these services as extensions on the theory that a few able companies would per-

form more satisfactorily than many smaller ones—that the few able companies could so consolidate their operations that the Government would benefit through reduced rates to the companies. It was pointed out that the pressure came from the affected localities, as would be indicated of a list of the speakers at the meetings was to be scanned.[6]

Patterson was particularly interested in learning the details of the award of the southern transcontinental route, CAM-33, to American. He assumed that the arrangement unfairly excluded those present-day small independents who were complaining the loudest. Hinshaw corrected this misinterpretation, reminding the investigator that the cornerstone of Brown's plan was the creation and expansion of passenger service throughout the country and that that could not be done without government assistance:

> Mr. Patterson next wanted to know why it was that AM 33 had but one bidder and that bidder dared, or was so sure, to bid the maximum price. It was pointed out that Section Four of the Watres Act required certain qualifications before a prospective bidder could be qualified to bid; furthermore, the advertisement contained certain requirements in the matter of speed, equipment, and seats to be furnished; that there were but five companies operating who could qualify as bidders; one operator was busy operating his route, two others combined for one of the routes, and the last two combined on the second route to be advertised; that one route had two bidders but the lower of the bids could not qualify and they might as well have dared to bid the full price because as it was with the full rate they would have to carry a high passenger average to break even; that it must be remembered that those lines protesting against the present day air mail structure were not in existence at the time of the advertisements; and that their protests came long after the awards were made.[7]

Hinshaw was concerned that Patterson saw little value in the air mail itself and, apparently, saw no correlation between the carriage of mail and the carriage of passengers, unlike officials in the Hoover administration. This was a recurring theme among the Democratic opposition concerning this public policy issue. Unlike his predecessor, Roosevelt never had a coherent national aviation policy. To Hinshaw the question of passengers was immaterial. The contract air mail carriers were compelled by Brown and the law to carry passengers on all of their routes. This they did in order to comply with the terms of their original contract and route certificates. "Hence the operators, under a bonded contract, could do nothing but follow the dictates of Mr. Brown and comply with their contractual terms," stated Hinshaw.

Patterson had already decided that the government was wasting money on a service as frivolous as the air mail, disregarding its role in fostering a new form of national transportation in the public interest. Hinshaw did not see the investigation leading to any useful conclusion. "The opinion prevails," he noted, "that Mr. Patterson had definitely convicted the industry as being of no value and a luxury for those that care to use it, that the industry has no place in the basic scheme of transportation facilities; that it may be possible for United Air Lines to carry the mail for a sum the government could spend but the rest of the operators could not—hence to require such a thing would be favoritism—that the investigation will end as they have all ended—not even suggesting an intelligent answer to the problem."[8]

On September 28, the Special Committee on Investigation of the Air Mail and Ocean Mail Contracts, under the chairmanship of Senator Black, began its work. The calm that followed was misleading. Black, desirous of unearthing as much incriminating evidence as possible, had sent out his research staff months earlier while the committee examined the uninteresting ocean mail contracts. The aviation holding companies got a taste of upcoming events when in late December they received an official questionnaire asking about stock acquisitions, salaries, bonuses, and profits. "We want to know the original background of the company so that we may know how the monopoly was worked out and the actual cash set-up of the companies seeking mail contracts," Black stated emphatically.[9]

By this time Braniff and Bowen were getting desperate. In September, Temple Bowen had approached A.P. Barrett requesting a merger of his line with American; he was flatly refused. Barrett pointedly reminded Bowen that he had bought him out once before and was not about to do it again. Tom and Paul Braniff were working as hard as possible to secure a contract for their struggling line, but with the highly restrictive NRA Air Transport Code soon coming into effect, they were running out of options. The Air Transport Code Authority would meet in February and likely codify the restrictions on routes and direct competition between city pairs served by the contractors, leaving Braniff and the other independents without any chance to compete directly. If this were to happen, Braniff and Bowen would soon be out of business. Braniff and Bowen hoped to convince the Post Office Department or the Black committee that if they could be given a route directly or indirectly through a subcontract, they could demonstrate their ability to fly the mail at a lower cost.

In October, Tom Braniff reminded A.G. Patterson as well as the Post Office that the administration now had the power to cancel or consolidate both contracts and route extensions. "Has it occurred to you that the Post Office Department has the authority to make the best possible test of the question as to whether or not the air mail carriers are overpaid?" wrote Braniff to Patterson. "They have the authority from Congress contained in the rider to the Independent Offices' Appropriations Bill giving them the authority to cancel contracts, and the Comptroller General has rendered them an opinion which in the estimation of our attorneys and ourselves clearly give the Post Office Department the right to summarily cancel so-called extensions which were granted under the previous regime." He suggested publicly and often that if the department canceled just one route and opened it to competitive bidding, "they would be amazed to learn how much money could be saved on carrying the mail."[10] Though Braniff and Bowen did have lower operating costs than the air mail contractors, they were not flying to the higher safety standards required by the Watres Act, nor were they flying their passengers in the larger multiengined aircraft prescribed by the department or paying their employees decent wages.

Braniff reminded Patterson that the year before they had offered to sublet all of CAM-3 from Chicago to Dallas–Fort Worth from United Air Lines but were refused by Philip Johnson. Through their political connections in the Post Office, however, Braniff and Temple Bowen finally found receptive ears. Second Assistant William Howes was a South Dakotan who had been an investor in Rapid Air Lines at one time and was interested in the affairs of the independents. In November he contacted Post Office Solicitor Karl Crowley and asked if it were possible for the department to extend the route along CAM-3 to several destinations between Oklahoma City and Fort Worth as yet without service. Howes wanted to know if such an extension would be legal and, if so, could it be subcontracted to serve Lawton, Oklahoma, and Wichita Falls, Texas.[11]

Crowley agreed that indeed the department had the power to create such an extension or consolidation of routes in the public interest. Subletting was also authorized; after all, this was how Brown had expanded the air mail network. United Air Lines suspected that the department wanted the route to go to tiny, independent Reed Airlines, which was affiliated with Braniff and Bowen through the Scheduled Airline Operators Association. Just as easily, it could have been given to Braniff. Regardless, former Fort Worth attorney Crowley had clearly reaffirmed the department's authority in these matters and was well aware that it also had the power to cancel contracts and extensions if so inclined. Rumored to be a business acquaintance of Temple Bowen, Crowley was well acquainted with the Democratic social and political circles in Fort Worth and was sympathetic to the plight of the independents—so sympathetic, in fact, that he was soon to assume the vanguard in their struggle.

To promote their plan, Braniff also offered to assist the investigation in any way possible through testimony or correspondence. The offer to Patterson was readily accepted.[12] Indeed, Patterson provided a formal letter of introduction for Paul Braniff to discuss with Joseph Eastman, commissioner of the ICC, "matters pertaining to air transportation." Patterson noted that "Mr. Braniff has been helpful and cooperative in furnishing this Committee with data and information relating to the investigation of air mail contracts."[13] The Braniff brothers needed all the help they could get; on January 1, 1934, dwindling revenues forced them to discontinue their service between Chicago and Kansas City and between Chicago and St. Louis, two extremely important routes.[14]

While the Braniffs were fighting a rear-guard action to save themselves from the brink of extinction by the impending regulations of the Air Transport Code Authority, the air mail contractors were also maneuvering for position. Colonel Brittin continued his fight for his own independence and sought approval from Senator Black. By this time, Northwest had managed to buy back the 22.5 percent of its outstanding shares held by TAT, leaving only AVCO as a major stockholder.

Brittin took his fight to Black, underscoring the problem of interlocking directorates in the airline industry. Through Brittin's efforts lobbying the members of Black's committee, he planted a story in the press in the name of the committee condemning "interlocking financial interests between air mail lines and threatening to put through legislation during the coming session that will force complete separation."[15] Brittin was pleased with the public endorsement by Black of his efforts to increase Northwest's independence. He was also pleased with the attitude of Black's chief investigator. "Mr. Patterson," he remarked, "is decidedly anti-monopolistic and very sympathetic toward the aims of the Northwest Airways to develop an independent transcontinental service that will be owned and controlled in the territory it serves."[16]

United, the largest of the air mail contractors, was developing its own plan to confront the coming investigation. Col. Paul Henderson, the former second assistant postmaster general and one of the founders of NAT, best expressed United's position. He, too, had no fondness for Walter Brown and felt that the air mail system as created by the Watres Act was flawed. He offered one solution—the one he had been offering since 1928 and one Brown prophesied in 1932: formal federal regulation. "Because of Walter Brown's high handed management of air mail from 1930 to and through 1932," stated Henderson, "there has developed in Congress a suspicion that all air mail matters may be questionable in character." He correctly surmised that most members were ill versed in the intricacies of the air mail question. "Such knowledge as most the members have," he concluded, "comes to them a bit at a time from other members, from disappointed independent air line operators and from other sources." This left Congress with a distorted and unfriendly view of the contractors.[17]

Henderson was actually somewhat sympathetic to the plight of many of the independent passenger lines. "Because of the fact that during Brown's entire administration there were no truly competitive contracts let for air mail, the independent, non-mail carrying operators in the country have become increasingly impatient with the situation and increasingly critical of all of us who enjoy mail contracts," he stated. "They know that although they may have tried to get consideration from the Government that their efforts have not met with success."[18]

In order to avoid future problems, Henderson suggested that United support the idea of route franchises in its discussions with Black and Congress. Underscoring Brown's understanding of the situation, Henderson stated, "From the beginning of air mail operations until now, air mail contracts and their following route certificates have practically served as franchises." The problem revolved around the matter of subsidies. As originally intended under the first Kelly Act, no subsidies were to be provided; the air mail was to pay for itself. Over time, with the understanding by Brown that the industry was too immature to survive and flourish without federal financial assistance, subsidy became a crucial part of air transportation, and with it came the risk of great politicization of future route decisions. Henderson wanted federal regulation to control competition, limit politicization, and provide industry stability and reasonable rates. By federal regulation Henderson meant "the issuance of certificates of convenience and necessity by the Federal Government for all interstate airlines running exclusively to the holder as long as he lives up to certain established requirements." He also recommended legislation to compel the Post Office Department to put air mail on all lines that would operate under these franchises at a reasonable fixed rate. Although Henderson harbored no illusions about the possibility of this plan actually coming to fruition, he felt that the forthcoming Senate hearings would produce comparable legislation.[19]

To this end Henderson met with Black in late December, much to the consternation of the other contractors, to help focus the committee's attention on these matters rather than on the perceived side issues of monopoly. He wished to discuss the problem of Northwest Airways' incursion into National Parks' territory in Montana and argue against unwarranted extensions. The result, he hoped, would be to focus the committee's attention on the problem of air mail reform while derailing Brittin's northern transcontinental plans. Henderson did not wish the committee to become sidetracked on secondary issues when he believed the entire air transportation system was ready for significant legislative change.

Regardless of the outcome of the forthcoming hearings, United was confident that it would remain in the clear; its contracts had been awarded through competitive bidding long before Walter Brown took office. Henderson and company thought the time was ripe to examine Brown's deeds honestly and with clear intentions. Unfortunately, Black and Patterson were fixated on the question of big business and monopoly. Remarked United's Washington, D.C., representative James P. Murray, "Col. Henderson reported that he had an interesting hour with Patterson, Senator Black's chief investigator of air mail contracts, but was unable to make any progress toward steering the investigation into the channel originally intended—viz—contracts and how obtained."[20] Instead, Murray understood Black's overriding obsession. "It was rumored that the 'hearings' would be announced but no witnesses called until after the Senate Committee had blared forth thru the press the sums of money made by prominent individuals in the industry," he stated.[21]

Just how accurate this prediction was would soon be seen. By early January 1934, with its work completed on the ocean mail, the special committee turned its attention to aviation matters and promised sensational revelations. On January 8, Black reconvened his committee. What followed was both serious drama and comic opera that generated garish daily headlines across the country. A succession of witnesses came forth who outlined Walter F. Brown's complicated machinations during the Hoover years. Few were complimentary. Brown's high-handedness and virtual dictatorship over the airlines were documented amid much fanfare.

Key to the apparent revelations of forced mergers, preferential treatment, and noncompetitive awarding of route extensions was the testimony of several small independent operators about a series of supposedly clandestine meetings between Brown (aided by Assistant Secretary of Commerce for Aeronautics William MacCracken) and the representatives of the three holding companies. These gatherings were, in fact, the well-publicized operators' meetings called by the Post Office in May and June 1930 to discuss the application of the new Watres Act.

Especially controversial were the remarks of Thomas H. McKee, former operator of the Wedell Williams Air Service of Louisiana, who told of these "secret" meetings of Post Office officials with the trusts. He testified that these "Spoils Conferences" following passage of the Watres Act deliberately excluded the small independents, and that when he attempted to join the meetings, MacCracken, who was chairing this meeting, "was anxious to get rid of me and invited me in a cordial way to get out of the room." According to McKee, the brief encounter at the meeting "gave me the definite impression that Mr. Brown had placed this whole transport operation in the hands of a fixed group with an axe to grind."[22] McKee and others testified that officials from the airlines controlled by UATC, North American, and AVCO were the sole industry representatives present. Wedell Williams, McKee claimed, was forced to sell out to American Airways. He failed to mention that Wedell Williams could have received a subcontract from American with the Post Office's blessing had they been able to work out a merger with Robertson. Others claimed they were "squeezed out by monopolists" (1447). None mentioned their poor financial condition or their inability to fly regular night service or meet other minimum Post Office requirements.

Black pressed other witnesses concerning the events of these secretive conferences and underscored the participants' ties to the interlocking directorates. Col. Paul Henderson, vice president of United Air Lines, confirmed that thousands of miles of new route extensions were never opened to bidding and admitted that the U.S. air map was drawn up at these meetings. Black asked him pointedly, "You understood that there were no competitive bids?" Henderson frankly replied, "No, none" (1457).

But Brown could not have opened these extensions to bidding even if he had wanted to; Congress had not authorized any new routes nor had provided the money necessary for more air mail contracts. In May 1930 there were 14,659 miles of air mail routes in the United States, and by May 1932 this had grown to 26,754 miles. Of that, 4,500 miles of lines were created by these extensions without competitive bidding as these were not new contracts. Henderson correctly asserted the crucial fact that as discriminating as these practices may have seemed, they were within the law (1462).

Compounding the damage done by these allegations was the revelation of potential illegal activity within the Post Office. James Maher, a Post Office clerk, testified that he had burned potential evidence. "We destroyed everything except the personal files Brown took with him" on the orders of the postmaster general's secretary, just two days before Brown left office. Maher did so, he claimed, despite reservations that "the next administration might want to refer to them" (1438).

The show took a strange twist ten days later when Brown returned to Washington. On January 19, he arrived with a large suitcase and proceeded immediately to the office of his successor, James Farley. There he deposited the contents.

Inside the bag were the missing documents, safely preserved, pertaining to the air mail contracts. According to Brown, he had found these "unexpectedly in a box with his personal papers, tightly secured." Absolving his former staff of any wrongdoing, Brown concluded, "There remains only one theory to wit, that these official files were surreptitiously placed among my personal papers at the instigation of someone who was engaged in a conspiracy of character assassination."[23]

With this crisis resolved but with suspicions raised, attention turned again to the dealings of the holding companies, producing a series of nasty shocks. First, America's greatest hero, Charles Lindbergh, was implicated in the alleged stock manipulations of North American. Lindbergh at that time was a precious advertising commodity whose services were desired by every airline.

His aeronautical expertise was just as valuable. An astute businessman, Clement Keys had enticed Lindbergh to provide his name and experience as technical advisor to TAT. Senator Black revealed that in addition to a very generous $10,000 annual salary, the "Lone Eagle" also received twenty-five thousand shares of TAT stock worth $250,000. As expected with Lindbergh associations, the value of the stock soared and Lindbergh was advised by Keys to sell his new shares quickly to turn a tidy profit. He was also advised by Keys to keep the stock deal quiet.[24] Still, like Brown's activity, Lindbergh's profit making may have appeared unseemly in the light of the existing economic conditions, but it too was legal.

The loudest bombshell was yet to come. On January 16 and 17, officials from UATC, the largest by far of the holding companies, were summoned before Senator Black. First up was Treasurer Charles W. Deeds. Subjected to intensive questioning, the thirty-one-year-old Deeds revealed that his two hundred shares of Pratt & Whitney stock, which he bought for $40 in 1926, was worth $5.6 million at its 1929 peak. He turned a $1.6 million profit when he sold off portions of his holdings, as did Rentschler and George Mead, when they allegedly engaged in a stock pool to inflate prices artificially.[25] As damning as this was, the testimony unearthed even greater supposed profiteering when Fred Rentschler was summoned.

Subjected to ardent questioning, the vice chairman and cofounder of UATC revealed that he had turned his original modest $254 investment in his new company into a startling $35,575,848 by 1929. Despite the subsequent collapse of the market, Rentschler still held $2.1 million worth of stock in various companies while continuing to receive a huge salary of $192,500, which had actually increased by 92 percent since 1927, even in the face of the ravaged economy.[26] Black and other committee members were appalled and infuriated by the profit taking, which was supported by federal funds. Pointedly, Black inquired, "Do you think it is right for the United States government to subsidize any company when the officers draw salaries and bonuses of several hundred thousand dollars?" An embarrassed Rentschler had no answer.[27]

Believing he had confirmation of his suppositions, Black was ready to call for action. Speaking to a radio audience over NBC, Black stated that the evidence his committee had gleaned over the past five months showed that the government should abandon its subsidy program, fly the mail itself, or completely revise the system of awarding contracts. Recalling the revelations of several witnesses, Black concluded that "when the air mail map had been redrafted it was found that the eighteen or more million dollars of taxpayers' money annually paid for the carriage of air mail was controlled more than 90 percent by four companies."[28] More fireworks were yet to come.

On January 30, several witnesses attempted to implicate Walter F. Brown in illegal stock dealings. Although quickly disproved, the allegations cast further doubts on the former postmaster general's integrity, and though legal, his possession of three thousand shares of International Mercantile Marine appeared questionable at the very least. Further testimony claimed that some vital correspondence between Brown and Secretary of the Treasury Andrew Mellon concerning the latter's interest in TAT was missing from Brown's recently discovered files.[29] Interestingly, Brown had yet to be called. The question of missing letters, however, would prove disastrous for one other unsuspecting individual.

Colonel Brittin of Northwest, who had earlier condemned the monopolies and supported total airline independence, was caught in a difficult position. In the ensuing document search, former Assistant Secretary of Commerce for Aeronautics William MacCracken, who was now an attorney for several airlines, including Northwest, refused to allow Senate investigators access to his files, citing attorney-client confidentiality. Black retaliated by having MacCracken and Brittin arrested for contempt by the Senate sergeant-at-arms. MacCracken refused to relent and appealed to the Supreme Court, where he eventually lost his argument. Brittin did not fight; he spent ten days in D.C. Jail for contempt of Congress for allegedly destroying subpoenaed documents.[30] Despite the assumptions of a massive coverup, Black's investigators recovered all of the missing papers after having literally pieced together Brittin's trash taken from his office; they found nothing but laundry receipts and other irrelevant papers.

By this time the press was in an antimonopoly hysteria, repeating the allegations of conspiracy, corruption, and favoritism in massive headlines in newspapers across the country. On the surface, a scandal rivaling the likes of the infamous Teapot Dome of 1923 seemed at hand, and the press and public readily accepted innuendo and half-truths as fact.

Sensing an excellent opportunity to exploit the frenzied situation to the fullest on behalf of the struggling independent passenger airlines, Post Office Solicitor Karl Crowley presented a forty-nine-page brief for Postmaster General Farley on February 6, 1934. In it he detailed his interpretation of the facts surrounding the air mail controversy, paying particular attention to the restricted operators' conferences held in the spring of 1930, now widely referred to as the "Spoils Conferences." Painting a bleak picture of a carefully chosen cabal huddled in secret conspiring to divide the air mail "spoils" among them, Crowley outlined all of the known facts surrounding the operators' meetings. He presented Brown's decisions to favor the large existing companies, which already had air mail contracts, as a conspiracy to prevent struggling independents from joining in this exclusive club.

Although there was a great deal of superficial truth in Crowley's assertions, he had overlooked Brown's express purpose in carrying out the Watres Act: to use the air mail to support those existing and still-struggling all-passenger lines, such as Transcontinental Air Transport, which were operating along important and natural trade routes. Crowley neglected entirely to state that none of the independents petitioning for contracts at this time had existed in viable form when the "Spoils Conferences" took place. Neither did he mention that Braniff and Bowen had at one time been air mail contractors who sold off their airlines to the so-called monopolies and promptly took the money to start new airlines in direct competition with the air mail lines that had existing contracts awarded through competitive bidding.[31]

Despite strong evidence and the legal opinion of the comptroller general to the contrary, Crowley asserted that the bid by United Avigation for the middle transcontinental route in the summer of 1930 was actually "responsible." In his opinion, therefore, the award of CAM-34 to TWA was fraudulent. Crowley went on to claim that because of the route extensions and the policy of exchanging air mail contracts for route certificates, the government paid approximately $47 million more than it needed to (12). How he arrived at that figure when the annual Post Office appropriation for air mail never changed under Brown's tenure was not explained. Crowley went on to cite as evidence the recent testimony concerning the alleged destruction of Post Office records as proof of guilt.

The solicitor then listed his numerous complaints. First, he stated that all existing air mail contracts and extensions were void because they were a product of a combination in restraint of trade. Second, in a wild assumption that ignored clear evidence to the contrary, he stated that all present air mail contracts "were executed as a result of a fraudulent, corrupt, collusive conspiracy to defraud the United States between the holders thereof and Post Office Department officials" (15).

In this Crowley was simply wrong. Every air mail contract with the exception of CAM-33 and CAM-34 and two irrelevant lines was awarded not by Brown but by his predecessor, and all of the contracts had been awarded through competitive bidding to the lowest responsible bidder and approved by an unsympathetic comptroller general. There were no exceptions, but this did not matter in the electric atmosphere generated in the Senate hearing room. Crowley presented Farley with a stark recommendation: "Since these contracts were procured as a result of fraud, conspiracy, and collusion between post office officials and the holders of such contracts, it is my recommendation that they be annulled (49).

Armed with this conclusion, Farley took Crowley and his report to the White House. By this time, President Roosevelt was becoming increasingly concerned by the recent events. In a private luncheon with Roosevelt, Senator

Black outlined his findings and reminded the president that it was within the chief executive's authority to cancel the contracts. Receiving Roosevelt's full support, Black was urged to press on.[32] Events began to move more quickly. Farley explained the events in his personal diary:

> Hearings on the Air Mail proposition had been going on for several weeks when I arranged to see the President on Thursday afternoon, February 8th, accompanied by First Assistant W.W. Howes, Second Assistant Harllee Branch, and Karl A. Crowley, Solicitor for the Department.
>
> We went over the situation with him and it was our advice to cancel the contracts and he said he was willing and that we must get the advice of the Attorney General. We went to [Homer] Cummings' office to place it before him and suggested we have a conference next morning at 10:30.
>
> A definite decision was reached as to the cancellation, everyone agreeing it was the thing to do, and while at that office an order was prepared for the cancellation of the contracts. It was agreed that the Attorney General and I would present it to the President after the Cabinet meeting on Friday and also that an Executive Order be prepared for his signature directing the Army and Commerce Department to take over the Air Mail.[33]

The meeting was held in private, and no comment was made to the press.[34] The reason was clear the next day.

On February 9, the president issued Executive Order 6591 declaring an emergency and canceling all domestic air mail contracts. Roosevelt directed that "the Postmaster General, Secretary of War, and Secretary of Commerce . . . cooperate to the end that necessary air mail service be afforded," and further ordered that "the Secretary of War place at the disposal of the Postmaster General such airplanes, landing fields, pilots, and other employees and equipment of the Army of the United States needed or required for the transportation of mail, during the present emergency, by air over routes and schedules prescribed by the Postmaster General."[35]

Once again, as in 1918, the army was to carry the mail, pending a completion of the hearings and the drafting of new legislation.

With their life's blood cut off by the stroke of a pen, the airlines struck back as best they could. Officials from United Air Lines were stunned by the allegations and the cancellations, for they thought that they were safe in the knowledge that their contracts were legally awarded well before Brown took office. William Patterson fired off an angry letter to Postmaster Farley:

> We have seen reference in the public press to the charge that contracts for the carriage of air mail were let pursuant to collusive agreements reached at a so-called conference of air mail operators called at the direction of Postmaster General Walter F. Brown in the spring of 1930. No such collusive agreements

were made by us. In this connection, we call your attention to the fact that the air mail contract covering this Company's Route No. 18 was awarded under the date of January 29, 1927, prior to the said conference and after competitive bidding in which the original contractors, our predecessors in interest, were the lowest qualified bidders.

As authority for your action, you appear to rely upon Section 432 of Title 39 of the United States Code, which provides for the annulment of mail contracts in certain cases of combinations or agreements to prevent bidding. We respectfully protest that that section furnishes no justification for the action you have taken in the case of this Company. We have at no time entered into any such combination or agreement.[36]

TWA also filed a protest in the form a lengthy letter to President Roosevelt and a suit against the government claiming that the cancellation was a breach of contract and unduly injurious to the airlines. The lawsuit was eventually dismissed, with the help of some back-door politicking from Crowley in order not to embarrass the president or Farley.[37]

Immediately, TWA played its trump card. The company called on its aviation advisor, Charles Lindbergh, and Lindbergh sent an open letter to Roosevelt. "Your present action does not discriminate between innocence and guilt and placed no premium on honest business," he stated. "Your order of cancellation of all air mail contracts condemns the largest portion of our commercial aviation without trial."[38] *Fortune* magazine condemned the action, which put out of work not only the big four but also several small operators and "kicked askew the underpinnings of a $250 million investment shared by 200,000 stockholders."[39] Roosevelt never forgave Lindbergh for this attack.

Charges and countercharges followed in an excited press as the administration was both vilified and praised for its action. In the vain hope of deflecting further criticism, Farley prepared a detailed open letter to Senator Black, edited by the president himself, repeating the administration's reasons for canceling the contracts.[40]

Quickly, though, public opinion began to turn against Roosevelt because of unforeseen events. Only now did Black call former postmaster general Brown to testify, which Brown did for several days, defending himself ably and patiently explaining his actions in detail. Cross-examinations by Sen. Warren R. Austin of Vermont, one of only two Republicans on the committee, cornered Crowley and Braniff about their testimony, exposing numerous flaws in their arguments. Farley was particularly embarrassed when he was forced to admit that he knew little about the air mail situation and that the cancellation was done in haste. By this time the press' attention was shifting to more dramatic events.

In an act of open defiance, American Airways vice president Eddie

When it entered service in 1934 with TWA, the Douglas DC-2 quickly superceded the Boeing 247 and set a new standard for speed and comfort. (Smithsonian, SI# A48080E)

Rickenbacker and TWA vice president Jack Frye took the opportunity to demonstrate why the Hoover administration had carefully spent the monies it had on developing a national air transportation system and the equipment to operate it. Despite the common assumption that monopolies restrict technical innovation, this was not the case in aviation. United had been flying its successful Boeing 247 for almost a year and had reaped great economic rewards as a result. Not to be outdone by their competition and fearful that any delay in improving their equipment could prove disastrous, Frye approached Boeing with the hope of purchasing 247s for TWA. Over the objections of William Boeing himself, the United Aircraft and Transport Corporation decided to sell these aircraft to Frye only after all of United Air Line's original order for fifty-nine had been delivered. Faced with overnight technological obsolescence, Frye turned to other aircraft manufacturers, requesting that they produce a better 247. Douglas Aircraft Company did exactly that.

In late 1933, the sole Douglas DC-1 took to the air and immediately demonstrated its dramatically superior performance over the 247 and all other competitors.[41] Stretching this excellent design to carry fourteen passengers, four more than the Boeing, Douglas produced the DC-2, which Frye and Rickenbacker promptly flew to Washington, D.C., on February 22, 1934, in a record-shattering thirteen hours. TWA president Richard Robbins pointedly invited Senator Black to inspect the new airliner upon its arrival in Washington; Black politely declined.[42]

B.C. Forbes, writing in the *New York American,* summarized the situation:

> Eddie Rickenbacker's record breaking flight (13 hours) from the Pacific to the Atlantic wasn't a stunt, but the result of painstaking development of airplanes, aviation equipment on ships and on land, the investment of millions of dollars in new inventions, airports, amazing scientific instruments to flying safe during the night and during fog, to make "blind landings" safe, to establish meteorological service far ahead of the government's etc.
>
> Up-to-date commercial aviation isn't child's play. It isn't a picayune business. It savors nothing of what Wall Street calls "fly-by-night" ventures.
>
> Rickenbacker's company, for example, sponsored by General Motors, has invested more money than it has ever collected from the government for carrying air mail and from all other sources combined. It cost $300,000 to create the Douglas ship America's premier ace flew. The company, never dreaming that its air mail contract would be annulled without even the opportunity to present the facts, placed orders for $3.5 million worth of these ultra modern eagles.
>
> . . . But the axe fell on it as on every other air mail carrying company, without its getting its day in court to prove its innocence.[43]

Four days later the *American* was even harsher in its judgment:

> Attempts by various spokesmen to justify the Government's action have, without exception, proved to be unconvincing pleas in EXCULPATION—NOT JUSTIFICATION in any sense of the word. They merely reveal the extent of the complications in which the government is involved because of its hasty and ill-considered action, and confirm the adverse judgment on the incident which is well nigh universal.
>
> THE NEW DEAL HAS BEEN WELCOMED IN MOST OF ITS PROCESSES AND PROVISIONS, BUT THERE ARE SOME INNOVATIONS WHICH THE AMERICAN PEOPLE WILL NEVER ADOPT!
>
> And one is the condemnation of a man—any man—without trial or even formal accusation. This is precisely what the Government is guilty of in its headlong cancellation of the air mail contracts. . . .
>
> The supposed guilty and the admittedly innocent have alike been struck down by a high-handed government which refuses to permit its conduct to be reviewed by ITS OWN COURTS, and is indifferent to the charge of injustice proceeding from ITS OWN CITIZENS.

Let us hope that the Government will soon reverse its hasty action and rectify its incomprehensible error.[44]

Roosevelt had asked the army to assume all responsibility for flying the air mail with only ten days' notice. Unprepared, with flying equipment inferior to the airlines, and with the nation suffering through the worst winter in decades, U.S. Army Air Corps pilots suffered several fatal accidents. Within a few weeks, twelve pilots were killed (eight in training) prompting Eastern chief Eddie Rickenbacker to condemn this loudly as "legalized murder."[45] The public outcry was overwhelming and forced Roosevelt to suspend the air corps' operation on March 10. Nine days later, the corps renewed its mail flights on a greatly reduced schedule.[46]

Stung by the public's angry reaction, Roosevelt, an astute politician who was suffering his first major setback after a year of triumphs, realized that a better solution was needed immediately—one that preserved the reputation of the administration and accomplished important reforms while placating the airline industry and keeping it alive. He proposed immediate temporary legislation to return the delivery of the air mail to private contractors for a period of three months. Once passed, the law would allow a renewal every three months, if necessary.[47]

While Congress hurried to prepare temporary legislation to tide the industry over, President Roosevelt also proposed a permanent change in the law. With the approval of Senators Black and McKellar, Farley and Howes drafted a letter for Roosevelt to send publicly to McKellar and Mead, chairmen of the post office committees in the Senate and House, respectively, outlining his plan. In the letter, the president called for the return of the air mail to the airlines under new contracts "to avoid the evils of the past" while encouraging the development of the entire industry. He suggested that all contracts be let for a period of three years after a fair and open bidding competition. New bidders were to be encouraged to participate and were therefore given a six-month grace period to qualify to fulfil the original bid. So that the airlines would operate strictly in accordance with the public interest, Roosevelt requested that the Interstate Commerce Commission rule on the question of public convenience and necessity and regulate subsequent air mail pay over the new routes. Ironically, Colonel Henderson got his wish for ICC control, but at a cost.

In the most controversial aspect of his proposal, the president wanted to proscribe from bidding all airlines that were part of holding companies or were in any way connected with the aviation monopolies. Now, for the first time, Roosevelt abandoned his cooperative approach to the question of industry monopolies as seen in his NRA and returned to a Progressive Democratic strategy. Trusts and monopolies were evil and must be destroyed. "I suggest," he stated, "that the proposed law prohibit the award of an air mail contract to any company having connections with subsidiaries, affiliates, associates, or holding companies, directly or indirectly, by stock ownership, interlocking directorates, interlocking officers, or otherwise, if said subsidiaries, affiliates, associates, or holding companies are engaged, directly or indirectly in the operation of competitive routes or in the manufacturing of aircraft, or other materials or accessories used generally in the aviation industry."[48]

The president incorrectly assumed that the vertically integrated aviation holding companies restricted the technological development of aircraft, thus providing another rationalization for the breakup of the aviation trusts. "Such legislation will relieve air transport companies from paralyzing monopolistic control which has heretofore often influenced them to buy planes and other equipment from associates and affiliates," he declared. "Real competition between the manufacturing companies will stimulate inventive genius, and should give to our people safer and better equipment both for commercial and military purposes."[49]

Roosevelt took this measure even further. In order to prevent any possible return of the aviation and airline monopolists, he wanted to forbid any individual who had participated in the operators' conferences in 1930 from future contracts. Assuming that the participants of the so-called Spoils Conference were acting in a criminal conspiracy to restrict competition, even though no charges were ever filed nor any individual brought to trial through due process, Roosevelt specifically stated, as noted in his own hand on the draft letter: "No air mail contract should be sublet or sold to another contracting company nor should a mail contractor be allowed to merge or consolidate with another company holding an air mail contract. Obviously, also no contract should be made with any companies, old or new, any of whose officers were party to the obtaining of former contracts under circumstances which were clearly contrary to good faith and public policy."[50] This amounted to an unconstitutional bill of attainder.

Immediately, Chairman Mead in the House and Chairman McKellar in the Senate introduced permanent legislation to redraw the air mail map. Immediately, too, Ernest R. Breech, president of North American Aviation, took exception to the president's proposal. Breech actually agreed with the prohibition against interlocking directorates and the problems of Wall Street domination. He agreed that control of the airlines by financiers and other non-aviation personnel was not in the best interest of the industry and that interlocking directorates could restrict competition. Access to capital, however, should not be curtailed, this the proposed legislation would do, to the ultimate harm of the industry.

Breech was quick to correct Roosevelt's erroneous assumption that the holding companies restricted technological development. As seen with the example of the Boeing 247, United Aircraft's refusal to sell any of these aircraft to TWA did not restrict aircraft development; it in fact, promoted it:

> During the past year there were three important developments of air transport planes in this country. Who brought out these developments? The Curtiss Condor, the first development, was developed for Eastern Air Transport by the Curtiss-Wright Corporation, which at that time was indirectly "affiliated" with EAT. The Boeing 247 in general use over United Air Lines, was developed by United Aircraft & Transport Corp. The TWA luxury liner was built by the Douglas Co. which was "indirectly affiliated" with T.W.A. What developments contributing to the advance of the aviation industry were brought out by the independent airlines which had no affiliation, direct or indirect, with manufacturing companies? Absolutely none!
>
> It is no accident that the above is true. These developments have been brought out by transport companies affiliated with manufacturing companies and none brought out by air transport companies not affiliated with manufacturing, for one reason, namely, it takes millions of dollars and complete cooperation in the exchange of technical knowledge and practical experience between the operator and the manufacturer to carry out the experimental and development work.[51]

Breech feared that the unwarranted abrogation of contracts, though legal, would open the industry once again to dangerous speculation, and that the routes pioneered by responsible companies would be taken by unscrupulous promoters, something Postmaster General Brown and the holding companies had fought hard to prevent (6). But Breech was most angered by Roosevelt's personal attack on the pioneer airline executives who were compelled to attend the operators' conference at the request of the postmaster general. "I think the grossest injustice done by this recommendation," he told the committee, "is the repeated condemnation of the pioneers of the air transport industry who, at the invitation of a Cabinet officer, met in the Postmaster General's office in Washington to discuss plans for the administration of the Watres Act and the future development of the air transport industry. . . . In view of all the charges of the Administration's officers in an effort to justify the cancellation order, most of the principal executives of air transport companies today would be excluded from ever being officers of an air mail carrying company in the future. . . . What tribunal, if any, is to determine this question of attainder of these officers, who have been so unfairly condemned without a hearing?" (2).

Breech had five recommendations: first, that all of the contracts be returned to their original holders; second, that a fixed pound-mile system of payment of 2 mills per pound be enacted, thus eliminating subsidies altogether; third, that a direct subsidy be paid to those contractors operating over thin routes; and fourth, that the air mail postage rate be reduced to five cents per half ounce. The fifth and most significant recommendation regarded the establishment of a unique federal commission dedicated strictly to the regulation of the air transportation industry, "where sufficient rules can be laid down for prevention of abuses." Four years later this is exactly what happened with the creation of the Civil Aeronautics Board.

The enactment of such legislation would protect the investment of millions of dollars by hundreds of thousands of stockholders and restore the public's faith in the government's ability to carry out fairly its contractual obligations. It would also not inhibit the Justice Department from prosecuting any person or organization that had committed any alleged criminal conspiracy to defraud the government. "Despite all that has happened to date," fumed Breech, "we still have faith that if the House and Senate Committees will take the time to give this problem fair consideration, the air mail and air transport industry may still survive and be spared the complete chaos which would be brought about by the legislation suggested" (8).

Breech's faith was misplaced. McKellar's committee had no intention of leaving the air mail contractors unpunished for their alleged crimes and followed Roosevelt's recommendations almost to the letter. During hearings, which ran concurrently with the Black committee's investigation, McKellar brought forth a host of witnesses, primarily from the present Post Office administration and the independent, nonmail carriers arguing for drastic changes in the air mail laws. The proposed bill, S. 3012, reaffirmed the requirement for competitive bidding for all routes, gave the Post Office responsibility for advertising competitions for new routes, and gave the Interstate Commerce Commission responsibility for determining the payment rates to the lowest responsible bidder. New contracts were to be for three years and at a maximum rate of forty cents per mile. All interlocking directorates and other monopolistic practices were to be abolished, and all the participants in the operators' conferences of 1930 were enjoined from participation in all future bids for a period of five years. Section 7 stated in part,

> No person shall be eligible to bid on or hold an air mail contract if such person, through its officers, has entered into any combination to prevent competitive bidding for carrying the mails, or has made any agreement or given or performed, or promised to give or perform, any consideration whatever to induce any person not to bid for any such contract, or has employed any Senator or Member of Congress or Government official or officer of any political party to seek to influence the awarding of contracts, or has, as an officer or director, any person who has heretofore entered into any combination to prevent the

making of any bids for carrying the mails, or which pays any officer . . . a sum in excess of $17,500 for a calendar year of full time service.[52]

In an astonishing clause, S. 3012 forbade the former contractors from filing suit against the government: "No person shall be eligible to bid for or hold an air mail contract if it or its predecessor is asserting or has any claim against the United States because of a prior annulment of any contract by the Postmaster General."[53] This punitive measure, designed by McKellar ostensibly to prevent the former, supposedly corrupt, air mail carriers from rebidding, went too far for the rest of the committee. Even Democratic members were angered by the clear vindictiveness of this measure. "That is about the most obnoxious thing I ever saw in a legislative bill," remarked Sen. M.M. Logan of Kentucky. "If the government canceled a contract on a man and that man felt he had a reasonable claim, we are saying to that man: 'We will not allow you to have any dealings with the Government.' It is entirely autocratic and unfair."[54] All of the other members except McKellar agreed. Supporting Chairman McKellar, Solicitor Crowley thought the clause appropriate. "I think it would have a salutary effect on some of these people who have secured illegal contracts to say to them that they have secured a contract in this way and if they are asserting a claim against the government we are not going to have anything to do with them," he asserted. Logan strenuously disagreed. "It might have a salutary effect on them," he said, "but I am wondering what it would do to the Constitution. We are living under the Constitution. If we are going to have a Government of men and not laws, that is probably all right" (73).

Charles Lindbergh strongly supported Logan's position, much to the discomfort of McKellar and the administration. In answering pointed questions from McKellar, Lindbergh stated, "The only point I have ever made is I feel that any organization or a citizen has a right to trial before being convicted or found guilty of a charge which if implied and not proven" (143). Eddie Rickenbacker, Richard Robbins, and William Patterson all testified against this provision. The clause did not survive.

Understandably, the independents testified in strong support for the entire bill but, with victory so close at hand, were anxious to protect their own interests. Representing Braniff Airlines and the Independents, as he had for many years, attorney William Denning sought a clarification of the qualifications for future bidders. Senator McKellar saw Walter Brown's measure to restrict bidding to airlines that had a minimum of six months of flying experience not as a reasonable requirement to prove responsibility but as "an old dodge" against the law. Braniff thought Brown's decision was deliberately discriminatory—until now.

In a remarkable about-face, Denning testified that Braniff now wanted to include a restriction prohibiting new entrant airlines with less than six months' experience in flying routes under 250 miles from bidding—now that Braniff Airways was well established. Using exactly the same argument that Brown and Glover had made four years earlier, Denning sought protection from cheap, irresponsible competition: "We feel in justice to the independent operators, who have been carrying on for a period of 3 or 4 years, that experience in operating successfully a high class passenger transport service on a daily service should be given some consideration as against an organized paper company" (393). Furthermore, Denning was no longer averse to noncompetitive bidding, provided that Braniff received an award:

> It seems to me that the Department would prefer to have some leeway in giving preference to experienced operators rather than having to take any company that might be organized, and, in order to get this air mail service into the hands of private operators, it seems to me something like that would be necessary. . . .
> . . . A great deal of discussion has been going on as to whether or not it should be by competitive bidding, or there should be something similar to the railroad mail bill. Now, the independent operators of the country that I speak for want to have an opportunity to bid, or else have the mail carrying awarded to him on a reasonable basis fixed by the Postmaster General or the Interstate Commerce Commission, without discrimination.

Denning's only complaint about the McKellar bill concerned the ICC's ability to lower rates in the same fashion as the Post Office under the Watres Act. He felt that this regulation placed an undue burden on the smaller lines. Braniff wanted the government to possess the ability to increase its rate of payment if necessary (395).

The major carriers belatedly approved the clause giving regulatory responsibility to the ICC. Following Henderson's six-year argument for federal regulation and Breech's recent recommendation, the Black-McKellar bill gave control of rate decisions to the ICC, although not to a body exclusively dedicated to aviation matters. "We favor governmental regulation by a non-political body," stated United president William Patterson, "but do not believe this should be the Interstate Commerce Commission. We believe it should be an independent aeronautical body created for the sole purpose of regulation of air transport and that it should have the power to award Federal certificates of convenience and necessity."

Patterson, Rickenbacker, and representatives of the rest of the former air mail lines correctly felt that the ICC would be overburdened with the dual tasks of regulating the railroads and the airways and would not be in a position to make timely, well-informed rate decisions. Furthermore, the ICC had no one in its employ who was knowledgeable about aviation matters (337). Nevertheless, some fair regulation was better than none because it would promote the continued rational development of aviation begun during the administration of the Watres Act.

Deliberations on S. 3012, cosponsored by Senators McKellar and Black, continued for months following the close of formal hearings on March 20, 1934. McKellar's proposed legislation ignored most of the entreaties of the former air mail carriers and followed Roosevelt's suggestion to the letter. So angry was TWA that Richard Robbins filed suit against the government for damages caused by the air mail cancellation. The airline had deferred filing its appeal of an earlier decision of the Second Circuit Court rejecting TWA's petition on the grounds that the court lacked jurisdiction, hoping that the Black-McKellar bill would address the arbitrary manner in which the contracts were annulled and the company's belief that the contracts had been improperly broken. It did not. Robbins declared the bill "a hastily devised and ill-conceived measure" that "fails miserably to deal with this immense problem in an intelligent manner. It is vindictive and punitive rather than constructive." He asserted further that TWA had been "wrongfully deprived of its rights and property" when its contract had been canceled. "We welcome a judicial investigation by an impartial tribunal," he said.[55]

Despite the week-long hearings, only the clause forbidding claims against the government had been removed. Robbins was bitterly disappointed. "The sponsors of this latest Bill," he said, "are either woefully ignorant of the most elementary principles of justice and rights guaranteed our citizens, as expressed in the Constitution of the United States, or else are determined to ignore the Constitution completely in their efforts to throw a smoke screen over the air mail cancellation bungle. Instead of rewriting their proposed legislation to meet the severe criticisms of every witness other than Government officials, this redraft is even more vindictive and punitive than the original measure."

Robbins labeled the proposed legislation a bill of attainder that would inflict punishment without a judicial trial. He condemned the provision prohibiting the former air mail contractors who attended Brown's operators' meetings from future bidding. This appeared most unjust. "Can any better method be found for the Post Office to advise the air mail carriers as to policy and plans by conference with the principal officials of the airlines affected?" asked Robbins. "Is it a crime to confer with a cabinet official by his invitation?"[56]

Robbins proposed a solution: return the contracts to their rightful owners under temporary provisions, as provided for in law, and allow those airlines charged with collusion a fair hearing. The impartial decision of the court would determine the outcome of the air mail crisis.[57]

The administration was not willing to be subjected to a humiliating public hearing but now was anxious to return the contracts to the airlines and defuse the crisis as swiftly as possible. While the Black-McKellar bill was debated, Congress and the Post Office worked desperately to find an interim solution to relieve the government of the onus of its questionable cancellations and the Army Air Corps of its burden of flying the mail. Under the temporary solution as suggested by the president, the commercial carriers would return to carrying mail, thus ending the crisis—but with restrictions designed to allow the administration to preserve its dignity.

On March 28, Postmaster General Farley announced that bids for temporary, three-month contracts for the carrying of mail would be accepted within the next three weeks. The bids were permitted based on existing law, and could be extended for three-month periods at the Post Office Department's discretion. Assuming the validity of the claims of fraud and collusion, no former contractors or participants in the Spoils Conference, with the exception of National Parks, were allowed to bid. Ironically, all of the bidders had to agree to comply with the existing NRA industry codes.

At noon, April 20, on the fourth floor of the Old Post Office Building in Washington, D.C., 150 representatives of the airlines crowded into the private office of Superintendent of Air Mail Stephen A. Cisler. They were gathered to hear the results of forty-five bids for the first seventeen air mail routes returned to civilian operation. Present were Postmaster General Farley, assorted government officials, and industry representatives. Not present were the individuals who attended the Spoils Conferences four years earlier. Also not present in name were the airlines these individuals represented. The big four, however, were there, but under new names, reflecting their corporate reorganization. American Airways became American Airlines; Eastern Air Transport, Eastern Air Lines; and Northwest Airways, Northwest Airlines. Others followed similar superficial changes. United kept its original title but lost its position as a managing company, having become an operating airline, as its four component parts were now completely subsumed as one legal entity. Two other former contractors remained unchanged in name but were reorganized from within.[58]

Despite the desperate pleas by the independents in the Black committee hearings, only a few showed up that day. Not unexpectedly, the awards were given essentially to the same airlines that had flown the routes before.[59] These airlines had the equipment, personnel, money, and infrastructure already in place along these routes, as Walter Brown had always asserted. Realistically, no independent airline stood a chance of flying the mail more efficiently or safely. The irony was not lost on many observers. American, Eastern, and TWA still flew their old routes. Only United, the one airline completely innocent of any possible charge of collusion, was denied a desired route, but this was expected, even by United.

Philip Johnson had appealed directly to President Roosevelt to tell United's side of the story. Despite a lengthy audience with the president in March, the administration refused to see Johnson's position. Stated Johnson, "The whole matter was a prodigious political blunder brought about by ignorance of the whole matter and with no wish to become enlightened on the part of the Administration men responsible for the action. We have done everything we can to protect the stockholders' interest, and I personally have spent some time with Mr. Roosevelt himself but to no real avail."[60]

Johnson was deeply disillusioned. "Our contracts were all let on the basis of open competitive bidding and we were never party to any arrangements with any other companies which smacked of collusion of fraud," he told First National Bank of Seattle vice president J.W. Spangler. "We have not been given the opportunity to have a fair hearing and as the result have instituted suit so as to get whatever relief we can in the courts."[61]

Unfortunately, in order that the cancellations be justified and that Braniff and Bowen receive contracts for United's routes, Solicitor Crowley and the department had to remain firm in their assumption of United's illicit complicity. For Crowley, United's mere presence at the 1930 operators' conference was sufficient proof of guilt.[62] No hearing was necessary. "The evidence in the possession of the Department having been sufficient to demonstrate the illegality of the contracts referred to, the conduct of a hearing would have served no useful purpose and been only the means of unnecessary delay," he stated.[63] Pending the outcome of their suit, United would be forced to abide by the new rules.[64]

United did indeed lose its route from Chicago to Dallas. Old CAM-3, so long coveted by the independents, was awarded to Braniff. Braniff benefited the most having won its fight for an air mail contract, but its operation of that route ran into considerable difficulty for several years. Braniff, as with the other independents, paid its pilots less than the industry average and now had to comply with NRA codes concerning labor. The Air Line Pilots Association filed complaints against Braniff almost immediately after the airline began flying the mail and won its complaints. Bowen too had immediate difficulties after winning a route in Texas. So poorly was the line operated that by 1936, Bowen sold his operation to Braniff.

Despite paralleling Braniff's new route to a large degree, American Airlines also won a contract, with different intermediate stops, from Chicago to Fort Worth. American, under E.L. Cord, benefited greatly. Cord, a Democrat and former independent airline operator, had not attended the Spoils Conferences. Through the good offices of the Texas delegation in Congress and the Post Office, American emerged the clear winner, gaining a parallel route to part of United's San Francisco–to–New York line between New York and Chicago. Cord also asked for and received a straighter southern transcontinental that bypassed Atlanta and went directly from Fort Worth to New York. In its place, a reborn Delta Air Lines was awarded the route from Atlanta to Dallas—Fort Worth. Eastern Air Lines' routes remained essentially unchanged.

Transcontinental and Western Air retained its middle transcontinental route, although it too was straightened, to the extent that it no longer connected Columbus, Ohio, with Chicago. It relinquished its air mail line from Los Angeles to San Francisco. The company lost approximately 40 percent of its previous year's income.[65] New entrant Pacific Seaboard was awarded the line from Chicago to New Orleans, and Hanford Tri-State Airlines was given much of Northwest's system, gaining a route from Chicago to Pembina, North Dakota, through Minneapolis–St. Paul. This was a pyrrhic victory, for, as with Bowen in Texas, Hanford was not in a strong enough financial condition to fly this route, just as former Postmaster Brown had suspected, and eventually sold its air mail route back to Northwest. Northwest did win part of its long sought after northern transcontinental, from Fargo to Seattle.

All of the winning bids were significantly lower than before, reductions averaging approximately 40 percent. The Post Office and administration could point with pride to the great reduction in expenditures, but others questioned the true cost. Senator Austin, the bête noir of the administration's air mail policy, condemned the original cancellations and attacked the probability that many of the new entrants were planning to use smaller, obsolete, though cheaper, equipment on their new lines. This, he reasoned, was needlessly risking the safety of the public for the saving of a few pennies. He also condemned the low bids noting that many of the airlines were operating at a loss before the cancellations and that under the new system they would receive far less than before. This, Austin believed, flew directly in the face of Roosevelt's NRA. "How can the Administration justify compelling corporations to do business for the government on a cost-minus basis," queried Austin, "when they have written into many of the N.R.A. codes the provisions which make it illegal to sell goods or services below cost?"[66]

Postmaster General Farley remained unbowed, reasserting his belief that the president had acted according to the law and that illegalities had indeed occurred under Brown, despite the preponderance of evidence to the contrary. Regardless of the ongoing debate, the administration held the advantage and was able to impose its own air mail policy over the objections of the industry and the Republican minority in Congress. Unwittingly, though, Farley's actions and the design of Senators Black and McKellar validated Walter Brown's program.

After the smoke had cleared, the large, financially stable firms were once again carrying the bulk of the nation's air mail over a rational route system that followed closely Brown's original network. Only those companies deemed "responsible" were permitted to fly the mail, and the entire system was regulated to prevent destructive competition, thereby preserving exclusive rights to the existing routes. As before, rates were controlled and the contracts administered according to department rules. Only now the Interstate Commerce Commission became involved. For all intents and purposes, the air mail system created by the new legislation replicated most of Brown's program—with one critical exception.

The most significant and last act in this drama would profoundly and permanently reshape the face of the American aviation industry and clearly reflected Wilsonian New Freedom attitudes. While Farley was giving out three-month temporary contracts, Senators Black and Kenneth McKellar were completing legislation that would assimilate the findings of the special committee with the needs of the Post Office into a coherent plan for the air mail and the route network across the United States. After much testy debate on the Senate floor, during which the complicity of Braniff and Crowley was questioned by Republicans, and following a lengthy discussion in the House and in conference, the Air Mail Act of 1934, modified as S. 3070, became Public Law No. 308 on June 12, 1934.

The act made the temporary contracts permanent, thus reestablishing Brown's route network system. Air mail rates were reduced from $.49 per mile to as low as $.08 on some routes. The average was $.395, still a significant drop from the $.45 paid under Brown's last rate revision plan—although, arguably, under Brown's former system, the rate would have naturally been lowered to that level. The public benefited from the lower rates and from the addition of extra mileage, including Colonel Brittin's long-awaited northern transcontinental line, which served nineteen new cities and four states. As expected, rates and routes were to be determined by the neutral decision of the ICC, which would be the sole arbiter in all such matters.[67] The Post Office was empowered to award contracts to the lowest responsible bidder as well as designating primary and secondary routes, but little more. The department could grant route extensions but only up to one hundred miles per contract.

Under the new permanent law, Postmaster General Farley was compelled to withdraw from the active sponsorship and regulation of the airline industry as these decisions were now to be made by the ICC. Fortunately for the industry, the work completed by Brown was too solidly in place for it to be undone, a fact the government tacitly acknowledged with passage of the Air Mail Act of 1934. The airlines fostered and created by Brown continued to dominate the industry, as they do today. Important for the airlines as well as the administration, however, the new legislation removed the stigma of questionable practices but at the cost of profits for the airlines.

Unfortunately, Colonel Brittin and many of the greatest airline leaders were now formally proscribed from the very industry they helped to create. The vehement objections of the former air mail carriers had fallen on deaf ears. Opponents of the punitive nature of the bill managed to insert a clause in the draft of the bill that permitted anyone to bid on contracts provided they met Post Office requirements. Farley strongly objected to this provision, for it would have publicly acknowledged that the administration had been in error in its reasons for the recent cancellations. "The Department," he wrote McKellar, "has insisted on bidders for new air mail contracts complying with the existing law which prohibits any company whose contracts have been annulled on the ground of fraud and collusion from bidding, and which also prohibits any company bidding from having as an officer or director any person who has entered into a combination or conspiracy to prevent competitive bidding. If the new air mail bill expressly provides for the exemption of such companies and such officers and directors from the penalties of existing law, it will have the effect of Congress, by law, exonerating companies and officers who participated in the collusive and fraudulent conferences of 1930."[68]

The clause was removed in conference. Now, as with the earlier temporary measure, no airline that had allegedly been involved in collusive bidding and no airline executive who had attended the Spoils Conferences would be permitted to bid on a contract. Furthermore, these executives were forbidden from working for any air mail carrier for the same length of time. Although they had never been formally charged, tried, or convicted of any crime, the industry leaders were punished ex post facto. Unfortunately for them, the airlines, the administration, the press, and the public were eager to put the air mail crisis behind them quickly, so ugly compromises were made in the name of salvaging the industry and the government's reputation.

The airlines sued the government following the air mail contract cancellations in February 1934, but with one exception, all withdrew their complaints by 1936. By then a quiet settlement had been reached whereby the government admitted no wrong doing but paid the air mail contractors for their services for January and February 1934. The one exception was William Patterson of United, who was outraged at the shabby treatment of his mentor Philip Johnson by the administration and continued his suit until 1942, when United also settled. United, too, was paid for its services in 1934, though the government was upheld in its right to annul the contracts. Most important for Patterson, Johnson, and former postmaster general Brown, the courts exonerated them, ruling that no fraud had occurred at the operators' conferences in 1930. By this time, however, the point was moot; the industry had moved on to other matters, now that World War II occupied the nation's interest.

Of even greater significance, however, the Air Mail Act of 1934 reflected the administration's New Freedom roots concerning monopoly. The vertically integrated holding company was now forbidden. The terms of the new act were clear:

> Section 7(a). After December 31, 1934, it shall be unlawful for any person holding an air mail contract to buy, acquire, hold, own, or control, directly or indirectly, any shares of stock or other interest in any other partnership, association, or corporation engaged directly or indirectly in any phase of the aviation industry, whether so engaged through air transportation of passengers, express, or mail, through the holding of an air mail contract, or through the manufacture or sale off airplanes, airplane parts, or other materials or accessories generally used in air transportation, and regardless of whether such buying, acquisition, holding, ownership, or control is done directly, or is accomplished indirectly, through an agent, subsidiary, associate, affiliate, or by any other device whatsoever.[69]

After December 31, 1934, all aviation holding companies were forbidden from receiving federal subsidy through the air mail, thus effectively destroying these organizations, which were heavily dependent upon the government for funding. The combines soon divested their interests. American, Eastern, and TWA sold off their holdings in other aircraft manufacturing firms. United, the most efficient and most thoroughly vertically integrated company, was hurt the most. UATC gave up United Air Lines and Boeing Aircraft Company, thus becoming the United Aircraft Corporation. So angry was William Boeing over the Black committee hearings and the subsequent act that he retired from all of his aviation enterprises, not wishing to deal with the federal government on any level.

As early as May 1934, United Aircraft had completed its formal reorganization plan to separate the transportation system from the holding company. Drafted by Philip Johnson, Joseph F. McCarthy, and Joseph P. Ripley, the plan outlined the eventual dissolution of UATC. With Boeing in Seattle and Pratt & Whitney in Hartford, United Aircraft formally divided its manufacturing companies along geographic lines. United Aircraft sold off all of its shares in Boeing Air Transport, Pacific Air Transport, Varney Air Lines, and National Air Transport. A new company, United Air Lines Transport Corporation, was formed with an authorized share capital of 1.2 million shares at a par value of five dollars a share. Eight days after passage of the Air Mail Act of 1934, on June 20, 1934, at a special stockholders meeting held at UATC's corporate headquarters on Park Avenue in Manhattan, the plan was formally adopted, thus ending a brief but highly influential enterprise in the history of U.S. aviation business.[70]

Thus, a short but turbulent period in American air transportation reached a watershed. Although the monopolistic holding companies are now gone, the oligopoly of airlines and manufacturers that existed under government regulation in the aftermath of the events of 1934 remains virtually intact and unchanged, even in this day of deregulation. The foundation built in those difficult Depression-era years has served the nation and its citizens well, with the federal government, as it was from the very beginning, ultimately in control.

From 1934 until 1938, the U.S. airline industry struggled on in the face of drastically declining federal revenue and continued confusion on the part of the government. The ICC proved unable to handle aviation matters to anyone's satisfaction and several hearings and commissions sought to revamp the industry along more clearly defined terms. The Post Office, with its authority greatly curtailed, no longer played an active role in the industry. During this time, President Roosevelt remained aloof from aviation matters, providing little direction.

With the advent of the superlative Douglas DC-3, a twenty-one-seat derivative of the DC-2, the airlines were slowly able to fight their way back to profitability, as this remarkable aircraft, which, in the words of American's C.R. Smith, was the first aircraft capable of flying just passengers and making a profit, first entered service in 1936. By the end of the decade, this aircraft came to dominate the industry as it would for years to come.

In the meantime, cooler heads prevailed in Congress and the administration. In 1938, Roosevelt signed into law the Civil Aeronautics Act, which provided for the unification of all federal regulation of commercial air transportation in the United States—exactly what Col. Paul Henderson had wanted for so long. The act created the Civil Aeronautics Board to regulate routes, fares, and restrict competition in order to promote the industry, exactly what Walter Brown had done eight years earlier. In addition, the new law established the Civil Aeronautics Administration, which was given the aviation responsibilities hitherto administered by the Commerce Department. Eventually the activities of this office became the responsibility of the Federal Aviation Administration.

By 1938, public policy toward the air transportation industry returned in essence to that which had existed eight years earlier under President Hoover and his farsighted postmaster general Walter Folger Brown. Under this law, the federal government once again legally protected the oligopoly of existing pioneering airlines operating in the public interest under certificates of convenience and necessity. The industry grew and prospered under this strict, rational control for the next four decades until President Jimmy Carter signed the Airline Deregulation Act of 1978, signifying the coming of age of the airline industry. Ironically, the deregulation of the airline industry was designed to remove the barriers for new crop of "independents" who had been denied entry into the government-controlled cartel dominated by United Air Lines,

American Airlines, and TWA. Just as ironically, since 1978, few new airlines have survived, whereas United and American remain dominant.

As from the very beginning of commercial aviation, this capital- and labor-intensive industry has reacted naturally to the forces of the free market in producing oligopoly. As before, the existence of oligopoly does not necessarily preclude competition, as the American public reaps the advantages of the world's best and most affordable air transportation system due in large part to the policies of the federal government.

Clearly, the actions and reactions of both Republican and Democratic administrations reflected old Progressive values placed within the context of a nascent aviation industry. These ideals profoundly affected the shape of American air transportation during its formation and infancy while guaranteeing its success during the most difficult of times and thereby ensuring its growth in the future. Progressivism did not die in 1914. It is with us today.

Notes

Chapter 1. Foundations

1. William M. Leary, *Aerial Pioneers: The U.S. Air Mail Service, 1918–1927* (Washington, D.C.: Smithsonian Institution Press, 1985), 34–38.

2. Ibid., 13.

3. Ibid., 14–15.

4. R.E.G. Davies, *Airlines of the United States Since 1914* (Washington, D.C.: Smithsonian Institution Press, 1982), 18.

5. Leary, *Aerial Pioneers*, 54.

6. Ibid., 79.

7. Davies, *Airlines of the United States*, 21.

8. Leary, *Aerial Pioneers*, 153.

9. Davies, *Airlines of the United States*, 24.

10. Leary, *Aerial Pioneers*, 171.

11. Davies, *Airlines of the United States*, 25–27.

12. Nick A. Komons, *Bonfires to Beacons: Federal Civil Aviation Policy Under the Air Commerce Act, 1926–1938* (Washington, D.C.: Smithsonian Institution Press, 1989), 22.

13. David D. Lee, "Herbert Hoover and the Golden Age of Aviation," in *Aviation's Golden Age: Portraits from the 1920's and 1930's*, ed. William Leary (Iowa City: University of Iowa Press, 1989), 130–31.

14. Lee, "Herbert Hoover," 129.

15. Ibid., 131.

16. Komons, *Bonfires to Beacons*, 46.

17. Ibid., 57–64.

18. Leary, *Aviation's Golden Age*, 222–23.

19. Ibid., 58–59.

20. House, *House Report 730*, 68th Cong., 1st sess., May 13, 1924, quoted in Paul T. David, *The Economics of Air Mail Transportation* (Washington, D.C.: Brookings Institution, 1934), 59.

21. David, *Economics of Air Mail Transportation,* 59.

22. *Webster's Third New International Dictionary* (Springfield, Mass.: G & C Merriam, 1965), 2279.

23. *Civil Aviation: A Report by the Joint Committee on Civil Aviation* (New York: McGraw-Hill, 1926), 94–95.

24. Department of Commerce, *Statement of Secretary Hoover on Commercial Aviation,* press release, September 24, 1925, 1, No. 741, Box 40, Cabinet Collection, Herbert C. Hoover Presidential Library and Archives, West Branch, Iowa (hereafter cited as HCHPLA).

25. Ibid., 1.

26. Department of Commerce, press release, January 24, 1926, 1.

27. *Civil Aviation,* 16.

28. Ibid., 20.

29. Komons, *Bonfires to Beacons,* 71.

30. Ibid., 72–74.

31. Ibid., 74.

32. Ibid., 76.

33. Ibid., 78.

34. Leary, *Aviation's Golden Age,* 41.

35. Ibid., 47–50.

36. Ibid., 43.

37. Komons, *Bonfires to Beacons,* 83.

Chapter 2. The Birth of an Industry

1. "Regulations for Air Mail Routes," *Aviation,* April 27, 1925, 458–59.

2. "Feeder Lines," *Aviation,* June 22, 1925, 689.

3. *Aviation,* June 15, 1925, 669.

4. Ibid., 661.

5. *Aviation,* September 28, 1925, 382.

6. *Aviation,* October 19, 1925, 552.

7. *Aviation,* August 17, 1925, 178.

8. Davies, *Airlines of the United States,* 39.

9. *Aviation,* April 5, 1926, 492.

10. *Aviation,* March 1, 1926, 292.

11. Davies, *Airlines of the United States,* 41.

12. "Clement M. Keys: He Bought a Company Nearly Insolvent," *Air Transportation,* July 27, 1929, 51.

13. Ibid., 51, 55.

14. *Aviation,* June 1, 1925, 598.

15. National Air Transport Listing Statement for the New York Stock Exchange, A-8687, May 10, 1929, Senate Special Committee on Investigation of Air Mail and Ocean Mail Contracts, Box 152, RG 46, National Archives and Records Administration, Washington, D.C. (hereafter cited as NARA).

16. National Air Transport, memorandum, April 6, 1927, Box 146, RG 46, NARA.

17. *Aviation,* May 24, 1926, 783, 804.

18. *Aviation,* May 10, 1926, 706.

19. Smith, Henry Ladd, 107.

20. *Aviation,* October 4, 1926, 598.

21. "Three Months Operation of Colonial Air Transport," *Aviation,* October 25, 1926, 703–5.

22. Davies, *Airlines of the United States,* 48.

23. Ibid., 42.

24. Ibid., 45–48.

25. Ibid., 47.

26. Frank J. Taylor, *High Horizons: Daredevil Flying Postmen to Modern Magic Carpet—The United Air Lines Story* (New York: McGraw-Hill, 1951), 21–22.

27. Patricia A. Michaelis, "L.H. Brittin," in *Encyclopedia of American Business History and Biography: The Airline Industry* by William Leary (New York: Bruccoli Clark Layman, 1992), 80–81.

28. Ibid., 54.

29. Ibid., 48.

30. "Harris M. Hanshue: Airline Operator and Manufacturer," *Air Transportation,* August 2, 1930, 27.

31. "The Los Angeles–Salt Lake City Air Mail Line," *Aviation,* April 5, 1926, 493; Davies, *Airlines of the United States,* 45.

32. David, *Economics of Air Mail Transportation,* 59–63.

33. Ibid., 64.

34. Ibid.

35. "Astonishing Air Mail Bids," *Aviation,* January 24, 1927, 170.

36. "Important Decision on Air Mail Bids," *Aviation,* March 21, 1927, 578.

37. "New Air Mail Bids Received on New York–Chicago Route," *Aviation,* April 4, 1927, 678.

38. "NAT Awarded New York–Chicago Contract," *Aviation,* April 11, 1927, 731.

39. Peter W. Bowers, *Boeing Aircraft Since 1916* (New York: Funk and Wagnalls, 1968), 7.

40. Davies, *Airlines of the United States,* 10–12.

41. Ibid., 27.

42. Ibid., 58.

43. Bowers, *Boeing Aircraft Since 1916,* 108.

44. Ibid., 109–17.

45. "Mr. Rentschler," *Bee Hive,* Summer 1956, 2–5.

46. Robert Schlaifer and S.D. Heron, *Development of Aircraft Engines and Fuels* (Boston: Harvard University, 1950), 162–70.

47. Ibid., 185.

48. Ibid., 189–90.

49. Bowers, *Boeing Aircraft Since 1916,* 100.

50. Bertha Boeing diary, January 28, 1927, Box 692, Boeing Company, Historical Services, Archives, Seattle, Washington (hereafter cited as Boeing).

51. Ibid., January 30, 1927.

52. Taylor, *High Horizons,* 29.

Chapter 3. The Aviation Industry Comes of Age

1. Paul R. Ignatius, "Every Flight for a Purpose," in *Charles A. Lindbergh: An American Life,* ed. Tom D. Crouch (Washington, D.C.: Smithsonian Institution Press, 1977), 17.

2. Ibid., 18.

3. "A Great Stimulus to Commercial Aviation," *Aviation,* June 6, 1927, 1213.

4. Keys to Tex Marshall, December 3, 1926, N.A.T./N.A.A., N.A.T. Correspondence File 1, Box 10, Record Unit (RU) 103, Keys Collection, National Air and Space Museum-Archives (hereafter cited as NASM Keys).

5. David, *Economics of Air Mail Transportation,* 69–70.

6. Richard P. Hallion, *Legacy of Flight: The Guggenheim Contribution to Commercial Aviation* (Seattle: University of Washington Press, 1977), 86–88.

7. "Guggenheim to Finance Passenger Services," *Aviation,* July 18, 1927, 151.

8. Ibid., 89.

9. Davies, *Airlines of the United States,* 65.

10. Keys for the record, memorandum, April 27, 1928, T.A.T.—Misc., Box 12, NASM Keys.

11. National Air Transport, memorandum, n.d., T.A.T.—Publicity, Box 12, NASM Keys.

12. Ibid.

13. Handwritten memorandum, Keys to the record, T.A.T—Publicity, Box 12, NASM Keys.

14. Ibid.

15. Ibid.

16. Ibid.

17. Keys to Henderson, April 4, 1928, T.A.T.—Henderson, Paul, Box 12, NASM Keys.

18. Keys to Thomas N. Dysert, confidential letter, April 4, 1928, T.A.T.—Cuthell, Hotchkiss, and Mills, Box 11, NASM Keys.

19. Dysart to Keys, April 7, 1928, T.A.T.—Cuthell, Hotchkiss, and Mills, Box 11, NASM Keys.

20. Keys to Dysart, April 9, 1928, T.A.T.—Cuthell, Hotchkiss, and Mills, Box 11, NASM Keys.

21. Ibid., 2.

22. Henderson to D.M. Shaeffer, telegram, April 11, 1928, T.A.T.—Henderson, Paul, Box 12, NASM Keys.

23. Hanshue to Chester W. Cuthell, April 24, 1928, NAA Transcontinental and Western Air, Box 143, RG 46, NARA.

24. Ibid.

25. Henderson to Keys, April 26, 1928, T.A.T.—Henderson, Paul, Box 12, NASM Keys.

26. Keys to Henderson, April 30, 1928, T.A.T.—Henderson, Paul, Box 12, NASM Keys.

27. Ibid.

28. North American Aviation Report Prepared for the Special Senate Committee, April 25, 1934, 81, NAA Transcontinental and Western Air, Box 143, RG 46, NARA.

29. Minutes, National Air Transport Board of Directors, June 1, 1928, 2, NAA Transcontinental and Western Air, Box 143, RG 46, NARA.

30. Keys to Seward Prosser/Bankers Trust Company, May 10, 1928, N.A.T./N.A.A., N.A.T. Correspondence File 1, Box 3, RU 103, NASM Keys.

31. Keys to Lindbergh, May 23, 1928, NAA Transcontinental and Western Air, Box 143, RG 46, NARA.

32. Keys to Lindbergh, confidential letter, June 6, 1928, N.A.T./N.A.A., N.A.T. Correspondence File 1, Box 3, RU 103, NASM Keys.

33. Henderson to Keys, October 17, 1928, T.A.T.—Henderson, Paul, Box 12, NASM Keys.

34. Keys to Cuthell, telegram, August 9, 1928, T.A.T.—Cuthell, C.W., Box 11, NASM Keys.

35. Ibid.

36. Keys for the record, memorandum, April 27, 1928, T.A.T.—Misc., Box 12, NASM Keys.

37. Ibid.

38. Keys to Henderson, April 30, 1928, T.A.T.—Henderson, Paul, Box 12, NASM Keys.

39. Keys to William Boeing, June 21, 1928, T.A.T.—Adams and Peck, Box 11, NASM Keys.

40. Ibid.

41. William E. Boeing to Keys, June 30, 1928, T.A.T.—Adams and Peck, Box 11, NASM Keys.

42. Keys to Cuthell, June 28, 1928, T.A.T.—Cuthell, C.W., Box 11, NASM Keys.

43. Keys to Cuthell, telegram, July 11, 1928, N.A.T./N.A.A., N.A.T. Correspondence File 1, Box 3, RU 103, NASM Keys.

Chapter 4. Consolidation

1. Elsbeth Freudenthal, *The Aviation Business* (New York: Vantage Press, 1940), 92.

2. David, *Economics of Air Mail Transportation*, 74–76.

3. Ibid., 77.

4. Ibid., 79, 81.

5. Joseph P. Ripley to Gerrard Winston of Shearman & Sterling, memorandum, Re: United Aircraft Financing, quoted in United Air Lines, *Corporate and Legal History of United Air Lines and Its Predecessors and Subsidiaries: 1925–1945* (Chicago: United Air Lines, 1953), 155.

6. M.C. Cross to Hyson, telegram, October 22, 1928, U.A.T.C. Copies of Boeing Correspondence (flashes and sales letters), Box 152, RG 46, NARA.

7. C.E. Mitchell to Joseph Ripley, telegram, October 22, 1928, U.A.T.C. Boeing—Reports and Exhibits, Box 152, RG 46, NARA.

8. Memorandum of Agreement between W.E. Boeing, National City Company, and Boeing Airplane & Transport Corporation, October 30, 1928, U.A.T.C. Copies of Boeing Correspondence (flashes and sales letters), Box 152, RG 46, NARA.

9. Draft letter to stockholders, n.d., U.A.T.C. National City Bank, Box 153, RG 46, NARA.

10. National City Bank to Committee on Listing and Securities, New York Curb Market (marginal notes), October 31, 1928; United Air Lines, *Corporate and Legal History of United Airlines,* 156 n. 14, quoted from the *Commercial and Financial Chronicle* 127 (November 10, 1928): 2671.

11. National City General Sales, Telegram Flash No. 3524, December 19, 1928, U.A.T.C. Boeing—Reports and Exhibits, Box 152, RG 46, NARA.

12. J.P. Ripley to Gordon Merier of National City—London, telegram, December 17, 1928, U.A.T.C. Boeing—Reports and Exhibits, Box 152, RG 46, NARA.

13. *New York Times,* December 16, 1928.

14. National City Company, sales letter, December 18, 1928, U.A.T.C. Copies of Correspondence (flashes and sales letters), Box 152, RG 46, NARA.

15. J.P. Ripley to M.H. Bradley, Treasurer, National City, memorandum, December 17, 1928, U.A.T.C. Boeing—Reports and Exhibits, Box 152, RG 46, NARA; United Air Lines, *Corporate and Legal History of United Air Lines,* 167.

16. Keys to Harry Chandler, November 7, 1928, T.A.T.—Misc., Box 12, NASM Keys.

17. Ibid.

18. C.M. Keys, interview, *Aviation,* December 15, 1928, 1990.

19. North American Aviation Circular, December 6, 1928, N.A.T/N.A.A., N.A.T. Correspondence File 1, Box 10, RU 103, NASM Keys.

20. Draft of article submitted to *Wall Street Journal,* by C.M. Keys, May 7, 1928, AVCO, Box 6B, NASM Keys.

21. Investigator's Report, North American Aviation, April 25, 1934, 1–2, 8, N.A.A., Inc. and Affiliated Companies, Box 145, RG 46, NARA.

22. "Sherman Mills Fairchild," *Air Transportation,* June 7, 1930, 30.

23. George R. Hahn to A.G. Patterson, January 30, 1934, George R. Hann, Box 125, RG 46, NARA.

24. "Form Pittsburgh Holding Concern," *Aviation,* December 29, 1928, 2103.

25. "1929 and the Aviation Corporation," unpublished Fairchild corporate history, 5–6, Sherman M. Fairchild Collection, Box 111, Manuscript Division, Library of Congress (hereafter cited as Fairchild Collection).

26. Sherman Fairchild, interview, July–August 1968, Box 113, Fairchild Collection.

27. Roland Palmedo and Sherman Fairchild, interview, October 20, 1965, unpublished transcript, Box 111, Fairchild Collection.

28. Fairchild to Clark, telegram, January 3, 1929, AVCO Correspondence, January—May 1929, Box 139, RG 46, NARA.

29. George Hann to Graham Grosvenor, February 11, 1929, AVCO Correspondence, January—May 1929, Box 139, RG 46, NARA.

30. "The Aviation Corporation Stock Issue," memorandum, February 21, 1929, AVCO Correspondence, January–May 1929, Box 139, RG 46, NARA.

31. Stock circular, the Aviation Corporation, March 7, 1929, W. Averell Harriman Collection, Box 1, Manuscript Division, Library of Congress (hereafter cited as Harriman Collection).

32. The Aviation Corporation Agreement, March 2, 1929, AVCO Excerpts from Minutes, Box 134, RG 46, NARA.

33. George Hann to Richard Mellon, cablegram, March 5, 1929, AVCO—William Dewey Loucks, Box 140, RG 46, NARA.

34. The Aviation Corporation, Closing Memorandum, March 19, 1929, AVCO Correspondence, January–May 1929, Box 139, RG 46, NARA.

35. Ibid.

36. Memorandum of decisions arrived at, Meeting of March 14, 1929, Box 1, Harriman Collection.

37. George Hann to Robert Lehman, March 22, 1929, AVCO—William Dewey Loucks, Box 140, RG 46, NARA.

38. George Hann to Graham Grosvenor, March 8, 1929, AVCO Correspondence, January–May 1929, Box 139, RG 46, NARA.

39. William B. Mayo to Benedict M. Holden of Colonial Air Transport, telegram, January 23, 1929, Colonial Air Transport (1926–1933), Box 135, RG 46, NARA.

40. John O'Ryan to Sen. James W. Wadsworth Jr. and Governor John H. Trumbull, memorandum, December 21, 1928, Colonial Air Transport (1926–1933), Box 135, RG 46, NARA.

41. John F. O'Ryan to William Mayo, January 25, 1929, Colonial Air Transport (1926–1933), Box 135, RG 46, NARA.

42. John F. O'Ryan to Wadsworth, March 12, 1929, Colonial Air Transport (1926–1933), Box 135, RG 46, NARA.

43. B.M. Holden to Stanley Knauss, telegram, Stout Air Services, April 1, 1929, Colonial Air Transport (1926–1933), Box 135, RG 46, NARA.

44. John H. Baker to John F. O'Ryan, April 9, 1929, Colonial Air Transport (1926–1933), Box 135, RG 46, NARA.

45. John F. O'Ryan to William D. Louckes, telegram, April 13, 1929, Colonial Air Transport (1926–1933), Box 135, RG 46, NARA.

46. John F. O'Ryan to Robert Lehman, April 29, 1929, Colonial Air Transport (1926–1933), Box 135, RG 46, NARA.

47. John F. O'Ryan to Governor Turnbull, memorandum, April 29, 1929, Colonial Air Transport (1926–1933), Box 135, RG 46, NARA.

48. Minutes of Board of Directors, Canadian Colonial Airways, May 20, 1929, AVCO—Colonial and Canadian Colonial, Box 134, RG 46, NARA.

49. James A. Walsh to Arthur J. Underhill, Boston News Bureau, April 25, 1929, Colonial Air Transport (1926–1933), Box 135, RG 46, NARA.

Chapter 5. 1929: The Calm before the Storm

1. Memorandum, Paul Henderson to Clement Keys, Oct. 12, 1928, TAT—Henderson, Paul, Box 12, NASM Keys.

2. Clement Keys to Paul Henderson, October 16, 1928, T.A.T.—Henderson, Paul, Box 12, NASM Keys.

3. Clement Keys to Paul Henderson, November 15, 1928, T.A.T.—Henderson, Paul, Box 12, NASM Keys.

4. Harvey S. Ford, "Walter Folger Brown," *Northwest Ohio Quarterly,* Summer 1954, 205.

5. Ibid., 200–202.

6. Anne Hard, "Uncle Sam's New Mail Man," *New York Herald Tribune,* April 7, 1929, 11–12.

7. Eugene P. Trani and David L. Wilson, *The Presidency of Warren G. Harding* (Lawrence: University Press of Kansas, 1977), 83–84.

8. Ford, "Walter Folger Brown," 204; Theodore G. Joslin, "Postmaster General Brown," *World's Work,* August 1930, 38–40.

9. Hainer Hinshaw to Mason Peters, March 13, 1929, AVCO Correspondence, January–May 1929, Box 139, RG 46, NARA.

10. List of Contractors and Rate of Pay, Schedule as of May 1, 1930, Entry 157, Box 3, RG 28, NARA.

11. David, *Economics of Air Mail Transportation,* 86–87.

12. W. Irving Glover to The Embry Riddle Company, May 8, 1929, AVCO, Post Office Correspondence—Brown, Glover, Coleman, Box 138, RG 46, NARA.

13. Post Office Press Release, May 27, 1929, Press Releases, Box 117, RG 46, NARA.

14. Post Office Department Press Release, July 22, 1929, Press Releases, Box 117, RG 46, NARA.

15. "Air Mail Rates Discussed in Capitol," *Aviation,* July 20, 1929, 188.

16. Post Office Department Press Release, April 25, 1929, Press Releases, Box 117, RG 46, NARA.

17. Post Office Press Release, May 10, 1929, Press Releases, Box 117, RG 46, NARA.

18. Ibid., 2.

19. William Gibbs McAdoo to Brice Clagett, May 11, 1929, William Gibbs McAdoo Collection, Box 343, Library of Congress (hereafter cited as McAdoo Collection).

20. Post Office Department Press Releases, May 25, 1929, May 29, 1929, Press Releases, Box 117, RG 46, NARA.

21. Post Office Department Press Release, June 12, 1929, Press Releases, Box 117, RG 46, NARA.

22. "Routes in the South Debated at Hearing," *Aviation,* June 22, 1929, 2202.

23. James A. Edgerton to William Gibbs McAdoo, July 9, 1929, Box 344, McAdoo Collection.

24. Davies, *Airlines of the United States,* 84–86.

25. W.B. Weisenburger to J.V. Magee, July 22, 1929, Thomas Hill, Box 126, RG 46, NARA.

26. J.V. Magee to Paul Henderson, July 26, 1929, Col. Paul Henderson, Box 126, RG 46, NARA.

27. Paul Henderson to Chester Cuthell, July 26, 1929, Col. Paul Henderson, Box 126, RG 46, NARA.

28. Hainer Hinshaw to George Hann, August 15, 1926, N.A.A. Correspondence of Pittsburgh Aviation Industries Corporation, Box 145, RG 46, NARA.

29. Post Office Department Press Release, August 15, 1929, Press Releases, Box 117, RG 46, NARA.

30. C.M. Keys to Harold Pitcairn, June 11, 1929, N.A.A.—Pitcairn, Box 145, RG 46, NARA.

31. Statement to the Press, June 27, 1929, Speeches and Articles, Box 10A, NASM Keys.

32. Minutes of Meeting of the Executive Committee of North American Aviation, June 27, 1929, N.A.A. Information, Box 145, RG 46, NARA.

33. Davies, *Airlines of the United States,* 85–87.

34. Chester W. Cuthell to C.M. Keys, September 28, 1928, T.A.T.—Cuthell, Hotchkiss, and Mills, Box 11, NASM Keys.

35. "Curtiss Extending Control Over Air Lines," *Western Flying* 6, no. 1 (July 1929): 152.

36. United Air Lines, *Corporate and Legal History of United Air Lines,* 45–52; Davies, *Airlines of the United States,* 52, 72.

37. "Sikorsky Interests and United Aircraft Merge," *Air Transportation,* July 27, 1929, 1, 32.

38. "United Aircraft Acquires the Assets of Avian Corp.," *Air Transportation,* August 17, 1929, 17.

39. "United Aircraft and Transport and Stearman Company Complete Merger," *Air Transportation,* August 10, 1929, 1.

40. "Chronology of Operation by Texas Air Transport, Inc.," Texas Air Transport File, C.R. Smith Museum, Archives, American Airlines, Fort Worth, Texas (hereafter cited as C.R. Smith Museum Archives).

41. Grady Barrett Jr. to Gregory Kennedy, Director, C.R. Smith Museum, American Airlines, n.d., C.R. Smith Museum Archives.

42. "Chronology of Operation by Texas Air Transport," 4.

43. Davies, *Airlines of the United States,* 106.

44. Paul Henderson to Clement Keys, January 25, 1929, Texas Air Transport, Box 11, NASM Keys.

45. Texas Air Transport Proposed List of Directors, February 9, 1929, "Chronology of Operation by Gulf Coast Airways, Inc.," Gulf Coast Airways File, C.R. Smith Museum Archives.

46. "Paul Braniff Air Transportation Taxi Co. of Oklahoma to Operate State Air Lines," *Aviation,* June 18, 1928, 1775; Davies, *Airlines of the United States,* 102.

47. George Hann to Graham Grosvenor, March 29, 1929, Box 1, Harriman Collection.

48. Walter H. Mayer to Hitt, Farwell & Co., April 16, 1929, AVCO Correspondence, January–May 1929, Box 139, RG 46, NARA.

49. Hitt, Farwell & Co. to W.H. Mayer, May 1, 1929, AVCO Correspondence, January–May 1929, Box 139, RG 46, NARA.

50. *The Aviation Corporation Statistical Memorandum,* August 6, 1929, AVCO Statistical Information, Box 138, RG 46, NARA.

51. George Hann to W.A. Harriman, telegram, June 17, 1929, Box 1, Harriman Collection.

52. Davies, *Airlines of the United States,* 112.

53. Mabel Walker Willebrandt to Gilbert Grosvenor, June 7, 1929, AVCO Correspondence, June–December 1929, Box 139, RG 46, NARA.

54. Roland Palmedo to M.C. Gutman, memorandum, Re: Aviation Listing, June 19, 1929, Box 45, Fairchild Collection.

55. Roland Palmedo to Committee on Stock List, New York Stock Exchange, June 26, 1929; the Aviation Corporation Listing Application, August 2, 1929, both Box 1, Harriman Collection.

56. W.D. Loucks to W.A. Harriman, August 27, 1929, William D. Loucks File, Box 71, Harriman Collection.

57. J.A. Talbot and Harris Hanshue to W. Dewey Louckes and Robert Law Jr., August 26, 1929, William D. Loucks File, Box 71, Harriman Collection.

58. William Dewey Loucks to G.W. Walker, confidential letter, September 12, 1929, William D. Loucks File, Box 71, Harriman Collection.

59. W. Dewey Loucks to George Hann, telegram cited in letter, September 11, 1929, AVCO—William Dewey Loucks, Box 140, RG 46, NARA.

60. George Hann to W. Dewey Loucks, September 12, 1929, AVCO—William Dewey Loucks, Box 140, RG 46, NARA.

61. William Dewey Louckes to Alexander B. Royce, April 16, 1929, Box 1, Harriman Collection.

62. Hainer Hinshaw to Mabel Walker Willebrandt, August 7, 1929, AVCO Correspondence, June–December 1929, Box 139, RG 46, NARA.

63. Transcript of Conference on Aviation Legislation, 15, AVCO Correspondence, June–December 1929, Box 39, RG 46, NARA. Subsequent references to this conference are cited in text with the page numbers in parentheses.

64. "Delegates to Kansas City Conference Discuss Problems of Transport Line Operators," *Air Transportation,* October 5, 1929, 16.

65. Ibid., 17.

66. Ibid., 22.

67. Ibid.

Chapter 6. The Post Office Takes Charge

1. Jordan Schwartz, *The New Dealers: Power Politics in the Age of Roosevelt* (New York: Alfred A. Knopf, 1993), 4–7.

2. Ibid., 13–18.

3. William Gibbs McAdoo to H.P. Wilson, April 2, 1929, Box 343, McAdoo Collection.

4. McAdoo to Brice Clagett, April 4, 1929, Box 343, McAdoo Collection.

5. McAdoo to Clagett, April 12, 1929, Box 343, McAdoo Collection.

6. McAdoo to James C. Edgerton, April 12, 1929, Box 343, McAdoo Collection.

7. McAdoo to Clagett, April 30, 1929, Box 343, McAdoo Collection.

8. McAdoo to Clagett, May 14, 1929, Box 343, McAdoo Collection.

9. Bernard Baruch to McAdoo, June 19, 1929, Box 344, McAdoo Collection.

10. McAdoo to Clagett, July 1, 1929, Box 344, McAdoo Collection.

11. McAdoo to H.P. Wilson, July 13, 1929, Box 344, McAdoo Collection.

12. Erle P. Halliburton to McAdoo, July 8, 1929, Box 344, McAdoo Collection.

13. McAdoo to Edgerton, August 7, 1929, Box 344, McAdoo Collection.

14. McAdoo to Halliburton, August 8, 1929, Box 345, McAdoo Collection.

15. Clagett to McAdoo, September 20, 1929, Box 345, McAdoo Collection.

16. Ibid.

17. McAdoo to Clagett, telegram, September 20, 1929, Box 344, McAdoo Collection.

18. McAdoo to Clagett, September 26, 1929, Box 346, McAdoo Collection.

19. Ibid.

20. Edgerton to McAdoo, October 2, 1929, Box 346, McAdoo Collection.

21. Erle P. Halliburton and W.G. McAdoo to Postmaster General, proposal, October 15, 1929, Box 555, McAdoo Collection.

22. Announcement, "The Southern Transcontinental Air Mail Route," by W.G. McAdoo and Erle P. Halliburton, n.d., Box 555, McAdoo Collection.

23. W. Irving Glover to W.G. McAdoo, October 25, 1929, Box 555, McAdoo Collection.

24. Clagett to McAdoo, October 25, 1929, Box 555, McAdoo Collection.

25. Ibid.

26. Unpublished Memorandum for the Press, November 22, 1929, Box 347, McAdoo Collection.

27. "New Transcontinental Air Mail Route Proposals Heard at Washington Meeting," *Air Transportation,* December 7, 1929, 44.

28. E.S. Evans to McAdoo, December 2, 1929, Box 347, McAdoo Collection.

29. McAdoo to Clagett, December 11, 1929, Box 347, McAdoo Collection.

30. Ibid., 2.

31. Ibid.

32. L.H. Brittin to Harold H. Emmons, January 15, 1929, Independent Companies—Northwest Airways, 1929, Box 156, RG 46, NARA.

33. Hainer Hinshaw to Dan W. Jones, June 24, 1929, AVCO Correspondence, June–December 1929, Box 139, RG 46, NARA.

34. "Air Mail Contracts and Rate Revision," *Aviation,* August 3, 1929, 249.

35. Ibid., 249–50.

36. Post Office Department Press Release, September 17, 1929, Press Releases, Box 117, RG 46, NARA.

37. Hinshaw to Robert J. Smith, September 24, 1929, Earl Wadsworth, Box 130, RG 46, NARA.

38. Philip G. Johnson to Hainer Hinshaw, September 12, 1929, U.A.T.C. Boeing Airplane Company, Box 152, RG 46, NARA.

39. Hainer Hinshaw to Robert J. Smith, September 24, 1929, AVCO Correspondence, June–December 1929, Box 139, RG 46, NARA.

40. "Secret Air Mail Conferences on in Washington," *Air Transportation,* October 5, 1929, 1.

41. L.H. Brittin to R.C. Lilly, telegram, October 6, 1929, Independent Companies—Northwest Airways, 1929, Box 156, RG 46, NARA.

42. McAdoo to Sen. Sam G. Bratton, October 4, 1929, Box 346, McAdoo Collection.

43. McAdoo to Clagett, October 4, 1929, Box 346, McAdoo Collection.

44. "Operators Divided In Mail Rate Parley," *Aviation,* October 12, 1929, 765.

45. Brittin to Lilly, telegram, October 15, 1929, Independent Companies—Northwest Airways, 1929, Box 156, RG 46, NARA.

46. "Mail Problem Puzzles Conferees," *Aviation,* October 26, 1929, 863.

47. "Advises Air Mail Mainly for Speed," *Washington Star,* October 9, 1929.

48. "Tex" Marshall to Paul Henderson, October 12, 1929, Col. Paul Henderson, Box 126, RG 46, NARA.

49. "Federal Aid to Aviation," *Boston Herald,* October 10, 1929.

50. "Mail Problem Puzzles Conferees," *Aviation,* October 26, 1929, 863.

51. Richard W. Robbins to Thurman Bane, November 27, 1929, N.A.A. Correspondence of Pittsburgh Aviation Industries Corporation, Box 145, RG 46, NARA.

52. William "Doc" Bishop to James Wooley, December 7, 1929, Col. Paul Henderson, Box 126, RG 46, NARA.

53. Hainer Hinshaw to Gilbert Grosvenor, December 7, 1929, Col. Paul Henderson, Box 126, RG 46, NARA.

54. William "Doc" Bishop to James Wooley, December 7, 1929, Col. Paul Henderson, Box 126, RG 46, NARA.

55. Paul Henderson to George Akerson, December 5, 1929, Col. Paul Henderson, Box 126, RG 46, NARA.

56. Henderson to Walter Newton, November 30, 1929, Col. Paul Henderson, Box 126, RG 46, NARA.

57. "Hoover In Conference with Keys and Henderson," *Air Transportation,* December 21, 1929, 1.

58. The White House, memorandum of telephone conversation, filed December 16, 1929, Presidential Papers, Aeronautics—Correspondence, 10–12, Box 56, HCHPLA.

59. Bishop to Wooley, December 10, 1929, Col. Paul Henderson, Box 126, RG 46, NARA.

60. Ibid.

61. Ibid.

62. Ibid.

63. Bishop to Wooley, December 7, 1929, Col. Paul Henderson, Box 126, RG 46, NARA.

64. Ibid.

Chapter 7. The Watres Act

1. "Securities Quotations: Week Ending January 4, 1930," *Air Transportation,* January 11, 1930, 44.

2. "T.A.T.-Maddux Has Net Deficit . . . ," *Aviation,* March 29, 1930, 660.

3. "Aviation Corporation Net Loss . . . ," *Air Transportation,* April 19, 1930, 2.

4. Minutes of Aviation Corporation Executive Advisory Committee, February 20, 1930, 4, Box 44, Fairchild Collection.

5. Clement Keys by the *Wall Street Journal,* interview, October 31, 1929, Speeches and Articles, Box 10A, NASM Keys.

6. Clement Keys by *Airway Age,* interview, December 10, 1929, Speeches and Articles, Box 10A, NASM Keys.

7. Clement Keys, interview, December 16, 1929, Speeches and Articles, Box 10A, NASM Keys.

8. "Air Fares Reduced 25 Per Cent," *Western Flying,* January 1930, 138.

9. "Transcontinental Air Transport," *Air Transportation,* November 30, 1929, 12.

10. Clement Keys to Graham Grosvenor, January 10, 1930, AVCO, Box 2B, NASM Keys.

11. "Los Angeles–New York Fare Cut to $159," *Air Transportation,* January 18, 1930, 6.

12. "T.A.T.-Maddux Air Lines Re-Organizes," *Western Flying,* March 1930, 116.

13. "W.A.E. Reduces Fares," *Air Transportation,* January 25, 1930, 3.

14. "Western Air Merging with Aero Corp.," *Western Flying,* March 1920, 116.

15. J. Gates Williams to W. Averell Harriman, November 21, 1929, Box 18, Harriman Collection.

16. Ibid.

17. Ibid., 4.

18. George R. Hann to Graham B. Grosvenor, November 25, 1929, Box 1, Harriman Collection.

19. Marginal note written by W. Averell Harriman on letter from Graham Grosvenor to Harriman, November 27, 1929, Box 1, Harriman Collection.

20. Frederick G. Coburn to John Hancock, November 26, 1929, Box 45, Fairchild Collection.

21. F.G. Coburn to Colonel T.H. Bane, November 26, 1929, Box 45, Fairchild Collection.

22. F.G. Coburn to Graham Grosvenor, November 29, 1929, Box 45, Fairchild Collection.

23. Sherman Fairchild to Gilbert Grosvenor and William D. Loucks, December 12, 1929, Box 45, Fairchild Collection.

24. Ibid.

25. Sherman Fairchild to William D. Loucks, January 15, 1930, Box 45, Fairchild Collection.

26. William Loucks to W. Averell Harriman, January 30, 1930, William D. Loucks File, Box 71, Harriman Collection.

27. Graham Grosvenor to AVCO Executive Committee, January 7, 1930, Box 1, Harriman Collection.

28. Hainer Hinshaw to Colonel L.H. Brittin, January 3, 1930, Independent Companies—Northwest Airways, 1930, Box 156, RG 46, NARA.

29. Address by Walter F. Brown, "Commercial Aviation and the Air Mail," before the Cleveland, Ohio, Chamber of Commerce, January 14, 1930, Presidential Papers, Cabinet Offices—Post Office 1929, Box 40, HCHPLA.

30. Post Office Department Press Release, January 15, 1930, Press Releases, Box 117, RG 46, NARA.

31. Hainer Hinshaw to L.H. Brittin, January 17, 1930, 1, Independent Companies—Northwest Airways, 1930, Box 156, RG 46, NARA. Subsequent references to this letter are cited in text with the page numbers in parentheses.

32. "The Postmaster General Speaks His Mind," *Aviation,* January 25, 1930, 141–42.

33. Memorandum based on testimony of Col. Paul Henderson before Special Senate Investigating Committee, Post Office Department Office of the Solicitor, March 12, 1934, Entry 42, UAL Suits, Folder 96252, Box 42, RG 28, NARA.

34. L.H. Brittin to Winsor Williams, February 8, 1930, Independent Companies—Northwest Airways, 1930, Box 156, RG 46, NARA.

35. Erle P. Halliburton to William Gibbs McAdoo, February 5, 1930, Box 348, McAdoo Collection.

36. Erle P. Halliburton to W. Irving Glover, telegram, February 15, 1930, Post Office Inspectors, Box 116, RG 46, NARA.

37. W. Irving Glover to Erle P. Halliburton, telegram, February 15, 1930, Post Office Inspectors, Box 116, RG 46, NARA.

38. Clifford Ball to Andrew J. White, February 14, 1930, Clifford Ball, Box 121, RG 46, NARA.

39. Testimony of Walter F. Brown, House, *Hearing Before the Committee on the Post Office and Post Roads on H.R. 9500,* 71st Cong., 2d sess., February 19, 1930, 3. Subsequent references to Brown's testimony are in cited in text with the page numbers in parentheses.

40. James C. Edgerton to William Gibbs McAdoo, February 21, 1930, Box 348, McAdoo Collection.

41. Richard Robbins to Walter F. Brown, March 15, 1930, Earl Wadsworth, Box 130, RG 46, NARA.

42. Joan Murphy to William P. MacCracken Jr., telegram, March 13, 1930, Presidential Papers, William P. MacCracken Jr. Papers (new acquisition), P.A.I.C., Box 22, HCHPLA (hereafter cited as MacCracken Papers).

43. William Bishop to James Wooley, memorandum, March 15, 1930, Col. Paul Henderson, Box 126, RG 46, NARA.

44. Ibid.

45. W. Irving Glover, report, March 15, 1930, Entry 42, Air Mail Legislation, Folder 96268, Box 46, RG 28, NARA.

46. William Bishop to James Wooley, memorandum, March 15, 1930, Col. Paul Henderson, Box 126, RG 46, NARA.

47. W. Irving Glover, report, March 15, 1930, Entry 42, Air Mail Legislation, Folder 96268, Box 46, RG 28, NARA.

48. Ibid.

49. William Bishop to James Wooley, memorandum, March 15, 1930, Col. Paul Henderson, Box 126, RG 46, NARA.

50. Ibid.

51. H.R. 9556, February 5, 1930, RG 233 71A-D35 Tray 11956.

52. William Bishop to James G. Wooley, telegram, March 17, 1930, Col. Paul Henderson, Box 126, RG 46, NARA.

53. James A. Edgerton to William Gibbs McAdoo, March 18, 1930, Box 348, McAdoo Collection.

54. Brice Clagett to William Gibbs McAdoo, March 19, 1930, Box 348, McAdoo Collection.

55. J.G.N. Nettleton to D.M. Shaeffer, March 20, 1930, Fess, Lehr, Box 124, RG 46, NARA.

56. William P. MacCracken to Richard W. Robbins, March 22, 1930, Presidential Papers, P.A.I.C., Box 22, MacCracken Papers.

57. William P. MacCracken to Harris M. Hanshue, March 22, 1930, Presidential Papers, Contracts and Bids August 1930, Box 4, MacCracken Papers.

58. John McCarl to David Hogg, March 31, 1930, Comptroller General's Decision and Extensions Granted, Box 113, RG 46, NARA.

59. William P. MacCracken to Harris M. Hanshue, March 22, 1930, 2, Presidential Papers, Contracts and Bids August 1930, Box 4, MacCracken Papers.

60. Report No. 966, to Accompany H.R. 9500, *Amend the Air Mail Act of February 2, 1925*, 71st Cong., 2d sess., March 24, 1930.

61. Ibid., "Minority Views."

62. Clyde Kelly to Judge Moore, March 24, 1930, Presidential Papers, P.A.I.C., Box 22, MacCracken Papers.

63. James A. Edgerton to William Gibbs McAdoo, March 28, 1930, Box 348, McAdoo Collection.

64. William Gibbs McAdoo to Brice Clagett, April 4, 1930, Box 348, McAdoo Collection.

65. William Bishop to James Woolsey, April 6, 1930, Col. Paul Henderson, Box 126, RG 46, NARA.

66. Richard Robbins to Walter F. Brown (unsent), April 2, 1930, Presidential Papers, P.A.I.C., Box 22, MacCracken Papers.

67. William Bishop to James Wooley, April 6, 1930, Col. Paul Henderson, Box 126, RG 46, NARA.

68. James A. Edgerton to William Gibbs McAdoo, April 8, 1930, Box 348, McAdoo Collection.

69. William Bishop to James Wooley, April 6, 1930, Col. Paul Henderson, Box 126, RG 46, NARA.

70. James A. Edgerton to William Gibbs McAdoo, April 8, 1930, Box 348, McAdoo Collection.

71. E.B. Wadsworth to Clifford Ball, April 8, 1930, Post Office Department, Air-mail—Cisler (N-P), Box 116, RG 46, NARA.

72. William P. MacCracken to Richard W. Robbins, April 12, 1930, Presidential Papers, P.A.I.C., Box 22, MacCracken Papers.

73. Post Office Department Press Release, April 12, 1930, Press Releases, Box 117, RG 46, NARA.

74. Hainer Hinshaw to Lewis H. Brittin, April 15, 1930, Independent Companies—Northwest Airways, 1930, Box 156, RG 46, NARA.

75. H.R. 11704, April 17, 1930, 71st Cong., 2d sess., Report No. 1209.

76. "Mileage Proposed As Basis for Air Mail Compensation," *United States Daily,* April 18, 1930.

77. H.R. 11704, April 17, 1930, 71st Cong., 2d sess., Report No. 1209.

78. Richard W. Robbins to William P. MacCracken Jr., April 19, 1930, Presidential Papers, P.A.I.C., Box 22, MacCracken Papers.

79. William P. MacCracken Jr. to Richard W. Robbins, April 23, 1930, Presidential Papers, P.A.I.C., Box 22, MacCracken Papers.

80. Sen. Lawrence C. Phipps to Richard W. Robbins, April 24, 1930, Presidential Papers, P.A.I.C., Box 22, MacCracken Papers.

81. George R. Hann to Walter F. Brown, April 24, 1930, Presidential Papers, P.A.I.C., Box 22, MacCracken Papers.

Chapter 8. Realignment

1. Hainer Hinshaw to Col. William G. Shauffler, February 1, 1930, AVCO re: Delta Air Lines, Hainer Hinshaw, and Misc., January 1929–October 1931, Box 140, RG 46, NARA.

2. George Hann to William Loucks, February 1, 1930, Box 45, Fairchild Collection.

3. Ibid.

4. George Hann to W. Averell Harriman, February 3, 1930, Box 1, Harriman Collection.

5. Ibid., 3.

6. Minutes of Meeting of Executive Advisory Committee, March 4, 1930, 4, Box 44, Fairchild Collection.

7. Minutes of Meeting of Executive Advisory Committee, February 20, 1930, 7, Box 44, Fairchild Collection.

8. Minutes of Meeting of Executive Advisory Committee, March 12, 1930, 5, Box 44, Fairchild Collection.

9. Interim Report of the Executive Advisory Committee to the Chairman of the Executive Committee, the Aviation Corporation, March 7, 1930, Box 45, Fairchild Collection.

10. Report from the Executive Advisory Committee to the Chairman of the Executive Committee, the Aviation Corporation, March 24, 1930, Articles, Brochures, and Ads, 1926–1929, Box 45, Fairchild Collection.

11. Report of Executive Advisory Committee, April 2, 1930, 5, Box 45, Fairchild Collection.

12. Minutes of Meeting of Executive Advisory Committee, March 21, 1930, 2, Box 44, Fairchild Collection.

13. Committee Report on the New York Organization and Transport Operations of the Aviation Corporation, April 9, 1930, 3, Box 17, Harriman Collection. Subsequent references to this report are cited in text with the page numbers in parentheses.

14. Executive Committee meeting, April 29, 1930, Supplement to Remarks, Air Mail Speech in Senate, Box 120, RG 46, NARA.

15. Ibid., 16.

16. Ibid., 16–17.

17. Ibid., 20, 21.

18. Chairman of the Executive Committee to Sanderson and Porter, April 17, 1930, AVCO—William Dewey Loucks, Box 140, RG 46, NARA.

19. United Air Lines, *Corporate and Legal History of United Air Lines,* 86.

20. "United Aircraft—N.A.T. Merger Proposed," *Air Transportation,* April 5, 1930, 1.

21. William P. MacCracken to Harris M. Hanshue, March 28, 1930, Presidential Papers, Contracts and Bids, 1930, March–July, Box 4, MacCracken Papers.

22. Clement Keys to J. Cheever Cowdin, January 1931, Cowdin, J. Cheever, Box 5, NASM Keys.

23. Clement M. Keys to Board of Directors of National Air Transport, memorandum, April 2, 1930, U.A.T.C. National Air Transport, Box 152, RG 46, NARA.

24. Howard E. Coffin to Frederick B. Rentschler, April 3, 1930, U.A.T.C. National Air Transport, Box 152, RG 46, NARA.

25. "N.A.T. Directors Refuse to Submit United Merger . . . ," *Air Transportation,* April 12, 1930, 1.

26. Frederick B. Rentschler to the Stockholders of National Air Transport, Inc., April 4, 1930, U.A.T.C. National Air Transport, Box 152, RG 46, NARA.

27. United Air Lines, *Corporate and Legal History of United Air Lines,* 88–89.

28. C.M. Keys to Stockholders, April 10, 1930, N.A.A. North American Copies of Correspondence, Box 146, RG 46, NARA.

29. McAdoo to Brice Clagett, April 3, 1930, Box 348, McAdoo Collection.

30. William Bishop to James Wooley, April 6, 1930, Col. Paul Henderson, Box 126, RG 46, NARA.

31. United Air Lines, *Corporate and Legal History of United Air Lines,* 88.

32. Howard Coffin to Stockholders, April 10, 1930, N.A.A. North American Copies of Correspondence, Box 146, RG 46, NARA.

33. Harold Pitcairn to C.M. Keys, April 11, 1930, N.A.A. North American Copies of Correspondence, Box 146, RG 46, NARA.

34. Minutes of Executive Advisory Committee, April 7, 1930, 4, Box 44, Fairchild Collection.

35. Clement Keys to Graham Grosvenor, April 12, 1930, AVCO, Box 2B, NASM Keys.

36. "N.A.T. and United Continue Controversy," *Aviation,* April 16, 1930, 826.

37. Clement Keys to C.W. Cuthell, telegram, April 16, 1930, N.A.A. North American Copies of Correspondence, Box 146, RG 46, NARA.

38. Clement Keys to C.W. Cuthell, telegram, April 19, 1930, N.A.A. North American Copies of Correspondence, Box 146, RG 46, NARA.

39. C.W. Cuthell to Clement Keys, telegram, April 23, 1930, N.A.A. North American Copies of Correspondence, Box 146, RG 46, NARA.

40. Frederick B. Rentschler to the Board of Directors, National Air Transport, April 23, 1930, U.A.T.C. National Air Transport, Box 152, RG 46, NARA.

41. James Edgerton to William Gibbs McAdoo, April 25, 1930, Box 348, McAdoo Collection.

Chapter 9. Drawing a New Map

1. David, *Economics of Air Mail Transportation,* 106.

2. Post Office Department Press Release, May 3, 1930, Box 348, McAdoo Collection.

3. "Watres Bill Signed," *Air Transportation,* May 10, 1930, 4.

4. Post Office Department Formula for Determining Rates, January 1, 1932, N.A.A. Eastern Air Transport, Box 143, RG 46, NARA.

5. Post Office Press Release, May 3, 1930, 2, Box 348, McAdoo Collection.

6. W. Irving Glover to E.B. Wadsworth, memorandum, May 15, 1930, Earl Wadsworth, Box 130, RG 46, NARA.

7. Post Office Department Press Release, May 19, 1930, Box 348, McAdoo Collection.

8. E.B. Wadsworth to W. Irving Glover, memorandum, May 20, 1930, Post Office Department, Airmail—Cisler (N-P), Box 116, RG 46, NARA.

9. Ibid., 2.

10. Minutes of Board of Directors Meeting, Eastern Air Transport, May 21, 1930, N.A.A. Eastern Air Transport, Box 143, RG 46, NARA.

11. Minutes of the Committee on Extensions of Air Mail Routes, May 23, 1930, Presidential Papers, Operators' Conference, 1930, Box 15, MacCracken Papers.

12. Hainer Hinshaw to L.H. Britten, telegram, May 21, 1930, Independent Companies—Northwest Airways, 1930, Box 156, RG 46, NARA.

13. James C. Edgerton to William Gibbs McAdoo, Box 348, McAdoo Collection.

14. William Denning to Tex Marshall, May 23, 1930, Denning, William I., Box 124, RG 46, NARA.

15. L.H. Brittin, memorandum, May 26, 1930, Independent Companies—Northwest Airways, 1930, Box 156, RG 46, NARA.

16. Ibid., 2.

17. L.H. Brittin to Mrs. R.R. Clarke, June 2, 1930, Independent Companies—Northwest Airways, 1930, Box 156, RG 46, NARA.

18. Ibid., 4.

19. L.H. Brittin to L. Piper, Inter Office Memorandum, May 27, 1930, Independent Companies—Northwest Airways, 1930, Box 156, RG 46, NARA.

20. L.H. Brittin to Mrs. R.R. Clarke, June 2, 1930, Independent Companies—Northwest Airways, 1930, Box 156, RG 46, NARA.

21. Minutes of Meeting, E.B. Wadsworth to W.I. Glover, June 5, 1930, Post Office Departmnet, Airmail—Cisler (N-P), Box 116, RG 46, NARA.

22. L.H. Brittin to A.R. Rogers, telegram, June 6, 1930, Independent Companies—Northwest Airways, 1930, Box 156, RG 46, NARA.

23. Hainer Hinshaw to Walter F. Brown, June 4, 1930, Earl Wadsworth, Personal Notes at "Spoils Conference," Box 130, RG 46, NARA.

24. William P. MacCracken to Chester Cuthell, June 6, 1930, Presidential Papers, Operators' Conference, 1930, Box 15, MacCracken Papers.

25. James Edgerton to William Gibbs McAdoo, June 10, 1930, Box 348, McADoo Collection.

26. L.H. Brittin to Mrs. R.R. Clarke, June 11, 1930, Independent Companies—Northwest Airways, 1930, Box 156, RG 46, NARA.

27. James C. Edgerton to William Gibbs McAdoo, June 10, 1930, Box 348, McAdoo Collection.

28. L.H. Brittin to Mrs. R.R. Clarke, June 11, 1930, Independent Companies—Northwest Airways, 1930, Box 156, RG 46, NARA.

29. Halliburton to MacCracken, telegram, July 8, 1930, Presidential Papers, Operators' Conference, 1930, Box 15, MacCracken Papers.

30. MacCracken to Halliburton, telegram, June 9, 1930, Presidential Papers, Operators' Conference, 1930, Box 15, MacCracken Papers.

31. Clagett to McAdoo, telegram, June 5, 1930, Box 348, McAdoo Collection.

32. McAdoo to Clagett, June 5, 1930, Box 348, McAdoo Collection.

33. Edgerton to McAdoo, June 10, 1930, Box 348, McAdoo Collection.

34. McAdoo to Halliburton, June 6, 1930, Box 348, McAdoo Collection.

35. McAdoo to Halliburton, June 18, 1930, Box 348, McAdoo Collection.

36. James C. Edgerton to William Gibbs McAdoo, June 2, 1930, Box 348, McAdoo Collection.

37. Clagett to McAdoo, June 6, 1930, Box 348, McAdoo Collection.

38. W. David Lewis and Wesley Phillips Newton, *Delta: The History of an Airline* (Athens: University of Georgia Press, 1979), 24–26.

39. C.E. Woolman to Walter F. Brown, June 6, 1930, AM 24, Case Files 1924–1934, RG 28, NARA.

40. Clagett to McAdoo, June 6, 1930, Box 348, McAdoo Collection.

41. McAdoo to Edgerton, June 16, 1930, Box 348, McAdoo Collection.

42. McAdoo to Clagett, June 16, 1930, Box 348, McAdoo Collection.

43. Lewis and Newton, *Delta,* 24.

44. Memorandum Brief in Support of the Eligibility of Delta Air Corporation to Karl Crowley, Solicitor of the Post Office Department, 1934, AM 24, Case Files 1924–1934, RG 28, NARA.

45. Memorandum of Basis for the Aviation Corporation Acquiring an Interest in Delta Air Service, July 25, 1930, AM 24, Case Files 1924–1934, RG 28, NARA.

46. Walter F. Brown to John McCarl, July 7, 1930, W.A. Letson, Box 127, RG 46, NARA.

47. J.R. McCarl to Walter F. Brown, July 24, 1930, Independent Companies—Northwest Airways, 1930, Box 156, RG 46, NARA.

48. William P. MacCracken, handwritten note, Presidential Papers, Operators' Conference, 1930, Box 15, MacCracken Papers.

49. Hainer Hinshaw to Earl B. Wadsworth, telegram, August 1, 1930, Post Office Department, Airmail—Cisler (N-P), Box 116, RG 46, NARA.

50. Post Office Department Press Release, August 2, 1930, Walter F. Brown Statement to the Press, Box 123, RG 46, NARA.

51. Advertisement for Air Mail Service, Post Office Department, August 2, 1930, Presidential Papers, Contracts and Bids, 1930, March–July, Box 4, MacCracken Papers.

52. Petition to W. Irving Glover, June 2, 1930, Thomas Hudson McKee, Box 128, RG 46, NARA.

53. Halliburton to U.S. Post Office, March 3, 1930, AVCO Misc., Box 140, RG 46, NARA.

54. Hainer Hinshaw to C.R. Smith, telegram, June 10, 1930, AVCO re: Delta Air Lines, Box 140, RG 46, NARA.

55. Halliburton to Daniel Schaeffer, telegram, n.d., Analysis of Cost of Operating Air Mail, Box 135, RG 46, NARA.

56. Halliburton to W.G. Skelly, telegram, August 4, 1930, Analysis of Cost of Operating Air Mail, Box 135, RG 46, NARA.

57. Hinshaw to F.G. Coburn, telegram, July 22, 1930, AVCO re: Delta Air Lines, Box 140, RG 46, NARA.

58. Memorandum of Agreement between American Airways, Inc., Southwest Air Fast Express Inc., and Erle P. Halliburton, August 23, 1930, AVCO—Southern Air Transport, Box 134, RG 46, NARA.

59. L.H. Brittin to Mrs. R.R. Clark, August 29, 1930, Independent Companies—Northwest Airways, 1930, Box 156, RG 46, NARA.

60. Post Office Department Press Release, August 25, 1930, Walter F. Brown Statement to the Press, Box 123, RG 46, NARA.

61. Contract between Robertson Aircraft Corporation and Southwest Air Fast Express and the Post Office Department, September 16, 1930, Presidential Papers, Contracts and Bids, 1930, March–July, Box 4, MacCracken Papers.

62. Daniel Shaeffer to T.A.T Executive Committee, memorandum, July 15, 1930, U.A.T.C. Copies of Correspondence, D.M. Shaeffer File, Box 154, RG 46, NARA.

63. J.A. Talbot to Harris M. Hanshue, telegram, May 21, 1930, Presidential Papers, Transcontinental and Western Air, 1930 May–October, Box 22, MacCracken Papers.

64. Harris M. Hanshue to Walter F. Brown, June 2, 1930, Presidential Papers, Transcontinental and Western Air, New York–California Route 1930, Box 26, MacCracken Papers.

65. Ibid., 5.

66. Ibid., 6.

67. Harris M. Hanshue to Harry Chandler, telegram, June 2, 1930, William P. MacCracken File, Box 127, RG 46, NARA.

68. Daniel Shaeffer to T.A.T Executive Committee, memorandum, July 15, 1930, U.A.T.C. Copies of Correspondence, D.M. Shaeffer File, Box 154, RG 46, NARA.

69. Memorandum of Agreement between Transcontinental Air Transport and

Western Air Express, July 15, 1930, Presidential Papers, Transcontinental and Western Air, New York–California Route 1930, Box 26, MacCracken Papers.

70. George R. Hann to Daniel Shaeffer, July 5, 1930, U.A.T.C. Copies of Correspondence, D.M. Shaeffer File, Box 154, RG 46 NARA.

71. Memorandum of Agreement between Transcontinental Air Transport and Western Air Express, August 22, 1930, N.A.A., W.A.E. Inc., General Information, Box 146, RG 46, NARA.

72. William Gibbs McAdoo to W.M. Kiplinger, August 13, 1930, Box 348, McAdoo Collection.

73. Herbert Hoover Jr. to Walter Folger Brown, August 24, 1930, Walter F. Brown Files—Not Found in Post Office Department Files, Box 123, RG 46, NARA.

74. Franklin Wallman, "Air Passenger Lines to Fight Mail Awards," *Baltimore Sun,* August 22, 1930.

75. Minutes of United States Airways Board of Directors Meeting, August 7, 1930, Presidential Papers, Contracts and Bids, 1930, March–July, Box 4, MacCracken Papers.

76. James D. Condon, to Walter F. Brown, August 23, 1930, AVCO re: Delta Air Lines, Box 140, RG 46, NARA.

77. W.A. Letson and J.D. Condon to W. Irving Glover, telegram, August 25, 1930, Entry 42, UAL Suits, Folder 96252, Box 42, RG 28, NARA.

78. W. Irving Glover to Chase Gove, August 26, 1930, Entry 42, UAL Suits, Folder 96252, Box 42, RG 28, NARA.

79. W. Irving Glover to Chase Gove, August 29, 1930, Aviation Bid/Comptroller's Letter and Post Office Report, Box 112, RG 46, NARA.

80. Chase Gove to W. Irving Glover, August 26, 1930, Post Office Department, Airmail—Cisler (N-P), Box 116, RG 46, NARA.

81. Chester Cuthell and Harris M. Hanshue to Walter F. Brown, August 23, 1930, Presidential Papers, Contracts and Bids, 1930, March–July, Box 4, MacCracken Papers.

82. Draft Protest, Chester Cuthell and Harris Hanshue to Walter F. Brown, n.d. (prepared by William P. MacCracken), Presidential Papers, Contracts and Bids, 1930, March–July, Box 4, MacCracken Papers.

83. William P. MacCracken Jr. to William H. White Jr., August 29, 1930, Presidential Papers, Transcontinental and Western Air, 1930 May–October, Box 22, MacCracken Papers.

84. Lawrence C. Phipps to Richard Robbins, telegram, September 11, 1930, William P. MacCracken File, Box 127, RG 46, NARA.

85. Richard Robbins to Lawrence C. Phipps, September 10, 1930, Presidential Papers, Transcontinental and Western Air, 1930 May–October, Box 22, MacCracken Papers.

86. George R. Hann to Harris M. Hanshue, September 20, 1930, Entry 42, UAL Suits, Folder 96252, Box 42, RG 28, NARA.

87. Post Office Department Press Release, October 1, 1930, Presidential Papers, Transcontinental and Western Air, New York–California Route 1930, Box 26, MacCracken Papers.

88. Subcontract, Transcontinental Air Transport and Western Air Express and Transcontinental and Western Air, October 24, 1930, Aviation Bid/Comptroller's Letter and Post Office Report, Box 112, RG 46, NARA.

89. William P. MacCracken Jr. to Chester W. Cuthell, October 22, 1930, Presidential Papers, Transcontinental and Western Air, 1930 May–October, Box 22, MacCracken Papers.

90. "New York–Los Angeles Passenger Line Opens," *Air Transportation,* November 1, 1930, 2.

91. Contract between American Airways, and Transcontinental Air Transport and Western Air Express, August 23, 1930, Presidential Papers, Transcontinental and Western Air, New York–California Route 1930, Box 26, MacCracken Papers.

92. A.O. Cushing, Treasurer, American Airways to Transcontinental Air Transport and Western Air Express, December 16, 1930, Presidential Papers, Contracts and Bids, 1930, March–July, Box 4, MacCracken Papers.

93. Harris M. Hanshue to William P. MacCracken Jr. and Jack Frye, n.d., Entry 42, UAL Suits, Folder 96252, Box 42, RG 28, NARA.

94. John R. McCarl to Walter F. Brown, October 9, 1930, Post Office Department, Airmail—Cisler (N-P), Box 116, RG 46, NARA.

95. John R. McCarl to Walter F. Brown, December 16, 1930, Presidential Papers, Transcontinental and Western Air, New York–California Route 1930, Box 26, MacCracken Papers.

96. Brown to McCarl, December 29, 1930, Presidential Papers, Contracts and Bids, 1930, March–July, Box 4, MacCracken Papers.

97. Ibid.

98. Ibid.

99. John R. McCarl to Walter F. Brown, January 10, 1931, Presidential Papers, Contracts and Bids, 1930, March–July, Box 4, MacCracken Papers.

Chapter 10. Reaction

1. W. Irving Glover to Northwest Airways, Inc., January 17, 1931, AVCO, Post Office Correspondence—Brown, Glover, Coleman, Box 138, RG 46, NARA.

2. Post Office Department Press Release, February 16, 1931, 4, AVCO Misc., Box 140, RG 46, NARA.

3. Ibid.

4. Ibid., 3.

5. Brittin to Julian Baird, February 17, 1931, Independent Companies—Northwest Airways, 1931, Box 156, RG 46, NARA.

6. MacCracken to Shaeffer, February 16, 1931, Presidential Papers, Air Mail Contract Rates, 1931–1932, Box 2, MacCracken Papers.

7. MacCracken to Shaeffer, February 17, 1931, Presidential Papers, Air Mail Contract Rates, 1931–1932, Box 2, MacCracken Papers.

8. MacCracken to Shaeffer, February 18, 1931, Presidential Papers, Air Mail Contract Rates, 1931–1932, Box 2, MacCracken Papers.

9. Brittin to Julian Baird, February 17, 1931, Independent Companies—Northwest Airways, 1931, Box 156, RG 46, NARA.

10. F. Robert van der Linden, *The Boeing 247: The First Modern Airliner* (Seattle: University of Washington Press, 1991), 23–53.

11. Brittin to Baird, February 17, 1931, 2, Independent Companies—Northwest Airways, 1931, Box 156, RG 46, NARA.

12. L.H. Brittin to Mrs. Clark, March 30, 1931, Independent Companies—Northwest Airways, 1931, Box 156, RG 46, NARA.

13. Clement Keys to Daniel Shaeffer, August 29, 1930, Clement Keys, Box 126, RG 46, NARA.

14. Ibid., 2.

15. Davies, *Airlines of the United States,* 154.

16. "A Super Airmail Service," *Aeronautical Industry,* December 13, 1930, 20.

17. Eugene Vidal to Walter F. Brown, January 16, 1931, Entry 155, Box 8, RG 26, NARA.

18. Ibid.

19. Eugene Vidal to Walter F. Brown, January 29, 1929, quoted in Fulton Lewis Report Synopsis, W. Irving Glover, Box 125, RG 46, NARA.

20. Ibid.

21. Clement M. Keys to C. Townsend Ludington, February 16, 1931, Ludington Philadelphia Flying Service, Box 9, NASM Keys.

22. C. Townsend Ludington to Clement M. Keys, February 20, 1931, Ludington Philadelphia Flying Service, Box 9, NASM Keys.

23. Extract of Senate Resolution, No, 394, January 21, 1931, Presidential Papers, Contracts and Bids, August 1930, Box 4, MacCracken Papers.

24. "Air Mail Inquisition," *Aviation,* April 1931, 201.

25. Paul Henderson to Thomas B. Eastland, April 20, 1931, Col. Paul Henderson, Box 126, RG 46, NARA.

26. Clement M. Keys to C. Townsend Ludington, March 4, 1931, 1–2, 5, Ludington Philadelphia Flying Service, Box 9, NASM Keys.

27. Ibid., 6.

28. C. Townsend Ludington to Clement M. Keys, March 27, 1931, Presidential Papers, New York–Washington Airport Company: Ludington, March–November 1931, Box 11, MacCracken Papers.

29. C. Townsend Ludington to William P. MacCracken Jr., March 25, 1931, Presidential Papers, New York–Washington Airport Company: Ludington, March–November 1931, Box 11, MacCracken Papers.

30. William P. MacCracken Jr. to C. Townsend Ludington, March 28, 1931, Presidential Papers, New York–Washington Airport Company: Ludington, March–November 1931, Box 11, MacCracken Papers.

31. George E. Hopkins, "E.L. Cord," in Leary, *Encyclopedia of American Business History and Biography,* 123–25.

32. N.S. Ludington to L.B. Manning, March 27, 1931, AVCO Correspondence, 1931, Box 139, RG 46, NARA.

33. Hopkins, "E.L. Cord," 124.

34. Ibid.

35. William M. Klein to West and Eckhart, memorandum, April 15, 1931, Entry 42, Air Mail Misc., Illinois ICC, Box 23, RG 28, NARA.

36. Ibid.

37. Horace J. Donnelly to Illinois Commerce Commission, telegram, April 21, 1931, Entry 42, Air Mail Misc., Illinois ICC, Box 23, RG 28, NARA.

38. Horace J. Donnelly, "The Status of an Air Mail Contractor Under the Laws of Illinois," memorandum, April 25, 1931, Entry 42, Robertson Airplane Service, Folder 96243, Box 37, RG 28, NARA.

39. Ibid.

40. Ibid.

41. Charles W. Hadley to Governor Louis L. Emmerson, May 21, 1931, Entry 42, Air Mail Misc., Illinois ICC, Box 23, RG 28, NARA.

42. Lucius B. Manning to Northwest Airways, May 4, 1931, Independents—Northwest Airways, 1931, Box 156, RG 46, NARA.

43. West and Eckhart to Horace Donnelly, May 14, 1931, Entry 42, Air Mail Misc., Illinois ICC, Box 23, RG 28, NARA.

44. "Two Chicago–E. St. Louis Plane Lines Get Permits," *St. Louis Post Dispatch*, August 27, 1931.

45. Post Office Department Press Release, April 30, 1931, W. Irving Glover, Box 125, RG 46, NARA.

46. Sen. Kenneth McKellar to W. Irving Glover, March 25, 1931, Entry 155, St. Louis, Box 14, RG 28, NARA.

47. Chase C. Gove to Sen. Kenneth McKellar, March 31, 1931, Entry 155, St. Louis, Box 14, RG 28, NARA.

48. Frank Robertson to Walter F. Brown, January 6, 1931, W.F. Brown, Box 123, RG 46, NARA.

49. Walter F. Brown to F.H. Robertson, January 16, 1931, W.F. Brown, Box 123, RG 46, NARA.

50. W. Irving Glover to Ernest Lee Jahncke, March 2, 1931, Exhibit 8, W. Irving Glover File—Not Found in Post Office Department, Box 125, RG 46, NARA.

51. Hainer Hinshaw to Graham B. Grosvenor, memorandum, March 4, 1931, AVCO Correspondence, 1931, Box 139, RG 46, NARA.

52. Robertson-Sachs Negotiations, summary of correspondence, May 4–28, 1931, William Sachs, Box 129, RG 46, NARA.

53. Silliman Evans to Hainer Hinshaw, telegram, May 27, 1931, AVCO Correspondence, 1931, Box 139, RG 46, NARA.

54. Hainer Hinshaw to Silliman Evans, telegram, May 27, 1931, AVCO Correspondence, 1931, Box 139, RG 46, NARA.

55. Frank H. Robertson to Walter F. Brown, June 6, 1931, AVCO Correspondence, 1931, Box 139, RG 46, NARA.

56. Dr. E.B. Clements to Walter Newton, July 28, 1931, Cabinet Offices—Post Office 1929, Box 41, HCHPLA.

57. Walter F. Brown to Walter H. Newton, July 31, 1931, Cabinet Offices—Post Office 1929, Box 41, HCHPLA.

58. Frank H. Robertson to Clement M. Keys, November 11, 1931, Texas Air Transport, Box 11, NASM Keys.

59. John H. Kelly to Sen. Peter Norbeck, June 10, 1931, Independent Companies—Hanford Airlines, Box 155, RG 46, NARA.

60. L.H. Brittin to W. Irving Glover, July 1, 1931, Independents—Northwest Airways, 1931, Box 156, RG 46, NARA.

61. W.F. Halley to Walter F. Brown, July 17, 1931, U.A.T.C. United Air Lines Routes, Box 153, RG 46, NARA.

62. Paul Henderson to Philip G. Johnson, August 3, 1931, Col. Paul Henderson, Box 126, RG 46, NARA.

63. Arch Coleman to J.S. Lincoln, August 25, 1931, Exhibit 5, Arch Coleman File Found in Post Office Department, Box 123, RG 46, NARA.

64. Memorandum of Meeting, July 11, 1931, Association of Air Transport Executives, Box 2B, NASM Keys.

65. Ibid.

66. Address of E.V. Savage to Non Air Mail Operators, July 10, 1931, Association of Air Transport Executives, Box 2B, NASM Keys.

67. Ibid., 3.

68. L.H. Brittin to R.C. Lilly and J.B. Baird, memorandum, July 25, 1931, Independents—Northwest Airways, 1931, Box 156, RG 46, NARA.

69. Walter F. Brown to Thomas B. Doe, July 7, 1931, Post Office Inspectors, Box 116, RG 46, NARA.

70. Ibid.

71. Fulton Lewis, "Airmail Monopoly Probe Demanded By Independents," *Washington Herald,* August 27, 1931.

72. Fulton Lewis, "Independent Operators Left Out in Award of 32 New Air-Mail Contracts," *Washington Herald,* August 19, 1931.

73. Clement M Keys to L.H. Brittin, et al, August 31, 1931, N.A.A. North American Copies of Correspondence, Box 146, RG 46, NARA.

74. Clement Keys to Paul Henderson, Col. Paul Henderson, Box 126, RG 46, NARA.

75. Hainer Hinshaw to W.A. Letson, November 24, 1931, AVCO Correspondence, 1931, Box 139, RG 46, NARA.

76. L.H. Brittin to R.C. Lilly, memorandum, August 20, 1931, Independents—Northwest Airways, 1931, Box 156, RG 46, NARA.

77. Ray Tucker, "Local Air Mail Line Is Costing $400,000 Too Much, Is Charged," *Washington Daily News,* August 23, 1931.

78. Fulton Lewis, "Brown 'Prostituting' Airmail, Asserts Representative Kelly; to Push Inquiry," *Washington Herald,* August 20, 1931.

79. H.W. Beck to T.B. Clement, September 11, 1931, N.A.A. North American Copies of Correspondence, Box 146, RG 46, NARA.

80. Ibid.

Chapter 11. Cord and Congress

1. "The News in Brief," *Western Flying,* August 1931, 17.

2. W.A. Patterson to P.G. Johnson, September 11, 1931, File 13, Box 3299, Boeing.

3. WA. Patterson to P.G. Johnson, September 15, 1931, File 13, Box 3299, Boeing.

4. Paul Henderson to Philip G. Johnson, August 3, 1931, Col. Paul Henderson, Box 126, RG 46, NARA.

5. Lyndol L. Young to L.B. Manning, telegram, September 11, 1931, AVCO Correspondence, 1931, Box 139, RG 46, NARA.

6. Lyndol L. Young to L.B. Manning, November 13, 1931, AVCO Correspondence, 1931, Box 139, RG 46, NARA.

7. Ibid.

8. E.L. Cord to L.B. Manning, November 12, 1931, Mark Requa, Box 129, RG 46, NARA.

9. Ibid.

10. Walter F. Brown to Mark L. Requa, November 7, 1931, AVCO Correspondence, 1931, Box 139, RG 46, NARA.

11. Ibid.

12. Hainer Hinshaw to W.M. Bishop, November 25, 1931, AVCO Correspondence, 1931, Box 139, RG 46, NARA.

13. Ibid.

14. Ibid.

15. William A. Mara to L.B. Manning, November 23, 1931, AVCO Correspondence, 1931, Box 139, RG 46, NARA.

16. Memorandum of Meeting, May 26, 1931, William P. MacCracken File, Box 127, RG 46, NARA.

17. Minutes of Meeting of Air Transport Executives, August 5, 1995, Association of Air Transport Executives, Box 2B, NASM Keys.

18. Richard W. Robbins to Daniel N. Casey, December 24, 1931, U.A.T.C. Copies of Correspondence, D.M. Shaeffer File, Box 154, RG 46, NARA.

19. Post Office Department Press Release, December 17, 1931, Press Releases, Post Office Department, Box 117, RG 46, NARA.

20. Ibid., 2.

21. W. Jefferson Davis to William Gibbs McAdoo, confidential memorandum, January 22, 1932, Box 358, McAdoo Collection.

22. Lyndol Young to E.L. Cord, February 14, 1932, AVCO Correspondence, 1932, Box 139, RG 46, NARA.

23. E.L. Cord to O.R. Fuller, January 27, 1932, AVCO Correspondence, 1932, Box 139, RG 46, NARA.

24. "Contract Offered at Half Rate for All Air Mail Lines," *United States Daily,* February 26, 1932.

25. George E. Hopkins, *The Airline Pilots: A Study in Elite Unionization* (Cambridge: Harvard University Press, 1971), 99–100.

26. Ibid., 103–6.

27. L.H. Brittin to R.C. Lilly, February 22, 1932, Independent Companies—Northwest Airways, 1932, Box 157, RG 46, NARA.

28. L.H. Brittin to R.C. Lilly, February 8, 1931, Independent Companies—Northwest Airways, 1932, Box 157, RG 46, NARA.

29. L.H. Brittin to R.C. Lilly, February 22, 1931, Independent Companies—Northwest Airways, 1932, Box 157, RG 46, NARA.

30. Ibid.

31. L.H. Brittin to R.C. Lilly, February 23, 1932, Kohler, Box 136, RG 46, NARA.

32. Ibid.

33. Arch Coleman to James M. Mead, February 27, 1932, as read by W. Irving Glover, in House, *Air Mail: Hearing Before the Committee on The Post Office and Post Roads,* 72d Cong., 1st sess., March 1, 2, 3, 4, 23, 1932, 3.

34. House, *Air Mail: Hearing Before the Committee on The Post Office and Post Roads,* 72d Cong., 1st sess., March 1, 2, 3, 4, 23, 1932, 5.

35. Ibid.

36. Ibid., 7–8.

37. Ibid., 7–8, 15.

38. L.H. Brittin to R.C. Lilly, March 1, 1932, Independent Companies—Northwest Airways, 1932, Box 157, RG 46, NARA.

39. House, *Air Mail: Hearing Before the Committee on The Post Office and Post Roads,* 72d Cong., 1st sess., March 1, 2, 3, 4, 23, 1932, 20–21.

40. William P. MacCracken to Daniel M. Shaeffer, March 5, 1932, Transcontinental and Western Air, November–December 1931, Box 23, MacCracken Papers.

41. House, *Air Mail: Hearing Before the Committee on The Post Office and Post Roads,* 72d Cong., 1st sess., March 1, 2, 3, 4, 23, 1932, 199.

42. Ibid.

43. Ibid.

44. The Aviation Corporation Annual Report for 1931, Box 1, Harriman Collection.

45. A.O. Cushy to W.A. Harriman, confidential memorandum, March 3, 1932, AVCO, Box 18, Harriman Collection.

46. Roland Palmedo and Sherman Fairchild interview, Box 111, Sherman Fairchild Collection.

47. Ibid.

48. Agreement of Sale, the Aviation Corporation, Century Air Lines, Inc., Century Pacific Lines Ltd., and E.L. Cord, March 31, 1932, Cord/Cohu File, Box 18, Harriman Collection.

49. Sanderson and Porter to W. Averell Harriman, March 14, 1932, AVCO, Box 18, Harriman Collection.

50. Ibid.

51. Ibid.

52. W.D. Loucks to W.A. Harriman, April 19, 1932, William Dewey Loucks File, Box 71, Harriman Collection.

53. W.D. Loucks to George R. Hann, June 7, 1932, AVCO—William Dewey Loucks, Box 140, RG 46, NARA.

54. Sherman M. Fairchild to W.A. Harriman, June 13, 1932, Box 18, W. Averell Harriman Collection, AVCO.

55. LaMotte T. Cohu to Roland Palmedo, October 10, 1932, Box 45, Fairchild Collection.

56. Chandler Henry to W.A. Harriman, October 1, 1932, AVCO, Box 18, Harriman Collection.

57. W.A. Harriman to the Board of Directors of the Aviation Corporation, October 10, 1932, William Dewey Loucks File, Box 71, Harriman Collection.

58. William D. Loucks to W.A. Harriman and Robert Lehman, June 9, 1932, William Dewey Loucks File, Box 71, Harriman Collection.

59. E.L. Cord to the Directors of the Thompson Aeronautical Corporation, telegram, n.d., AVCO Correspondence, 1932, Box 139, RG 46, NARA.

60. Robert Lehman to E.L. Cord, telegram, October 8, 1932, AVCO Correspondence, 1932, Box 139, RG 46, NARA.

61. Proposal, the Aviation Corporation to North American Aviation, November 1, 1932, AVCO Correspondence, 1932, Box 139, RG 46, NARA.

62. Raymond Pruitt plan for proxy war, November 5, 1932, AVCO Correspondence, 1932, Box 139, RG 46, NARA.

63. E.L. Cord, "E.L. Cord and the Future of the Aviation Corporation," E.F. Hutton & Company, New York, November 14, 1932, Cord-Cohu Contest, Box 137, RG 46, NARA.

64. "Interview with Mr. Talbot in the Late Afternoon of November 11, 1932," memorandum, November 11, 1932, AVCO Correspondence, 1932, Box 139, RG 46, NARA.

65. Notice of Special Meeting of Stockholders, the Aviation Corporation, November 10, 1932, AVCO, Box 18, Harriman Collection.

66. La Motte T. Cohu to the Stockholders of the Aviation Corporation, open letter, November 14, 1932, Box 45, Sherman M. Fairchild Collection.

67. Agreement, AVCO and Cord, November 17, 1932, Box 1, Harriman Collection.

68. Minutes, Meeting of the Board of Directors of the Aviation Corporation, March 15, 1933, AVCO, Box 18, Harriman Collection.

Chapter 12. The Democrats Take Control

1. T.E. Braniff to P.G. Johnson, December 23, 1932, Col. Paul Henderson, Box 126, RG 46, NARA.

2. James MacGregor Burns, *Roosevelt: The Lion and the Fox, 1882–1940* (New York: Harcourt, Brace & World, 1956), 134–38.

3. Ibid., 139–40.

4. J.P. Murray, daily report, December 17, 1932, Murray, James P. (reports), Box 30, Boeing.

5. George Wheat to Philip Johnson, n.d., Pioneer Air Transport Operator's Association, Box 137, RG 46, NARA.

6. T.B. Doe to H.A. Talbot Jr., September 14, 1932, N.A.A. North American Copies of Correspondence, Box 146, RG 46, NARA.

7. *New York Times*, January 27, 1933.

8. Hainer Hinshaw to W.A. Patterson, January 23, 1933, Col. Paul Henderson, Box 126, RG 46, NARA.

9. Ibid.

10. Walter F. Brown to James M. Mead, January 30, 1933, Independent Companies—Northwest Airways, 1933, Box 157, RG 46, NARA.

11. Ibid.

12. L.H. Brittin to R.C. Lilly, January 24, 1933, Independent Companies—Northwest Airways, 1933, Box 157, RG 46, NARA.

13. *New York Times,* February 1, 1933.

14. L.H. Brittin to R.C. Lilly, February 16, 1933, Independent Companies—Northwest Airways, 1933, Box 157, RG 46, NARA.

15. Harry E. Collins, Pioneer Air Transport Operators Association to W.A. Letson, March 2, 1933, Pioneer Air Transport Operator's Association, Box 137, RG 46, NARA.

16. Walter F. Brown to Sen. Joseph T. Robinson, February 3, 1933, Pioneer Air Transport Operator's Association, Box 137, RG 46, NARA.

17. van der Linden, *Boeing 247,* 74–75.

18. Henry Ladd Smith, 325.

19. L.H. Brittin to R.C. Lilly, February 23, 1933, Independent Companies—Northwest Airways, 1933, Box 157, RG 46, NARA.

20. John B. Crane, *Report, An Analysis of the Air Mail System in the United States* (Cambridge: Harvard University, December 2, 1932), C-8.

21. Ibid., A-4

22. Ibid., 6.

23. Ibid., A-4

24. L.H. Brittin to R.C. Lilly, March 17, 1933, Independent Companies—Northwest Airways, 1933, Box 157, RG 46, NARA.

25. Ibid.

26. House Committee on the Post Office and Post Roads, Report, *A Resolution Authorizing an Investigation of the Expenditures of the Post Office Department,* 72d Cong., 2d sess., February 21, 1933.

27. Remarks of Hon. Clyde Kelly in the House of Representatives, March 3, 1933, Presidential Papers, Transcontinental and Western Air, 1933, Box 24, MacCracken Papers.

28. Resume of Former Mead and Kelly Air Mail Bill, March 15, 1933, Microfilm Collection, Reel 14, Aeronautical Chamber of Commerce Papers, National Air and Space Museum, Washington, D.C.

29. House Committee on the Post Office and Post Roads, Hearing, *A Bill to Amend the Air Mail Act of February 2, 1925,* 73d Cong., 2d sess., April 20, 1933 to March 21, 1934, 1.

30. T.B. Clement to Richard Robbins, March 14, 1933, Presidential Papers, Transcontinental and Western Air, Kelly Bill 1933, Box 25, MacCracken Papers.

31. J.H. Schoonmaker Jr. to Stockholders, General Aviation Corporation, March 1933, Presidential Papers, Transcontinental and Western Air, 1933, Box 24, MacCracken Papers.

32. L.H. Brittin to R.C. Lilly, January 24, 1933, Independent Companies—Northwest Airways, 1933, Box 157, RG 46, NARA.

33. Ibid., 8–10.

34. Ibid., 15–17.

35. F.B. Rentschler to P.G. Johnson, memorandum, March 3, 1933, U.A.T.C. Miscellaneous Copies of Correspondence, Box 154, RG 46, NARA.

36. L.B. Manning to Rep. A.J. Sabath, April 21, 1933, AVCO Correspondence, 1933, Box 139, RG 46, NARA.

37. L.B. Manning to R.S. Pruitt, telegram, April 25, 1933, AVCO Correspondence, 1933, Box 139, RG 46, NARA.

38. L.H. Brittin to R.C. Lilly, March 31, 1933, Independent Companies—Northwest Airways, 1933, Box 157, RG 46, NARA.

39. Ibid., 2.

40. L.H. Brittin to R.C. Lilly, May 11, 1933, Independent Companies—Northwest Airways, 1933, Box 157, RG 46, NARA.

41. L.H. Brittin to R.C. Lilly, May 21, 1933, Independent Companies—Northwest Airways, 1933, Box 157, RG 46, NARA.

42. L.H. Brittin to R.C. Lilly, June 2, 1933, Independent Companies—Northwest Airways, 1933, Box 157, RG 46, NARA.

43. L.H. Brittin to R.C. Lilly, telegram, August 17, 1933, Independent Companies—Northwest Airways, 1933, Box 157, RG 46, NARA.

44. L.H. Brittin to R.C. Lilly, August 25, 1933, Independent Companies—Northwest Airways, 1933, Box 157, RG 46, NARA.

45. W.A. Patterson to P.G. Johnson, memorandum, September 6, 1933, File 13, Box 3303, Boeing.

46. Ibid.

47. Ibid., 2.

48. Ibid.

49. "Airlines Continue Up-Curve," *Western Flying*, April 1933, 22.

50. Ellis Hawley, *The New Deal and the Problem of Monopoly* (Princeton, N.J.: Princeton University Press, 1966), 32, 53–71.

51. "The Code of the Airlines," *Western Flying*, October 1933, 8.

52. L.H. Brittin to R.C. Lilly, telegram, August 1, 1933, Independent Companies—Northwest Airways, 1933, Box 157, RG 46, NARA.

53. L.H. Brittin to Croil Hunter, August 1933, Independent Companies—Northwest Airways, 1933, Box 157, RG 46, NARA.

54. L.H. Brittin to E.E. Hughes, Assistant Deputy Adminstrator, September 12, 1933, Independent Companies—Northwest Airways, Miscellaneous Data and Letters for File, Box 156, RG 46, NARA.

55. L.H. Brittin to R.C. Lilly, September 2, 1933, 1, 2, Independent Companies—Northwest Airways, 1933, Box 157, RG 46, NARA.

56. Ibid., 2.

57. "Code of the Airlines," 8–10.

58. W.A. Patterson to P.G. Johnson, memorandum, "Post Office Department Meeting," September 6, 1933, 6., U.A.T.C. Miscellaneous Copies of Correspondence, Box 154, RG 46, NARA.

59. "Aviation's Codes," *Western Flying*, September 1933, 19.

60. Thomas Braniff to the Administrator, National Recovery Administration, September 8, 1933, Independent Companies—Braniff, Box 155, RG 46, NARA.

61. Ibid., 5–6.

62. "The Air Transport Code," memorandum, n.d., Microfilm Collection, Reel 14, Aeronautical Chamber of Commerce records, National Air and Space Museum.

Chapter 13. Congress Assumes Command

1. Roger K. Newman, *Hugo Black: A Biography* (New York: Pantheon Books, 1995); Arthur Schlesinger Jr., *The Age of Roosevelt: The Coming of the New Deal* (Houghton Mifflin, Boston, 1959), 446–49.

2. Eastern Air Transport, Memorandum for the Record, July 19, 1932, N.A.A. North American Copies of Correspondence, Box 146, RG 46, NARA.

3. Hugo Black, "Those U.S. Mail Contracts," speech, National Broadcasting Company, published by the *Evening Star,* January 24, 1934, General Information, Box 114, RG 46, NARA.

4. *New York Times,* February 16, 1933.

5. *New York Times,* February 11, 1933.

6. Hainer Hinshaw to P.G. Johnson, memorandum, June 1, 1933, 1, U.A.T.C., United Air Lines Routes, Box 153, RG 46, NARA.

7. Ibid., 2.

8. Ibid., 3.

9. *New York Times,* December 23, 1933.

10. Thomas Braniff to A.G. Patterson, October 4, 1933, Independent Companies—Braniff, Box 155, RG 46, NARA.

11. W.W. Howes to Karl Crowley, November 10, 1933, Entry 42, Air Mail Misc., Domestic, 96337, Box 66, RG 46, NARA.

12. Paul Braniff to A.G. Patterson, November 29, 1933, A.G. Patterson to Paul R. Braniff, telegram, December 6, 1933, Independent Companies—Braniff, Box 155, RG 46, NARA.

13. A.G. Patterson to Joseph B. Eastman, December 22, 1933, Independent Companies—Braniff, Box 155, RG 46, NARA.

14. W.A. Patterson to P.G. Johnson, telegram, January 3, 1934, File 5, Box 3295, Boeing.

15. L.H. Brittin to R.C. Lilly, telegram, November 17, 1933, Independent Companies—Northwest Airways, 1933, Box 157, RG 46, NARA.

16. L.H. Brittin to R.C. Lilly, November 18, 1933, Independent Companies—Northwest Airways, 1933, Box 157, RG 46, NARA.

17. Paul Henderson to P.G. Johnson, memorandum, November 10, 1933, U.A.T.C., United Air Lines Routes, Box 153, RG 46, NARA.

18. Ibid.

19. Ibid., 4–5.

20. J.P. Murray, daily report, December 20, 1933, Col. Paul Henderson, Box 126, RG 46, NARA.

21. J.P. Murray, daily report, January 2, 1934, Col. Paul Henderson, Box 126, RG 46, NARA.

22. Senate Special Committee on Investigation of Air Mail and Ocean Mail Contracts, Hearings, *A Resolution Creating a Special Committee of the Senate to Investigate Air Mail and Ocean Mail Contracts,* 73d Cong., 2d sess., September 26, 1933, to May 25, 1934, part 6, 1442. Subsequent references to the Senate Special Committee are cited in text with the page numbers in parentheses.

23. *New York Times,* January 20, 1934.

24. C.M. Keys to C.A. Lindbergh, June 6, 1928, reported in *New York Times,* January 16, 1934.

25. Senate Special Committee, *Resolution Creating a Special Committee,* part 6, 1695.

26. G.R. Simonson, ed., *The History of the American Aircraft Industry: An Anthology* (Cambridge: MIT Press, 1968), 87–93.

27. Senate Special Committee, *Resolution Creating a Special Committee,* 1795–1828.

28. *New York Times,* January 25, 1934.

29. *New York Times,* February 1, 1934.

30. "Air Mail Investigation," *Aviation,* March 1934, 91.

31. Crowley Report to the Postmaster General, February 6, 1934, 10, Entry 42, Air Mail Misc., 80096, Box 23, RG 28, NARA. Subsequent references to the Crowley report are cited in text with the page numbers in parentheses.

32. *New York Times,* January 26, 1934.

33. James A. Farley diary, February 10, 1934, Microfilm Reel 1, James A. Farley Collection, Library of Congress (hereafter cited as Farley Collection).

34. *New York Times,* February 9, 1934.

35. Samuel I. Rosenman, ed., *The Public Papers and Addresses of Franklin D. Roosevelt,* vol. 3 (New York: Macmillan, 1938), 93.

36. William A. Patterson to James A. Farley, February 16, 1934, U.A.T.C., United Air Lines Routes, Box 153, RG 46, NARA.

37. *New York Times,* February 11, 1934.

38. *New York Times,* February 12, 1934.

39. Davies, *Airlines of the United States,* 156–57.

40. James A. Farley to Hugo L. Black, February 13, 1934, Special Correspondence, Presidential File, F.D.R. 1934, Box 34, Farley Collection.

41. van der Linden, *Boeing 247,* 88–92.

42. Richard W. Robbins to Hugo L. Black, February 21, 1934, Hugo L. Black to Richard Robbins, February 23, 1934, N.A.A. Transcontinental and Western Air, Box 143, RG 46, NARA.

43. B.C. Forbes, "Modern Flying No Child's Play, Facts Reveal," New York *American,* February 21, 1934.

44. "Let Us Hasten to Rectify an Inexcusable Error," New York *American,* February 25, 1934.

45. *New York Times,* February 19, 1934.

46. Rosenman, "The Army Stops Flying the Mail," in *Public Papers and Addresses of Franklin D. Roosevelt,* 141.

47. Ibid., 142 n.

48. Franklin D. Roosevelt to Chairman Kenneth McKellar, March 7, 1934, Entry 42, Air Mail Legislation, Folder 96268, Box 46, RG 28, NARA.

49. Ibid., 2.

50. Franklin D. Roosevelt to Sen. Kenneth McKellar, draft letter, March 7, 1934, Microfilm Reel 1, Farley Collection.

51. Statement of Ernest R. Breech, commenting on President Roosevelt's letter dated March 7, 1934, 3–4, Aircraft Investigations—Black Committee, Box 1, NASM Keys. Subsequent references to Breech's statement are cited in text with the page numbers in parentheses.

52. S. 3012, 73d Cong., 2d sess.

53. Ibid.

54. Testimony of W.W. Howes, U.S. Congress, Senate, *Revision of Air Mail Laws, Hearings Before the Committee on Post Offices and Post Roads, S. 3012, A Bill to Revise the Air Mail Laws,* 73d Cong., 2d Sess., March 12 to March 20, 1934, 46–47. Subsequent references to this testimony are cited in text with the page number in parentheses.

55. Statement of Richard W. Robbins, March 13, 1934, T.W.A. Press Release, Aircraft Investigations—Black Committee, Box 1, NASM Keys.

56. Statement of Richard W. Robbins, March 25, 1934, T.W.A. Press Release, 4, Aircraft Investigations—Black Committee, Box 1, NASM Keys.

57. Ibid., 4–5.

58. "Spring Opening: Formal Prelude to an Air Mail Shuffle," *Aviation,* May 1934, 135, Post Office Department Press Release, April 21, 1934, General Correspondence, Box 2, Farley Collection.

59. "Up from Chaos," *Aviation,* November 1934, 339.

60. P.G. Johnson to J.W. Spangler, April 23, 1934, File 7, Box 3300, Boeing.

61. Ibid.

62. Memorandum of Conference between Attorney General Homer Cummings, Solicitor Karl Crowley, et al., April 3, 1934, Entry 42, Kohler Aviation Corp., Folder 96221, Box 34, RG 28, NARA.

63. Karl A. Crowley to Cornelius V. Mitchell, May 17, 1934, Entry 42, Kohler Aviation Corp., Folder 96221, Box 34, RG 28, NARA.

64. P.G. Johnson to J.W. Spangler, April 23, 1934, File 7, Box 3300, Boeing.

65. Davies, *Airlines of the United States,* 173.

66. *Congressional Record,* April 24, 1934, 7450–51.

67. "A New Law for Air Transport," *Aviation,* July 1934, 205.

68. James A. Farley to Kenneth McKellar, May 14, 1934, Entry 42, Air Mail Legislation, Folder 96268, Box 46, RG 28, NARA.

69. Ibid., 206.

70. Plan of Reorganization, United Aircraft & Transport Corporation, May 14, 1934, Financial Information, File 21, Box 3296, Boeing.

Bibliography

Primary Sources

Archives

The Boeing Company, Historical Services, Archives, Seattle, Washington

The archives preserves the records, files, correspondence, and photographs of the Boeing Airplane Company, United Air Lines and its predecessors, and United Aircraft and Transport Corporation. The records are thorough and are the only such source left, as no other aircraft manufacturer has preserved its documentary record.

C.R. Smith Museum, American Airlines, Fort Worth, Texas

The museum's archival holdings include records of the formation of the Aviation Corporation and American Airways/Airlines.

Herbert C. Hoover Presidential Library and Archives, West Branch, Iowa

The library and archives contain the papers of Herbert Hoover as both Secretary of Commerce and President. The archival collection includes the William P. MacCracken Jr. Papers and a file on Walter Folger Brown, which is small but useful. Hoover left little concerning his involvement with aviation, though that which remains is valuable. MacCracken's thorough papers provide indispensable information concerning the airline industry.

Manuscript Division, Library of Congress, Washington, D.C.

Many of the most prominent names in the formation of the U.S. air transportation industry left their papers to the Library of Congress. The most valuable are the papers of Sherman Fairchild, W. Averill Harriman, and William Gibbs McAdoo. Surprisingly, the papers of Hugo Black and Charles McNary contain little concerning their air mail investigations.

Records Consulted:

Hugo Black Collection
William E. Borah Collection
Sherman M. Fairchild Collection
James A. Farley Collection
W. Averill Harriman Collection
Jesse Jones Collection
William Gibbs McAdoo Collection
Charles McNary Collection
Mabel Walker Willebrandt Collection

National Air and Space Museum-Archives, Washington, D.C.

The Keys Collection provides a detailed documentation of the early years of U.S. aviation, particularly concerning the formation of Transcontinental Air Transport. The Aeronautical Chamber of Commerce records are large and contain information of particular value concerning the industry's lobbying efforts and the implementation of the aviation's codes under the National Recovery Administration.

Records Consulted:

Aeronautical Chamber of Commerce Papers, Microfilm Collection
Clement M. Keys Collection

National Archives and Records Administration, Washington,D.C.

The records preserved by NARA contain the bulk of material used in this work. RG 46, which preserves the Black committee papers, contains a treasure house of material on the airline industry and most of the individuals in business and government up to 1933, as the committee's investigators subpoenaed and copied all of the corporate correspondence they deemed necessary. RG 28 contains all of the available records from the Post Office Department, particularly those concerning the issuance and enforcement of contracts. The early records from the Solicitor's Office are also quite useful, as they contain several files on the contract controversies.

Records Consulted:

Record Group 28. Office of the Second Assistant Postmaster General, Division of Air Mail Service, Contract Air Mail—Case Files 1924–1934.
Record Group 28. Entry 42. Office of the Solicitor—Investigation of Air Mail/ Ocean Mail
Record Group 28. Entries 155 and 157. Correspondence Related to Air Mail Routes and Stops.
Record Group 28. Entry 160. General Correspondence of Superintendent, Division of Air Mail Service; Correspondence Related to Reduction of Air Mail Rates.
Record Group 46. U.S. Senate. Special Committee on Investigation of Air Mail and Ocean Mail Contracts, 1934.

Record Group 151. Records of the Bureau of Foreign and Domestic Commerce.
Record Group 233. United States House of Representatives.

United Airlines Archives, Chicago, Illinois

Housed at corporate headquarters, this rudimentary archival collection contains a small but highly useful amount of material concerning Boeing Air Transport, some of United Air Lines' corporate papers, and a small amount of correspondence concerning air mail contracts.

United Technologies, Archival and Historical Resource Center, East Hartford, Connecticut

The center contains the records of the former United Aircraft and Transport Corporation, including transcripts and notes of the Technical Advisory Committee meetings.

University of Texas at Dallas, Aviation History Collection, Dallas, Texas

UT-Dallas specializes in preserving records concerning all aspects of aviation history, including the airline industry. They house the Braniff Airlines Collection, which consists of the company's public relations papers.

Other records exist but do not provide much useful additional information. Walter F. Brown's papers are housed at the Ohio Historical Society. Unfortunately, Brown was a careful politician throughout most of his life and did not keep his correspondence. His papers primarily consist of his records concerning legal attempts to clear his name after 1934. The records of Northwest Airlines are preserved by the Minnesota Historical Society and are quite good. However, the Black committee copied all of Northwest's correspondence relative to the air mail up to 1933. These records are currently preserved in the National Archives. Other airlines and aircraft manufacturers have either not preserved their records or have closed them to all public access.

Secondary Sources

Books

Abramson, Rudy. *Spanning the Century: The Life of W. Averill Harriman, 1891–1986.* New York: William Morrow, 1992.

Baker, Richard A., and Roger H. Davidson, eds. *First Among Equals: Outstanding Senate Leaders of the Twentieth Century.* Washington, D.C.: Congressional Quarterly, 1991.

Barber, William J. *From New Era to New Deal: Herbert Hoover, the Economists, and American Economic Policy, 1921–1933.* New York: Cambridge University Press, 1985.

Borden, Norman E., Jr. *Air Mail Emergency: 1934.* Freeport, Maine: Bond Wheelwright, 1968.

Bowers, Peter W. *Boeing Aircraft Since 1916.* New York: Funk and Wagnalls, 1968.

Brooks, Peter W. *The Modern Airliner: Its Origins and Development.* Manhattan, Kans.: Sunflower University Press, 1982.

Brown, Dorothy M. *Mabel Walker Willebrandt: A Study of Power, Loyalty, and Law.* Knoxville: University of Tennessee Press, 1984.

Burkhardt, Robert. *CAB—The Civil Aeronautics Board.* Dulles International Airport: Green Hill Publishing, 1974.

Burner, David. *Herbert Hoover: A Public Life.* New York: Atheneum, 1984.

Burns, James MacGregor. *Roosevelt: The Lion and the Fox, 1882–1940.* New York: Harcourt, Brace & World, 1956.

Caves, Richard E. *Air Transport and Its Regulators: An Industry Study.* Cambridge: Harvard University Press, 1961.

Civil Aviation: A Report by the Joint Committee on Civil Aviation. New York: McGraw-Hill, 1926.

Crane, John B. *Report, An Analysis of the Air Mail System in the United States.* Cambridge: Harvard University, December 2, 1932.

Crouch, Tom D., ed. *Charles A. Lindbergh: An American Life.* Washington, D.C.: Smithsonian Institution Press, 1977.

David, Paul T. *The Economics of Air Mail Transportation.* Washington, D.C.: Brookings Institution, 1934.

Davies, R.E.G. *Airlines of the United States Since 1914.* London: Putnam, 1972; Washington, D.C.: Smithsonian Institution Press, 1982.

———. *Delta: An Airline and Its Aircraft.* Miami: Paladwr Press, 1990.

Davis, Kenneth S. *FDR: The New Deal Years, 1933–1937.* New York: Random House, 1986.

Farley, James A. *Behind the Ballots: The Personal History of a Politician.* New York: Harcourt, Brace, 1938.

———. *Jim Farley's Story: The Roosevelt Years.* New York: McGraw Hill Book, 1948.

Fausold, Martin L. *The Presidency of Herbert C. Hoover.* Lawrence: University of Kansas Press, 1985.

Fausold, Martin L., and Mazuzan George T. *The Hoover Presidency: A Reappraisal.* Albany: State University of New York Press, 1974.

Financial Handbook of the American Aviation Industry. New York: Commercial National Bank and Trust Company of New York, 1929.

Francillon, Rene J. *McDonnell Douglas Aircraft Since 1920.* London: Putnam, 1979.

Frederick, John H. *Commercial Air Transportation.* Homewood, Ill.: Richard D. Irwin, 1961.

Freidel, Frank. *Franklin D. Roosevelt: A Rendezvous with Destiny.* Boston: Little, Brown, 1990.

Freudenthal, Elsbeth. *The Aviation Business.* New York: Vantage Press, 1940.

Fuller, Wayne E. *The American Mail: Enlarger of the Common Life.* Chicago: University of Chicago Press, 1972.

Gelfand, Lawrence E., ed. *Herbert Hoover: The Great War and Its Aftermath, 1914–1923.* Iowa City: University of Iowa Press, 1979.

Hallion, Richard P. *Legacy of Flight: The Guggenheim Contribution to American Aviation.* Seattle: University of Washington Press, 1977.

Hawley, Ellis W. *The Great War and the Search for a Modern Order: A History of the American People and Their Institution, 1917–1933.* New York: St. Martin's Press, 1979.

———. *Herbert Hoover and the Crisis of American Capitalism.* Cambridge, Mass.: Schenkman Publishing, 1973.

———. *Herbert Hoover and the Historians.* West Branch, Iowa: Herbert Hoover Presidential Library, 1989.

———. *The New Deal and the Problem of Monopoly: A Study in Economic Ambivalence.* Princeton, N.J.: Princeton University Press, 1966.

———. "Three Facets of Hooverian Associationalism: Lumber, Aviation, and Movies, 1921–1930." In McGraw, *Regulation in Perspective*, 95–123.

Hawley, Ellis W., ed. *Herbert Hoover as Secretary of Commerce: Studies in New Era Thought and Practice.* Iowa City: University of Iowa Press, 1981.

Herbert Hoover Reassessed: Essays Commemorating the Inauguration of Our Thirty-First President. Washington, D.C.: Government Printing Office, 1981.

Hicks, John D. *Republican Ascendancy: 1921–1933.* New York: Harper and Brothers, 1960.

Himmelberg, Robert F. *The Origins of the National Recovery Administration: Business, Government, and the Trade Association Issue, 1921–1933.* New York: Fordham University Press, 1976.

Hopkins, George E. *The Airline Pilots: A Study in Elite Unionization.* Cambridge: Harvard University Press, 1971.

———. *Flying the Line: The First Half Century of the Air Line Pilots Association.* Washington, D.C.: ALPA, 1982.

Hoover, Herbert. *Public Papers of the Presidents of the United States: Herbert Hoover, Containing the Public Messages, Speeches, and Statements of the President, March 4 to December 31, 1929.* Washington, D.C.: Government Printing Office, 1974.

Hurley, Alfred. *Billy Mitchell.* New York: Franklin Watts, 1964.

Jordan, William A. *Airline Regulation in America: Effects and Imperfections.* Baltimore: Johns Hopkins University Press, 1970.

Keller, Morton. *Regulating a New Economy: Public Policy and Economic Change in America, 1900–1933.* Cambridge: Harvard University Press, 1990.

Kennedy, Thomas H. *An Introduction to the Economics of Air Transportation.* New York: Macmillan, 1924.

Kohlmeier, Louis M., Jr. *The Regulators: Watchdog Agencies and the Public Interest.* New York: Harper & Row, 1969.

Kolko, Gabriel. *Triumph of Conservatism: A Reinterpretation of American History, 1900–1916.* New York: Free Press of Glencoe, 1963.

Komons, Nick A. *Bonfires to Beacons: Federal Civil Aviation Policy Under the Air Commerce Act, 1926–1938.* Washington, D.C.: Government Printing Office, 1978.

Krog, Carl E. *Herbert Hoover and the Republican Era: A Reconsideration.* Lanham, Md.: University Press of America, 1984.

Lawrence, Charles L. *Our National Aviation Program.* New York: Aeronautical Chamber of Commerce, 1932.

Leary, William M. *Aerial Pioneers: The U.S. Air Mail Service, 1918–1927*. Washington, D.C.: Smithsonian Institution Press, 1985.

————. *Encyclopedia of America Business History and Biography: The Airline Industry*. New York: Bruccoli Clark Layman, 1992.

Leary, William M., ed. *Aviation's Golden Age*. Iowa City: University of Iowa Press, 1989.

Leuchtenburg, William E. *Franklin D. Roosevelt and the New Deal: 1932–1940*. New York: Harper Colophon Books, 1963.

————. *The Perils of Prosperity, 1914–1932*. Chicago: University of Chicago Press, 1958.

Lewis, W. David, and Wesley Phillips Newton. *Delta: The History of an Airline*. Athens: University of Georgia Press, 1979.

Lyons, Eugene. *Herbert Hoover: A Biography*. Garden City, N.Y.: Doubleday, 1964.

McGraw, Thomas K., ed. *Regulation in Perspective: Historical Essays*. Boston: Division of Research, Graduate School of Business Administration, Harvard University, 1981.

Mansfield, Harold. *Vision: A Saga of the Sky*. New York: Duell, Sloan and Pierce, 1956.

Marvin, Langdon P. *Air Mail Subsidy Separation*. Washington, D.C.: Georgetown University Law Journal, 1952.

Mead, Cary Hoge. *Wings Over the World: The Life of George Jackson Mead*, Wauwatosa, Wisc.: Swannet Press, 1971.

Miller, Ronald E., and David Sawers. *The Technical Development of Modern Aviation*. London: Routledge and Kegan Paul, 1968.

Murray, Robert K. *The Harding Era; Warren G. Harding and His Administration*. Minneapolis: University of Minnesota Press, 1969.

Myers, William Starr, ed. *State Papers and Other Public Writings of Herbert Hoover, 1929–1931*. Vol. 1. Garden City, N.Y.: Doubleday, Doran, 1934.

————. *State Papers and Other Public Writings of Herbert Hoover, 1931–1933*. Vol. 2. Garden City, N.Y.: Doubleday, Doran & Company, 1934.

Myers, William Starr, and Walter H. Newton. *The Hoover Administration: A Documented Narrative*. New York: Charles Scribner's Sons, 1936.

Nash, Lee. *Understanding Herbert Hoover: Ten Perspectives*. Stanford, Calif.: Hoover Institution Press, 1987.

Newman, Roger K. *Hugo Black: A Biography*. New York: Pantheon Books, 1995.

Osborn, Michael, and Joseph Riggs. *Mr. Mac: William P. MacCracken, Jr., A Biography. On Aviation—Law—Optometry*. Memphis: Southern College of Optometry, 1970.

Puffer, Claude E. *Air Transportation*. Philadelphia: Blakiston, 1941.

Rae, John B. *Climb to Greatness: The American Aircraft Industry, 1920–1960*. Cambridge: MIT Press, 1968.

Rentschler, Frederick B. *An Account of Pratt and Whitney Aircraft Company: 1920–1950*. Hartford, Conn.: United Technologies, 1950.

Reeves, Earl. *Aviation's Place in Tomorrow's Business*. New York: B.C. Forbes Publishing, 1930.

Rhyne, Charles S. *Civil Aeronautics Act Annotated with the Legislative History Which Produced It and the Precedents Upon Which It Is Based*. Washington, D.C.: National Law Book, 1939.

Rickenbacker, Edward V. *Rickenbacker: An Autobiography.* Englewood Cliffs, N.J.: Prentice-Hall, 1967.

Rosenman, Samuel I., ed. *The Public Papers and Addresses of Franklin D. Roosevelt.* Vol. 3. New York: Macmillan, 1938.

Scheele, Carl H. *A Short History of the Mail Service.* Washington, D.C.: Smithsonian Institution Press, 1970.

Schlaifer, Robert, and S.D. Heron. *Development of Aircraft Engines and Fuels.* Boston: Harvard University, 1950.

Schlesinger, Arthur, Jr. *The Age of Roosevelt: The Coming of the New Deal.* Boston: Houghton Mifflin, 1959.

Schriftgiesser, Karl. *This Was Normalcy; An Account of Party Politics During Twelve Republican Years: 1920–1932.* Boston: Little, Brown, 1948.

Schwartz, Jordan A. *The Interregnum of Despair: Hoover, Congress and the Depression.* Urbana: University of Illinois Press, 1970.

———. *The New Dealers: Power Politics in the Age of Roosevelt.* New York: Alfred A. Knopf, 1993.

Serling, Robert J. *From the Captain to the Colonel: An Informal History of Eastern Airlines.* New York: Dial Press, 1980.

———. *Howard Hughes's Airline: An Informal History of TWA.* New York: St. Martin's Press, 1983.

———. *The Only Way to Fly: The Story of Western Airlines, America's Senior Air Carrier.* Garden City, N.Y.: Doubleday and Company, 1976.

Simonson, G.R., ed. *The History of the American Aircraft Industry: An Anthology.* Cambridge: MIT Press, 1968.

Smith, Gene. *The Shattered Dream; Herbert Hoover and the Great Depression.* New York: Morrow, 1970.

Smith, Henry Ladd. *Airways: The History of Commercial Aviation in the United States.* New York: Knopf, 1942.

Sobel, Robert. *Herbert Hoover at the Onset of the Great Depression, 1929–1930.* Philadelphia: J.B. Lippincott, 1975.

Solberg, Carl. *Conquest of the Skies: A History of Commercial Aviation in America.* Boston: Little, Brown, 1979.

Sorrell, Lewis C., and Harry A. Wheeler. *Passenger Transport in the United States, 1920–1950.* Chicago: Railway Business Association, 1944.

Spencer, Francis A. *Air Mail Payment and the Government.* Washington, D.C.: Brookings Institution, 1941.

Taylor, Frank J. *High Horizons: Daredevil Flying Postmen to Modern Magic Carpet—The United Air Lines Story.* New York: McGraw-Hill, 1951.

Trani, Eugene P., and David L. Wilson. *The Presidency of Warren G. Harding.* Lawrence: Regents Press of Kansas, 1977.

United Air Lines. *Corporate and Legal History of United Air Lines and Its Predecessors and Subsidiaries, 1925–1945.* Chicago: Twentieth Century Press, 1953.

U.S. Congress. House. *Air Mail, Hearing on H.R. 7213 and H.R. 8337.* 70th Cong., 1st sess., January 12, 13, 1928.

————. *Hearing Before the Committee on the Post Office and Post Roads on H.R. 9500.* 71st Cong., 2d sess., February 19, 1930.

————. *Hearing on H.R. 8390 and 9841.* 72d Cong., 1st sess., March 1, 2, 3, 4, 23, 1932.

————. *H. Res. 359.* 72d Cong., 2d sess., January 20, 1933.

————. Report. *Investigation of the United States Postal Air Mail Service Pursuant to H. Res. 226.* 72d Cong., 2d sess., February 21, 1933.

————. Report. *A Resolution Authorizing an Investigation of the Expenditures of the Post Office Department.* 72d Cong., 2d sess., February 21, 1933.

U.S. Congress. House. Committee on the Post Office and Post Roads. Hearing. *A Bill to Amend the Air Mail Act of February 2, 1925.* 73d Cong., 2d sess., April 20, 1933 to March 21, 1934.

U.S. Congress. Senate. *Air Mail Contracts, Letter from the Postmaster General, In Response to Senate Resolution No. 394, Certain Information Relative to Air Mail Contracts, Existing Air Mail Routes in the United States, New Routes to Be Established, and Names of Officers and Attorneys That Have Been Employees of the United States Government Within the Past Five Years, Document No. 315.* 71st Cong., 3d sess., February 17, 1931.

————. *Report of the Federal Aviation Commission.* 74th Cong., 1st sess., 1935.

————. *A Resolution Creating a Special Committee of the Senate to Investigate Air Mail and Ocean Mail Contracts.* 73d Cong., 2d sess., 1933.

————. *Revision of Air Mail Laws, Hearings Before the Committee on Post Offices and Post Roads, S. 3012, A Bill to Revise the Air Mail Laws.* 73d Cong., 2d sess., March 12 to March 20, 1934.

————. *S. Res. 48, Resolution, To Investigate Air and Ocean Mail Contracts, Use of Mail Tubes, Proposed Postal Rate Increases, and the Erection of Public Building in Small Towns.* 72d Cong., 1st sess., December 9, 1931.

U.S. Congress. Senate. Special Committee on Investigation of Air Mail and Ocean Mail Contracts. Hearings. *Investigation of Air Mail and Ocean Mail Contracts.* 73d Cong., 2d sess., September 26, 1933 to May 25, 1934.

van der Linden, F. Robert. *The Boeing 247: The First Modern Airliner.* Seattle: University of Washington Press, 1991.

Warren, Harris G. *Herbert Hoover and the Great Depression.* New York: Oxford University Press, 1959.

Whitnah, Donald. *Safer Skyways: Federal Control of Aviation, 1926–1966.* Ames: Iowa State University Press, 1981.

Wilbur, Ray Lyman, and Arthur Mastick Hyde. *The Hoover Policies.* New York: Charles Scribner's Sons, 1937.

Wilson, Joan H. *Herbert Hoover, Forgotten Progressive.* Boston: Little, Brown, 1975.

Wooley, James G., and Earl W. Hill. *Airplane Transportation.* Hollywood: Hartwell Publishing, 1929.

Articles

"Advises Air Mail Mainly for Speed." *Washington Star,* October 9, 1929.

"Advocates Government Aid on Natural Routes." *Airway Age,* November 1929, 49.

"Air Fares Reduced 25 Per Cent." *Western Flying* 7 (January 1930): 138.

"Airlines Continue Up-Curve." *Western Flying* 13 (April 1933): 22.

"Air Mail Contracts and Rate Revision." *Aviation* 27 (August 3, 1929): 249.

"The Air Mail Fathers Commercial Aviation." *Aviation* 21 (October 18, 1926): 668.

"Air Mail Inquisition." *Aviation* 30 (April 1931): 201.

"Air Mail Investigation." *Aviation* 33 (March 1934): 91.

"The Air Mail Pioneers." *Aviation* 21 (October 25, 1926): 701.

"Air Mail Rates Discussed in Capitol." *Aviation* 27 (July 20, 1929): 188.

"Airmail to Help Aviation." *Aircraft Age,* June 1930, 4.

"The Astonishing Air Mail Bids." *Aviation* 22 (January 24, 1927): 170.

"Aviation Corporation Net Loss . . ." *Air Transportation,* April 19, 1930, 2.

"Aviation's Codes." *Western Flying* 13 (September 1933): 19.

"Clement M. Keys: He Bought a Company Nearly Insolvent." *Air Transportation,* July 27, 1929, 51.

"The Code of the Airlines." *Western Flying* 13 (October 1933): 8–10.

"Contract Offered at Half Rate for All Air Mail Lines." *United States Daily,* February 26, 1932.

"Control of Flying." *Aviation* 20 (June 7, 1926): 867.

"Curtiss Extending Control Over Air Lines." *Western Flying* 6 (July 1929): 152.

"Delegates to Kansas City Conference Discuss Problems of Transport Line Operators." *Air Transportation,* October 5, 1929, 16–22.

"Federal Aid to Aviation." *Boston Herald,* October 10, 1929.

"Feeder Lines." *Aviation* 18 (June 22, 1925): 689.

Forbes, B.C. "Modern Flying No Child's Play, Facts Reveal." *New York American,* February 21, 1934.

Ford, Harvey S. "Walter Folger Brown." *Northwest Ohio Quarterly* (Summer 1954): 204–5.

"Form Pittsburgh Holding Concern." *Aviation* 25 (December 29, 1929): 2103.

"Graham G. Grosvenor." *Air Transportation,* July 6, 1929, 44.

"A Great Stimulus to Commercial Aviation." *Aviation* 22 (June 6, 1927): 1213.

"Guggenheim to Finance Passenger Services." *Aviation* 23 (July 18, 1927): 151.

Hard, Anne. "Uncle Sam's New Air Mail Man." *New York Herald Tribune,* April 7, 1929, 11–12.

"Harris Hanshue: Airline Operators and Manufacturer." *Air Transportation,* August 2, 1930, 27.

Hawley, Ellis W. "Herbert Hoover and the Sherman Act, 1921–1933." *Iowa Law Review* 74, no. 5 (1989): 1067–1103.

———. "Herbert Hoover, the Commerce Secretariat, and the Vision of the Associative State, 1921–1928." *Journal of American History* 61 (June 1974): 116–40.

"Hoover in Conference with Keys and Henderson." *Air Transportation,* December 21, 1929, 1.

"Important Decisions on Air Mail Bids." *Aviation* 22 (March 21, 1927): 578.

Joslin, Theodore. "Postmaster General Brown." *World's Work,* August 1930, 38–40.

Lee, David D. "Herbert Hoover and the Rise of Commercial Aviation, 1921–1926." *Business History Review* 58 (1984): 78–102.

"Let Us Hasten to Rectify an Inexcusable Error." *New York American,* February 25, 1934.

Lewis, Fulton. "Airmail Monopoly Probe Demanded by Independents." *Washington Herald,* August 27, 1931.

———. "Brown 'Prostituting' Airmail, Asserts Representative Kelly; to Push Inquiry." *Washington Herald,* August 20, 1931.

"Los Angeles–New York Fare Cut to $159." *Air Transportation,* January 18, 1930, 6.

"The Los Angeles–Salt Lake City Air Mail Line." *Aviation* 20 (April 5, 1926): 493.

"Mail Problem Puzzles Conferees." *Aviation* 27 (October 26, 1929): 863.

"Mileage Proposed as Basis for Air Mail Compensation." *United States Daily,* April 18, 1930.

"Mr. Rentschler." *Bee Hive* (Summer 1956): 2–6.

"N.A.T. and United Continue Controversy." *Aviation* 28 (April 16, 1930): 826.

"N.A.T. Awarded New York–Chicago Route." *Aviation* 22 (April 11, 1927): 731.

"N.A.T. Directors Refuse to Submit United Merger . . ." *Air Transportation,* April 12, 1930, 1.

Nevill, John T. "The First National Air Traffic Conference." *Air Transportation,* September 28, 1929, 653.

"New Air Mail Bids Received on New York–Chicago Route." *Aviation* 22 (April 4, 1927): 678.

"The New Air Mail Rate." *Aviation* 22 (February 21, 1927): 361.

"A New Law for Air Transport." *Aviation* 33 (July 1934): 205.

"The News in Brief." *Western Flying* 10 (August 1931): 17.

"New Transcontinental Air Mail Route Proposals Heard at Washington Meeting." *Air Transportation,* December 7, 1929, 44.

"New York Central to Enter Air Travel Field." *New York Herald Tribune,* July 28, 1928.

"New York–Los Angeles Passenger Line Opens." *Air Transportation,* November 1, 1930, 2.

"Operators Divided in Mail Rate Parley." *Aviation* 27 (October 12, 1929): 765.

"Paul Braniff Air Transportation Taxi Co. of Oklahoma to Operate State Air Lines." *Aviation* 24 (June 18, 1928): 1775.

Pettus, Clay. "First National Air Traffic Conference." *Aircraft Age,* October 1929, 6.

"The Postmaster General Speaks His Mind." *Aviation* 28 (January 25, 1930): 141–42.

"Regulation for Air Mail Routes." *Aviation* 18 (April 27, 1925): 458–59.

"Resume Hearings on Air Mail Routes." *Aviation* 27 (November 2, 1929): 907.

"Routes in the South Debated at Hearing." *Aviation* 26 (June 22, 1929): 202.

"Secret Air Mail Conferences on in Washington." *Air Transportation,* October 5, 1929, 1.

"Securities Quotations: Week Ending January 4, 1930." *Air Transportation,* January 11, 1930, 44.

"Sherman Mills Fairchild." *Air Transportation,* June 7, 1930, 30.

"Sikorsky Interests and United Aircraft Merge." *Air Transportation,* July 27, 1929, 1, 32.

Spencer, T.T. "Air Mail Controversy of 1934." *Mid America* 62 (October 1980): 161–72.

"Spring Opening: Formal Prelude to an Air Mail Shuffle." *Aviation* 33 (May 1934): 135.

"A Super Airmail Service." *Aeronautical Industry,* December 13, 1930, 20.

"T.A.T.-Maddux Air Lines Re-Organizes." *Western Flying* 7 (March 1930): 116.

"T.A.T.-Maddux Has Net Deficit . . ." *Aviation* 28 (March 29, 1930): 660.

"Three Months Operation of Colonial Air Transport." *Aviation* 21 (October 25, 1926): 703–5.

"Transcontinental Air Transport." *Air Transportation,* November 30, 1929, 12.

Tucker, Ray. "Local Air Mail Line Is Costing $400,000 Too Much, Is Charged." *Washington Daily News,* August 23, 1931.

"Two Chicago–E. St. Louis Plane Lines Get Permits." *St. Louis Post Dispatch,* August 27, 1931.

"United Aircraft Acquires Assets of Avion Corp." *Air Transportation,* August 17, 1929, 17.

"United Aircraft–N.A.T. Merger Proposed." *Air Transportation,* April 5, 1930, 1.

"Up from Chaos." *Aviation* 33 (November 1934): 339.

"W.A.E. Reduces Fares." *Air Transportation,* January 25, 1930, 3.

Wallman, Franklin. "Air Passenger Lines to Fight Mail Awards." *Baltimore Sun,* August 22, 1930.

"Watres Bill Signed." *Air Transportation,* May 10, 1930, 4.

"Western Air Merging with Aero Corp." *Western Flying* 7 (March 1930): 116.

Index

Illustrations are referenced by italicized page numbers.